READING MONARCH'S WRITING:

The Poetry of Henry VIII, Mary Stuart, Elizabeth I, and James VI/I

MEDIEVAL AND RENAISSANCE
TEXTS AND STUDIES

VOLUME 2 3 4

READING MONARCH'S WRITING:

The Poetry of Henry VIII, Mary Stuart, Elizabeth I, and James VI/I

edited by

Peter C. Herman

Arizona Center for Medieval and Renaissance Studies
Tempe, Arizona
2002

Library of Congress Cataloging-in-Publication Data
Reading monarch's writing : the poetry of Henry VIII, Mary Stuart, Elizabeth I,
and James VI/I / edited by Peter C. Herman.
    p. cm. — (Medieval & Renaissance texts & studies ; v. 234)
    Includes bibliographical references and index.
    ISBN 0-86698-276-0 (acid-free paper)
    1. Kings' and rulers' writings, English—History and criticism. 2. Kings' and
rulers' writings, Scottish—History and criticism. 3. English poetry—Early
modern, 1500-1700—History and criticism. 4. Henry VIII, King of England,
1491-1547—Literary art. 5. Mary, Queen of Scots, 1542-1587—Literary art. 6.
Elizabeth I, Queen of England, 1533-1603—Literary art. 7. James I, King of
England, 1566-1625—Literary art. I. Herman, Peter C., 1958- . II. Medieval &
Renaissance Texts & Studies (Series) ; v. 234.
PR120.K54 R43 2001
821'.30992351—dc21   2001022436

∞
This book is made to last.
It is set in Goudy, smyth-sewn,
and printed on acid-free paper
to library specifications.

Printed in the United States of America

For Alison and Jonathan

CONTENTS

PART II
SELECTED POEMS OF TUDOR/STUART MONARCHS

LIST OF ILLUSTRATIONS

ACKNOWLEDGEMENTS

The first person I need to thank is David Richardson. Some years ago, he asked me to write on Henry VIII for the *Dictionary of Literary Biography*, and his request first led me to think about Henry VIII's poetry. This volume is the end, if unexpected, result of that commission. Second, I thank the contributors to this volume, which has been from the start a truly co-operative venture. In order of appearance, I am grateful to Ray Siemens for agreeing to co-write the essay on Henry VIII and for allowing me to adapt his forthcoming edition of Henry VIII's poems; Lisa Hopkins for contributing her essay on Mary's verse and for vetting my translations; Jennifer Summit for answering "yes" at a key moment in this volume's gestation and for allowing me to reproduce her transcriptions of Elizabeth's "Doubt of Future Foes"; Leah Marcus for her help with Elizabeth's poetry and her instructing me on how to interpret manuscripts; Constance Jordan for agreeing to write on Elizabeth's French verses and for her general support in this and other matters; Sandra Bell for contributing her fine essay on James's verse and her help with annotating James's poetry; and Robert Appelbaum for agreeing to write on James's *Lepanto* and his friendship over the years. I am very grateful to Marianne Pade and Henry T. Summerson for help with a particularly difficult identification. I also need to thank Professor Bob Bjork, Laura Gross, and Karen Lemiski for their professionalism and patience as this volume crept toward completion.

Three parts of *Reading Monarchs Writing* have been published elsewhere. Jennifer Summit's " 'The Arte of a Ladies Penne': Elizabeth I and the Poetics of Queenship" first appeared in *English Literary Renaissance* 26 (1996): 395–422, and Robert Appelbaum's "War and Peace in the *Lepanto*" first appeared in *Modern Philology* 97.3 (2000): 333–63. Both essays are reprinted here with the kind permission of the editors. Unless otherwise noted, Elizabeth I's poetry is reprinted from *Elizabeth I: Collected Works*, ed. Leah Marcus, Janel Mueller, and Mary Beth Rose (Chicago: University of Chicago Press, 2000). I am indebted to the editors and to Allan Thomas of the University of Chicago Press for granting me permission.

PART I

Figure 1: Detail of a block "H" from the Henry VIII manuscript.
Reproduced by permission of The British Library,
MS. Add. 31922, f14^v–15^r, 18^v.

PETER C. HERMAN & RAY G. SIEMENS

Reading Monarchs Writing:
Introduction

THIS ANTHOLOGY EXAMINES A BODY OF VERSE that has received surprisingly little attention: the poetry of Tudor and Stuart monarchs Henry VIII, Mary, Queen of Scots, Elizabeth I, and James VI/I. Despite all the enabling work that has been done on the intersections of poetry and politics in such "courtly makers" as Wyatt, Surrey, and Sidney, among many others, critics seem to have neglected the fact that *monarchs* also wrote verse. Although James's works have received some attention (due, in no small part, to Ben Jonson's recognition of his monarch's poetic activities),[1] virtually nothing has been written on Henry VIII's lyrics. As for Mary Stuart, while she remains a popular figure outside of academia, and while her verse has remained continuously available, critics have all but ignored her verse.[2] And while Elizabeth's speeches have come under in-

---

[1] See Jonathan Goldberg, *James I and the Politics of Literature* (Stanford: Stanford University Press, 1989), 17–24, and Kevin Sharpe, "The King's Writ: Royal Authors and Royal Authority in Early Modern England," in *Culture and Politics in Early Stuart England*, ed. Kevin Sharpe and Peter Lake (Stanford: Stanford University Press, 1993), 117–38. In addition, see Daniel Fischlin and Mark Fortier, eds., *Royal Subjects: The Writings of James VI and I* (Detroit: Wayne State University Press, forthcoming), Peter C. Herman, " 'Best of Poets, Best of Kings': King James VI/I and the Scene of Monarchic Verse," forthcoming in *Royal Subjects*; and Daniel Fischlin, " 'Like a Mercenary Poët': The Politics and Poetics of James VI's *Lepanto*," *Essays on Older Scots Literature*, ed. Sally Mapstone (East Linton: Tuckwell Press, forthcoming), vol. 3: 9.

[2] See in this volume Peter C. Herman, " 'mes subjectz, mon ame assubjectie': The

creasing scrutiny, her poetry too remains nearly unexamined. (Steven May, for example, cites only one item on Elizabeth's poetry in his "Recent Studies in Elizabeth I" — a single page from his own book on courtier verse.)[3] This neglect is surprising for a number of reasons.

To begin, there is a minor tradition of English monarchs writing verse. Richard I, during the last years of his father's reign, lived in the courts of Provence and, according to Walpole, practiced their poetic arts.[4] Edward II wrote a lament in verse;[5] Richard II commissioned an epitaph for himself which compares him to Homer,[6] and Henry VI is supposed to have written "Kingdomes are bote cares," a proverbial poem on the nature of worldly vanity.[7] Closer to home, Henry VIII's mother, Elizabeth of York, may have written the short poem "My heart is set upon a lusty pin,"[8] and Henry's first wife, Katherine of Aragon, also has a lyric ascribed to her.[9] Moreover, Margaret of Austria — whom Henry's father proposed to marry, and whose Burgundian court culture Henry admired and imitated — wrote many lyrics as well, chiefly in the tradition of the courtly love lyric.[10] Marguerite de Navarre was also both a poet and a

---

Problematic (of) Subjectivity in Mary Stuart's Sonnets," n. 2 and n. 4. After completing work on *Reading Monarchs Writing*, however, I had the good fortune of reading Sarah Dunnigan's published and forthcoming work on Mary (see " 'mes subjectz,' " note 2).

[3] May, "Recent Studies in Elizabeth I," *English Literary Renaissance* 23.2 (1993): 348. Ilona Bell devotes five pages to Elizabeth's verse in *Elizabethan Women and the Poetry of Courtship* (Cambridge: Cambridge University Press, 1998), 108–13.

[4] Horace Walpole, *A Catalogue of the Royal and Noble Authors of England* (London, 1758), 2.

[5] "Lamentatio gloriosi Regis Edwardi de Karnarvan, quam edidit tempore suae incarcerationis," Walpole, *Royal and Noble Authors*, 4; Thomas Tanner, *Bibliotheca Britannica* (London: Guliemus Bowyer, 1748), 253.

[6] Gervase Matthew, *The Court of Richard II* (New York: Norton, 1968), 22.

[7] This attribution may be suspect. Sir John Harington, *Nugæ Antiquæ: Being a Miscellaneous Collection of Original Papers in Prose and Verse*, ed. Henry Harington (London: W. Frederick, 1775), vol. 2: 247.

[8] From *Oxford, Bodleian Rawlinson MS C.8* (155ᵛ–156ʳ). For a full discussion of this ascription, see Julia Boffey, *Manuscripts of English Courtly Love Lyrics in the Later Middle Ages*. Manuscript Studies 1 (Woodbridge, Suffolk: D. S. Brewer, 1985), 83–84.

[9] The poetic voice of "Whilles lyue or breth is in my brest" (*London British Library Additional MS 31,92*, 54ᵛ–55ʳ), a lyric seemingly intended to be sung by a woman in praise of her lover's performance at a running of the ring, appears to be that of Katherine of Aragon; the matter of the poem, as well as marginal notations in the manuscript, suggest that the male lover, the "lord," is Henry.

[10] See Ghislaine DeBoom, *Margarite d'Autriche-Savoie et la Pre-Renaisance* (Paris: Librarie E-Droz, 1935), 123 ff., and E. W. Ives, *Anne Boleyn* (Oxford: Basil Blackwell, 1986), 26 ff., for discussion and examples of Margaret's lyrics. On the importance of Bur-

great queen, and in all likelihood Mary, Elizabeth and James knew about her literary bent. There is, in short, nothing surprising or unprecedented about a monarch turning his or her hand to lyric poetry.

The neglect also seems to be a relatively modern phenomenon, as monarchic verse constituted a recognized (sub?)genre during the early modern era. For example, in a letter dated 1609 and addressed to King James I's eldest son, Prince Henry, Sir John Harington mentions and reproduces:[11]

A special verse of King Henry the Eight, when he conceived love for Anna Bulleign. And hereof I entertain no doubt of the Author, for, if I had no better reason than the rhyme, it were sufficient to think that no other than suche a King could write suche a sonnet; but of this my father oft gave me good assurance, who was in his household. This sonnet was sunge to the Lady Anne at his commaundment, and here followeth:

> THE eagle's force subdues eache byrd that flyes;
> What metal can resyst the flaminge fyre?
> Dothe not the sunne dazzle the cleareste eyes,
> And melt the ice, and make the froste retyre?
> The hardest stones are peircede thro wyth tools;
> The wysest are, with Princes, made but fools.

While in all likelihood, Henry VIII did not write these lines,[12] the metaphors the speaker uses to describe himself (an eagle, a fire, the sun, the highly phallic piercing tool) are all associated with authority and in particular, with authority establishing its pre-eminence through the use of some kind of *force*, irresistable flame, blinding incandescence, melting heat, and probing incision. These are the metaphors, in other words, that a prince *ought* to use when composing verse, and therefore Harrington is sure, even, as he says, if had he no other basis than the words themselves,

---

gundy to the early Tudors, see Gordon Kipling, *The triumph of honour: Burgundian origins of the Elizabethan Renaissance* (The Hague: Leiden University Press, 1977).

[11] Harington, *Nugæ Antiquæ*, vol. 2: 248.

[12] Nonetheless, William Byrd set them to music in *Psalmes, Songs, and Sonnets* (1611; B1'). See also Thomas Warton, *The History of English Poetry From the Close of the Eleventh to the Commencement of the Eighteenth Century* (1781), rev. ed. (London: Thomas Tegg, 1824), vol. 3: 342–43. They also appear in *A Mirror for Magistrates* (1563; Lily B. Campbell, ed., *A Mirror for Magistrates* [Cambridge: Cambridge University Press, 1938]) as lines 85–91 of Thomas Churchyard's "Shore's Wife" (376; see also E. H. Fellowes, *English Madrigal Verse, 1588–1632*, 3rd ed. [Oxford: Clarendon Press, 1967], 685).

that *only* "A King could write suche a sonnet." In addition, the last line's reference to "Princes" carries with it the assumption that Henry is revealing his identity explicitly, thus turning a conventional lyric into a royal performance.

While aesthetics surely plays some role in the marginalization of monarchic verse — most of these poems are competent at best, one or two, we must admit, are downright terrible — the absence of masterpieces should not prevent our taking these texts seriously. Lack of poetic merit has certainly not stopped critics from according serious and sustained attention to other less than wondrous poetic texts, such as the *Mirror for Magistrates* or Robert Sidney's sonnets. Nor is there a problem of establishing a reliable canon. While as Harington's mistaken ascription attests and as Leah Marcus's contribution will later show, poems circulated under a monarch's name that were not written by a monarch, the existence of spurious texts should not obscure the fact that the canon of monarchic verse rests on a solid foundation.

Granted, we do not have a holograph of Henry VIII's lyrics, yet we have indisputable firsthand evidence that Henry wrote lyrics (Hall records that during a progress in the second year of his reign, Henry exercised "hym self daily in shotyng, singing, daunsyng, wrastelyng, casting of the barre, plaiyng at the recorder, flute, virginals, and in setting of songes, [and] makyng of balettes" [515]), and in a letter written to Wolsey, Richard Pace noted that the royal almoner incorporated "Pastime with Good Company" and another lyric, "I love unloved, such is mine adventure," into his sermon while preaching in the King's hall in March of 1521.[13] The anonymous interlude *Youth* (c. 1514) employs Henry's lyrics, specifically those which present his persona of the youthful lover (given exemplification in other courtly entertainments as well), and identifies Henry with the interlude's protagonist.[14] And the lyric, "Though Some Say that Youth Rules Me," concludes with an assertion of Henry's royal authorship that perfectly coincides with his proclivity for public performance: "Thus says the King, the eighth Harry, / Though some say that youth rules me." Furthermore, the compiler of the *Henry VIII Manuscript*, our primary source for Henry's lyrics,[15] carefully separated Henry's contributions from

---

[13] *Letter and Papers: Henry VIII* 3.1, #1188, 447.

[14] Ian Lancashire, ed., *Two Tudor Interludes: The Interlude of Youth, Hick Scorner* (Manchester: Manchester University Press, 1980), 54.

[15] See "A Selection of Henry VIII's Lyrics," in this volume, n. 1.

the others.[16] For everyone else, attribution appears following the music and verse of each piece; but in Henry's case, "The Kynge H. VIII." is given centred at the top of the leaf on which each piece begins. In one instance, the block "H" even incorporates a little portrait of the king (figure 1).

The case for Elizabeth's and James's responsibility for their verse is indisputable because for both Elizabeth and James, we have copies of their poems in their own handwriting,[17] plus James published his verse under his name. The situation with Mary appears less certain, as her sonnets were not only published without her permission, but as part of Buchanan's book arguing for Mary's responsibility for her husband's murder. Yet Mary never disclaimed responsibility for the Casket Sonnets (as they came to be known), and even her defenders, including the French ambassador to England, La Mothe Fénelon, who knew and praised Mary's poetry, did not assert that the poems are forgeries.[18]

There are no good reasons, in sum, for ignoring this poetry, and the omission of monarchic verse from our considerations of early modern lyric poetry means that we have inadvertently created an incomplete history of the lyric's place in early modern culture, and in particular, in the cultural poetics of the early modern court. Starting (more or less) with the seminal articles by Arthur Marotti and Louis A. Montrose, literary critics of both new and old historicist leanings have continuously explored how the conventions of lyric verse are ideally suited to describe the hopes and frustrations of a courtier seeking favor.[19] Indeed, the commonplace of "love is

---

[16] On King James's manipulation of the appearance of his poems so as to emphasize their royal origin, see Peter C. Herman, " 'Best of Poets, Best of Kings': King James VI/I and the Scene of Monarchic Verse," forthcoming in *Royal Subjects: The Writings of King James VI/I* (Detroit: Wayne State University Press).

[17] Elizabeth's French verses exist in her own hand. For the provenance of her other lyrics, see the notes to her poems in this edition. As for James, in addition to his printed volumes, MS. Bodley 165 contains an Anglo-Scots versions of many of James's poems, some of them unpublished, in James's hand. In addition, a manuscript in the British Museum (MS. Add. 24195), entitled *All the kings short poesis that ar not printed*, while produced by Prince Charles and James's Groom of the Chamber, Thomas Carey, contains corrections by the king (James Craigie, "Introduction," *The Poems of James VI of Scotland* [Edinburgh: Blackwell, 1955], vol. 2: xxiii).

[18] See Herman, "mes subjectz," n. 58.

[19] The bibliography on this topic is huge. However, the following may be considered a preliminary list of essential works on the politics of early modern literature: Jonathan Goldberg, *James I and the Politics of Literature* (Stanford: Stanford University Press, 1989); Stephen J. Greenblatt, *Renaissance Self-Fashioning: From More to Shakespeare* (Chicago:

not love" has grown so established that Heather Dubrow devotes *Echoes of Desire* to resituating the Petrarchan lyric within the discourses of desire, arguing that in the Petrarchan lyric, love remains very much love and not always politics.[20] Yet despite the fascination with the nexus of poetry and power, almost no one has investigated what happens when poetry gets written by the person *in* power, the person dispensing rather than seeking favor, or the complex relations between a courtier's use of erotic tropes and a monarch's use of them. If, as Montrose rightly observes, "The otiose love-talk of the shepherd masks the busy negotiation of the courtier; the shepherd is a courtly poet prosecuting his courtship in pastoral forms,"[21] what happens when the otiose love-talk is articulated not by a courtier, but by a king or a queen? Answering these questions constitutes the project of this anthology.

§

Peter C. Herman and Ray G. Siemens propose that Henry VIII's lyrics directly respond to the anxieties caused by the crowning of a new king

---

University of Chicago Press, 1980); Greenblatt, *Shakespearean Negotiations* (Berkeley: University of California Press, 1988); Daniel Javitch, *Poetry and Courtliness in Renaissance England* (Princeton: Princeton University Press, 1978); Ann R. Jones and Peter Stallybrass, "The Politics of *Astrophil and Stella*," *Studies in English Literature* 24 (1984): 53–68; David Scott Kastan, " 'Proud Majesty Made a Subject': Shakespeare and the Spectacle of Rule," *Shakespeare Quarterly* 37 (1986): 459–75; Arthur F. Marotti, " 'Love is not Love': Elizabethan Sonnet Sequences and the Social Order," *English Literary History* 49 (1982): 396–428; Steven May, *The Elizabethan Courtier Poets: The Poems and Their Contexts* (Columbia: University of Missouri Press, 1991); Louis A. Montrose, " 'Eliza, Queene of Shepherds,' and the Pastoral of Power," *English Literary Renaissance* 10 (1980): 153–82; Montrose, " 'The perfecte paterne of a Poet': The Poetics of Courtship in *The Shepheardes Calender*," *Texas Studies in Literature and Language* 21 (1979): 34–67; David Norbrook, *Poetry and Politics in the English Renaissance* (London: Routledge & Kegan Paul, 1984); Annabel Patterson, *Pastoral and Ideology: Virgil to Valéry* (Berkeley: University of California Press, 1987); Maureen Quilligan, "Sidney and His Queen," in *The Historical Renaissance: New Essays on Tudor and Stuart Literature and Culture*, ed. Heather Dubrow and Richard Strier (Chicago: University of Chicago Press, 1988), 171–96; Kevin Sharpe and Steven Zwicker, eds., *The Politics of Discourse* (Berkeley: University of California Press, 1985); Steven N. Zwicker, *Lines of Authority: Political and English Literary Culture, 1649–1689* (Ithaca: Cornell University Press, 1993).

[20] Dubrow reminds us that as much as "Petrarchism and anti-Petrarchism are . . . about subjects like politics, history, or the relationships among men, . . . they are always—and often primarily—about love, desire, and gender as well" (*Echoes of Desire: English Petrarchism and Its Counterdiscourses* [Ithaca: Cornell University Press, 1995], 10).

[21] Montrose, " 'Eliza, Queene of Shepherds,' and the Pastoral of Power," 155.

whose policies and personality differ radically from the previous monarch's. As such, Henry VIII has the (admittedly unlikely) distinction of being the first "courtly maker" to use verse as a device for both talking about and actually *doing* politics. In such lyrics as "Pastime with Good Company" and "Though Some Say that Youth Rules Me," the king uses his verse, which he intended for public performance, both to defend himself and to assert his independence. Such lines as "So God be pleased, this life will I" and "Thus says the king, the eighth Harry / Though some say [that youth rules me" remind Henry's audience that his desires are the desires of a king. The line, then, functions as a claim to power, to independence. Yet Henry's songs are not the assured assertions of a firmly established king. Instead, they often function as an element in the process by which Henry established his independence. Defenses perforce imply the existence of attacks, and the very fact that Henry felt compelled to assert his right to play strongly implies the existence of a "they" Henry had to take into account who wanted to refrain the king's liberty and to have him disdain merry company; specifically, Henry used his lyrics as vehicles for establishing his independence from Henry VII's policies, if not from Henry VII himself, and for articulating as forcefully as possible that he, and only he, rules the land. Henry VIII's lyrics thus constitute an unrecognized watershed in the history of the Renaissance lyric.

Lisa Hopkins, in "Writing to Control: The Verse of Mary, Queen of Scots," explores the tension between expressivity and formality in Mary's poetry, noting how Mary consistently points towards her regality in her earlier and later verse. Indeed, throughout her verse, there is no doubt that Mary writes as the "Reine de France Marie," which is how she signed her first surviving poem, the "Quatrain Written in the Mass Book Belong to her Aunt Anne of Lorraine, Duchess of Aerschot." This regal tone is, fittingly enough, even more audible when Mary addresses her sister queen, Elizabeth I, in particular her sonnet, "Un seul penser qui me profite et nuit," and it is present even in her religious poetry, in which Mary evinces a sense of her monarchic status through her directly addressing God without the need for any intermediary, like two monarchs speaking together.

In " 'mes subjectz, mon ame assubjectie': The Problematic (of) Subjectivity in Mary Stuart's Sonnets," Peter C. Herman examines Mary Stuart's Sonnets to Bothwell (included among the Casket Letters) as an example of how monarchic verse can yield unexpected consequences. On the one hand, Herman proposes that Mary's position as queen allowed her to adopt the masculine position as the ardent, desiring lover. Her queenship, in other words, allowed Mary to become a desiring subject rather than the desired object. But a monarch can never be a subject, especially not an absolute monarch, and so, Mary's articulation of her personal subjectivity led to the destruction of her political subjectivity.

Elizabeth I of England was praised by her contemporaries as an accomplished poet in several genres, yet few poems have survived attributed to her. Leah S. Marcus surveys her known poetic production, discusses the courtier ethos that caused her poems — as well as many by her courtiers — to be concealed from a broader public, and considers issues of attribution arising from the appearance of her known poems in manuscript sources. As a case in point, previous editors have assumed that the striking through of an attribution to the queen in manuscript collections was a good sign that she was not the author. But even poems known to be authored by her are regularly so treated in manuscript collections that are close to the court, not because of uncertainty over authorship, but because of reticence to admit the queen's authorship in a forum more public than the Privy Chamber. Once we are aware of the ways in which her poems circulated (and failed to circulate) we can re-evaluate previous evidence and, with luck, uncover additional presently unattributed verses that may well have been authored by the queen.

Jennifer Summit takes up the proposition that Elizabeth I was a central figure for the literature of her age. But while criticism has focused on the works produced for or about the queen, it has left unexplored the fact that Elizabeth I wrote and circulated poetry herself. Celebrated in her own age as a female poet worthy of Sappho's mantle, Elizabeth demands a new assessment of what it meant to write as a woman in the Elizabethan period. Elizabeth's "The Doubt of Future Foes," a poem that George Puttenham presents as the most "beautiful and gorgeous" of its age, brings together the gendered concerns of Elizabethan poetics, the courtly practice of coterie manuscript circulation, and the historical occasion of Elizabeth's struggle with Mary Queen of Scots. In so doing, it not only illuminates the postures and meanings available to the female poet in the Elizabethan period, it also shows how these could become the unexpected bases of a claim to supreme cultural and literary authority.

Constance Jordan argues that Elizabeth's recently recovered French verses, "Avecq l'aveugler si estrange," reflects upon the English queen's part in the execution of Mary, Queen of Scots. These verses narrate a spiritual crisis and its resolution in the confidence of having done the right thing. It moves from lamenting the unseeing ignorance that is occasioned by self-division, as the speaker's body and soul fail to cohere in a union of flesh and spirit, to the visionary blindness of spiritual peace to which this union is the precondition. Intermediate reflections focus on justice, a meliorative form of blindness. The scope of the speaker's reflections is essentially Pauline, determined by a creative play between her earthly state of seeing through a glass darkly and the enlightened state she finally attains. Looking beyond the world's vicissitudes, she sees the supra-phenomenal world, whatever is true, changeless, and thus redemptive. In short, having shattered the glass of darkness, her vision is blinded by the light of heaven. This light is consistent with the earthly justice that condemns those who are treasonous — most important, it has condemned Mary, Queen of Scots. In addition, "Avecq l'aveugler si estrange" recalls the imagery Elizabeth employed in her earlier poem, "The doubt of future foes," which in turn was sparked by Mary's poetic plea for safe harbor, "J'ai vu la nef."

In her chapter, "Kingcraft and Poetry: James VI's Cultural Policy," Sandra J. Bell examines James VI's first collection of poetry, *The Essayes of a Prentise, in the Divine Art of Poesie* (1584), as a reaction against the Reformation satires which flourished during the reign of his mother, Mary Stuart. In addition, James's volume constitutes an attempt to develop a new direction for Scottish poetry as well as a monarch-centric court culture. *The Essayes of a Prentise* includes James's poetic treatise on Scottish poetry and a variety of poems which lead his followers away from direct discussion of political topics and toward a more Continental style. Bell addresses the connection of poetry and politics, the problematic media of poetry and print, and the specific questions raised when the poet is a monarch.

Robert Appelbaum, in "War and Peace in *The Lepanto* of James VI/I," reads James's mini-epic as not only the representation of what appeared to be a glorious military victory but also as an implicit argument about the justice of just wars. Appelbaum seeks to underscore the complexities entailed in James's poem, raising questions about what it might mean for someone like James — who was among other things a man of peace — to write a heroic poem about someone else's victory in someone else's war. In addition, Appelbaum raises questions about what it means for a monarch to be writing heroic verse in the first place, doing so after the fashion not of great kings but of great poets writing in the service of great kings.

Finally, as very little of this verse is easily available, the second part of this volume contains a selection of monarchic verse, in particular the poems discussed by the various contributors. We are also mindful, how-

ever, of how the older principles of editing early modern texts, which assumed the existence of a single, pure text that the contemporary editor
had to reconstruct from many corrupt copies, have been put into question.
For most monarchic verse, this is not an issue, because the poems exist
only in a single version. Elizabeth's "Doubt of Future Foes," however, is
the exception that proves the rule; we have numerous manuscript versions
and early published versions. Rather than conflating the various versions
(as earlier editors of *King Lear* and *Doctor Faustus* have done), we present
each of the variants, so readers can compare and contrast the differing versions for themselves.

Monarchic verse thus illustrates the limitations of Michel Foucault's
famous rhetorical question, "What matter who's speaking?"[22] In this
case, nothing matters more than who is speaking, for the speaker *defines*,
to paraphrase Foucault, "the modes of existence of this discourse" and
"where ... it comes from; how it is circulated; [and] who controls it."[23]
The meaning of the verse *derives* from the speaker's identity, and Henry,
Mary, Elizabeth, and James consciously manipulate their verse so that it
reflected their royal position. In sum, we hope that the recovery of these
poems will significantly alter our present sense of the place of lyric poetry
in early modern courtly culture, and we hope that these poems will start
to find their way on to a syllabus or two.

Peter C. Herman, San Diego State University
Ray G. Siemens, Malaspina University-College

---

[22] Michel Foucault, "What is an Author?" in *Language, Counter-Memory, Practice: Selected Essays and Interviews*, ed. Donald F. Bouchard (Ithaca: Cornell University Press, 1977), 138.

[23] Foucault, "What is an Author?" 138.

PETER C. HERMAN & RAY G. SIEMENS

Henry VIII and the
Poetry of Politics

Youth must have some dalliance,
Of good or ill some pastance.
[Henry VIII, "Pastime With Good Company"]

I'm 'Enery the 'Eighth ! am
'Enery the Eighth I am I am
[Herman's Hermits]

IN THE SUMMER OF 1499, Desiderius Erasmus stayed at the Greenwich country house of his former pupil and present patron, William Blount, Lord Mountjoy. One day, Thomas More dropped by and invited his friend to take a walk to the nearby village of Eltham. Without first warning Erasmus, More led his friend to Eltham Palace, which served as the royal nursery. Because Prince Arthur happened to be in Wales, everyone's attention focused on the eight-year-old Prince Henry, Duke of York, who would soon be King Henry VIII. More, who had prepared for the occasion by bringing a small literary gift, bowed to the young prince and presented his offering. Erasmus, caught entirely unawares and not a little peeved at More for this surprise, mumbled his excuses and promised to remedy the omission another time. However, during the meal Erasmus received a note from Henry "challenging something from his pen," and the eminent humanist complied several days later with an exceedingly tedious panegyric to the prince, the prince's father, England in general, and a great deal else besides.[1]

This anecdote, recalled in a letter Erasmus wrote in 1523 to Johannes Botzheim, says a great deal about its author, about Thomas More, and about Henry VIII. It shows that the prince, doubtless encouraged by his tutor, John Skelton (who might have sparked the young prince's challenge), liked the company of the learned, thereby prefiguring his patronage of humanist endeavors. More ominously, this anecdote also shows how even as child, Henry injected an element of threat into his literary doings. It was not enough for the young prince merely to accept Erasmus's apologies and promises; instead, Henry imperiously challenges, that is to say, he *commands*, Erasmus to come up with something, and the flustered guest clearly understood the note as much more than a child's whim. Twenty years later, Erasmus interpreted the incident as a prediction of Henry's future glory, writing that even as a child Henry had "already something of royalty in his demeanor, in which there was a certain dignity combined with a singular courtesy." But by 1523, Erasmus depended on Henry for patronage, so it was politic of him to forget how he spent three days slaving over Henry's demand. Indeed, the event so traumatized him that he neither wrote nor read poetry again (which given his poem's dreariness may have been a good thing). Power, as we shall see, figures as an abiding concern in Henry's literary endeavors.

Many contemporary historians and literary historians, such as J. J. Scarisbrick, C. S. Lewis, and John Stevens, characterize the early Henrician court as obsessed by games, chivalric role-playing, and light allegory. As Scarisbrick puts it, the newly crowned Henry VIII "was a prodigy, a sun-king, a *stupor mundi*. He lived in, and crowned, a world of lavish allegory, mythology and romance."[2] A world in which, as Stevens says, "people acted out their aspirations to a leisured and gracious life, where Lady Courtesy led the dance and Beauty, Simplesse, Swete-lokyng, Fraunchise, Mirth and Gladness danced with her" (152). This picture of the early Henrician court as a fundamentally innocent idyll has its roots in a misreading of Edward Hall's lengthy, detailed accounts of Henry's court and his very detailed accounts of the many spectacles.[3] Hall's seemingly un-

---

[1] Carolly Erickson, *Great Harry* (New York: Summit Books, 1980), 27.

[2] J. J. Scarisbrick, *Henry VIII* (Berkeley: University of California Press, 1968), 20.

[3] On Hall's initially implicit, but later very explicit, criticism of Henry VIII, see Peter C. Herman, "Henrician Historiography and the Voice of the People: The Cases of

critical tone in his early chapters on Henry VIII have led most later critics to assume that the chronicler entirely endorses the king's activities (which is not true) and to assume that Henry's lyrics emanate from the putatively untroubled atmosphere of festivity and chivalry marking the first decade or so of Henry's reign. Thus, the one critic (John Stevens) who deigned to note their existence dismisses them as light, after-dinner entertainment, as another element of the "game" of courtly love. While such literary historians as Sidney Anglo and W. R. Streitberger have done important archival work on the place and organization of the Henrician court's pageantry, for the most part they have preferred to stay away from analyzing Henry's literary activities and entertainments as ideological vehicles.[4]

Skiles Howard has demonstrated brilliantly how the masques and disguisings of the early Henrician court constituted "a privileged site for the production of hierarchy and gender difference,"[5] to which we can add the production of political authority as well. Take, for example, the *Chateau Vert* spectacle produced by Wolsey for the amusement and benefit of the king by "certain noble men from the Emperor" on Shrovetide, 1522 (630).[6] Recalling the passage in the *Roman de la Rose* in which the fortress containing the rose is under siege by the god of love and his followers [ll. 3267 ff.],[7] as reported by Hall the dignitaries were ushered into a "great chamber" in which a castle had been constructed, and significantly, this castle is a monument to female power: "and on every Tower was a banner, one banner was of iii. rent hartes, the other was a ladies hand gripyng a mans harte, the third banner was a ladies hand turnyng a mannes hart" [631].) The women inhabiting this castle assumed the allegorical names of Beauty, Honor, Perseverance, Kindness, Constancy, Bounty, Mercy and

More and Hall," *Texas Studies in Literature and Language* 39: 3 (1997): 270–76.

[4] Sydney Anglo, *Spectacle, Pageantry and Early Tudor Policy* (Oxford: Oxford University Press, 1969; repr. 1997) and W. R. Streitberger, *Court Revels, 1485–1559* (Toronto: University of Toronto Press, 1994).

[5] Skiles Howard, " 'Ascending the Riche Mount': Performing Hierarchy and Gender in the Henrician Masque," in Peter C. Herman, *Rethinking the Henrician Era: New Essays on Early Tudor Texts and Contexts* (Urbana: University of Illinois Press, 1994), 17.

[6] Edward Hall, *Hall's Chronicle Containing the History of England during the Reign of Henry the Fourth and the Succeeding Monarchs to the End of the Reign of Henry the Eighth* [original title: *The Union of the Two Noble and Illustre Famelies of Lancastre & Yorke*], ed. Sir Henry Ellis (London: J. Johnson et al., 1809). All references are given parenthetically, and we have silently modernized the usages of i/j and u/v.

[7] *Roman de la Rose*, trans. Charles Dahlberg (Princeton: Princeton University Press, 1971).

Pity, the feminine virtues, in other words, and they are guarded by other ladies named Danger, Disdain, Jealousy, Unkindness, Scorne, Malebouche [Bad Mouth or Speech], and Strangeness. (Hall also records that these ladies "were tired [attired] to women of Inde" [631] which ensures that the feminine enemies of the king's will are identified absolutely with the Other.) Then, men entered with the allegorical names of Morus, Nobleness, Youth, Attendence, Loyalty, Pleasure, Gentleness, and Liberty, the king, "the chief of this compaignie," adopting the disguise of Ardent Desire. Hall describes the action thus:

> *Ardent Desire* . . . so moved the ladies to geve over the Castle, but *Scorne* and Disdain saied they would helde the place, then *Desire* saied the ladies should be wonne and came and encouraged the knightes, then the lordes ranne to the castle, (at whiche tyme out was shot a greate peale of gunnes) and the ladies defended the castle with Rose water and Comfittes, and the lordes threwe in Dates and Orenges, and other fruites made for pleasure, but at the last the place was wonne, but the Lady *Scorne* and her compaignie stubbernely defended them with boows and balles, til they were driven out of the place and fled. Then the lordes toke the ladies of honor as prisoners by the handes, and brought them doune, and daunced together very pleasauntly, which much pleased the straungers. . . . (631)

Howard rightly sees in this production a paradigm for how dance constitutes a rehearsal for gender roles, yet we also need to remember that Wolsey produced the "assault on the *Chateau Vert*" for the benefit of the king and of Charles V's ambassadors (the "straungers" of Hall's report). In other words, alongside figuring gender, the evening of playacting also constituted a demonstration of the king's *political* authority.[8] The king — conquering hero that he is — answers the challenge to his desires by asserting that "the ladies should be wonne" and encouraging his "knights" to enact a "battle" that concludes with a mock rape. The reassertion of male dominance at the "battle's" conclusion emblematizes the reassertion of the king's dominance over the (literally feminized) enemies who dared to defy him; the king's sexual potency, in other words, symbolizes his political po-

---

[8] On how Jonson's masques refigured the authority of the Stuart court, see Stephen Orgel, *The Illusion of Power: Political Theater in the English Renaissance* (Berkeley: University of California Press, 1975).

tency. No doubt there was much laughter and good cheer at the actual event, but when Hall writes that the ladies were led "as prisoner by the handes," could anyone present at the scene not have understood that Wolsey also intended a lesson about masculine/royal authority for both the court and the Emperor's representatives?

The underlying politics of this playacting exemplifies the intertwining, if not the outright collapse, of the private and the public characterizing the early Henrician court,[9] and we propose to investigate how Henry VIII's lyrics perform similar ideological work. If, as Seth Lerer posits, "[t]he literary products of [this] period expose confusions and conflations among poetry and drama, private letters and public performances,"[10] Henry's literary products *enact*, if not initiate, precisely this confusion. Moreover, they not only constitute a site for the "confusion of personal and political power," as Foley describes Henry's miniatures,[11] they also blend together the construction of masculinity and political authority. Thus, in the "Assault on the Chateau Vert," Henry displays both his personal and his professional virility. Consequently, even though Henry's lyrics were (at some level) pure entertainment, describing and inventing a world of pastime with good company, as Lewis and Stevens have it, they are not *merely* light diversions. Like Henry's masques and disguisings, his lyrics also constitute vehicles for depicting the hierarchy of the court and for both defending and reinforcing the power of his monarchy. In no way do we claim that Henry VIII is as skillful a poet as Wyatt or even (in his own peculiar way) John Skelton. Instead, we claim that Henry VIII's lyrics become much more interesting than previously allowed when looked at as interventions in the cultural poetics of the early Tudor court.

Although no direct evidence unambiguously connects Henry's lyrics to specific situations and events, nonetheless it makes sense to situate these poems within the context of the early Henrician court. The *Ritson MS*, which contains "Pastime with Good Company," dates from around 1510, and the *Henry VIII MS* (the name arising from its containing the bulk of Henry's songs) from around 1522.[12] Several pointed and touching refer-

---

[9] See David Starkey, "Intimacy and Innovation: the Rise of the Privy Chamber, 1485–1547," *The English Court: From the Wars of the Roses to the Civil War*, ed. David Starkey (London: Longman, 1987); Seth Lerer, *Courtly Letters in the Age of Henry VIII: Literary Culture and the Arts of Deceit* (Cambridge: Cambridge University Press, 1997).

[10] Lerer, *Courtly Letters*, 38.

[11] Stephen M. Foley, *Sir Thomas Wyatt* (Boston: Twayne, 1990), 36.

[12] On the dating of Henry's lyrics, see Ray G. Siemens, "New Evidence on Wyatt's

ences to Queen Katherine had to have been penned well before their marriage cooled in the early 1520s.[13] Therefore, it is likely that Henry's writing dates from circa 1510 to 1515, and even likelier that he wrote some of
them in the period just after he ascended to the Crown, and as we will
see, Henry's lyrics not only engage the issues facing the new king, but they
also reflect his somewhat tenuous hold on power at the start of his reign.

I

Henry's lyrics can be grouped into two non-exclusive categories by the poetic personae adopted by their author: in the first group, the speaker ex-
pounds upon and defends the virtues of ostensibly youthful pastimes, and
in the second group, the speaker prescribes or fulfills the proper actions of
the courtly lover.

In the latter poems, Henry often adopts the role of the faithful lover.
In "Oh, My Heart," for instance, the speaker mourns (in not very complex verse) his imminent (and reasonless) departure from his lady:

> Oh, my heart and, oh, my heart,
> My heart it is so sore,
> Since I must from my love depart,
> And know no cause wherefore.

Other poems reiterate the speaker's ostensibly rock-solid devotion. In
"Green Grows the Holly," Henry asserts that just:

> As the holly grows green
>   And never changes hue,
> So I am — ever have been —
> unto my lady true. (ll. 5–8)

And in "Without Discord," the speaker pleads for reconciliation:

'Ah robyn,' in British Library Additional MS 31, 922," *Notes and Queries* n.s. 46.2
(1999): 189–91, and Siemens, "Thomas Wyatt, Anne Boleyn, and Henry VIII's Lyric
'Pastime with Good Company,'" *Notes and Queries* n.s. 44 (1997): 26–27.

  [13] E.g., I hurt no man, I do no wrong, / I love true where I did marry ("Though
Some Say that Youth Rules Me") and The daisy delectable, / The violet waning and
blue, / You are not variable — / I love you and no more ("Whereto Should I Express").
All references to Henry's poems are to this volume.

> Without discord,
> And both accord,
> > Now let us be.
> Both hearts, alone,
> To set in one
> > Best seems me.
> For when one, sole,
> Is in the dole
> > Of love's pain,
> Then help must have
> Himself to save
> And love to obtain. (ll. 1–12)

Taken as a whole, many of Henry's poems overlap especially in their defense of pastime, constituting a rebuttal and defense of the activities of the
Lover. "If Love Now Reigned as it Has Been" asserts that, despite its
pains, "Noble men then would surely ensearch / All ways whereby they
might it reach" (ll. 2–3) — love being the obvious province of the noble,
the aristocratic. Henry reiterates this point in "Though That Men Do Call
it Dotage": "Love maintains all noble courage; / Who love disdains is all
of the village[14]" (ll. 13–14).

These lyrics seem like trifles until we remember that, unlike the lyrics
of later Henrician poet-courtiers such as Wyatt or the various contributors
to such miscellanies as the *Devonshire Manuscript*, there was nothing private about Henry's literary amusements. Instead, Henry's lyrics constituted
public *performances* — even more specifically, monarchic performances —
with accompaniment of at least two other singers (as evidenced by the settings in the manuscript that is the sole witness to the majority of his lyrics) for the whole court, which would also include ambassadorial retinues.
Moreover, Henry's lyrics constitute monarchic performances in a number
of ways.

The first of these is found in an examination of some of the ways Henry's adopting the persona of the courtly lover might intervene in the politics of the early Henrician court. As noted, according to the politicized
poetics of the 1510s and 1520s, the allegorical figures of the Lover and the
Warrior are inextricably tied together, both being expressions of Henry's
masculinity; at the same time that Henry constructs himself as the Lover,

---

[14] Viillage = villainage, peasantry.

he is also restarting the Hundred Years War with plans to re-invade France. And Henry's construction of himself as a chivalric lover reflects his overall absorption in neo-chivalric pastimes, such as jousting and tilts, that will culminate in his trying to act out a chivalric fantasy by invading France. As Hall, our most detailed source for this period, writes at the start of his chapter on Henry's second year:

> [The king exercised] hym self daily in shotyng, singing dau[n]syng, wrastelyng, casting of the barre, plaiying at the recorders, flute, virginal, and in setting of songes, makyng of balettes, & dyd set. ii. goodly masses, every of them fyve partes, whiche were songe oftentimes in hys chapel, and afterwardes in diverse other places. And whan he came to Okyng, there were kept both Justes and Turneys: the rest of thys progresse was spent in huntyng, hawkyng and shotyng. (515)

While it may appear that Henry is merely recreating himself on this progress, the setting of songs and making of ballads — presumably including the type of compositions represented in the *Henry VIII MS* — are part of Henry's fashioning himself as a figure from a chivalric romance. To take one step further Lerer's insight that Henry's masques and disguisings "exemplify his understanding of the theatrical nature of both love and politics: his recognition that the court remains a world of masks,"[15] Henry's adoption of the persona of the Lover reflects his intuition that play is also a way of *doing* politics. Henry's love songs enact, in other words, precisely the conflation of "sexual and political potency, virility and kingship," that marks Holbein's much later portrait of Henry VIII commemorating the birth of Edward, in which the king's phallus, his ability to conceive, is the central focus.[16]

The expressions of faithfulness, and the desire to dispel "discord" and achieve "accord" are, no doubt, generic traits of the courtly lyric, but they take on further resonance when we remember that at the time Henry probably composed these lyrics, he was anything but faithful to Katherine of Aragon, his wife. The author of *Youth*, the interlude in which a young Henry VIII is depicted, portrays its protagonist as a regular frequenter of brothels, and associates him with Lady Lechery; in representing a King,

---

[15] Lerer, *Courtly Letters*, 41.

[16] Louis A. Montrose, "Elizabethan Subject and the Spenserian Text," *Literary Theory/Renaissance Texts* (Baltimore: The Johns Hopkins University Press, 1986), 315.

however, one assumes the author would take great care to avoid such a negative representation, especially if it were not true.[17] But there is evidence to confirm his extra-marital exploits. Henry had an affair with a Belgian woman while on the continent in 1513 and, "had clad himself and his court in mourning" because he had to leave her.[18] Though Hall records "a louing metyng" between Henry, who rushed home ahead of his troops, and Katherine upon his return (567), Peter Martyr notes the following year that Henry had "boasted of and cast in [Katherine's] face the fact of his own infidelity."[19] In that year as well, Henry was secretly inquiring about a divorce from Katherine, with the hope of marrying another, the daughter of the French Duke of Bourbon.[20] He also first met Elizabeth Blount in 1514.[21] Henry, a "freshe youth ... in the chaynes of loue" (Hall 703), fell for her and, in 1519, she bore him a child;[22] interestingly, it was her excellence in singing, dancing, and other pastimes which Henry enjoyed that attracted him to her (Hall 703).

In addition, as the correspondence of the Spanish ambassador, Luis Carroz, illustrates, the private life and indiscretions of the King (as well as the state of the Queen's reproductive organs) were not only public, but the subject of intense observation and speculation. Despite the ambassador's report on 25 May 1510 that the King and Katherine "adore" each other,

---

[17] We know that Henry, disguised as one of his yeomen of the guard, visited the King's Head Tavern in Cheapside to see the watch on a midsummer's night, 1510 (Roman Dyboski, *Songs, Carols, and other Miscellaneous Poems* [London: Early English Text Society, 1907], 156). In the interlude, Youth is introduced by Riot and Pride to Lady Lechery (ll. 387 ff.) on the way to a tavern, and Youth and Lechery exchange vows to meet again (ll. 464–70). Similarly, Youth is characterized as someone who spends much time in the Stews, a brothel quarter (ll. 701–2, and notes (*Two Tudor Interludes: The Interludes of Youth and Hick Scorner*, ed. Ian Lancashire [Manchester: Manchester University Press, 1980]).

[18] *Calender of State Papers and Manuscripts, Relating to English Affairs, Existing in the Archives and Collections of Venice and in other Libraries of Northern Italy*, ed. Rawdon Brown (London: Longmans, Green, Reader & Dyer, 1867), vol. 2: 152.

[19] *Calender of State Papers, Venice*, vol. 2: 152.

[20] See the letter from Vetor Lippomano (*Calendar of State Papers, Venice* 1: 188), and Betty Behrens, "A Note on Henry VIII's Divorce Project of 1514," *Bulletin of the Institute of Historical Research* 11 (1933–34): 163–64.

[21] Scarisbrick, *Henry VIII*, 147.

[22] Later, Henry had Anne Boleyn's sister, Mary, as mistress. It has also been suggested that Henry was involved with Mary and Anne's mother (*Letters and Papers of Henry VIII*, vol. 4: 329); when confronted with a rumour of these affairs, Henry denied the affair with the mother, and Cromwell immediately denied the affair with Mary. See Paul Friedmann, *Anne Boleyn* (London: MacMillan, 1884), appendix B.

in his next letter, dated 29 May 1510, Carroz informs Ferdinand of the king's sexual adventuring:[23]

> What lately has happened is that two sisters of the Duke of Buck-ingham, both married, lived in the palace. The one of them is the favorite of the Queen, and the other, it is said, is very much liked by the King, who went after her [y andava tras ella]. Another ver-sion is that the love intrigues were not of the King, but of a young man, his favourite, of the name of Conton [Compton], who had been the late King's butler. This Conton carried on the love in-trigue, as it is said, for the King, and that is the more credible ver-sion, for the King has shown great displeasure at which I am going to tell.

Carroz's gossip concerns how the King got found out and his displeasure at having his infidelities revealed. Henry's bedhopping, of course, lends an ironic air to his pleadings for reconciliation and his assertions of eternal truth and fidelity. Yet in addition to the domestic comedy (everyone in the court probably knowing that even as the king swears eternal fealty, he is carrying on a "love intrigue"), there might be a more serious, diplo-matic overtone to Henry's adoption of this persona before the court.

At the same time that Henry is either chasing other women or having his friends act for him, he was also assiduously attempting to enlist his father-in-law as an ally in his planned wars. Immediately upon his acces-sion, he wrote to Ferdinand asking if he would be willing to attack France (Ferdinand evidently told Henry to restrain himself), and he tried three times between 1510 and 1512 to carry on a military adventure of one type or another with him. In each case, however, Ferdinand pulled out without bothering to tell Henry first.[24] The probable connections to Henry's lyr-ics are twofold. Like the jousts and tourneys, Henry's songs are part of his attempt to construct his image as the ideal chivalric king who is both lover and warrior, as we have seen. The songs, in other words, are directed at both the court *and* the foreign ambassadors, and of course help symbo-lize and project his masculinity. But also, having his infidelities broad-casted surely would not help Henry enlist his father-in-law's aid in going

---

[23] *Supplement to Volume I and Volume II of Letters, Dispatches, and State Papers Related to the Negotiations between England and Spain*, ed. G. A. Bergenroth (London: Public Record Office, 1868), 35, 39.

[24] Scarisbrick, *Henry VIII*, 24–34.

to war. Without meaning to underestimate the extent of masculine privilege or Ferdinand's paternal affections, when Henry swears "So I am — ever have been — / unto my lady true," it is distinctly possible that he also has Katherine's father — whose approval Henry clearly desired — in mind as his audience. The love songs could, therefore, be construed as a form of poetic diplomacy, using verse not only to enhance Henry's masculine image, but also to create the public illusion of marital bliss for the purpose of reassuring his father-in-law that he is indeed treating his daughter well and therefore should be trusted in other endeavors as well.[25] In other words, Henry is drawing upon and manipulating the generic conventions of the courtly love lyric to provide an acceptable face for marital relations, which themselves are suggestive of national political strength, stability, and Henry's ability to deal with political discord.

Alongside the diplomatic overtones, Henry's songs also reveal their monarchic perspective by the way in which the poems deal with the issue of power. From the Provençal poets onward, power conventionally is delegated to the female object of desire. The male (at least superficially)[26] continuously begs the woman for grace in language that could just as easily describe the quest for the monarch's or the lord's patronage of favor. "Love lyrics," as Marotti writes, "could express figuratively the realities of suit, service, and recompense with which ambitious men were insistently concerned as well as the frustrations and disappointments experienced on socially competitive environments."[27] Hence the parallel between political and erotic experience that Wyatt, his contemporaries, and his followers found so productive.[28]

Henry's "Alac! Alac! What Shall I Do?" (Alac! Alac! What shall I do?

---

[25] It is also possible, if these songs were composed after Ferdinand's repeated abandonments of Henry's forces, that they have an ironic counterpoint, i.e., that I am faithful, and you are not.

[26] See Nancy J. Vickers, "Diana Described: Scattered Woman and Scattered Rhyme," *Critical Inquiry* 8 (1981): 265–79, and Maureen Quilligan, "Sidney and his Queen," in *The Historical Renaissance: New Essays on Tudor and Stuart Literature and Culture*, ed. Heather Dubrow and Richard Strier (Chicago: University of Chicago Press, 1988), 171–96.

[27] Marotti, " 'Love is Not Love,' " 398.

[28] On the use of private miscellanies as forms of social protest, see Paul G. Remley, "Mary Shelton and Her Tudor Literary Milieu," in Herman, *Rethinking the Henrician Era*, 40–77.

/ For care is cast in to my heart / And true love locked thereto")[29] — and
its companion, "Hey Nonny Nonny, Nonny Nonny No!" — provide an
example of this. The two lyrics, taken together, provide one of the rare instances of male poets writing in a female voice.[30] In "Hey Nonny," the
speaker hears a maid "Right piteously complain" and then rehearses what
he hears:

> She said, alas,
>   Without trespass,
>   Her dear heart was untrue.
> In every place,
>   I know he has
> Forsaken me for a new. (ll. 9–14)

The inversion of the conventional assumption of male fidelity and female
lability (as Wyatt puts it, "continuously seeking with a continual change")
is interesting enough, and we will return to it. Right now, however, we
want to note that the lyric also inverts the language conventionally used
to describe the power relations between the desirer and the desired. The
female voice complains:

> And now I may,
>   In no manner away,
>   Obtain that I do sue.
> So ever and aye
>   Without denay [deny]
> My own sweet heart, adieu. (ll. 21–26)

To state the obvious, Henry-as-king is the object of everyone's desire. He
is the person sued, not the person suing, for favor. Nowhere is this made
more evident than in "If Love Now Reigned as it Has Been," where Henry offers a riddle to his audience: "To lovers I put now sure this case: /
Which of their loves does get them grace?" One must remember that Henry's audience would have known this question came from their monarch,
and just as the lady must "sue" the male, so now the elder disdainers must
sue the youthful, regal lover for political and amorous "grace," the two

---

[29] On the relationship between these two poems, see note 13 of Siemens's selection
of Henry's poems in this volume.

[30] See Elizabeth Harvey, *Ventriloquized Voices: Feminist Theory and Renaissance Texts*
(New York: Routledge, 1992).

being conflated. If, in the court of love, the choice lady offers the best grace to her suitor, in the court itself it is the king who offers grace, thus this lyric combines Henry's literary personae and his actual position.

Actions associated with grace in Henry's lyrics include what we expect of courtiers — suing, purchasing, and so forth[31] — not of a monarch, except in the guise of the courtly lover; here, likely as narrator, Henry is not the subservient lover, and the erotic story is adjusted accordingly. The *lady*, not the male lover, is now the one complaining that she cannot "In no manner away, / Obtain that I do sue" (ll. 22–23). It would have been impossible for Henry to constitute himself as a desiring subject for the simple reason that Henry is *not* a subject (even to the Pope, as the Reformation will later make clear).[32] Consequently, Henry alters the conventions of erotic verse so that they not only accord with his own position at the top of the hierarchy, but also reminds everyone, through the fact of public performance, that he is indeed the king, and kings do not sue, even in matters of the heart.

Yet the story ends happily. After overhearing the Lady complain, the royal speaker suddenly, almost miraculously, appears and makes everything better, though of course without apologizing for his previous indiscretions:

> She had not said
> > But, at abraid, [suddenly]
> > Her dear heart was full near
> And said good maid,
> > Be not dismayed,
> > My love, my darling dear. (ll. 45–50)

In addition, the song also suggests the culture of surveillance that is beginning to develop in Henry's court. One has a sense that the royal speaker can observe his desiring subject(s) without revealing his presence, and then, through an act of will, of power, suddenly make things better. The underlying implication, one that will be developed in "Pastime with Good

---

[31] Consider Henry's "Though That Men Do Call it Dotage" (l. 17), his "Who So That Wyll for Grace Sue" (l. 1), his "Without Discord" (ll. 19–20), and his "Lusty Youth Should us Ensue" (in which "disdainers . . . sue to get them grace" [ll. 14–15]).

[32] On the conflict between erotic and political subjectivity in Mary Stuart's verse, see Peter C. Herman's essay in this volume, " 'mes subjectz, mon ame assubjectie': The Problematic (of) Subjectivity in Mary Stuart's Sonnets."

Company" and "Though Some Say that Youth Rules Me," is that this power can be used for other, less benign, purposes as well.

This note of threat, so strangely foreign to conventional lyric verse, is amplified by the oddly discordant note in the ending:

> In arms he hent [held]
> That lady gent
> In voiding care and moan.
> The day they spent
> To their intent
> In wilderness, alone.

This seems like a traditionally comedic conclusion with the lovers in each others arms. Yet two points need to be made. First, the song only allows the pair one day of "voiding care and moan," implying that there will be more "care and moan" in the future. Second, Henry reinforces this implication by situating the ending "In wilderness." Stevens glosses this word as "the country" (398), yet the *OED* records no such use before 1644, and virtually all previous usages are some variation on "a tract of solitude and savageness" (1.b).[33] Assuming that both Henry and his audience would have had no trouble associating at some level Henry's lyrics with the court, this moment anticipates Wyatt's and Surrey's much later court satires, only this time it is Wyatt's "Caesar" and Surrey's "Sardanapalus" registering, however briefly and allusively, the dangers of courtly life.

This use of "wilderness" also imports a sense of sexuality's dangers, and perhaps also Henry's or his culture's distrust of women. The two themes come together again in "Whereto Should I Express," which begins with the royal speaker bemoaning his departure from his lady:

> Whereto should I express
> My inward heaviness?
> No mirth can make me fain,
> 'Till that we meet again. (ll. 1–4)

This seemingly conventional lyric, however, strays toward the unconventional near the end. At first, the speaker (anticipating Donne's "A Valediction Forbidding Mourning") reverses conventional gender expectations and asserts that "You are not variable," ascribing to the woman, in other

---

[33] See also the definitions in the online Early Modern English Dictionary Database, http://www.chass.utoronto.ca:8080/english/emed/patterweb.html.

words, the fixedness more usually associated with masculinity. The next stanza, however, makes clear that the beloved's invariability is not due to any unusual merit on her part, but results instead from the royal speaker's act of will. "*I* make you fast and sure," the speaker sings. Even when admitting a degree of powerlessness, in other words (the speaker must leave even though he doesn't want to), the poem very firmly reminds the audience that the speaker, however much in the throes of love melancholy, remains very much in charge.

The speaker's monarchic position similarly manifests itself in several of the lyrics in which Henry defends himself. The first three lines of "Pastime with Good Company," sound, for example, like a mere declaration of high spirits:

> Pastime with good company,
> I love and shall until I die.
> Grudge who likes, but none deny. (ll. 1–3)

In this text, Henry implicitly adopts the persona of Youth addressing the aged disdainers opposing his actions. According to convention, though, in the relationship of Youth and Old Age, it is Youth who is (putatively) subservient. However, when Henry invokes this convention, in effect he redefines it to endow Youth with the authority of his kingship. The fourth line — "So God be pleased, thus live will I," with manuscript variants also urging an equivalently possible reading of "So God be pleased, this life will I" — transforms the song into a vehicle through which Henry establishes his independence, "thus live [or "life"] will I" serving to remind one and all that these desires are the desires of the king.[34] The line, then, functions as a claim to power, to independence. It is not simply a declaration of high spirits; and no matter how frivolous the circumstances of performance, it would be hard for any courtier or lady mindful of the very few practical limitations on royal power to miss the overtone of threat vibrating in the last line of the burden:

> For my pastance:
> Hunt, sing, and dance.
> My heart is set!
> All goodly sport

---

[34] That "Grudge who likes" echoes the Burgundian motto *groigne qui groine* reinforces the regality of the statement.

> For my comfort.
> Who shall me *let*? (ll. 5–10; my emphasis)[35]

Similarly, in "Lusty Youth Should Us Ensue [imitate]," Henry uses a song that superficially appears to be an *apologia* for sowing wild oats to emphasize once more his royal independence:

> For they would have him his liberty refrain,
> And all merry company for to disdain.
> But I will not do whatsoever they say,
> But follow his mind in all that we may. (ll. 5–8)

Who will stop me from doing whatever I choose to do?, the king warbles to the assembled company.

Yet Henry's assertions of authority in these texts also evince a substratum of genuine insecurity. Defenses imply the existence of attacks, and the very fact that Henry felt compelled to assert his right to choose strongly suggests the existence of an unignorable "they" who wanted to restrain the king's liberty. While, as we have noted, we cannot precisely connect a particular lyric with a particular event, it is nonetheless interesting that Henry wrote these songs at about the same time that he began to separate himself from his father's domestic policies through extravagant spending, lavish entertaining, seeming indifference to the minutiae of government, and, perhaps most importantly, the instigation of a belligerent foreign policy diametrically opposed to Henry VII's pacific aims. Even though Henry's accession was widely (and wildly) celebrated, Henry's policies and pastimes very quickly developed significant opposition from some members of the nobility, as well as from humanists. Although Henry ultimately prevailed, he could not have realized that then, and we need to situate Henry's seemingly apolitical lyrics within the real, if ultimately overcome, resistance to his policies and preferred modes of recreation.

Hall records that while many applauded the king's pastimes, such as his taking part in tournaments, the older members of the court disapproved because of the dangers posed to the king and therefore the country:

> the ancient fathers much doubted [the prudence of Henry's hobby],
> considering the tender youth of the king, and divers chances of
> horses and armour: in so much that it was openly spoken, that

---

[35] Let = prevent.

steel was not so strong, but it might be broken, nor no horse could
be so sure of foot, but he may fall. (520)

In addition, many of the old guard were particularly unhappy with the
young King's desire to reverse his father's pacific policies and go to war for
the sake of chivalric honor. Henry's reign may have begun with a grand
sense of sweeping out the old and celebrating the new, yet a number of
Henry VII's advisors retained their place on the council, and they resisted
Henry's desire to involve England in a costly foreign venture.[36] But resistance emanated from more than a group of old spoilsports. Polydore Vergil
reports that Henry's initial proposal to join Ferdinand in his campaign
against the French in Italy met at first with considerable dissent:

> King Henry then summoned to London a council of his nobles.
> When they were assembled there the good king, full of devotion to
> the church, publicly expained how he had been requested by both
> Pope Julius and King Ferdinand his father-in-law to take up arms in
> defence of the church. For this reason he had summoned his no-
> bles, so that when asked they might speak their minds, whereby he
> could decide this weighty business from the general views of all.
> And to enable them to give their opinions, he questioned each
> separately. *After a long debate, many came to the conclusion on several
> grounds that there was no need to take up arms then*; because in the
> war against the French the pope had as allies King Ferdinand and
> the Venetians, whose support of the papal arms ought to be the
> more eager since it closely concerned their own interests; also be-
> cause England was far distant from Italy, and her assistance could
> only with difficulty be sent there; finally because, if they entered
> the war, being so far removed from Italy and Spain, it might per-
> haps happen that, the French having been evicted from Italy, the
> whole burden of the war would fall on this country, which would
> thus be involved in war while its allies were enjoying peace. *This
> view seemed correct to many*, but nevertheless the king scarcely
> agreed with it, for, owing to his confidence in his own resolution,
> he considered it to be dishonourable to him if so great a war waged

---

[36] The three are Thomas Ruthall, royal secretary from 1500 to 1516, William War-
ham, Chancellor of Oxford from 1506 until his death, and Richard Fox, Keeper of the
Privy seal. Dominic Baker-Smith, " 'Inglorious glory': 1513 and the Humanist Attack on
Chivalry," in *Chivalry in the Renaissance*, ed. Sydney Anglo (Woodbridge, England: Boy-
dell, 1990), 131–32.

against the Roman church should come to an end before some efforts of his own had been employed to end it. Wherefore the religious and most valiant prince, not unmindful that it was his duty to
seek fame by military skill, preferred so justifiable a war rather than
peace.[37] (my emphasis)

Thomas Wolsey also initially balked at the king's warmongering, mainly
because of the expense. In a report to Bishop Fox, Wolsey groused about
the malign influence of Sir Edward Howard, "by whose wanton means his
Grace spendeth much money, and is more disposed to war than peace."[38]
A French Papal diplomat noted that the king was a "youngling, car[ing]
for nothing but girls and hunting, and wast[ing] his father's patrimo-
ny,"[39] and the Bishops of Durham and Winchester commented (a bit
more charitably) that he "is young and does not care to occupy himself
with anything but the pleasures of his age."[40]

   In 1512, Henry's youthful disregard for danger also ran into considerable resistance from his councilors. Henry announced that since "his
English subjects were of such high spirits that they tended to fight less
willingly and less successfully under any commander other than their
king," the obvious course was for him to lead the troops personally.[41]
Significantly, Henry had to browbeat his nobles into agreeing with him:

> Wherefore he again summoned a council of nobles and there was
> a general discussion concerning the newly proposed expedition.
> *Many considered it too perilous that the king in the first flush of his
> youthful maturity in arms should expose himself to the danger of so great
> a war.* They accordingly thought that a commander of the army
> should be appointed who would conduct the war according to the
> king's wishes. *This view was thoroughly approved by many but not by
> the king, who held to his original opinion* and argued that it behooved
> him to enter upon his first military experience in so important and
> difficult a war in order that he might, by a signal start to his mar-

---

[37] *The Anglica Historia of Polydore Vergil, A.D. 1485–1537*, ed. Denys Hay (London:
Royal Historical Society, 1950; Camden Society, 3rd series, vol. 74), 161.

[38] Quoted in Baker-Smith, " 'Inglorious glory,' " 136.

[39] *Letters and Papers of Henry VIII*, vol. 2: 292.

[40] *Calendar of Letters, Despatches, and State Papers Relating to the Negotiations Between
English and Spain*, ed. G. A. Bergenroth et al. (London: Longmans, 1862), vol. 1.2: 40–
41.

[41] *Anglica Historia*, 197.

tial knowledge, create such a fine opinion about his valour among all men that they would clearly understand that his ambition was not merely to equal but indeed to exceed the glorious deeds of his ancestors ... [H]e persistently asserted that he wished with the approval of all to take charge of the matter himself; if this were conceded he was sure that at no point would he be deprived of divine assistance in undertaking so meritorious a war. When the nobles saw that the king, on account of the confidence he had in his own great valour, *they were unable not to agree with him.*[42] (my emphasis)

Vergil indirectly implies his distance from Henry's glorious, yet politically irresponsible, desires through careful diction and irony. It is Henry's "confidence" — overconfidence? — that leads to their agreement, yet an agreement that is hedged by the double negative: "*non* potuere *non* in eius tandem sentientiam ire" (198).

Henry eventually got his war, but only after King Louis refused peace, saying via Henry's ambassador that he "would not by any means agree to making peace on the terms which the pope demanded."[43] And even then Henry achieved permission for only a limited intervention as Ferdinand's ally. In addition, Henry could not have remained either ignorant or untouched by the humanist disapproval of war and chivalry expressed in such popular texts as More's *Utopia* and Erasmus' adage deconstructing the eagle as a noble creature, *Scarabeus Aquilam Querit*. The king might metaphorically twist Colet's arm after his impolitic sermon denouncing war, but others were less immediately pliable.[44]

Then there is the matter of Thomas Wolsey. Vergil (like Hall and so many others) hated the Cardinal, but it is important that his rise also occasioned resistance among Henry's counselors:

Wolsey [conducted] all business at his own pleasure, since no one at all was of more value to the king. It was certainly as a result of this that several leading counselors, when they saw so much power coming into the hands of one man, withdrew gradually from the court. Canterbury and Winchester were among the first to leave, going into their dioceses. But before they left, *like truly responsible*

---

[42] *Anglica Historia*, 199. See also Starkey's rather fanciful renarration of this incident in *The Reign of Henry VIII: Personalities and Politics* (London: George Philip, 1985), 49.

[43] *Anglica Historia*, 163. See also Starkey, *The Reign of Henry VIII*, 49.

[44] Baker-Smith, " 'Inglorious glory,' " 138–40.

statesmen, they earnestly urged the king not to suffer any servant to be greater than his master: they borrowed this saying from Christ, who, in the gospel according to St. John, says to his disciples, "Verily, verily, I say unto you, the servant is not greater than his lord." Aware at all events that these remarks were directed at Wolsey, Henry replied to them that he would make it his first business diligently to ensure that any servant of his was obedient and not autocratic. Then Thomas duke of Norfolk retired to his estates; and afterwards even Charles [Brandon] duke of Suffolk followed the others.[45]

The implication of the last sentence is that despite Henry's assurances, Wolsey continued on his autocratic path. Furthermore, if Canterbury and Winchester act as "truly responsible statesmen" by warning Henry, then Henry by implication acts irresponsibly by not heeding their advice.

Consequently, the curious defensiveness radiating from a number of Henry's lyrics becomes more understandable. It would have been clear to Henry that not only his elders, but also the humanists whose favor he courted, as well as a certain amount of public opinion, disapproved of his chivalric role-playing and his warmongering. Henry thus uses the persona of Youth to pre-empt or answer criticism of how he chooses to conduct his life, but goes against the generic expectations of Youth by asserting his royal right to do exactly as he pleases. Henry concludes "Pastime," for example, by assuring his audience that "The best ensue. / The worst eschew. / My mind shall be. / Virtue to use. / Vice to refuse. / Thus shall I use me!" (ll. 25–30). Similarly, in "The Time of Youth is to Be Spent," Henry explicitly takes on his critics and defends his chivalric games as encouraging virtue:

> The time of youth is to be spent,
> But vice in it should be forfent. [forbidden]
> Pastimes there be I note truly
> Which one may use and vice deny.
> And they be pleasant to God and man:
> Those should we covet [desire] when we can.
> As feats of arms, and such other
> Whereby activeness one may utter.
> Comparisons in them may lawfully be set,

---

[45] *Anglica Historica,* 231–33.

> For, thereby, courage is surely out fet. [gained]
> Virtue it is, then, youth for to spend
> In good disports which it does fend.

In "Lusty Youth Should Us Ensue," Henry once again defends himself, this time against all "disdainers." It is possible, however, that Henry uses this lyric to react explicitly against the breaking up of his group of "minions" in the reorganization of the court. When Henry first came to power, he brought with him a cohort of friends, "young gentlemen," as Hall calls them (581), who — with Henry — acted in a manner that the king's counsel found utterly inimical to the dignity of their position and the king's person. In what must have seemed like a classic example of Old Age restraining Youth, the counsel met secretly to put a stop to this state of affairs. As Hall reports:

> the kynges counsaill secretly communed together of the kynges gentrenes & liberalitee to all persones: by the whiche they perceived that certain young men in his privie chamber not regardyng his estate nor degree, were so familier and homely with hum, and plaied such light touches with hym that they forgat thmeselfes: ... yet the kinges counsail thought it not mete to be suffred for the kynges honor, & therfor thei altogether came to the king, beseching him al these enormities and lightnes to redres. To whom the kung answered, that he had chosen them of his counsaill, both for the maintenaunce of his honor, & for the defence of all thyng that might blemishe thesame: wherefore it they sawe any about hym misuse theimselfes, he committed it to their reformacion. (598)

The result was that "the kynges minions" were banished and "foure sad and auncient knightes, put into the kynges privie chamber" (598).[46] While Henry appears to have acquiesced to the replacement of his partners in male bonding and youthful exuberance with what must have seemed like chaperones, "Lusty Youth Should Us Ensue" offers a slightly different view on this:

> Lusty Youth should us ensue.
> His merry heart shall sure all [i.e., disdainers] rue.
> For whatsoever they do him tell
> It is not for him, we know it well.

---

[46] Lerer, *Courtly Letters*, 42–43; Starkey, "Intimacy and Innovation," 80–81.

> For they would have him his liberty refrain,
> *And all merry company for to disdain.*
> But I will not do whatsoever they say,
> But follow his mind in all that we may.
>   (ll. 1–8; my emphasis)

The next two stanzas constitute a *defense* of not just Youth's "pastance," but of Henry's "merry company":

> How should youth himself best use
> But all disdainers for to refuse?
> Youth has as chief assurance
> Honest mirth with virtue's pastance.
>
> For in them consists great honour,
> Though that disdainers would therein put error.
> For they do sue to get them grace,
> All only riches to purchase. (ll. 9–16)

And yet, for the rest of the song, Henry, perhaps bowing to the inevitable, grants that the disdainers have a point, and that he will work towards balance:

> With good order, counsel, and equity,
> Good Lord grant us our mansion to be.
> For without their good guidance
> Youth should fall in great mischance.
>
> For Youth is frail and prompt to do
> As well vices as virtues to ensue.
> Wherefore by these he must be guided,
> And virtue's pastance must therein be used.
>
> Now unto God this prayer we make,
> That this rude play may well betake
> And that we may our faults amend
> And bliss obtain at our last end. Amen. (ll. 17–28)

Whether or not one finds the final turn to religion convincing, this lyric offers a masterful diplomatic performance. Henry must have felt humiliated by the actions of his elders, although he clearly believed that he had no choice but to submit. Henry's actions before his elders, as recorded by Hall and in his lyric, demonstrate Henry's trying to turn this successful affront to his authority to his advantage by essentially arguing both sides of the issue. That is to say, Henry initially rebuts his elders by calling them "disdainers" and by asserting once more his royal will ("I will not ..."). Yet (assuming the king penned this lyric after the counsel's actions), Henry turns, admits that youth is indeed frail and in need of guidance. Hence the final turn to religion, which makes *Henry* the originator of his merry company's banishment. The lyric concludes, in other words, with Henry turning a corrosion of royal authority into a strengthening of it.

It is "Though Some Say That Youth Rules Me," however, that is the most interesting because it is the most overt example of Henry using a parlor song as a vehicle for simultaneously rebutting and reassuring his elders. The song begins in a seemingly defensive, if not apologetic, mood:

> Though some say that youth rules me,
>> I trust in age to tarry.
> God and my right, and my duty,
>> From them shall I never vary,
>> Though some say that youth rules me. (ll. 1–5)

Yet Henry's incorporation of his royal motto, "Dieu et mon droit," in the third line both reassures his audience that the king is mindful of his royal position and also reminds them of the power invested in the crown. In the next stanza, Henry furthers his offensive by asking his critics how they acted in their youth: "I pray you all that aged be / How well did you *your* youth carry?" (ll. 6–7; my emphasis). Henry ends this lyric with a strategically placed revelation of the author's name and, most importantly, his title:

> Then soon discuss that hence we must
>> Pray we to God and Saint Mary
> That all amend, and here an end.
>> Thus says the King, the eighth Harry,
>> Though some say that youth rules me. (ll. 16–20)

More than "Pastime with Good Company," this song deserves the title of "The King's Ballad" because it would be inconceivable for anyone other than Henry VIII to perform it. And, for this reason, this lyric is the most deeply political of Henry's efforts. What begins as a somewhat sheepish defense hearkening back to the conventional Youth-Age debates of medieval poetry becomes an overt assertion of royal power and royal prerogative. It is the *king* — and the eighth of that name to sit on England's throne, a position which gives him the collective authority of the previous seven (not the least being Henry V) — who issues this defense of his life; and by including this self-referential allusion to his position and his name's history, Henry VIII forcefully reminds his listeners that if youth rules the king, it is the king who rules everyone else.

In conclusion, Henry's lyrics are not just the remnants of an early Tudor parlor game. Instead, they directly respond to the anxieties caused by the crowning of a new king whose policies and personality differ radically from the previous monarch's. Henry VIII has the (admittedly unlikely) distinction of being the first English king to use vernacular courtly verse as a device for both talking about and actually *doing* politics; specifically, Henry used his lyrics as vehicles for establishing his independence from Henry VII's policies, if not from Henry VII himself, and for articulating as forcefully as possible that he, and only he, rules the land. Henry VIII's lyrics thus constitute an unrecognized watershed in the history of Renaissance the lyric.

Peter C. Herman, San Diego State University
Ray G. Siemens, Malaspina University-College

LISA HOPKINS

Writing to Control:
The Verse of Mary, Queen of Scots

THE EARLIEST KNOWN PIECE OF POETRY by Mary, Queen of Scots dates
from 1559, when she was seventeen, and queen not only of Scotland but
also of France. After the death of her father, James V of Scotland, shortly
after her birth, the country had been plunged into turmoil, and ravaged by
the attacks of the English king, Henry VIII, who sought the infant Mary
as a bride for his son, Edward, and sent an army to secure her in what became known as "The Rough Wooing." The young queen's mother, Mary
of Guise, already had been compelled to abandon in France the son of her
first marriage. He later died in childhood, and she had also lost in infancy
the two sons she had borne James. Determined not to lose this last, precious child, she negotiated through her Guise-Lorraine relatives a betroth-
al to Francis, eldest son of Henri II, and at the age of five the young
queen, with five small attendants also called Mary, left her kingdom for
the safety of France and the care of her powerful Guise grandmother and
uncles (one of whom was later to be immortalised in Marlowe's The Massa-
cre at Paris). As first "reine-dauphine" and later queen of France, she
became thoroughly steeped in French court culture, and it is against this
background, and in particular the tuition which she received from Ronsard
and the other members of the Pléiade, that her use and development of a
poetic voice and persona must be understood. In one sense, to write poetry
in such surroundings may be said to have come naturally to her; equally,
however, the kind of poetry which she had been trained to write was consciously artificial. It is in this tension between expressivity and formality

that the chief interest of Mary's poetry may be felt to lie.

Mary's first surviving poem is, like all her work, in French; she forgot her Scots after her departure at the age of five, and French remained throughout her life the language which she used and preferred. Headed "Quatrain écrit dans le livre de Messe de sa tante Anne de Lorraine, La duchesse d'Aerschot" (Quatrain Written in the Mass Book Belonging to Her Aunt Anne of Lorraine, Duchess of Aerschot),[1] it runs as follows:

> Si ce lieu est pour écrire ordonné
> Ce qu'il vous plaît avoir en souvenance,
> Je vous requiers que lieu me soit donné
> Et que nul temps m'en ôte l'ordonnance.
> Reine de France Marie.

This has been most recently translated thus:

> If I am ordered to write in this space
> Because you're pleased by such a souvenir,
> I ask of you always to save my place
> And ne'er withdraw the order I have here.
> Mary Queen of France.[2]

More literally, however, it might well be rendered thus:

> If this place is ordered for writing
> That which it pleases you to have in remembrance,
> I require of you that this place be given me
> And that no time take away the ordering from me.

Though it is less polished, I shall prefer for the moment to work with my own translation, since it highlights certain aspects of the poem which seem to me to be both distinctive in themselves and which also recur as keynotes throughout her compositions. The presence of these elements means that, though the poem itself is brief, I think that both it and the circumstances of its composition are worth spending some time on.

The lines should not be considered in isolation from their physical

---

[1] This translation is taken from Robin Bell, *Bittersweet Within My Heart: The Collected Poems of Mary, Queen of Scots* (London: Pavilion, 1992), 15. All subsequent quotations from Mary's poems, either in the original or in translation, will be taken from this edition unless otherwise specified. As Bell has translated the poems into verse, I have sometimes provided a more literal rendition of my own.

[2] Bell, *Bittersweet Within My Heart*, 14–15.

location. They are written in a Mass book, thus setting a pattern for Mary's later compositions on the leaves of her Book of Hours[3] (others of her poems are similarly tied, albeit in different ways, to concrete physical objects or locations). Though God is not directly mentioned, the poem is implicitly situated within a context of both personal and public piety (specifically the Catholicism to which Mary was so controversially to adhere throughout her life), as, again, much of her subsequent verse would be. Equally, though, the poem's presence in this particular Mass book imbues it with clear political significance. It belonged to "Her Aunt Anne of Lorraine, Duchess of Aerschot," a member of Mary's mother's family, the House of Guise and Lorraine. Appropriately enough, it may seem, Robin Bell's handsomely-illustrated edition includes beneath the poem a double portrait of Mary's parents, James V of Scotland and Mary of Guise. In the painting, the light falls from the left, illuminating the golden background of the lion of Scotland much more brightly than the complex quarterings of the House of Guise-Lorraine, and picking out the gold Latin lettering which names in full the king but not the queen. The inclusion of this image serves to point up the striking contrast of the absolute absence of the paternal line in Mary's poem and signature. Written in the French of her mother's family rather than the Scots of her father's, it is addressed to her mother's sister, and signed not as we would know her, "Mary, Queen of Scots," but "Reine de France Marie." It thus triply encodes that completeness of identification with France and with her Guise mother which would so thoroughly undo her when circumstances forced her to return to Scotland — and this even though the writing of verse was in fact a tradition in the Scottish royal family, practised first and most notably by her ancestor James I in *The King's Quair*, but also by her father James V.[4]

The subscription "Reine de France Marie" underlines not only the adopted nationality but also the status of the writer, and the poem itself plays with the language of command, ending its first line with "ordonné"

---

[3] See Bell, *Bittersweet Within My Heart*, 111, for the details of these. He notes that the original is preserved in the M. E. Saltykov-Schedrin Library in St. Petersburg, MS Lat Q. V.I. 112, and that there are photographs of the pages with poems on in the Advocates' Library of the National Library of Scotland, MS 81.55. The English translations given after each poem are by Bell.

[4] James V's Usher, and later his Lord Lyon King-of-Arms, was Sir David Lindsay of the Mount, author of *Ane Satyre of the Thrie Estaitis*. Lindsay's surviving poems include "The Answer to the Kingis Flyting," a piece of occasional verse in response to a poem by James himself.

and its last with "ordonnance." Robin Bell identifies this as "the first known example of Mary's fondness for wordplay. She plays on ordonné / ordonnance, just as eight years later she plays on sujets / assujettie in the sonnet to Bothwell 'Entre ses mains et en son plein pouvoir.'"[5] The authorship of that alleged "sonnet to Bothwell" is of course much disputed, but the presence in it of punning on words associated with Mary's own regal status certainly would accord with her practice in this early quatrain. Here the tone moves with extraordinary rapidity from the opening uncertainty of "Si" ("If") to the triumphant conclusion of "Et que nul temps m'en ôte l'ordonnance" ("And that no time take away the ordering from me"). The poem as a whole is structured by verbs of control and request — "ce lieu est ... ordonné" ("this place is ordered"), "Ce qu'il vous plaît" ("what it pleases you"), "Je vous requiers" (I request you), "que lieu me soit donné" ("that place be given me"). These are all the verbs used in the first three lines, and it is worth noting that, although Bell's translation begins with "If I am ordered," in the original version Mary herself is *never* the subject of a command: instead, "this place is ... ordered," "I request you," and, in "que lieu me soit donné," "let place be given me." This last example introduces the subjunctive into the poem, and the subjunctive construction continues into the final line in a way which dissipates the sense of its original dependence on the main clause and gives it instead the ring of a free-standing statement.

Formally, the logic of the grammar all depends on the opening words of the second couplet, "Je vous requiers" ("I require you"), which ostensibly invest power in the hands of the Duchess Anne. It is she who must see that "lieu me soit donné" ("place be given me"). When we move on to "Et que nul temps m'en ôte l'ordonnance" ("And that no time take away the ordering from me"), though, the subject of the verb "ôte" ("take away") is clearly "temps" ("time"), not "vous" ("you"). The Duchess Anne's supremacy has been displaced by Time's; moreover, Time has a rival for control — Mary herself, from whom Time cannot take "l'ordonnance" ("the ordering"). Indeed Mary's power was already implicit in the previous line: the Duchess Anne may be able to ensure that "lieu me soit donné" ("place be given me"), but her action is already dependent on the fact that Mary "requires" ("requiers") it. The seventeen-year-old who signed herself "Reine de France Marie" sounds a confident note indeed, even in the face of Time.

---

[5] Bell, *Bittersweet Within My Heart*, 14.

The rather unexpected mention of time — in a poem which has previously concentrated so exclusively on place — draws attention to another facet of Mary's exercise of control. Her education at the French court had introduced her to the poetic fashions of the Pléiade,[6] and this is a self-consciously sophisticated exercise in approved poetic diction and devices. Although its presence in a Mass book, and its overt references to itself as merely something for the Duchess to "avoir en souvenance" ("have in remembrance"), seem to suggest a throwaway, impromptu composition, it is carefully crafted into regular pentameters (with 'ôte' pronounced as two syllables) and an abab rhyme scheme, while the time-place contrast is not only pointed in itself but also clearly in line with the Petrarchan obsession with time and its relation to the written.[7] The pun on "ordonné" / "ordonnance" highlights this other aspect of "ordonnance," the writer's control of the poem. This desire to achieve ordering in words, even when in no other aspect of her life, was never to leave Mary, Queen of Scots; nor was the implicit valuing of the very act of writing itself, implied by the absence of any object for the verb "écrire" ("to write") in the opening line, which allows it to stand as an act valued for itself alone. Thus, though these lines were written at what was perhaps the happiest period of a life which was never to know much happiness again, their continuity with Mary's later writing is nevertheless striking. She was always to value the ordering act of writing as an exercise of skill suitable to her education and status; and she was always to do so, too, in the implicit or explicit context of her adherence to the Catholic faith.

---

[6] An unusual but illuminating approach to her relationship with the members of the *Pleiade* is offered in Helen Smailes and Duncan Thomson, *The Queen's Image: A Celebration of Mary Queen of Scots* (Edinburgh: Scottish National Portrait Gallery, 1987). They discuss Ronsard's poem about an actual portrait of the Queen (33), and the influence of Chatelard and Ronsard on nineteenth-century history paintings of Mary (74), as well as the nineteenth-century forger W. H. Ireland's faked "Chatelard" poems about the queen (78). They also reproduce John Rogers Herbert's 1830s reworking of Louis Ducis's portrait of Mary as Saint Cecilia listening to Rizzio playing his setting of "her" poem "Adieu plaisant pays de France" (80; the poem was not in fact by Mary). In addition, they quote part of Southwell's poem on Mary (136).

[7] For Petrarch and the Pléiade, see most recently Lachlan Mackinnon, "Petrarch's Heir," a review of Ronsard's *Oeuvres Complètes*, *Times Literary Supplement*, 19 January 1996, 28–29. Julian Sharman in his edition of Mary's verses notes her lifelong fondness for poetry, born partly of her early association with the Pléiade; he comments on Philip II's choice of Garcilaso de la Vega as an ambassador to her (*The Poems of Mary Queen of Scots* [London: Pickering, 1873], 3) and on her ownership of books of poetry (5), but he dismisses her relationship with Brantôme in particular as merely one of flattery, calling the poet's praise of her Latin inaccurate and insincere (7).

To illustrate this continuity, one can place beside this earliest of her poems a two-verse one from much later in her life. "Versets" ("Verses"), written in 1582, was not identified as Mary's until three hundred years later,[8] but its similarities to the Mass-book lines are immediately obvious:

> Celui vraiment n'a point de courtoisie
> Qui en bon lieu ne montre son savoir;
> Etant requis d'écrire en poésie,
> Il vaudrait mieux du tout n'en point avoir.
>
> A man is lacking in civility
> If, when time calls, he fails to show his wit.
> And when the occasion merits poetry
> He would far rather have no part of it.

Here the situation posited is virtually identical to that of the Mass-book sonnet: the poem concerns a person "Etant requis d'écrire en poésie" ("Being required to write in poetry"). This time, though, there is no explicit reference to Mary herself, and indeed pronouns and adjectives are consistently masculine throughout the poem, as indicated in Bell's translation by the opening words, "A man," picking up on the masculine gender of the French "celui." It thus becomes less a personal statement than a generalisation, although one which could certainly be read as operating within the old-fashioned convention which subsumes women within the generic category "man" (as is indeed still reflected in the rules of modern French grammar, where plural forms which refer to both genders together are always masculine). Equally, there is no named commissioner of the verses here; Bell translates "when the occasion merits poetry," but even this imparts a concreteness absent in the original, where the fact of being "requis" ("required") is merely a *donnée*, never explained.

Though the personal dynamic of the situation is not expanded upon, however, the social codes which govern it are quite clear. As in Mary's

---

[8] Bell, *Bittersweet Within My Heart*, 93. Bell's translation also occurs on this page, with the original on the preceding one. In each case, these lines are immediately followed by another quatrain ("Les dieux, les cieux, la mort et la haine et l'envie"), discovered at the same time as this one, and, in Bell's edition, printed as though the two together might form part of the same poem. However, since neither meter nor rhyme scheme is the same, I have assumed the second couplet to be a separate entity, although the two together would provide a suggestive contrast between the assured, social (and masculine-gendered) voice of the first and the persecuted, person-oriented and female persona of the second.

first poem, we again find reference to "lieu," the "place" (rather mislead-
ingly translated by Bell as "time") where poetry is to be displayed, though
this time the "place" is a less tangible object than the Mass book was on
the first occasion. Indeed this verse could read almost as a gloss on the
first poem, explicating the unstated code of "courtoisie" ("courtesy") and
value for "savoir" ("learning") which inform the Mass book lines; and
these two crucial concepts are themselves clarified by their prominent
positions at the end of the first two lines and their consequent associations
with their rhyme-words, "poésie" ("poetry") and "avoir" ("to have").
These two pairings may well be thought to be interestingly counter-
pointed: while "courtoisie" and "poésie" chime together as inextricably
connected, "savoir" and "avoir" ("to know" and "to have") are more
problematically linked in their denoting of inner qualities and outward
possessions. Given the poem's status as a product of Mary's imprisonment,
one might well ponder the way that "du tout n'en point avoir" ("to have
nothing at all of any of it") — the overwhelmingly negative phrases which
are grouped together to provide the poem's conclusion — is set against the
value-laden words "courtoisie," "savoir," and "poésie," the legacies of a
courtly, cultured education which is ineradicable even in adversity.

Such spirit may, at first sight, be hard to find in the poem which was
found at the same time as this one, and which Robin Bell prints immediately below it:

> Les dieux, les cieux, la mort et la haine et l'envie
> Sont sourds, ires, cruels, animés contre moi.
> Prier, souffrir, pleurer, à chacun être amie,
> Sont les remèdes seuls qu'en tant d'ennuis je vois.
>
> [The gods, the heavens, death, envy and hate rail on;
> They are deaf, angry, cruel, marshalled against me.
> To pray, weep, suffer, be a friend to everyone
> Are the only cures for the many woes I see.]

This may well seem to represent Mary's darkest hour, and to bear no
single remaining trace of that confident girl who defied Time and signed
herself "Reine de France Marie." However harassed and despairing the
poem's tone, however, its structure still encodes a recognisable element of
control over the situation, echoing the "ordonnance" provided by the act
of writing in the Mass book. The complex dodecasyllabic metre forces a
careful reading which does not merely list the forces opposed to Mary but
also verbally separates and isolates them, an effect which is reinforced by

the double "et" of the first line, and which is clearly working to suggest that even if Mary is almost overwhelmed by evils, she has at least not lost her intellectual purchase on the apprehension and description of them. The rhythm continues to be important, and to create the impression that she can, at least, still exercise the control of crafting language. In the second line, the caesura after "cruels" is followed by an abrupt change of tempo suitable to the more active and impassioned attitude suggested by "animés": this alexandrine, unlike Pope's wounded snake, thus whiplashes back, but the vehemence with which Mary's enemies are thus endowed must perforce be equalled by her own vigor as the writer of the line. Similarly, though she chooses to stress her own passivity in the next line — "Prier, souffrir, pleurer, à chacun être amie" ("To pray, to suffer, to cry, to be a friend to everybody") — her decision to "être amie" ("to be a friend") quietly affirms her status. She who will choose to be a friend must still have power (and could indeed choose to be an enemy); and it is worthwhile noting that it is only superhuman or abstract forces which she imagines opposing her — the only other humans mentioned in the poem are denoted by the "chacun" whom she will befriend. It is perhaps in that understated decision that we hear most clearly that it is, indeed, "Reine de France Marie" who is speaking still.

The regal tone is, fittingly enough, even more audible when Mary, Queen of Scots addresses her sister queen, Elizabeth I. From the moment that, at the behest of her father-in-law Henri II of France, Mary claimed the English throne on the death of Catholic Mary Tudor, dismissing Protestant Elizabeth as a bastard, she made Elizabeth her enemy, though on her first arrival in Scotland there were uneasy gestures at cousinly reconciliation (punctuated by such surprising and straining incidents as Elizabeth's suggestion that Mary should marry her own discarded suitor the Earl of Leicester, and Mary's unwelcome decision to take as her actual husband their mutual cousin Darnley, an English subject). Part of these intermittent and halting civilities consisted of the sending of verses, something which inaugurated a tendency for the two queens to image each other in poetry for the remainder of their relationship.

An early poem which Mary is said to have dispatched along with a diamond to the English court is lost, except in Latin translations,[9] but a Sonnet to Elizabeth survives in both French and Italian versions. The French, which would undoubtedly have been the language of the original

---

[9] See Bell, *Bittersweet Within My Heart*, 21–25.

composition, begins "Un seul penser qui me profite et nuit" ("One thought, that is my torment and delight"; the complete poem, with translation, is reproduced elsewhere in this book). From the outset, the language and imagery of this arguably most technically accomplished and mellifluous of all Mary's poems belong recognisably to the poetic traditions of the Pléiade in which Mary had been educated at the court of France. The opening quatrain is structured primarily around classic Petrarchan paradoxes — "me profite et nuit" ("that profits and harms me"), "amer et doux" ("bitter and sweet"), "le doute et l'espoir" ("fear and hope") — and the groupings of contrarieties here strikingly offset the sudden switch to the sustained, single-minded plea of the second quatrain, with its relentless emphasis on Mary's overwhelming desire to see Elizabeth. The double use of "suit" and "ensuit" (both, roughly, "follows") further underlines the sense of insistence, as does the grammatical unity of the quatrain with its "Donc ... C'est que" ("Therefore" ... "It's because") structure. With the sestet, though, the poem switches again, as indeed befits its opening announcement that "Un seul penser ... change en mon coeur sans cesse" ("A single thought changes incessantly within my heart"). Dropping the personal tone of the plea for a meeting, Mary reverts to a more conventional poetic voice with the image of the ship so beloved of Petrarchan tradition.[10] As customarily, this connotes instability and the changeability of Fortune, and also affords Mary an opportunity for disclaiming fear or doubt of Elizabeth personally and displacing her anxieties onto the figure of Fortune.[11] Once more, we hear a poetic voice aware both of its training and its status, fearing no human power, but only those above.

The power whom Mary feared and reverenced most was of course her God, the "Seigneur et Père Souverain" (Lord and Sovereign Father) as she terms him in a phrase richly suggestive of ascendancy in both spiritual and temporal hierarchies.[12] Bell points to the importance of the phrase "hum-

---

[10] This use of an image at once conventional and strongly visual accords with her practice in the choice of themes for her embroideries. See for instance Jane Roberts, *Royal Artists from Mary Queen of Scots to the Present Day* (London: Grafton Books, 1987), 40–41.

[11] Bell suggests that Elizabeth's line "No forreine bannisht wight shall ancre in this port" (from the "The Doubt of Future Foes") is a direct response to Mary's ship imagery (*Bittersweet Within My Heart*, 62).

[12] This occurs in her "Méditation sur l'inconstance et vanité du monde ..." ("Meditation on the inconstancy and vanity of the world"). See Bell, *Bittersweet Within My Heart*, 72.

ble et dévot" ("humble and devout") in the religious poetry which she
wrote during her long incarceration,[13] and in her addresses to her God
"Reine de France Marie" did indeed adopt, uniquely, the language of
humility. He is, indeed, the only being in whom she can acknowledge a
title greater than her own, and she does so very early indeed in a sonnet
written in 1583, well into the period of her imprisonment, which begins
"Donne, Seigneur, donne-moi patience" ("Give me, O Lord, the patience
to progress"). Though this poem does indeed acknowledge God as "Seigneur" ("Lord"), it is equally remarkable that it does so in the course of is-
suing a series of commands to him. Every verb relating to God is either an
imperative or, equally associated with commmand, a subjunctive —
"Donne" ("Give"), "Renforce" ("Reinforce"), "Que ton esprit me con-
duise en ta loi" ("Let your spirit guide me in your law"), "Reluis"
("Relight"), "m'ôte" ("take from me"), "Ne permet" ("Do not permit"),
"Délivre-moi" ("Deliver me"), and "prouve-moi" ("try me").

To some extent the traditional format of prayer allows for precisely this
sequence of instructions to God: "Give us this day our daily bread, and
forgive us our trespasses." The Lord's prayer, however, also includes recip-
rocal acknowledgement — "Our Father, which art in heaven, hallowed be
thy name." Equally notable is a silent but powerful omission from the per-
sonnel of Mary's religious verse: though a devout and lifelong Catholic,
she never addresses the intercessory figure of her own namesake the Virgin, but speaks instead directly to God. Though in one sense this may
seem to take her closer to the prayer practices of Protestantism than of her
own religion, is perhaps influenced by the desire, which may also be present in the preference for masculine pronouns, to avoid flaunting too openly the image of feminine power so demonised by those who inveighed
against female rule. Equally, though, it can be seen as arising from a simple sense of her own status, which precludes the need for any intermediary
when two sovereigns speak. The woman who had herself been hymned as
a "Déesse" ("Goddess") by Ronsard could speak direct to a God;[14] she
is, after all, "Reine de France Marie."

This continuing awareness of her own position is perhaps most clearly

---

[13] Bell, *Bittersweet Within My Heart*, 80.

[14] See Antonia Fraser, *Mary Queen of Scots* [1969] (London: Granada, 1970), 104.
Mary may also have been the recipient of poems from her second husband, Darnley;
three, one in English and two in Scots, are reproduced, translated and commented on by
Caroline Bingham in her recent biography *Darnley* (London: Constable, 1995), 92–96.

illustrated in one of the quatrains which she wrote in her Book of Hours:[15]

> En feinte mes amis changent leur bienveillance.
> Tout le bien qu'ils me font est désirer ma mort,
> Et comme si, mourant, j'étais en défaillance
> Dessus mes vêtements ils ont jeté le sort.
>
> [With feigned goodwill my friends change toward me,
> All the good they do me is to wish me dead,
> As if, while I lay dying helplessly,
> They cast lots for my garments round my bed.][16]

Bell's translation, quoted above, is unusually misleading here, for in order to find a rhyme for "dead" he has introduced, without any warrant in the original, the idea of a "bed." While the speaker of Mary's poem is certainly dying, they are not doing so in a bed: the second couplet could be more literally rendered as "And as if, dying, I were failing, / Beneath my garments they cast lots." The motif is, then, clearly recognisable as referring to the story of Christ on the cross, as the soldiers diced for the seamless robe. Mary is not actually equating herself with her saviour — to do so would be sacrilegious — for the adjective "mourant" ("dying") which describes the poem's speaker is masculine; nevertheless, she has adopted his persona, just as elsewhere in the Book of Hours she speaks in the voice of the book itself.[17]

There are, however, some poems ostensibly written by Mary that adopt a very different tone. The notorious Casket Letters included a sequence of twelve sonnets.[18] Antonia Fraser, arguing that these were not in fact by Mary, comments that "Brantôme and Ronsard, who both had intimate

---

[15] The intimate status of this object is clearly indicated by the fact that it was kept in her personal cupboard, along with her toiletries; see David H. Caldwell and Rosalind K. Marshall, *The Queen's World* (Edinburgh: Scottish National Portrait Gallery, 1987), 4.

[16] Bell, *Bittersweet Within My Heart*. The original is on page 90 and the translation on page 91.

[17] See Bell, *Bittersweet Within My Heart*, 88, first poem and note.

[18] On the Casket Letters, see especially Fraser, *Mary Queen of Scots*, 463ff. Fraser sees the twelve sonnets as essentially one poem (464 and 477), but does not explain why. She calls many of the "casket" documents "manifestly absurd when applied to the relationship possible between Queen Mary and Bothwell" (466), and sees them essentially as a palimpsest of original material written by Mary, love-letters and love-poems written to Bothwell by another woman, and forged material. Suggestively, she finds "a genuine Marian ring [where] the tone is regal" (476).

knowledge of Mary's earlier verses, indignantly denied that these poems could have been by Mary Stuart," and herself opines that "[t]hese long turgid verses are certainly remarkably unlike Mary's known poetic efforts, her early simple poems and her later more complicated poetry, which tends to be extremely courtly in phrase and analogy, as might be expected from the atmosphere of the High Renaissance in which she had been educated."[19] Fraser attributes the poems to an "other woman," an unnamed mistress of Bothwell's, who she finds more plausible as the author of lines like those which marvel at Bothwell's wealth and which express a frantic jealousy about his sexual fidelity. Interestingly, though, Fraser treats the claims of one sonnet, "Entre ses mains et en son plain pouvoir," rather more seriously, remarking that "[t]he only lines in the total of 158 which might seem to apply to Mary, and to Mary only, are those in which she describes how she has subjected herself, her son, her country and her subjects to Bothwell."[20] Even here, Fraser finds that "third line has an odd ring," and wonders if "sujets" has been interpolated to replace a word which may originally have been monosyllabic, and which was less suggestive of royal authorship. However, as Bell points out, "sujets / assujettie" ("subjects / subjected") is an example of punning quite typical of Mary,[21] and this sonnet is frequently singled out from the others allegedly found in the casket.[22] I think, therefore, that it merits consideration.[23]

---

[19] Fraser, *Mary Queen of Scots*, 477–78.

[20] Fraser, *Mary Queen of Scots*, 478.

[21] Bell, *Bittersweet Within My Heart*, 14n.

[22] Jenny Wormald, who believes the Casket Letters to be genuine, comments that "[t]he woman portrayed in the letters and the sonnet is a woman utterly dominated by a man, one who would renounce everything for him, who masochistically dwells on her sacrifice — 'my peace, my subjects, my subjected soul' " (*Mary Queen of Scots: A Study in Failure* [London: Collins & Brown, 1991], 177). Whether Wormald is referring to Sonnet 7 alone or to the Bothwell poems as a whole is, though, unfortunately rendered unclear by her description of the casket's contents as "eight letters from Mary to Bothwell, a long sonnet expressing her emotions, and two marriage contracts between her and Bothwell" (*Mary Queen of Scots*, 176). The nonsensical phrase "a long sonnet" leaves open the possibility that Wormald, like Fraser, regards the poems as essentially a single entity, and the same suggestion is made in Rosalind K. Marshall's book *Queen of Scots* (Edinburgh: HMSO, 1986), where the casket's contents are described as "eight letters and a long poem" (180). H. Armstrong Davison, in *The Casket Letters* (London: Vision Press, 1965), similarly opines that "the whole constitutes a single continuous poem" (69) which he terms a "love-ballad" (99); comparing the poems unfavorably with Mary's earlier elegy for her husband Francis (206), he objects particularly to the "sujets / assujettie" line, which on grounds of sense, scansion and context he proposes emending to "mon pays jetté" (211–12). Clifford Bax, in *The Silver Casket* (London: Home & Van

The sonnet begins "Entre ses mains et en son plein pouvoir" ("Into his hands and wholly in his power"), and it differs from the majority of the "casket" sonnets by never addressing Bothwell directly. Though that is also the case in the first and fourth of the twelve, the second, third, sixth, eighth, tenth, eleventh, and the unfinished twelfth all speak throughout straight to "vous" ("you"), and the fifth and ninth do so at the end ("Entre ses mains" is the seventh in the series). Moreover, this strikes a less abject note than any of the other sonnets.[24] Though Mary begins by openly asserting her subjection, the very length and nature of the list of what she has offered him in itself underlines her own impor-tance: "mon fils, mon honneur et ma vie, / Mon pays, mes sujets, mon ame assujettie" ("my son, my honour and my life, / My country, my sub-jects, my subjected soul"). The poem is, too, full of the language of will and power, leaving no doubt that its speaker does not only actively desire, but also has a clear agenda of her own: "n'ai autre vouloir" ("I have no other wish"), "Suivre je veux" ("I wish to follow"), "je n'ai autre envie" ("I have no other longing"), "Jamais ne veux changer" ("I never wish to alter"), "je ferai de ma foi telle preuve" ("I shall make such proof of my faith"). This woman may be overtly submissive, but she also formulates her own wants very clearly indeed, and outlines a firm plan (indicated by the simple future tense of "je ferai") for obtaining them.

Her strategy, interestingly, will be not dissimilar to that outlined by Sir Philip Sidney in the first sonnet of *Astrophil and Stella*: "Knowledge might

---

Thal, 1946), not only believed himself in Mary's authorship but considered acceptance of it uncontroversial (7).

[23] Some at least of these poems were shown to the Duke of Norfolk, a prospective suitor for Mary's hand. He seems to have believed in their authenticity, which suggests that the tone and diction of them appeared plausible to a contemporary of Mary's. Inter-estingly, he termed them ballads: "[t]he said letters and ballads," the duke wrote to Eliza-beth with disgust on 11th October, "do discover such inordinate love between her and Bothwell, her loathsomeness and abhorring of her husband that was murdered, in such sort as every good and godly man cannot but detest and abhor the same ... the matter contained in them being such as could hardly be invented or devised by any other than herself' " (Neville Williams, *A Tudor Tragedy: Thomas Howard Fourth Duke of Norfolk* [London: Barrie & Jenkins, 1964], 137). A roughly analogous argument from plausibility and "mindset" is offered ingeniously, if not entirely convincingly, by Jenny Wormald, who argues that the poems' image of the woman adoring a bad man was *not* culturally familiar, and hence would have been unlikely to be deployed by forgers (*Mary Queen of Scots*, 177–78).

[24] Wormald (*Mary Queen of Scots*, 125) comments on Mary's consistent sense of her own royal dignity.

pity win, and pity grace obtain."[25] If the verbs deployed by the female speaker signify desire, those which she applies to the "he" of the poem are most crucially concerned with knowledge: "lui faire appercevoir" ("to make him notice"), and "Qu'il connaîtra" ("That he will know"). The man may have the "plein pouvoir" ("full power"), but it is in fact the woman who will structure and inform the thought processes which will condition his use of it. Equally, she will disdain the tactics of others ("comme autres ont fait", "as others have done") and will precisely not descend to the "pleurs ou feinte obéissance" ("tears or feigned obedience") which characterise the abject tones of others of these sonnets (and do indeed work to reinforce Antonia Fraser's theory of two separate hands). Instead, she will demonstrate her constancy by deeds ("diverses épreuves"). The speaker thus explicitly posits for herself a role different from, indeed superior to, that of other women.

The poem itself implicitly constitutes a display of such superior status, for it is artfully crafted in a way appropriate to a disciple of the writers of the Pléiade. From the outset, the assonance of "entre" and "en" and "mains" and "plein" joins with the alliteration of "plein pouvoir" to demonstrate a clear sense of tight control exercised over language, rhythm and sound. The Ciceronian triple of the second line — "mon fils, mon honneur et ma vie" ("my son, my honour and my life") is triumphantly capped by yet another triple as the speaker declares that she is in fact in a position to offer even more than this — "mon pays, mes sujets, mon âme assujettie" ("my country, my subjects, my subjected soul"). The daring enjambement at the end of this line to "Et toute à lui" ("And [either 'I am' or 'my soul is'] all his") further underlines the sense of self-worth that can allow the speaker herself to be the climax of this splendid series of gifts, while the "sujet / assujettie" pun underlines still more the sense of the writer's control of the poem. The woman who can write thus is still in command, and will certainly not resort to an "obéissance" ("obedience") which one would indeed have to think feigned. Here, as opposed, I think, to the remainder of the "casket" sonnets, it is not hard to feel that the writer might indeed have been "Reine de France Marie."

---

[25] *Sir Philip Sidney: Selected Poems*, ed. Katherine Duncan-Jones (Oxford: Oxford University Press, 1973), 117. This poem of course predates Sidney's, but the comparison still seems to me suggestive of the ways in which this sonnet operates within structures and assumptions which are at least to a certain extent conventional rather than personal — and also the extent to which the speaker's voice in the "casket" sonnet appropriates a tone not conventionally feminine.

Yet if Queen Mary could speak as an equal to her aunt, to Elizabeth I, to God, and perhaps even to her lover, there remains one addressee before whom her poetic voice quailed. In 1583 her early friend Ronsard dedicated a volume of his poetry to her, which she received in the prison to which Elizabeth had confined her after her flight to England. She thanked him with a present of money and a silver vase celebrating the Muses; but she had originally intended to send him a poem, too, in reply. After some unsuccessful drafts, she abandoned the attempt, and the difficulty she found in the task is also clearly signalled by the fact that what survives of her efforts is, for her, unusually obscure. Bell, indeed, thinks something must be missing: in his transcription of the original, he has indicated a need to insert "te" into the first line of the second stanza to make Ronsard himself the object of Mary's praises.[26] I do not, however, think this can be right. In the first stanza, the "roi / De ton roi allié" ("king / Allied to your king") who nourished Ronsard in his youth can only be James V of Scotland, the father whom Mary never knew because he died when she was only six days old. Though her early poetry showed so much more affiliation to the French culture of her mother, it was this father who transmitted to Mary her claims both to Scotland and England, and after whom she had named her son; he had, too, been both patron of poets and minor versifier himself. It is, I think, he of whom she is, uniquely, speaking in the second stanza. It seems more likely that it is not Ronsard (whom she has earlier called by the familiar form of "tu") but James whom she terms a "brave prince."

Equally, Bell's translation of the final couplet seems to be misleading, and a significant distortion of the original. "But that he'd fain be succoured in his woes" is very strange indeed as a rendition of "Mais qu'il a bien voulu empêcher des malheurs," which is literally "But that he much wanted to prevent misfortunes." Moreover, Bell's use of the present, and indeed the expectation of the future, works to suggest that it is Mary herself who is the prince who hopes for succour. While Elizabeth I may have thought of herself as having the heart and stomach of a king, Mary does not so readily forget her gender, and certainly would not refer to herself in French as "il." It is a male prince of whom she is speaking, and surely it is, once again, her father. It is perhaps appropriate that this figure, so noticeably absent elsewhere in her life and writing, should surface here. This

---

[26] Bell, *Bittersweet Within My Heart*. The original is on page 102 and the translation on page 103.

is a poem to Ronsard, who clearly stands for Mary as an originary, authoritative figure in her own relationship to the processes of poetic composition. Apart from the biographical coincidence of his relationship with her father, it is only fitting for the memory of the real father to be evoked by that of the literary guide. In a sense, then, it is perhaps doubly the *nom-du-père* which has intervened to prevent completion and dispatch of this poem by a daughter both literal and literary. And yet, even in apparent uncertainty, Mary can still use the tone of command. Ronsard is "tu" to her, and she reminds him, albeit graciously, of the favours he has received from both sides of her family; in her bestowal of the title "brave prince," she overtly and carefully deploys the privilege of naming, and the command "Ne scrivez" ("Do not write") reminds us that this is a writer who is a patron too. For even in the imagined presence of the King of Scotland, this is a poetess who never forgets that she is first and foremost "Reine de France Marie," and for whom writing remains, in a chaotic life, the one area where she can exercise queenship and control.

Sheffield Hallam University

PETER C. HERMAN

"mes subjectz, mon ame assubjectie:
The Problematic (of) Subjectivity
in Mary Stuart's Sonnets

> *Subject*: 2. One who is under the dominion of a monarch or
> reigning prince; one who owes allegiance to a govern-
> ment or ruling power, is subject to its laws and enjoys
> its protection.
> 3. A person (rarely a thing) that is the control or under
> the dominion of another; one who owes obedience *to*
> another.
> . . . . .
> 6.b. A thing having real independent existence.
> 9. The mind, as the subject in which ideas inhere; that to
> which all mental representations or operations are at-
> tributed; the thinking or cognizing agent. (*OED*)

STRANGELY, THE INTEREST IN RECOVERING early modern women's writing
has passed over the poems of Mary Stuart, conventionally known as Mary,
Queen of Scots (1542–1587). Even though Mary enjoyed a reputation as
a poet during her life as a poet,[1] and despte the fairly large number of edi-

---

[1] Pierre Brantôme recorded in his biography of Mary that "Above all, she loved

tions of her works (including Betty Travitsky's selection of Mary's verse in her 1981 anthology, *The Paradise of Women*), her verse has remained practically *terra incognita*.[2] Indeed, she is so marginalized an author that as of

poetry and poets, especially M. de Ronsard, M. du Bellay, and M. de Mainson-Fleur, who all made beautiful poems and elegies upon her. She was a poet herself and composed verses, of which I have seen some that were fine and well done. . . . [Her poems were] beautiful and dainty" (*Recueil des Dames* [Paris: Gallimard, 1991], 72–73, my translation). And in the late nineteenth century, Agnes Strickland, author of the momentous *Lives of the Queens of Scotland* (10 volumes), refers to her as "the poet-Queen" (quoted in *Queen Mary's Book: A Collection of Poems and Essays by Mary Queen of Scots*, ed. P. Stewart-Mackenzie Arbuthnot [London: George Bell, 1907], 152).

[2] *The Paradise of Women: Writings by Englishwomen of the Renaissance* (Westport, CT: Greenwood Press, 1981). None of the major treatments of gender and of early modern women writers mention Mary Stuart or include her in their lists of women authors. I have consulted, among other texts, Elaine V. Beilin, *Redeeming Eve: Women Writers of the English Renaissance* (Princeton: Princeton University Press, 1987); Linda Woodbridge, *Women and the English Renaissance: Literature and the Nature of Womankind 1540–1620* (Urbana: University of Illinois Press, 1984); *Women in the Renaissance: Selections from "English Literary Renaissance,"* ed. Kirby Farrell, Elizabeth H. Hageman, and Arthur F. Kinney (Amherst: University of Massachusetts Press, 1988); and *Rewriting the Renaissance: The Discourses of Sexual Difference in Early Modern Europe*, ed. Margaret W. Ferguson, Maureen Quilligan and Nancy J. Vickers (Chicago: University of Chicago Press, 1986). Mary is also not mentioned in *English Literary Renaissance*'s otherwise synoptic bibliographies of women in the Renaissance; see Elizabeth Hageman, "Recent Studies in Women Writers of Tudor England (1945–1984)" and "Recent Studies of Women Writers of Tudor England (1984–April 1990)," in *Women in the Renaissance*, 228–44, 258–64, and Georgianna M. Ziegler, "Recent Studies in Women Writers of Tudor England, 1485–1603 (1990 to mid-1993)," *English Literary Renaissance* 24.1 (1994): 229–42.

Histories of Scottish literature similarly ignore Mary's literary work: Maurice Lindsay, *History of Scottish Literature* (London: Robert Hale, 1977); David McCordick, ed., *Scottish Literature: An Anthology* (New York: Peter Lang, 1996); and Robert Watson, *The Literature of Scotland* (London: MacMillan, 1984) do not even mention Mary. *The History of Scottish Literature (Origins to 1600)*, ed. R. D. S. Jack (Aberdeen: Aberdeen University Press, 1987), vol. 1, does include Mary in the index, but the entry concerns "Discrediting of, in poetry," and the short article on Mary in Trevor Royle, *The MacMillan Companion to Scottish Literature* (London: MacMillan, 1983), talks excusively about her reign. There is nothing about her writing poetry.

Since completing this article, I have become aware of Sarah Dunnigan's work exploring various aspects of Mary's poetry: "Rewriting the Renaissance Language of Love and Desire: The 'Bodily Burdein' in the Poetry of Mary, Queen of Scots," *Gramma* 4 (1996): 183–95; "The Creation and Self-Creation Mary Queen of Scots: Rhetoric, Sovereignty, and Female Controversies in Sixteenth Century Scottish poetry," *Scotlands* 5.2 (1998): 65–88; " 'O venus soverane': Erotic Politics and Poetic Practice at the Courts of Mary, Queen of Scots and James VI," *Terranglian Territories*, ed. Susanne Hagemann (Frankfurt: Peter Lang, 2000), 161–77; "Reclaiming the Languages of Love and Desire in the Scottish Renaissance: Mary, Queen of Scots and the Female-Voiced Love Lyric 1567–87," *Proceedings of the Eighth International Conference on Medieval and Renaissance Scottish Lan-*

this writing (November 2001), the MLA bibliography does not record a single article on her or her works.[3] The neglect is even stranger, given the flurry of books that started appearing towards the middle of nineteenth century devoted specifically to Mary's literary achievements and the Casket Letters.[4] Unlike Elizabeth Carey, Aemelia Lanyer, or Margaret Cavendish, Mary's poetic works were never really lost or relegated to the obscurity of a single scholarly edition. Yet contemporary scholars have ignored her. Why?

One reason might be the uncertain provenance of many of her poems, the sonnets to her lover and, for a short time, husband, James Hepburn, Earl of Bothwell, in particular. Granted, the originals of the Casket Letters mysteriously disappeared, and the Letters themselves were originally published by Mary's arch-enemy, George Buchanan. Yet no-one involved with their original discovery and dissemination considered them fakes, including those who had a vested interest in declaring them forgeries, such as the French ambassador, La Mothe Fénelon.[5] In addition, most recent his-

---

guage and Literature, ed. Sally Mapstone and Juliette Woods (East Linten, Scotland: Tuckwell Press, forthcoming); and *Eros and Poetry and the Courts of Mary Queen of Scots and James VI* (Basingstoke: Macmillan, forthcoming). I am grateful to Professor Dunnigan for allowing me to see her work, much of it in advance of publication.

[3] So far as I know, Jennifer Summit is the first contemporary scholar to take Mary's poetry seriously, and she analyzes the political implications of Mary's 1568 sonnet to Elizabeth along with Elizabeth's response to Mary's poem in "Doubt of Future Foes." See her article, " 'The Arte of a Ladies Pen,' " in this volume.

[4] *The Poems of Mary Queen of Scots*, ed. Julian Sharman (London: Basil Montague Pickering, 1873); T. F. Henderson, *The Casket Letters and Mary Queen of Scots* (Edinburgh: Adams and Charles Black, 1889); Andrew Lang, *The Mystery of Mary Stuart* (London, 1901; repr. New York: AMS, 1970); Arbuthnot, *Queen Mary's Book*; *The Poems of Mary Queen of Scots to the Early of Bothwell* (Haarlem: Enschedé en Zonen, 1932); *The Letters and Poems by Mary Stuart, Queen of Scots*, ed. Clifford Bax (New York: Philosophical Library, 1947); M. H. Armstrong Davison, *The Casket Letters: A Solution to the Mystery of Mary Queen of Scots and the Murder of Lord Darnley* (London: Vision Press, 1965). The most recent, albeit deeply flawed, edition of Mary's verse is Robin Bell, *Bittersweet Within My Heart: The Collected Poems of Mary, Queen of Scots* (London: Pavilion, 1992). Mary's popularity outside of academia puts into stark relief her non-presence within it. None of the writers or the editions of her work cited above are by mainstream academics and they have been published by non-academic presses. Nor has she received the kind of scholarly bibliography that, for example, Kevin Sharpe has published on Charles I. The best, and most detailed, biography remains Antonia Fraser's *Mary Queen of Scots* (New York: Delacorte Press, 1969).

[5] See the quote from Fénelon at the end of this essay. Brantôme, however, asserted that the Sonnets to Bothwell could not be by Mary because they are "too coarse and too badly polished [trop grossiers et mal polis] to have come from her beautiful making," and Ronsard thought so too: "M. de Ronsard was of my opinion as to this one day when we

torians accept Mary's authorship of these works.[6] A more interesting reason for Mary's absence from the academic stage might be that Mary's sonnets fall outside conventional disciplinary boundaries: as a French educated Scots queen writing sonnets that were published (as an indictment)
in both French as well Anglicized Scots in England and Scotland, both
Mary and her work transect a number of national literatures without precisely belonging to any. And I suspect a third is Mary Stuart's embarrassing irrationality in love and her disastrous lack of political common sense,
including her habit of plotting against Elizabeth. A role model, in other
words, she is not.

Whatever the reasons for her exclusion from the canon of early modern women writers, her absence is entirely unjustified. Mary had a genuine, lifelong interest in poetry, and what has been recovered of her library
shows that she collected "the largest vernacular collection known in Scotland up to her time," including works by Ronsard, Scève, a translation of
Ovid's *Epistles*, Du Bellay's *Olive*, the unfortunate Châstelard's "French

---

were reading and discussing them" (*Recueil des Dames*, 73). Yet Brantôme was writing
hagiography, and admitting Mary's authorship would not help his idealizing purpose. Yet
even if the sonnets *are* fakes, they remain important texts because, as we will see, Mary's
poems in many ways follow the same forms and themes that Louise Labé explored in her
sonnets. If someone, presumably male, forged them, it would mean that this person recognized that when women wrote Petrarchan lyric verse, they followed different conventions than those followed by men. In other words, the forger had to have thought, "what
would a Petrarchan poem written by a woman look like?" and the results are these sonnets. If these poems are indeed fakes, then they testify to the contemporary recognition
of a distinctly feminine lyric voice.

    [6] "What it all amounts to is this. Outright forgery of the originals — as opposed to
the odd interpolation in the copies — can only have been done by the Scots; and to
suggest that her Scottish enemies forged something that they were then very unwilling
to use, and managed in the process to fool Mary's own son and cousin, both of whom
knew her handwriting, into believing that they were undoubtedly genuine, simply does
not make sense" (Jenny Wormald, *Mary Queen of Scots: A Study in Failure* [London:
George Philip, 1988], 177; see also 178). On the other hand, Antonia Fraser seems to
doubt their authenticity, but mainly on the grounds of a highly literal reading of some of
the poems' tropes, e.g., "There are references also to Bothwell's wealth, which were
unthinkable for Mary to make. To her Bothwell was a comparatively poor man ..."
(*Mary Queen of Scots* [New York: Delacorte Press, 1970], 404). Fraser follows the equally
literal commentary by M. H. Armstrong Davison, who avers that these poems were
written by "the 'other woman'," e.g., his commentary on "Entre ses mains": "We can
be quite certain that Mary never wrote these lines, for the statement that she put her
son in Bothwell's full power was absolutely untrue" (*The Casket Letters: A Solution to the
Mystery of Mary Queen of Scots and the Murder of Lord Darnley* [Washington, DC: University Press of Washington, 1965], 211). See also Lisa Hopkins' essay in this volume,
"Writing to Control: The Verse of Mary, Queen of Scots," notes 18 and 22.

Sonnatis in Writ,"[7] Boiardo's *Orlando in Love*, Ariosto's *Orlando Furioso*, and a copy of Bandello's tales (which included the source material for both *Hamlet* and *Romeo and Juliet*).[8] More importantly, Mary produced a signifi-cant amount of verse in a variety of genres and for a variety of occasions. In other words, Mary, like Henry VIII and Elizabeth, had a more than cas-ual interest in poetry, and she turned to it regularly, in particular in mo-ments of personal crisis, such as the death of her first husband, Francis II. Furthermore, Mary, again like Henry VIII and Elizabeth (as well as her son, James), knew how to use verse for political ends.[9]

Even so, as Anne Rosalind Jones writes, "gender expectations" inev-itably shaped a woman's "choice of genres and their sense of an audience. ... Female-authored Neoplatonism might pass, because it emphasized the spiritual ascent of the lover and the superiority of the beloved in ways that presented no threat to ideologies of feminine chastity and masculine auth-ority."[10] A good deal of Mary's literary work, as Lisa Hopkins has shown, appears to comply (at least superficially) with these restrictions, in particu-lar her later religious meditations. But Mary also produced a convention breaking sequence, the sonnets to Bothwell, which puts her among the small group of women to write Petrarchan sequences from a woman's per-spective.[11] That alone should make these poems worthy of greater notice.

---

[7] Pierre de Châstelard, a French poet who accompanied Mary to Scotland, hid himself twice in Mary's bedchamber. The first time he was let off with a warning. The second time, however, he was executed, but not before he bade farewell to "the most cruel princess of the world" (Wormald, *Mary Queen of Scots*, 136).

[8] John Durkan, "The Library of Mary, Queen of Scots," *Mary Stewart, Queen in Three Kingdoms*, ed. Michael Lynch (Oxford: Blackwell, 1988), 77–78. It is worth noting that Louise Labé is not included among the poets that we know Mary Stuart read, although it is always possible that the book somehow slipped through the cracks.

[9] See also the essays in this volume by Lisa Hopkins and Jennifer Summit. On James, see Sandra J. Bell and Robert Appelbaum, also in this volume, and my "Best of Poets, Best of Kings": King James VI/I and the Scene of Monarchic Verse," in *Royal Subjects: Essays on the Writings of James (VI)*, ed. Daniel Fischlin (Detroit: Wayne State University Press, forthcoming).

[10] Jones, "City Women and their Audiences: Louise Labé and Veronica Franco," *Rewriting the Renaissance*, 299, 300.

[11] Some critics and historians are unsure if Mary wrote a sequence or one "long son-net expressing her emotions," as Jenny Wormald has it (*Mary Queen of Scots*, 176). The notion that the poems constitute a single poem may have started with how they were first described. In Moray's *The Book of Articles*, he recounted the production of the Cas-ket Letters thus: "seven writings, *being copied*, weare red in Frenche, and a due collation made thereof as neare as could be by reading and inspection, and made to accord with the originals, which the said Erle of Murray required to be redelivered, and did thereupon

However, in addition to writing as a woman, Mary also wrote as a monarch, and the combination turns this sequence into a fascinatingly complicated, even contradictory, intervention into Petrarchan poetics.

Discussions of Petrarchism have tended to construct a binary opposition between the political and the non-political. The former line of inquiry is still best represented by Arthur F. Marotti, who argued that Petrarchan erotic language is really coded political language, hence Petrarchan poetry often figures the courtier's negotiations of power and ambition. Love is not love, in other words, but politics.[12] Recently, however, Heather Dubrow has argued that sometimes love really is love: "both Petrarchism and anti-Petrarchism are indeed often about subjects like politics, history, or the relationships among men, but they are always — and often primarily — about love, desire, and gender as well."[13] Both critics are, of course, right (Dubrow does not so much rebut Marotti as redress the balance). What makes Mary's sonnets so fascinating is that they manage to conflate these two positions. Mary's sonnets *are* about desire. They clearly and forthrightly express her passion for Bothwell. As such, therefore, they ought to be situated within the context of the tense relationship between the woman writer and Petrarchism as these poems show what happens when traditional Petrarchan roles are reversed and the speaking "I" becomes the "I" of a woman. Mary's sonnets demonstrate, as Deborah

---

deliver the copies being collationed, the tenours of which vii wrytinges hereafter follow in order, *the first being in manner of a sonnett*, 'O Dieux ayez de moy etc' " (quoted in Lang, *The Mystery of Mary Stuart*, 275; emphases in the original). Also, the journal of the Privy Council considers them one text: "And before those articles were read, there were produced sundry lettres written in French, supposed to be written by the Quene of Scotts own hand, to the Erle Bothwell; and therwith also one long sonnet ... " (quoted in Henderson, *The Casket Letters*, 188).

Yet however they were described, the person who translated Buchanan's *Detectioune* (1572) and prepared the Casket Letters for publication clearly considered them a collection of discrete poems. He calls them "Certaine French Sonnettes written by the quene of Scottes to Bothwell" (sig. Q.iiii), and separates each poem by a line of blank space. My guess is that the sonnets were written on a manuscript without any breaks between them, and so they were thought to be one poem rather than a sequence of twelve poems. The publisher, however, perhaps because he was more used to the conventions of manuscript transmission, interpreted the original text as a sequence, not a long poem.

[12] Arthur Marotti, " 'Love is not love': Elizabethan Sonnet Sequences and the Social Order," *ELH* 49 (1982): 396–428.

[13] Heather Dubrow, *Echoes of Desire: English Petrarchism and Its Counterdiscourses* (Ithaca, NY: Cornell University Press, 1995), 10

L. Baker puts it, what happens when "the conventionally gendered object of desire becomes a desiring subject."[14]

But to invoke Freud's example of the courtier who responded to Louis XV's demand that someone make him the "subject" of a joke by asserting "*le roi n'est pas sujet*,"[15] the transformation of a monarch into a subject, even a desiring subject, is highly problematic because it contradicts Mary's monarchic status. Because Mary Stuart can never be a private citizen, because she will always be — whether she liked it or not — primarily Mary, Queen of Scots as well as Mary, Queen Dowager of France (she married François II in 1559, the year before his death), that is to say, because Mary is twice a monarch, the sexual desire and the privileging of *personal* desire openly (and ardently) expressed in these works inescapably have very serious political ramifications. The effects of reversing Petrarchan roles and expressing desire depends, as we shall see, upon the political situation, one might even say interpellation, of the speaking subject. It is one thing for a private citizen, such as Louise Labé, to reverse Petrarchan roles. It is quite another for a queen to do so, and even though Mary doubtless intended her sonnets to remain private documents,[16] Mary not only wrote from a monarchic perspective, but her political stature allowed her both the freedom and the language to create these texts. The irony is that it is precisely Mary's monarchic status that made this desire so threatening once the sonnets were forced into the public sphere.

I

I want to begin by discussing the gender politics of Mary's sonnets. To point out the obvious, Mary's sex precedes her political position, and

---

[14] Baker, *The Subject of Desire: Petrarchan Poetics and the Female Voice in Louise Labé* (West Lafayette, IN: Purdue University Press, 1996), 7.

[15] "Wit and its Relation to the Unconscious," in *The Basic Writings of Sigmund Freud*, ed. A. A. Brill (New York: Random House, 1938), 650.

[16] In fact, most of Mary's verse seems to have been written for her eyes alone or for one other person. For example, she scribbled verses into a book of hours during her imprisonment, and she sent her meditation on religion to Leslie, Bishop of Ross, in response to his book of consolations. According to Leslie, Mary "sent a Testimony of her diligent perusing the first Trety of the Godly meditations, out of which she had drawn summary collections, and put the same in French meetre" (quoted in *Queen Mary's Book*, 106–7). Arbuthnot adds that "It is fortunate for us that it occurred to Leslie to publish this and two other poems of Mary's in his own book, as they would otherwise have been lost to the world" (*Queen Mary's Book*, 107).

many critics have pointed out the problematics of a woman writing Petrarchan poetry. The Renaissance love lyric is a genre, according to Gary
Waller, "entirely structured by male categories" and which réquired "the
fixing of the female as a body which is the subject of power, requiring her
passivity as the object of anguish or manipulation."[17] Or, as Jones puts
it, "The amorous discourses available to [women] had been constructed by
male writers, who represented women as the silent objects of love rather
than its active, articulate pursuers."[18] Petrarchan verse is, arguably, a
genre largely predicated upon the suppression of feminine voice and
agency. Yet Mary wrote sonnets that explicitly invert the expected relations, at least the expected relations in Petrarchan poetics, between men
and women. Rather than portraying herself as either the passive recipient
of male attentions or the passive mourner of an unconstant male (as, say,
Mary Wroth does), Mary often adopts the masculine position of the active,
desiring agent. As the anonymous translator of Mary's "French Sonnettes"
puts it, "she here prefereth hir self in deserving to beloved of Bothwell"
(Ane Detectioune, sig. Q.iiii).

First, Mary inverts the conventional understanding of constancy. As
Jones points out, constancy was usually figured as a feminine trait associated with the refusal of sexual favors; constancy is supposed "to be admired or overcome by men's uses of rhetoric."[19] Mary, however, turns
this convention on its head in a number of ways. As perhaps one would
expect, Mary regularly constructs herself as a rock, unmoved and un-
moveable in her love. The opening sonnet "O dieux," begins by asking
divine assistance in proving that her love does not seem "vain" to Bothwell but firm ("ne lui semble vain / De mon amour et ferme affection"),[20] and it concludes with Mary asking "What is left to prove my
constancy?" [Que reste il plus pour prouver ma constance?] In "Entre ses
mains," Mary asserts that her love will never change, no matter what
"tempête ou bonace" — storm or fair weather — they face, and she concludes "Mon amour croît" by promising that she will soon prove to him

---

[17] Gary Waller, "Struggling into Discourse: The Emergence of Renaissance Women's
Writing," in Silent but for the Word: Tudor Women as Patrons, Translators, and Writers of
Religious Works, ed. Margaret Hannay (Kent, OH: Kent State University Press, 1985),
248.

[18] Anne R. Jones, The Currency of Eros: Women's Love Lyric in Europe, 1540–1620
(Bloomington: Indiana University Press, 1990), 1.

[19] See Jones, "City Women," 304.

[20] All references to Mary's verse are to the modernized versions in this edition.

"ma constance," that Bothwell will find her (like Elizabeth) without change, semper eadem: "et sans changer me trouvera tout une."[21] In the third sonnet, "Elle pour son honneur," she accuses Lady Bothwell of *misusing* her "constancy" for her own "profit,"[22] and in "Vous la croyez," she once again accuses Bothwell of doubting her "ferme constance." The difference, however, is that Mary is not asserting her "constance" in chastity, but in erotic pursuit. Her purpose, as she says in "De vous je dis," is *"to win you* [Bothwell] in spite of all envy" [*De vous gagner* malgré toute l'envie; my emphasis]. Analogously to Louise Labé's addresses to a lover she thinks has abandoned her, Mary maneuvers "both inside and outside ideologies of the feminine" in order to win her lover back,[23] which brings us to Mary's second inversion of expectations.

Not only does she adopt the traditionally masculine position of the desiring lover, but Mary explicitly asserts that she will use masculine rather than feminine strategies to prove her "constance." Mary concludes "Entre ses mains," for instance, by saying that "he will know my constancy [il connaîtra ... ma constance]" not by "my tears or feigned obedience [Non par mes pleurs ou fainte obéissance"], i.e., through stereotypically feminine trickery or passivity, but by various *deeds* ("Divers épreuves"), i.e., through masculine action and straightforwardness. Mary repeats this desire to prove in "Mon amour croît," when she again combines the assertion of constancy with assuming the male duty of seeking honor: "For him I wish to search for honor / And will do so much that he will truly know" [Pour lui je veux rechercher la grandeur, / Et ferai tant qu'en vrai connaîtra] that Mary loves him. The emphasis, again, is on *doing*, on action, rather than passively hoping that Bothwell will leave his wife and return to her, and most of the poems include some reference to some action that Mary took on behalf of her love.[24] For Bothwell, she *leaves* her family, allies, and friends, she *risks* her name and conscience, and she *writes* about the differences between herself and her rival.[25]

---

[21] Given the strained relations between Elizabeth and Mary, one wonders if Mary intended to appropriate rhetoric of constancy for her own purposes.

[22] The Anglo-Scots reads: "Sche useth constancy for hyr awin profit," sig. R.iii.

[23] Jones, "City Women," 305.

[24] Lang also notes that "The queen throughout is much more the pursuer than the pursued. Bothwell is cold, careless, breaks promises is contemptuously negligent, does not write, is suspicious, prefers his wedded wife to his mistress. ... The passion, in the Letters, is all on the side of Mary" (*The Mystery of Mary Stuart*, 350–51).

[25] "Pour lui touts mes parents j'ai quitté & amies" ("Pour lui aussie"); "J'ai hazardé

The corollary of Mary's adoption of an active, masculine position is her explicitly distancing herself from traditionally feminine traits and methods. In "Vous la croyez," Mary accuses Bothwell of thinking of her as a "typical" woman:

Vous las croyez, las trop je l'aperçois
Et vous doutez de ma ferme constance,
O mon seul bien et ma seul espérance,
Et ne vous puis assurer de ma foi
Vous m'estimez légère qui le voy,
Et si n'avez en moi nulle assurance
Et soupçonner mon coeur sans apparence
Vous défiant à trop grand tort de moi.
Vous ignorez l'amour que je vous porte,
Vous soupçonnez qu'autre amour me transporte,
Vous estimez mes paroles du vent,
Vous dépeignez de cire mon las coeur,
Vous me pensez femme sans jugement.
Et tout cela augmente mon ardeur.

[You believe her, alas, too well I see you do
And you doubt my firm constancy,
O my sole wealth and my sole hope.
And I cannot make you sure of my faith.
I see that you judge me light,
And so you do not have any confidence in me
And you distrust my heart without any evidence,
Your distrust does me great wrong
You do not realize the love I bear for you.
You suspect that some other love transports me.
You consider my words mere wind.
You think my heart malleable as wax.
You think me a woman without judgment.
And all this increases my passion.]

Bothwell, in other words, assumes that Mary is fickle, that she is faithless, and most interestingly, that she is not very smart, but the poem itself im-

---

pour lui et nom et conscience" ("O dieux"); "J'ai mis la main au papier pour escrire / D'un difference que je voulu transcrire" ("Ne vous voyant").

plies that Mary does not conform to these gender stereotypes, arguing that she is constant, that her heart is as solid as a rock, and that she is, to paraphrase the French, une femme *avec* jugement.

However, if Mary consistently aggregates to herself the male role of the constant, ardent, lover (while relegating Lady Jean Gordon to the realm of the feminine and the fictive), she assigns Bothwell the role of the *inconstant* lover. In a complete reversal of the endless recitations of female inconstancy and male dependability, now Bothwell is the fickle one whose loyalty and faith Mary is consistently uncertain of. In "Elle, pour son honneur," she accuses him of doubting *her* constancy: "vous doutez ma constance," and in "Et maintenant elle commence à voir," Mary asserts that Bothwell is now returning to his wife:

> Ses pleurs, ses plaintes remplies de fictions,
> Et ses hauts cris et lamentations,
> Ont tant gagné que par vous sont gardées
> Ses lettres écrites auxquelles vous donnez foi
> Et si l'aimez et croyez plus que moi.

> [Her tears, her plaints filled with fictions,
> And her great cries and laments,
> Have so won you that you keep
> Her letters and believe them.
> And so you love and believe her more than me.]

And "Vous la croyez" plays on Mary turning the charge of inconstancy back at Bothwell ("You believe her, alas, too well I see you do / And you doubt my firm constancy"). The final, unfinished sonnet begins with Mary writing because Bothwell has not shown up, even though he promised he would: "Not seeing you, as you had promised, / I have put my hand to paper to write" [Ne vous voyant selon qu'avez promis, / J'ai mis la main au papier pour écrire].

Along the same lines, the inversion of masculine and feminine positions also pertains to the homosocial triangles illuminated by Eve Kosofsky Sedgewick.[26] Rather than exemplifying the male traffic in women, exemplified for Sedgwick by the first eighteen of Shakespeare's sonnets, Mary's mini-sequence exemplifes female traffic in men! The drama of the se-

---

[26] Eve Kosofsky Sedgwick, *Between Men: English Literature and Male Homosocial Desire* (New York: Columbia University Press, 1985), 28–48.

quence lies in both Mary's expressions of explicitly physical desire for Bothwell and in Mary's competition for Bothwell's affections with Lady Jean Gordon, the man's wife:

> Elle, pour son honneur, vous doit obéissance.
> Moi, vous obéissant, j'en puis recevoir blâme,
> N'etant, à mon regret, comme elle, votre femme.
>
> [She, for her honor, owes you obedience
> I, in obeying you, can receive only blame,
> Not being, to my regret, like her, your wife.]

As much as Mary clearly despises her rival, she still allows her the same agency that she grants herself. In "Et maintenant elle commence" (a poem we will return to below), rather than constructing her rival as a passive, suffering figure to whom Bothwell returns, Mary records Lady Jean actively wooing her husband back:

> Et voudrait bien mon ami décevoir
> Par les écrits tout fardés de savoir
> Qui pourtant n'est en son esprit croissant
> Ains empruntés de quelque auteur éluissant . . .
>
> [And she would now deceive my beloved
> Through writings all painted with learning,
> Which could not have come from her mind
> But cribbed from some dazzling author . . .]

Furthermore, in another example of male inconstancy, the sonnet records that the "feigned" letters accomplish the task of getting Bothwell back:

> Et ses hauts cris et lamentations
> Ont tant gangé que par vous sont gardées
> Ses lettres écrites auxquelles vous donnez foi
> Et si l'aimez et croyez plus que moi.
>
> [And her great cries and laments,
> Have so won you that you keep
> Her letters and believe them.
> And so you love and believe her more than me.]

Significantly, Bothwell *responds* in these sonnets, he does not *initiate*, and what's more, he responds to the traditional means used to "woo" women, i.e., feigning. Ironically, he has done what Sidney's Astrophil so ardently wishes Stella would do: he has read, and she has obtained his pity and his grace. Finally, it is worth noting that Bothwell, like Petrarch's Laura and to a lesser extent, like Sidney's Stella, is silent. "The basic configuration" of Shakespeare's sequence, Sedgwick writes, "includes a stylized female who functions as a subject of action but not of thought," and Mary reverses this role.[27] Curiously reversing her political passivity, in Mary's poetry, women act and men respond.[28] If Mary prefers herself in deserving of Bothwell's love, Bothwell is not the one doing the preferring. To invert Nancy Vickers's formulation, Mary's speech, really, Mary and Lady Gordon's speech, seems to require *his* silence.[29]

Finally, Mary contradicts the traditional roles assigned to women by including and privileging physical desire. It is very important that Mary refers to Bothwell as her "ami," to herself as "votre amie," and uses the verb "aimer" to describe her emotions towards, all of which had erotic overtones. Randle Cotgrave, in 1611, for instance, would define "ami" thus: "A friend; a lover, a paramour; a loving mate, a deere companion."[30] And Mary will use the verb "aimer" to specifically describe sex. In addition to the already remarkable spectacle of an early modern woman writing explicitly erotic, as opposed to Neoplatonic, poetry, Mary also ap-

---

[27] Sedgwick, *Between Men*, 33.

[28] Compare the role of passivity in Marguerite de Navarre's verse, which is linked to her faith in God. See Robert Cottrell, *The Grammar of Silence: A Reading of Marguerite de Navarre's Poetry* (Washington, DC: Catholic University of America Press, 1986). Even though everyone at the time, including her brother, François, recognized Marguerite's diplomatic abilities and importance, I am not aware of any studies of how Marguerite's position as queen shapes her verse, although one possible reason for the concentration upon religion to the exclusion of politics might be, as Susan Snyder suggests, that the title, Queen of Navarre, "carried with it a fairly limited sovereignty, such power as there was residing with her husband Henri de Navarre, with the kingdom itself being largely under Spanish rule" (Snyder, "Guilty Sisters: Marguerite de Navarre, Elizabeth of England, and the *Miroir de l'âme pécheresse*," *Renaissance Quarterly* 50.2 [1997]: 443). See also Gary Ferguson, *Mirroring Belief: Marguerite de Navarre's Devotional Poetry* (Edinburgh: University of Edinburgh Press, 1992) and Anne Lake Prescott, "The Peal of the Valois and Elizabeth I: Marguerite de Navarre's *Miroir* and Tudor England," in *Silent But for the Word*, ed. Margaret P. Hannay (Kent, OH: Kent State University Press, 1985), 61–76. I am grateful to Professor François Rigolot for alerting me to this connection and bringing Cottrell and Ferguson's books to my attention.

[29] Nancy Vickers, "Diana Described: Scattered Woman and Scattered Rhyme," *Writing and Sexual Difference*, ed. Elizabeth Abel (Chicago: University of Chicago Press, 1982), 108–9.

[30] Randle Cotgrave, *A Dictionarie of the French and English Tongues* (London, 1611), sig. Dvir.

propriates the standard Petrarchan trope of freezing/burning in "Quand
vous l'aimiez" and deploys it to a very different end:

> Quand vous l'aimiez, elle usait de froideur,
> Si vous soufriez pour l'amour passion
> Qui vient d'aimer de trop d'affection,
> Son doigt montrait la tristesse de coeur,
> N'ayant plaisir de votre grande ardeur

> [When you made love to her, she lay frigid
> So that you suffered a passionate love for her
> That comes from loving with too much emotion,
> Her hand showed her heart's discontent,
> Taking no pleasure in your great ardor.]

The metaphor no longer describes the lover's divided internal state, nor
does coldness signal the purity of the beloved's soul. Instead, Mary appropriates this trope to denounce Lady Gordon's frigidity ("froideur"), approve of Bothwell's performance in bed (his "grand ardeur"), and imply
her own sexual responsiveness. She concludes with some rather mean comments about Lady Jean Gordon's taste in clothes:

> En ses habits, montrait sans fiction
> Qu'elle n'avait peur qu'imperfection
> Peut l'effacer hors de ce loyal coeur.

> [In her clothes, she showed without fiction
> That she never feared that poor taste
> Would erase love from a loyal heart.]

And yet, as much as Mary challenges traditional gender roles, she also
confirms them in the abuse she heaps upon Bothwell's wife. As we have
seen, Mary asserts that Lady Jean Gordon uses tears ("pleurs") and feigned
obedience ("Feinte obeissance") in order to manipulate Bothwell. Ironically, given that she is writing verse, Mary associates the feminine with
falsity, and this assumption underlies one of the most remarkable poems in
the sequence (while I have cited lines of this poem previously, its importance requires that I quote here the poem in its entirety):

> Et maintenant elle commence à voir
> Qu'elle était bien de mauvais jugement
> De n'estimer l'amour d'un tel amant
> Et voudrait bien mon ami décevoir

Par les écrits tout fardés de savoir
Qui pourtant n'est en son esprit croissant
Ains empruntés de quelque auteur éluissant,
A fait très bien un envoi sans l'avoir
Et toutefois ses paroles fardées,
Ses pleurs, ses plaintes remplies de fictions,
Et ses hauts cris et lamentations,
Ont tant gagné que par vous sont gardées
Ses lettres écrites auxquelles vous donnez foi
Et si l'aimez et croyez plus que moi.

[And now she starts to see
That she had very bad judgment
Not to value the love of such a lover;
And she would now deceive my beloved
Through writings all painted with learning,
Which could not have come from her mind
But cribbed from some dazzling author.
She crafted well a letter without having the brains.
And yet her filched words,
Her tears, her plaints filled with fictions,
And her great cries and laments,
Have so won you that you keep
Her letters and believe them.]

Imitation in early modern culture is, of course, a massive and complicated topic. Even so, it is neither an exaggeration nor a simplification to
assert that early modern poetics was primarily concerned with investigat-
ing the relationship between *imitatio* and originality, with the emphasis at
the start on *imitatio*. According to Joel Spingarn, "The imitations of the
classics became, in a word, the basis of literary creation [and] a dogma of
literary criticism in the Cinquecento."[31] Mary, as noted above, was a
great reader of the poetry produced by the Pléiade, Ronsard was even her
tutor for a while, and as perhaps one would expect, questions over the imitation of nature and classical writers and the relationship between origi-

---

[31] Joel Spingarn, *A History of Literary Criticism in the Renaissance* (New York: Columbia University Press, 1938), 131; Arthur F. Kinney, *Continental Humanist Poetics: Studies
in Erasmus, Castiglione, Marguerite de Navarre, Rabelais and Cervantes* (Amherst: University
of Massachusetts Press, 1989), 19 and *passim*.

nality and imitation figured significantly in the Pléiade's poetics. While Du Bellay, for instance, argued for the importance of the vernacular and for the necessity of achieving a literature that would equal the accomplishments of the past, this had to be achieved *through* imitation, not through pure originality. The only way, he asserts in his *Défence et Illustration de la Langue Française*, that French can create its own achievement is through imitation of the classical past: "sans l'immitation des Grecz & Romains nous ne pouvons donner à nostre Langue l'excellence & lumiere des autres plus fameuses," and "le moyen de l'enrichir & illustrer ... est l'imitation des Grecz & Romains."[32] Given the presence of his works in Mary's library and his personal relationship with her, it is particularly important that Ronsard also emphasized the centrality of the importance of classical imitation for both young poets for for himself. In the preface to the 1550 volume of the *Odes*, he proclaimed himself "imitateur des poetes Grecs" in that he "redit souvent memes mots, memes sentences, & memes trais de vers,"[33] and in the *Hylas*, he compared himself to a bee, selecting the finest passages from different "flowers" and then fashioning his work from them.[34]

And yet, despite the conventional, if complex, valorization of imita-

---

[32] Cited in Grahame Castor, *Pléiade Poetics: A Study in Sixteenth-Century Thought and Terminology* (Cambridge: Cambridge University Press, 1964), 67. On the complexities of du Bellay's views on imitation, see Margaret W. Ferguson, *Trials of Desires: Renaissance Defences of Poetry* (New Haven: Yale University Press, 1983), 23–28; as well as Terence Cave, *The Cornucopian Text: Problems of Writing in the French Renaissance* (Oxford: Clarendon Press, 1979), 60–77.

[33] Quoted in Castor, *Pléiade Poetics*, 71.

[34] Mon Passerat, je resemble à l'Abeille
Qui va cuillant tantost la freur vermeille,
Tantost la jaune: errant de pré en pré
Volle en la part quit plus luy vient à gré,
Contre l'Hiver amassant force vivres.
Ainsy courant & feuilletant mes livres,
J'amasse, trie & choisis le plus beau,
Qu'en cent couleurs je peints en un tableau,
Tantost en l'autre: & mastre en ma peinture,
Sans me forcer j'imite la Nature.

(*Hylas*, in Ronsard, *Oeuvres complètes*, ed. P. Laumonier [Paris: Société des Textes Français Modernes, 1914–75], Vol. 15: 252).

According to Thomas Greene, this passage evokes "a kind of capricious errancy that leads the poet on an apparently irregular itinerary from meadow, text to text, but that permits him to appear finally as a master-painter, selecting and combining with the skill of nature" (*The Light in Troy: Imitation and Discovery in Renaissance Poetry* [New Haven: Yale University Press, 1982], 199).

tion, Mary's sonnet *condemns* imitation as the refuge of an inferior mind, and in so doing, Mary implicitly proposes a radically new relationship between imitation, originality, and composition that anticipates by about thirty years the Muse's injunction in *Astrophil and Stella*'s sonnet 1 to "look in thy heart and write." In direct contrast to the theories put forward by Du Bellay et al., Mary figures drawing on other writers as pure theft and a sign of her rival's insincerity and lack of intelligence. In order to deceive her lover ("mon ami"), Bothwell, Lady Gordon must resort to the literary products of someone who is really talented (an "auteur éluissant"). Imitation, the picking and choosing of the best passages, Mary describes as relying on "stolen words; paroles fardées," or as the Anglo-Scots puts it, on "paintit learning." According to Mary's sense of poetics, there has to be a correspondence between the writer's sentiments, the writer's abilities, and the words on the page. Consequently, she condemns Lady Gordon's use of words and phrases that *could not* have come from her mind, because, according to Mary, Lady Gordon does not have the brains ("sans l'avoir") for such writing.

Interestingly, Mary accompanies her privileging of originality over imitation with a condemnation of fiction, which she associates with duplicity.[35] Just as Lady Gordon's words are stolen, her tears and sighs are "remplies de fictions," "full of dissimulation" in the Anglo-Scots, and one finds the same dichotomy in other poems as well. In "De vous je dis," Mary asserts that her love for Bothwell is "no fiction [nulle fiction]"; in "Quand vous l'aimiez," Lady Gordon's clothes show "without fiction [sens fiction]" her bad taste; and in "Entre ses mains," Mary asserts that Bothwell will know her constancy through concrete evidence, not by feigning, "Non par ... feinte." Mary, on the other hand, figures herself as the epitome of truth, whose words are original to her, not "stolen" or "cribbed" from someone else. Given our feminist perspective, Mary's constitution of herself as a desiring subject who privileges originality over copying sounds like an entirely positive challenge to the patriarchal construction of women as passive, intellectually deficient, generally inferior creatures, but at the same time, Mary's "subjectification" of herself is highly problematic, even dangerous.

---

[35] On Renaissance distrust of fiction, see William Nelson, *Fact or Fiction: The Dilemma of the Renaissance Storyteller* (Cambridge, MA: Harvard University Press, 1973) and Peter C. Herman, *Squitter-wits and Muse-haters: Sidney, Spenser, Milton and Renaissance Antipoetic Sentiment* (Detroit: Wayne State University Press, 1996).

II

Many critics have noted how early modern culture denied women subjectivity and agency. In both England and Scotland, the law did not recognize women (unless they were widows) as individuals. Rather, as a category women existed only in relation to, and underneath, men. Assuming that T. E.'s *The Lawes Resolution of Women's Rights* (1632) is a valid guide to the situation circa 1567, women were granted only a subordinate place in English legal discourse.[36] In her sonnets, though, Mary implicitly challenges this formulation by constituting herself as a full-fledged subject who has agency and desire, just as men do. How did Mary achieve the independence of mind to defy these proscriptions and write in such an original fashion? Anne R. Jones , also asks "What enabled [Louise Labé and Veronica Franco] to depart from ideals of modesty and silence?"[37] and she speculates that their non-aristocratic position allowed these women the freedom, the psychic space, as it were, to reverse gender roles, since the aristocracy is "the class to which early treatises on women's intellectual activity were most often dedicated."[38] For Mary, I suggest that her status as a monarch, something that Mary was highly conscious of throughout her life,[39] allowed her to depart from the conventions of feminine chastity and silence. If Labé remained below the aim of these early treatises, then Mary Stuart remained *above* them. T. E. explains the incorporation of the wife by the husband by the fact that women have no recognized political power: "Women have no voyse in Parliament, They make no Lawes, they consent to none, they abrogate none."[40] But Mary, as a monarch, most certainly does have a voice in parliament and certainly has the right to make and break laws.[41] In this sense, Louis XV's courtier is wrong: the monarch, even a female monarch, *is* a subject.

In another sense, however, the courtier was entirely correct. To say that Mary "subjectifies" herself means that she grants herself the subjectivity, the agency, to challenge the inferior position of women. This is

---

[36] While it is a little unclear which context would apply, I have chosen to situate Mary within English legal discourse because her poems were made public in England, and Mary was subsequently judged (and executed) under English law.

[37] Jones, "City Women," 301.

[38] Jones, "City Women," 301.

[39] Wormald, *Mary Queen of Scots*, 125, 147.

[40] Sig. B3^v.

[41] Much, it must be said, to John Knox's horror.

exactly what Labé does in her work. The problem is that subjectification can also entail exactly the opposite. The word itself, "sub-ject," means "that which is *thrown under*,"[42] and the transformation into a "subject" can also mean the stripping away of agency, of personhood. The courtier meant that the French king is subject to, inferior to, nobody, that subjecthood is inimical to the very nature of monarchy because the monarch is obeyed rather than obeys.[43] What happens in Mary's sonnets is that these two meanings of subjectivity collide. Mary's monarchic status grants her the language and the ability to equal masculine subjectivity. But, ironically, she uses this empowering subjectivity to *dis*empower herself. That is to say, while Mary's political subjectivity enabled her to assert her sexual subjectivity, her sexual subjectivity leads Mary to subjectify herself in the literal sense, to throw herself under someone else's will, with disastrous results. In the end, the monarch is not, *cannot* be, a subject.

While, as we have seen, Mary often refuses the passive role usually assigned to women, all of her actions are *for* Bothwell, never for herself, a fact that she emphasizes by her habit of reiterating the phrase "pour lui," "for him" in successive lines. In "O dieux," the first sonnet, she repeats the phrase four times in the closing sestet:

> Pour lui tous mes amis j'estime moins que rien
> Et de mes enemies je veux espérer bien.
> J'ai hasardé pour lui et nom et conscience:
> Je veux pour lui au monde renoncer:
> Je veux mourir pour lui avancer.
> Que reste il plus pour prouver ma constance?

> [For him I value all my friends as less than nothing
> And of my enemies I hope well.

---

[42] Margreta de Grazia, Maureen Quilligan, and Peter Stallybrass, "Introduction," in *Subject and Object in Renaissance Culture*, ed. de Grazia, Quilligan, and Stallybrass (Cambridge: Cambridge University Press, 1996), 5.

[43] The nationality is important because the joke depends upon French rather than English theories of monarchy. The former is more absolutist, whereas the latter is better described as a mixed monarchy in which the "king-in-parliament" is supreme rather than the king alone. See, for example, J. G. A. Pocock, *The Ancient Constitution and the Feudal Law: A Study of English Historical Thought in the Seventeenth Century* (New York: Norton, 1967); Glenn Burgess, *The Politics of the Ancient Constitution: An Introduction to English Political Thought, 1603–1642* (University Park: Pennsylvania State University Press, 1992); and Constance Jordan, *Shakespeare's Monarchies: Ruler and Subject in the Romances* (Ithaca, NY: Cornell University Press, 1997), 3–4.

I have risked for him fame and conscience:
I would for him renounce the world:
I would die to advance him.
What is left to prove my constancy?]

In "Mon amour croît," Mary begins three of the four lines of the concluding quatrain with this phrase:

Pour lui j'attends toute bonne fortune.
Pour lui je veux garder santé et vie.
Pour lui tout vertu de suivre j'ai envie,
Et sans changer me trouvera toute une

[For him I await good fortune.
For him I wish to keep good health and long life.
For him I wish to follow each virtue
And he will find me always without change.]

To be sure, Mary's self-subjection, her consistently acting "pour lui," constitutes another expression of her desire for Bothwell, and so there is an
element of empowerment implicitly present. But the politics of Mary's self-
subjection turn her acting "pour lui" into something completely different.

The problematic is also intimated by Mary's equally consistent use of
the formal "vous" rather than the intimate "tu" to refer to Bothwell.
While the rules for usage were not formalized until the seventeenth century, and while in medieval French the two pronouns were used inter-
changeably, by the early modern period "vous" was more and more associated with the court and with signaling a hierarchical relationship. One
conventionally used "vous" to address a superior, not the opposite. For instance, Mary always used "vous" when addressing Elizabeth, in particular
when submitting (or at least claiming that she is submitting) to Elizabeth's
will.[44] Furthermore, the convention in love poetry seems to have been
use "tu" to signal intimacy. Pernette du Guillet, for instance, whose
Rymes (1545) were very popular, in her epigrams consistently addresses the
object of her desire as "tu."[45] And yet, Mary without exception addresses

---

[44] "Je me sousmetay à vos commandemants," and "Vous aurés fayt une profitable
conqueste de moy" (quoted in Lang, The Mystery of Mary Stuart, 352).

[45] E.g., Epigram IV: "Ton eloquence, avecques ta faconde, / Et hault sçavoir, auquel
tu es appris, / Demonstre assez le bien en toy compris" ("Your eloquence and your eloquent speech / And the high learning you devote yourself to / Show forth love's height,
summed up in you"; Pernette du Guillet, Rymes, ed. Victor E. Graham [Geneva: Drosz,

Bothwell as "vous" rather than "tu." For example, she begins "Elle, pour son honneur":

> Elle, pour son honneur, *vous* doit obéissance.
> Moi, *vous* obéissant, j'en puis recevoir blâme,
> N'etant, à mon regret, comme elle, *votre* femme.

> [She, for her honor, owes you obedience
> I, in obeying you, can receive only blame,
> not being, to my regret, like her, your wife.]
>   (my emphasis)

The same happens in "Par vous, mon coeur":

> Par *vous*, mon coeur, et par *votre* alliance
> Elle a remis sa mainson en honneur
> Elle a joui par *vous* de la grandeur
> Dont tous les siens n'ont nulle assurance
> De *vous*, mon bien, elle a eu la constance,
> Et a gagné pour un temps *votre* coeur.
> Par *vous* elle a eu plaisir et bonheur,
> Et par *vous* a reçu honneur et réverence,
> Et n'a perdu sinon la jouissance
> D'un fâcheux sot qu'elle aimait chèrement

> [Through you, my love, and through your marriage,
> She restored honor to her house.
> She enjoyed through you such greatness
> Of which her family never had assurance.
> From you, my love, she has had constancy
> And for a while won your heart.
> From you she had pleasure and good fortune,
> And from you she received honor and reverence;

1968], 11. Translation by Anne Rosalind Jones, "The Lyonnais Neoplatonist: Pernette du Gillet," in *Women Writers of the Renaissance and Reformation*, ed. Katharina M. Wilson [Athens: University of Georgia Press, 1987], 224). Professor François Rigolot informs me that Labé's *personae* also use "tu," although she "sometimes shifts from 'tu' to 'vous' when she wants to distance herself from her unfaithful lover" (private correspondence). Pernette du Gillet will also occasionally use "vous," as in Chanson IX ("Je suis le Journée / Vous, Amy, le Jour"; "I am the Daytime \ You, my love, the day" (Graham, *Rymes*, 82; Jones, "The Lyonnais Neoplatonist," 226), but she mostly employs the less formal "tu."

> And she lost nothing but the pleasures
> Of a tiresome fool she once loved dearly.]
>   (my emphasis)

Certainly, Mary's use of "vous" rather than "tu" along with her repeated declarations that she does everything "pour lui," for her man, could be construed as an almost classic example of the "subversion-containment" paradigm explored in Stephen J. Greenblatt's earlier work.[46] By using "vous," which implies respect, distance, and the authority of the addressee, Mary contains her subversions of gender roles and gender relations by reinscribing masculine superiority. Bothwell may be the (silenced) object of her expressed sexual desire, yet she still refers to him as a superior. Even so, the connotations are, I think, more politically explosive than simply illustrating Mary's internalization of early modern gender codes.

At several points in her sequence Mary invokes a cliché of Petrarchan discourse: the avowal of service and obedience to the beloved. In particular, "De vous je dis":

> De vous je dis seul soutien de ma vie
> Tant seulement je cherche m'assurer,
> Et si ose de moi tant présumer
> De vous gagner malgré tout l'envie.
> Car c'est le seul désir de votre chère amie,
> De vous servir et loyalement aimer,
> Et tous malheur moins que rien estimer
> Et votre volonté de la mienne suivre.
> Vous connaîtrez avec obéissance
> De mon loyal devoir n'omettant la science
> A quoi j'étudierai pour toujours vous complaire,
> Sans aimer rien que vous, sous la sujétion
> De qui je veux, sans nulle fiction,
> Vivre et mourir et à ce j'obtempère.
>
> [Of you, I say, the sole support of my life,
> I only seek an assured commitment
> And yet I dare presume so much of myself

---

[46] The "subversion-containment" model received its fullest articulation in "Invisible Bullets," in *Shakespearean Negotiations: The Circulation of Social Energy in Renaissance England* (Berkeley: University of California Press, 1988), 21–65.

To win you in spite of all envy.
Because the sole desire of your dear lover
Is to loyally serve and love you
And to consider all misfortunes less than nothing.
And for my will to follow yours.
By this, you will know the obedience
In my loyal devotion, never forgetting
Always to study how best to please you,
Loving no-one but you, under the subjection
Of the one whom I, with no fiction,
Live and die for, and obey.]

Mary once more puts herself in the active position by daring "To win you in spite of all envy." But having constituted herself as a subject in terms of agency, she reverses herself by declaring herself Bothwell's "subject." Furthermore, she asserts in this sonnet that her sole desire is to "serve" ("De vous servir") and "obey" Bothwell, and in "Elle pour son honneur," Mary does the same ("Moi, vous obéissant").[47]

Mary's language here would be perfectly conventional if she occupied the conventional subject position of the sonneteer. As Marotti pointed out in " 'Love is not Love,' " "Love lyrics could express figuratively the realities of suit, service, and recompense with which ambitious men were insistently concerned as well as the frustrations and disappointments experienced in socially competitive environments ... [R]ivalry with peers for status, money and power could be fictionalized as the wooing of a woman of superior station."[48] And not only a woman, as demonstrated by Wyatt's "Tagus, Farewell," his love letter to Henry VIII. This language, in other words, conventionally reflects the subservient status, be it erotically, politically, or both, of the speaker. Thus, Mary is doing considerably more than reinscribing masculine superiority and feminine inferiority. Her adoption of what for anybody else (anybody, that is to say, who is not a monarch) would have been a purely conventional position implicitly entails Mary's abandonment of the superior position of monarch, a fact to which Mary draws attention by concluding her poem with the verb "obtempère," which Cotgrave defines as to "obey" and "to be at the com-

---

[47] The contrast is to Bothwell's wife, who *owes* Bothwell the deference of a wife/servant to a husband/lord ("Elle pour son honneur vous doibt obeissance").

[48] Marotti, " 'Love is Not Love,' " 398.

maund of."[49] Needless to say, monarchs were not supposed to "be at the
commaund of" anybody (except of God), especially French monarchs, who
were more absolutist in their political theory than their English or Scots
counterparts.[50] They are supposed to command, not be commanded; to
be obeyed, not to obey. As Mary herself puts it in her "Essay on the Science of Government": "For God has chosen kings and commanded the
people to obey them, and kings have appointed and constituted princes
and nobles to assist them in their labours, and not to dictate to them."[51]
But if these lines gain their power, their *energia*, as Sidney might put it,[52]
from Mary's privileging of her erotic subjectivity over her political identity, at other times in the sequence, Mary employs the opposite strategy of
explicitly using her monarchic power in order to entice her lover. Mary
ends "Pour lui aussi" by stating that she has "gambled rank and conscience" (j'ai hazardé grandeur & consience) for Bothwell for one end alone:
"l'alliance." The translation of this term is tricky, as it can refer to marriage or friendship. Mary herself uses the word in the former sense in "Par
vous mon coeur," when she disparagingly says that Lady Jean Gordon received everything from her marriage to Bothwell: "Through you, my love,
and through your marriage / She restored honor to her house" [Par vous
mon coeur et par votre alliance / Elle a remis sa maison en honneur]. Using this sense, the final line of "Pour lui aussi," "Brief de vous seul je
cherche l'alliance," could be construed as "In short, I have sought to

---

[49] Cotgrave, *A Dictionarie of the French and English Tongues*, sig. Kkk iiiiiv.

[50] On England as a mixed monarchy, see Z. S. Fink, *The Classical Republicans: An Essay on the Recovery of a Pattern of Thought in Seventeenth-Century England* (Evanston: University of Illinois Press, 1945); John Guy, "The Henrician Age," *The Varieties of British
Political Thought, 1500–1800* (Cambridge: Cambridge University Press, 1993), 13–46, esp.
17–19; Donald W. Hanson, *From Kingdom to Commonwealth: The Development of Civic
Consciousness in English Political Thought* (Cambridge, MA: Harvard University Press,
1970), 240–52; and Robert Eccleshall, *Order and Reason in Politics: Theories of Absolute
and Limited Monarchy in Early Modern England* (Oxford: Oxford University Press 1978).

[51] The date of this essay is uncertain. While its original editor, Prince Alexander La-
banoff, dates it at 1566 (*Receuil des Lettres et Memoires de Marie Stuart*, 7 vols. [London:
Charles Dolman, 1844]), the year before Mary wrote her sonnets, Arbuthnot argues that
"it seems on the whole more probable that it was written during her captivity" (*Queen
Mary's Book*, 132). On the other hand, Arbuthnot is also not the most reliable source,
as she omits Mary's sonnets from her collection. As Travitsky writes, "Arbuthnot's basis
for selection is rather arbitrary: she includes some doubtful pieces but excludes the love
sonnets, apparently because she prefers not to think of Mary as Bothwell's mistress" (*The
Paradise of Women*, 192).

[52] Sir Philip Sidney, *An Apology for Poetry*, ed. Forrest G. Robinson (Indianapolis:
Bobbs-Merrill, 1977), 81.

marry you alone," and so I have decided to translate this sentence thus. But "alliance" had additional connotations during this period. It could also mean *political* alliance, and that may have been the primary meaning during the Renaissance. Cotgrave, for instance, gives the following definition of "alliance": "Alliance; confederation, fellowship, combination; agreement, consent; a league of friendship" (sig. D iiiir). Edmond Huguet's *Dictionnaire de la Langue Française du Seizième Siècle* gives Rabelais as an example of this meaning's currency: "Comment Pantagruel arriva en l'isle Ennaisin et des etranges alliances du pays." Moreover, the Anglo-Scots translation of this line is "I seke the aliance of you onely," which suggests that for the anonymous translator, Mary is seeking something more along the lines of a political alignment than something more private. For Mary to "cherche l'alliance" with Bothwell alone, therefore, casts the personal into the arena of state, which makes perfect sense, as a monarch's marriage *is* a matter of state, and her desire to marry Bothwell is a political matter that will have political overtones. Mary signals her awareness of this fact in "O dieux" when she asserts that "I would die to advance him" [Je veux mourir pour lui avancer]. Given the fact that the author of these lines was the queen, however embattled, of Scotland, one must assume that "avancer" means *political* advancement, e.g., honors at court, peerages, money, political influence, etc. for not only Bothwell, but for his family and followers. Mary's language, in sum, demonstrates her awareness (at some level) that her personal desires are in fact an intervention into the complicated morass of Scottish factional politics, and this is certainly how her nobles interpreted her seeking an "alliance" with James Hepburn, Earl of Bothwell.

Without diminishing in any way the man's culpability in the murder of Mary's husband, Darnley, the objection among the aristocracy to his marrying the queen arose less from horror at the blood on his hands and more from his destroying the delicate balance of power among Scotland's constantly feuding nobles. Although Bothwell's family had a history of trying to rise by wooing widowed queens,[53] they had not counted on the problems resulting from success. With Bothwell's coronation and being created Duke of Orkney came of course the rise of his friends and family,[54] but the Scots nobility were more concerned with Bothwell's sudden

---

[53] Wormald, *Mary Queen of Scots*, 45.

[54] "At his investure, four of his followers were, as was customary, knighted. His cousin, James Cockburn of Langton; the Captain of Dunbar, Patrick Hay of Whitelaw;

increase of power over them than with avenging Darnley's untimely demise. Notwithstanding their earlier support of Bothwell's marriage to the queen,

> the forces of aristocratic reaction were coalescing against his meteoric rise. Furious at the realization that Bothwell — one of their own number — had made himself a virtual dictator, on 1 May a party of dissidents gathered at Stirling. They vowed in yet another communal bond to strive by all means in their power to set their queen at liberty, and defend her son Prince James. . . . The pattern of Scotish politics was forming once more into the same shapes of family alliances and feuds, in which the power of one noble could not be allowed to grow unchecked . . .[55]

Doubtless, there is considerable truth to Bothwell's challenge to the confederate lords who were about to separate him from Mary: "What harm have I done them? I never wished to displease any, but have sought to gratify them all. Their words proceed from envy of my favour. But Fortune is free to any who can win her. There is not a man of them but wishes himself in my place!"[56]

When, therefore, Mary writes the following quatrain, she is not only explicitly invoking her position as queen, she uses her power to promise exactly what her nobility feared most:[57]

> Entre ses mains et en son plein pouvoir
> Je mets mons fils, mon honneur et ma vie,
> Mon pays, mes sujets, mon âme assujettie
> Et toute à lui, ...
>
> [Into his hands and his absolute power
> I place my son, my honor and my life,
> My country, my subjects, my subjected soul
> Are all for him, ...]

---

the nominee for Edinburgh Castle, Patrick Hepburn of Beanston; and James Ormiston of the ilk, better known as the Black Laird, were chosen for the accolade" (Robert Gore-Browne, *Lord Bothwell and Mary Queen of Scots: A Study of the Life, Character and Times of James Hepburn, 4th Earl of Bothwell* [New York: Doubleday, 1937], 355).

[55] Fraser, *Mary Queen of Scots*, 320.

[56] Quoted in Gore-Browne, *Lord Bothwell and Mary Queen of Scots*, 375–76.

[57] See also Hopkins' analysis of this sonnet.

What seems to be extreme rhetoric also has extreme political consequences. Her son, we need to remember, is the future James VI, and the
country she offers to place in his hands is not an abstraction, as in "My
mind to me a little kingdom is," but a very real place. By declaring that
everything is his, Mary is not only declaring Bothwell the king of Scotland,
she in effect is also abdicating her throne by giving him her "subjects."

This is an offer that only a queen can make, and yet, paradoxically, she
uses her position as monarch to undermine her position as monarch.
Whereas Henry VIII used the lyric as a means of furthering his power,
Mary uses poetry to articulate her personal subjectivity while destroying
her political subjectivity. Moreover, Mary clearly knows this, and her sonnets play on their employment of seemingly cliché devices that suddenly
seem very different when articulated by a monarch. Promises of advancement and declarations of loyal service cannot be taken very seriously when
given by a struggling courtier; but they have to be taken seriously when
put forward by a monarch, even more so when the monarch offers to make
the Hepburns Scotland's royal family. The same applies to Mary's avowals
of loyal service, since they invert the conventional relationship between
subject and monarch. Bothwell ought to be declaring *his* desire to serve his
queen, not the other way around. It is no wonder, then, that when the
Casket Letters were finally made public in Buchanan's *Ane Detectioun of
the duinges of Marie Quene of Scottes* (1571), La Mothe Fénelon, the French
ambassador to England, wrote that "Rhymes in French had been added
which are worse than all the rest," even though they never allude to
Darnley or his murder.[58]

§

In conclusion, Mary's sonnets demonstrate that the meaning of Petrarchan
erotic rhetoric changes significantly depending upon the political position
of the speaker. As in Henry VIII's lyrics, seemingly innocuous or innocent
lines become fraught with meaning because the speaker is not a subject,
but a monarch. Furthermore, also like Henry VIII, Mary clearly sensed this
fact and wrote from a monarchic perspective. The results, however, were
diametrically opposed, as Mary's articulation of sexual agency led her to ig-

---

[58] Quoted in R. H. Mahon, *The Indictment of Mary Queen of Scots* (Cambridge:
Cambridge University Press, 1923), 25.

nore the central fact that the monarch is not a subject. Ironically, Mary's position allowed her the freedom to express precisely the desires that would start the chain of events that would lead to her deposition and, ultimately, her execution at the hands of a woman infinitely more skilled at manipulating the politics of desire: Elizabeth I.[59]

San Diego State University

---

[59] I gratefully acknowledge Professor François Rigolot's reading this essay and his consequently saving me from many an embarrassing error.

JENNIFER SUMMIT

"The Arte of a Ladies Penne":
Elizabeth I and the Poetics of Queenship

I

In the third book of *The Arte of English Poesie* George Puttenham asks "who in any age haue bene the most commended writers in our English Poesie," and the names he offers in response — among them, Chaucer, Wyatt, Sidney, and Ralegh — describe the beginnings of a high-literary history in English.[1] But when it comes to naming the greatest poet of all time, Puttenham brushes these canonical figures aside in favor of none other than Elizabeth I: "last in recitall and first in degree is the Queene our soueraigne Lady, whose learned, delicate, noble Muse, easily surmounteth all the rest that haue written before her time or sence" (77). To support this extraordinary statement Puttenham reproduces in full Elizabeth's enigmatic poem, "The Doubt of Future Foes," claiming that it represents

[1] I owe sincere gratitude to those who have helped to shape this essay and the larger work of which it forms part: Simon Firth, Jonathan Goldberg, Helen Hackett, Robert Matz, David Riggs, Jennifer Tucker, and many others, including audiences at The Johns Hopkins University, the University of Mississippi, the University of London, and the University of California, Berkeley, at which earlier versions of this paper were delivered; a version was also delivered at the 1995 Modern Language Association Convention. The American Association of University Women generously supported my research. This essay first appeared in *English Literary Renaissance* 26 (1995): 395–422, and is reprinted here by the kind permission of the editors.

The Arte of English Poesie, facs. repr. ed. Baxter Hathaway (Kent, OH: Kent State University Press, 1970), 77; all subsequent references to the *Arte*, unless otherwise noted, are to this edition, with page numbers cited in the text parenthetically.

nothing short of "the most bewtifull and gorgious" of all of English poetry
(254). Despite the exhaustive critical attention that Puttenham's text has
received in the past decade, this passage has attracted surprisingly little
notice, except to be dismissed as the piece of flattery that it undoubtedly
is.[2] But the specific form this flattery takes is as significant as it is unexpected, reflecting the importance of a fact that was more widely recognized in his age than it has been in our own: the queen was a poet.

Few would now doubt that Elizabeth played a major role in the formation of Elizabethan literature, after New Historicist work has prepared us
to notice the queen's shaping influence on early modern culture, as well
as the complicated relationship between poetry and monarchy that per-
sisted throughout Elizabeth's reign.[3] Left almost totally unexplored, however, has been the queen's own use of poetry, as well as the literary-histori-
cal implications of the fact that the Elizabethan period was presided over
by a poetry-writing queen. Part of the responsibility for this critical over-
sight, as Susan Frye has recently suggested, must lie in the uneven attention that the queen's writing has received from editors.[4] In an important
survey of Elizabeth's poetry, Steven W. May argues that the queen wrote
more than has been recognized previously, and he expands her corpus to
as many as fifteen original verses in English, French, and Latin, including
addresses and responses to her courtiers, an elegy, and a poem that was

---

[2] On Puttenham's place in recent Renaissance studies, see Jonathan Crewe, *Hidden Designs: The Critical Profession and Renaissance Literature* (New York: Methuen, 1986), 71; Derek Attridge, "Puttenham's Perplexity: Nature, Art, and the Supplement in Renais-sance Poetic Theory," in *Literary Theory/Renaissance Texts*, ed. Patricia Parker and David Quint (Baltimore: Johns Hopkins University Press, 1986), 275.

[3] Influential examples of this work include Louis Adrian Montrose, "The Elizabethan Subject and the Spenserian Text," in *Literary Theory/Renaissance Texts*, and Leah S. Marcus, *Puzzling Shakespeare: Local Reading and its Discontents* (Berkeley: University of California Press, 1988), especially chapter 2, "Elizabeth." Recent work assessing Eliza-beth's literary influence includes Carole Levin, *"The Heart and Stomach of a King:" Eliza-beth I and the Politics of Sex and Power* (Philadelphia: University of Pennsylvania Press, 1994) and Helen Hackett, *Virgin Mother, Maiden Queen: Elizabeth I and the Cult of the Vir-gin Mary* (London: Macmillan, 1995).

[4] Susan Frye, *Elizabeth I: The Competition for Representation* (Oxford: Oxford Univer-sity Press, 1993), 9; *The Poems of Queen Elizabeth I*, ed., Leicester Bradner (Providence, RI: Brown University Press, 1964), used to be the only edition of Elizabeth's poetry; how-ever, Leah Marcus, Janel Mueller, and Mary Beth Rose have recently published a major edition of Elizabeth's writings, speeches, verses, prayers and poems, *Elizabeth I: Collected Works*, ed. Leah S. Marcus, Janel Mueller, and Mary Beth Rose (Chicago: University of Chicago Press, 2000).

printed later as a ballad.[5] But Elizabeth's poems challenge editorial efforts to establish textual authenticity or even, in some cases, clear attribution. Because they circulated largely in manuscript and survive within multiple sources, the poems are subject to considerable textual ambiguity; and thus, like most coterie poetry of the period, they resist the efforts of modern editors who seek to establish authenticity on the basis of a single, original text.[6] Moreover, Elizabeth's poetry was often copied and preserved in collections of speeches and court records or in county archives, documents that are easily overlooked as specimens of literary culture.[7]

If Elizabeth's surviving poems don't always look like poetry to modern eyes, Elizabeth herself doesn't look like a poet. To the contrary, while the New Historicism has established the queen's importance as a figure in English literary history, the models of writing that it has produced often close off the possibility of seeing Elizabeth as a poet herself. To take a highly influential example, Louis Adrian Montrose's account of "the Elizabethan subject" in Spenser's poetry contends that "the male subject / poet puts into question the female monarch's claim to shape herself and her subjects" by making her the "subject" of his verse and thereby subjecting her to a violent debasement that is both textual and sexual.[8] What makes Spenser a poet — his masculine aggression — would also appear to disqualify Elizabeth from occupying that same position because she is a woman. Like other early modern women, Queen Elizabeth I is instead far more readily seen as the silent subject of poetry by men, a view that has found unlikely support in some feminist work. Philippa Berry's recent analysis of

---

[5] Steven W. May, *The Elizabethan Courtier Poets: The Poems and their Contexts* (Columbia: University of Missouri Press, 1991), 47, 317–18; May also provides the best bibliography available on Elizabeth I — which stresses the need for further analysis of her poetry — in "Recent Studies in Elizabeth I," *English Literary Renaissance* 23 (1993): 345–54.

[6] One poem alternatively known as "The Ladies Comfortable and Pleasant Answer," "Ah Silly Pugge, wert thou so afraid," and "On fortune," e.g., exists in versions so dramatically different as to make it impossible to secure an original or authoritative text, if any single one exists. (See Walter Oakeshott, *The Queen and the Poet* [London: Faber and Faber, 1960], L. G. Black, "A Lost Poem by Queen Elizabeth I," *Times Literary Supplement* 23 May 1968, 535, and Steven W. May, *Sir Walter Ralegh* [Boston: Twayne, 1989], 140n12.) See also the notes by Marcus, Mueller, and Rose to these poems in this volume. For a critique of editorial practice that is grounded in theories of final authorial intention, see Jerome McGann, *A Critique of Modern Textual Criticism* (Charlottesville: University Press of Virginia, 1983).

[7] An example is the Inner Temple Library MS Petyt 538 vol. 10, which brings together Elizabeth's poetry and her speeches and is discussed below.

[8] Montrose, "The Elizabethan Subject," 303, 324.

Elizabeth's literary influence, which importantly stresses the femininity of Elizabeth's court and its conventions, nonetheless joins Montrose in representing poetic practice as an inscription of masculine desire that objectifies and immobilizes women, including the queen. From this perspective Berry advances the argument that Elizabeth could only have been excluded from literary agency: "What is most striking about the queen, in vivid contrast to the repeated rhetorical emissions *about* her which were produced by many of her masculine subjects, is the dearth of her own texts, her own speech. From the literary perspective, what chiefly remains of Elizabeth Tudor is her silence."[9]

If this view of Elizabeth as a "silent" female subject reflects current assumptions about the gender of Renaissance literary authority, it is not shared by Elizabeth's contemporaries. In 1598 Francis Meres celebrated the queen as "an excellent Poet herself," and, even after her death removed the incentive to flatter, Edmund Bolton's *Hypercritica* (1610-17) classifies her among "the best Authors for written English," taking as his example "The Doubt of Future Foes."[10] The textual acts of sexual aggression that Montrose illuminates in Spenser's verse did not necessarily consign Elizabeth to a position of "subjected" silence: indeed, in *The Teares of the Muses* Spenser praises the queen as a "most peereless Poëtresse."[11] To these contemporary observers, Elizabeth's position as a female monarch is not inconsistent with that of a poet; it made her uniquely qualified for it. The queen sanctioned and encouraged this recognition of her poetic activity, and even wrote an "Art of Poetry" herself; among Elizabeth's surviving poetic efforts is the partial verse translation of Horace's *Ars Poetica*.[12]

---

[9] Philippa Berry, *Of Chastity and Power: Elizabethan Literature and the Unmarried Queen* (London: Routledge, 1989), 7. Despite this representation of Elizabeth's literary practice, Berry's study provides a useful corrective to the critical assumption that Elizabeth occupied a masculine sphere of power by pointing to the ways in which the queen surrounded herself with women and self-consciously figured her femininity.

[10] Francis Meres, *A Comparative Discourse of our English Poets, with the Greek, Latine, and Italian Poets* (1598) and Edmund Bolton, *Hypercritica* (1610-1617), reprinted in *Ancient Critical Essays Upon English Poets and Poesy*, ed. Joseph Haslewood (London, 1811), 2: 155, 246-48.

[11] Edmund Spenser, "The Teares of the Muses," in *Poetical Works*, ed. J. C. Smith and E. de Selincourt (Oxford: Oxford University Press, 1985), 486.

[12] This translation is reprinted in Bradner, *Poems of Queen Elizabeth I*; see also *Queen Elizabeth's Englishings of Boethius, "De Consolatione Philosophiae," A.D. 1598; Plutarch, "De Curiositate," A.D. 1598; Horace, "De Arte Poetica" (partial), A.D. 1598*, ed. Caroline Pemberton, EETS (London, 1899).

As a poet, Elizabeth followed the example of other poet-monarchs such as James VI/I and her father, Henry VIII.[13] But where James and Henry use the tropes of Petrarchism to craft themselves as male lovers, Elizabeth cultivates a poetic persona that is notable for its femininity. To the more familiar figurations of her royal persona — Elizabeth as amazon, Diana, Astraea — we must add one more, Elizabeth as Sappho.[14] The dedication to Spenser's 1569 translation of John van der Noodt's *Theatre for Worldlings* not only praises the queen for her "learning, knowledge, counsell, iudgement, and eloquence," but also claims that she is "so instructed in the divine Arte of Poetrie, that you may woorthily be called the second *sappho*."[15] And in the *Partheniades*, the manuscript sequence of poems that Puttenham presented to Elizabeth as a new year's gift in 1579 and to which he frequently refers in *The Arte of English Poesy*, the queen attracts similar praise: "Oft youre self, w[ith] Ladye Sapphoes pen / In sweet measures, of poesye t'endite / The rare affectes of your heavenly sprighte."[16] While Joan DeJean has argued that early modern invocations of Sappho usually work to repudiate her in favor of masculine literary ancestors, in these instances Sappho secures Elizabeth's own poetic practice in a female literary genealogy.[17]

---

[13] See Kevin Sharpe, "The King's Writ: Royal Authors and Royal Authority in Early Modern England," in *Culture and Politics in Early Stuart England*, ed. Kevin Sharpe and Peter Lake (London: Macmillan, 1994) and Seth Lerer, *Courtly Letters in the Age of Henry VIII: Literary Culture and the Arts of Deceit* (Cambridge: Cambridge University Press, 1997), 87–121. On the poetry of Henry VIII, see Herman and Siemens, "Henry VIII and the Poetry of Politics," in this volume.

[14] On these various personifications of the queen's authority (but notably excluding Sappho), see Winfried Schleiner, "*Divina Virago*: Queen Elizabeth as Amazon," *Studies in Philology* 75 (1978): 163–80; and Frances A. Yates, *Astraea: The Imperial Theme in the Sixteenth Century* (London: Pimlico, 1975).

[15] John van der Noodt, *A Theatre Wherein be Represented as wel the Miseries & Calamities that Follow the Voluptuous Worldlings, as also the Greate Ioyes and Pleasures which the Faithfull do Enioy* (London, 1569); see also J. W. Saunders, "From Manuscript to Print: A Note on the Circulation of Poetic MSS in the Sixteenth Century," *Proceedings of the Leeds Philosophical and Literary Society* 6 (1951): 508, and on Spenser's translation see Crewe, *Hidden Designs*, 93–118.

[16] British Museum Cotton Vesp. E. VIII, folio 169r; the *Partheniades* are also reprinted by Haslewood, *Ancient Critical Essays*, 1: xix–xxxviii.

[17] Joan DeJean, *Fictions of Sappho, 1546–1937* (Chicago: University of Chicago Press, 1989); on other early modern representations of Sappho, see Elizabeth D. Harvey, *Ventriloquized Voices: Feminist Theory and English Renaissance Texts* (London: Routledge, 1992), chapter 4: "Ventriloquizing Sappho, or the Lesbian Muse." See also Paula Blank, "Comparing Sappho to Philaenis: John Donne's 'Homopoetics,' " *PMLA* 110 (1995): 358–68.

If Elizabeth counters assumptions about the masculinity of poetry in early modern literary culture, she also challenges us to redefine what we mean by "early modern woman writer." In one critical model that has found wide acceptance in the past, the de facto masculinity of the Renaissance poet, together with humanist injunctions against women's public or erotic self-expression, could only have disqualified women from writing poetry. Those who dared to take up the pen performed an oppositional act against the conditions of privacy and silence to which they were bound.[18] But recent research into the material conditions of women's writing in the period suggests the need to reconsider the opposition between masculine writing on the one hand and feminine decorum on the other. In her valuable work on Jacobean women's production and circulation of manuscripts, Margaret Ezell illuminates a form of writing that was apparently consistent with feminine privacy, and examples of women writers such as Lady Anne Southwell and Elizabeth Egerton reveal that early modern poetry itself was no more inherently masculine than poetry by women was inherently oppositional.[19] In Elizabeth I we find a female poet who is neither silenced and marginalized nor oppositional in her writing; rather, she occupies the central position within Elizabethan culture. While the queen was hardly typical of women writers in her day, she sheds important light on the cultural meanings that attached to and defined the figure of the woman writer in her age, at the same time that she endows this figure with more cultural authority than has been previously believed possible. In crafting herself as a female poet Elizabeth called on a set of tropes and postures that were conventionally identified with women writers — in particular, the privacy and enclosure that humanism famously assigned to women. But by cultivating the persona of the female poet as a representation of her royal authority, she also employed that persona toward decidedly public ends.

The doubleness of this stance comes to the fore in Puttenham's representation of Elizabeth as both the female poet who is "the most gorgious and bewtifull" and the English poet whose talent "easily surmounteth all

---

[18] Juliet Fleming offers a provocative critique of this "oppositional" model in her review of Barbara Lewalski's *Writing Women in Jacobean England*, *The Huntington Library Quarterly* 57 (1994): 202–4.

[19] See Margaret J. M. Ezell, *The Patriarch's Wife: Literary Evidence and the History of the Family* (Chapel Hill: University of North Carolina Press, 1987), and "Elizabeth Delaval's Spiritual Heroine: Thoughts on Redefining Manuscript Texts by Early Modern Women Writers," *English Manuscript Studies, 1100–1700* 3 (1992): 216–37.

the rest." By presenting Elizabeth's position as a female poet as central to her royal persona, Puttenham reveals himself to be perhaps the queen's best reader. Moreover, by presenting Elizabeth as the greatest English poet of all time, he also makes her the unexpected centerpiece of *The Arte of English Poesie* itself, not as a dedicatee alone but also as an exemplum. In the passage I cite above, Puttenham makes Elizabeth's poetic practice define the project of a broader English poetics. He thereby provokes a question that opens up an unexpectedly new avenue for both feminist and historicist inquiry in early modern England: what would it mean to take Puttenham seriously when he claims that "the art of English Poetry" finds its ultimate model in what he calls, in reference to Elizabeth, "the arte of a ladies penne" (255)?

II

To start, it would mean reappraising the influential reading of Puttenham that takes *The Arte of English Poesie* to be the handbook of ambitious male courtier-poets who wooed their queen in verse.[20] While such a reading valuably brings into relief the myriad ways in which Puttenham's work upholds masculine privilege, it also obscures the ways in which *The Arte* defines the courtier-poet through his proximity to, and indeed identification with, an imaginary gathering of women writers — or as Puttenham calls them, "gentlewomen makers" — of whom the queen is the most visible representative. Puttenham openly addresses his work not to courtiers alone but most pointedly to "Ladies and young Gentlewomen" who desire "for their own priuate recreation to make now and then ditties of pleasure" (170).[21] The femininity of this art is reflected in Puttenham's discussion of poetic figures, which he describes as decorations similar to the "courtly habillements" of "great Madames of honour" (149) and "the crimson tainte, which should be laid vpon a Ladies lips" (150). Given this comparison of poetic ornament to feminine ornament, Puttenham asserts that it is in "the pretie Poesies and devices of Ladies, and Gentlewomen makers" that figurative language finds a natural place (256).

---

[20] Such is the influential argument of David Norbrook, *Poetry and Politics in the English Renaissance* (London: Routledge and Kegan Paul, 1984) and Daniel Javitch, *Poetry and Courtliness in Renaissance England* (Princeton: Princeton University Press, 1976).

[21] Javitch discusses the importance of the female readership in the Elizabethan court (but not the practices of the female poet) in *Poetry and Courtliness in Renaissance England*, 28–29.

When literary critics of a later age rejected what they saw as the ef-
feminacy of Elizabethan writing they made Elizabeth herself its embodiment, as did Richard Flecknoe when he scornfully noted that the style "of
Queen Elizabeths dayes" was "flaunting and pufted like her Apparell."[22]
Puttenham's *Arte of English Poesie* lends ammunition to such a charge by
making Elizabeth the exemplary poet in his discussion "Of Poetic Ornament," which defines the art of poetry as one of beautiful seeming ("*beau
semblant*"). Such an art would appear to be exemplified in Elizabeth's
"Doubt of Future Foes," since, being "desciphered by the arte of a ladies
penne," as Puttenham puts it, the poem reflects the beauty of its maker,
"her selfe beyng the most gorgious and bewtifull" (255).[23]

But the poem itself is hardly what we expect of "the pretie Poesies and
devises of ladies, and Gentlewomen makers." For all its supposed beauty,
the poem also takes as its subject a scene of unexpected violence and men-
ace; under its thin veneer of figurative language, it advances what amounts
to a death threat to Mary Queen of Scots. If "The Doubt of Future Foes"
defines a feminized and feminine art of ornament and beauty, idleness and
"private recreation," it also compels a reexamination of these terms'
meanings and uses within Puttenham's poetics.

In Puttenham's words, "the ditty is as followeth:"

The doubt of future foes, exiles my present ioy,
And wit me warnes to shun such snares as threaten mine annoy,
For falshood novv doth flow, and subiect faith doth ebbe,
Which would not be, if reason rul'd or wisdome weu'd the webbe.
But clowdes of tois untried, do cloake aspiring mindes,
Which turne to raigne of late repent, by course of changed
vvindes.
The toppe of hope supposed, the roote of ruth vvil be,

[22] Cited in Wesley Trimpi, *Ben Jonson's Poem's: A Study in Plain Style* (Stanford:
Stanford University Press, 1962), 251–52; for a discussion of how the "masculine" style
of Jacobean writing was seen to supplant the "feminine" style of Elizabethan writing, see
Patricia Parker, "Virile Style," in *Premodern Sexualities*, ed. Carla Freccero and Louise
Fradenburg (New York: Routledge, 1996). I am grateful to Patricia Parker for sharing this
reference and her work on this topic with me.

[23] Relevant to this discussion of the feminization of poetic ornament is John
Guillory's observation that "the development in the early modern period of new
discourses of truth (the scientific) occasioned ... the epistemological bracketing of the
poetic genres as 'fiction,' and the identification of ornament as defining the linguistic
difference of those genres." See Guillory, *Cultural Capital: The Problem of Literary Canon
Formation* (Chicago: University of Chicago Press, 1993), 213.

And frutelesse all their graffed guiles, as shortly ye shall see.
Then dazeld eyes vvith pride, vvhich great ambition blinds,
Shalbe unseeld by vvorthy wights, vvhose foresight falshood finds,
The daughter of debate, that eke discord doth sovve
Shal reap no gaine where formor rule hath taught stil peace to growe.
No forreine bannisht vvight shall ancre in this port,
Our realme it brookes no strangers force, let them elsvvhere resort.
Our rusty svvorde vvith rest, shall first his edge employ,
To polle their toppes that seeke, such change and gape for ioy.
    (255–56)

The poem's subject is recognizable from one of the most fraught political dramas of Elizabeth's reign: the "daughter of debate," as Puttenham explains, refers to the Queen of Scots, who was Elizabeth's cousin and Catholic rival for the throne; and as the poem foretells, she was indeed beheaded for treason on 8 February 1587, after her long captivity in England. This reference is supported by the poem's textual history: surviving manuscripts of "The Doubt of Future Foes" place its composition at around 1570, within two years after Mary fled Scotland to seek the refuge that she apparently expected to find in England's borders. Because of fears that she would amass armies of Catholic supporters and pose a threat to Elizabeth, Mary was instead imprisoned for nineteen years before she was finally beheaded in 1587.[24] Expressing the royal speaker's "doubt" about the intentions of her "foes" and brandishing an imaginary "sworde" in her protection, the poem would appear to wage a threat against a fellow queen, and to predict future events with deadly accuracy. For Puttenham's readers in 1589 those events would still be a recent memory. Yet for Puttenham, "The Doubt of Future Foes" is an example of "poeticall Ornament," a "ditty … passing sweete and harmonicall," and "the most bewtifull and gorgious of all others." For *whom* is this poem "sweete and harmonicall," we might well ask: on what grounds could it possibly be classified as the most "bewtiful and gorgious" poem in English?

---

[24] On the Mary Queen of Scots affair, see J. E. Neale, *Queen Elizabeth I* (London: Jonathan Cape, 1934) and *Elizabeth and Her Parliaments, 1559–1581* (London: Jonathan Cape, 1953), 226–34, 241–90; see also Alison Plowden, *Two Queens in One Isle: The Deadly Relationship of Queen Elizabeth I and Mary Queen of Scots* (Sussex: Harvester Press, 1984).

These questions return us to *The Arte of English Poesie*, in which the poetic figure of "the gorgious" exemplifies the complexity of the art of poetic beauty, "*beau* semblant." "The gorgious," as Puttenham explains in the passage that introduces "The Doubt of Future Foes," takes its name and meaning from the work of marble polishers, whose art shears away the outer roughness of the stone to leave a mirror-like surface, "so smooth and cleare as ye may see your face in it." At the same time that it clarifies the stone's surface, the "gorgious" art embellishes the stone's native dullness, Puttenham continues, just as "rich and gorgeous apparell" embellishes "the bare and naked body" (254). Both dressing up and shearing away, the figure of "the gorgious" implies an ability to cloak and to reveal at the same time.

By offering "The Doubt of Future Foes" as the embodiment of poetic "gorgiousness," Puttenham invites readers to note the poem's concern with questions of cloaking and revelation. In her attempt to confound her foes, the speaker promises to uncloak "aspiring minds," to clear away "clowdes of toies," to "unseal" eyes formerly blinded, and to root out "falsehood" and hidden "snares." The poem thereby creates an opposition between outward appearances and inner meanings, as the speaker worries that her "foes" hide their threatening intentions under pleasant facades, and then resolves to expose and eradicate them with a threat of violence. The terms in which "The Doubt of Future Foes" describes the speaker's "foes" were frequently used to describe the art of poetry: poems, after all, were commonly referred to as "toyes" and figurative language as a cloud, as when Spenser describes his *Faerie Queene* as being "clowdily enwrapped in Allegorical devices."[25] Yet while "The Doubt of Future Foes" offers to uncloak hidden meanings such as those concealed in "clowdes of toies," it does so in a language that is itself glutted with figures — figures of weaving, storms, plants, and gardeners. While she claims to stand against poetic "falsehood," the speaker also shows herself to be an aficionada of its language.

If the poem's figurative language explains Puttenham's decision to call it "the most bewtiful and gorgious" of all others, it also recalls us to the proximity of the art of "*beau*-semblant" to that of "*fals*-semblant" in Puttenham's famous discussion of allegory. *Allegoria*, the chief figure in *The Arte of English Poesie*, is the art of dissimulation, of "speak[ing] otherwise than we thinke ... under covert and darke termes" (197). This skill par-

---

[25] *Poetical Works*, 407.

ticularly befitted the Queen of Scots affair, as Puttenham suggests in his description of the poem's context:

> Our soueraigne Lady perceiuing how by the Sc. Q. residence within this Realme at so greate libertie and ease . . . bred secret factions among her people. . . . The Queene our soueraigne Lady to declare that she was nothing ignorant [of] those secret [practizes], though she had long with great wisdome and pacience dissembled it, writeth this ditty most sweet and sententious, not hiding from all such aspiring minds the daunger of their ambition and disloyaltie, which afterward fell out most truly by th'exemplary chastisement of sundry persons. (255)

In Puttenham's account, "The Doubt of Future Foes" cannily manipulates the appearances of secrecy and disclosure. The poem is not a straightforward declaration of knowledge but rather a declaration of a lack of ignorance: the queen wrote it "to declare that she was nothing ignorant [of] those secret [practices]." It isn't an outright revelation but a strategic decision not to hide, in "not hiding from all such aspiring minds the daunger of their ambition and disloyaltie." And it isn't so much a renunciation of dissemblance — "though she had long with great wisdome and pacience dissembled it" — as an effort to foreground the queen's dissemblance, to show how her "ignorance" is merely a cover. While the poem itself seeks to reveal the truth of the foes' "secret practices," it asks the reader to supply that truth through the process of interpreting the queen's cloaking language.

Puttenham takes up this burden of interpretation in another text he wrote for Elizabeth. Following the trial and execution of Mary Stuart a long manuscript was circulated under the various titles, "A Defence of the Honorable Sentence and Execution of the Queene of Scotes" and "An Apologie or True Defense of her Ma[jesty's] Hono[r] and Good Renowne," announcing itself to be "writen by GEORGE PUTTENHAM to the service of her ma[jesty]."[26] Both the "Defence of the Honorable Sentence"

---

[26] The text has been printed as "A Justificacion of Queene Elizabeth in Relacion to the Affaire of Mary Queene of Scottes" (1587–1588) in *Accounts and Papers Relating to Mary Queen of Scots*, ed. Allan J. Crosby and John Bruce (London, 1867); in the discussion that follows, citations are to this edition, with page numbers noted parenthetically; the manuscripts are: British Museum Add. MS 48027, folios 451–76; and British Museum Harl. 831; the Additional MS contains this marginal gloss at the title: "It is thought that this book was made by George Puttenham" (451r); the complete title of the Harleian MS is as follows: "An apologie or true defence of her Ma[jesties] hono[r] and

and *The Arte of English Poesy* choose to foreground Elizabeth's relationship
with Mary Queen of Scots as the center of production for the queen's dark
and figurative language.[27] In *The Arte of English Poesie* the "covert and
dark terms" of allegory enable monarchs to dissemble, a critical ability in
the art of rulership: "*Qui nescit dissimulare nescit regnare*" (197). The ruler's
use of "covert and dark termes" is also the premise of "A Defence of the
Honorable Sentence and Execution of the Queene of Scotes," which aims
to explain those terms to readers, "to the intent that no part of her Majesty's behaviour or doings therein should be *covered or hidden*" in relation to
the Queen of Scots affair (68; emphasis added). Puttenham's aim in the
"Defense" is therefore, he explains, "to have laied open and unfoulded
even the most secreat partes of the sayd cause, whiche hath fallen out
from the beginning of this businesse betwene her Maiestie and the sayd
Scottische Quene" (69). The trial and execution of Mary Queen of Scots
is to the "Defense" what "The Doubt of Future Foes" is to *The Arte of
English Poesie*; both the poem and the trial position the queen as the auth-
or of a discourse of covert but controversial meaning that will necessitate
a written defense or explanation. And in both Puttenham offers his work
as the gloss on Elizabeth's dark text. But while Puttenham promises to
"lay open" "even the most secreat partes of the sayd cause," in the course
of the text he is compelled to admit the extent to which the queen's deal-
ings with the Scottish queen are an open secret: "Nor this entent of her
Majesties was so close or secrete, but that manie about her haue bene
made acquainted with it by her own regall mouthe" (75). Indeed, the
queen's "secreats" are coextensive with those matters "which her Majestie
was not unwilling should be bruted and spred abroad" (74). What makes

---

good renowne against all such as haue unduelie sought or shall seek to blemish the same
with any injustice, crueltie, or other unprincely behaviour in any parte of her Ma[jesties]
proceedings against the late Scotisch Queene. Be it for her first surprince, imprisonment,
process, attaynder, or death. By uery firme reasons, authorities warrantable by the law of
God and of man. Writen by GEORGE PUTTENHAM to the servece of her Ma[jestie]
and for large satisfaction of all such persons both princely and private who by ignorance
of the case, or partiallitie of mind shall happen to be irresolute and not well satisfied in
the said cause."

[27] The relation between these two texts has not been examined, with the exception
of the introductory notes to Gladys Doidge Willcock and Alice Walker's edition of *The
Arte of English Poesie* (Cambridge: Cambridge University Press, 1936); on the connection
between the "Defense" and the *Arte*, see especially pages xviii, xxii–xliv; on the "Defense" as "royal propaganda no doubt approved if not commissioned by Elizabeth," see
May, *The Elizabethan Courtier Poets*, 33.

those secrets "covered or hidden," in other words, does not necessarily keep them from public knowledge.

Renaissance discourses of secrecy, as several recent studies have established, manipulated the appearances of public and private knowledge. In the Tudor and Stuart vogue for the "secret" arts of miniatures and sonnets, Patricia Fumerton discerns the effort to create a private self both within and beyond the artifice of public display, while Richard Rambuss analyses Spenser's poetics of secrecy to conclude that its primary effort is less to hide a material secret than to craft that hiddenness as a flagrant display.[28] Such insights can illuminate the doubleness of Puttenham's "Defence of the Honorable Sentence" and its promise to "lay open" the queen's secrets. Puttenham's effort in the "Defense" is not to disclose the queen's secrets, the substance of which he claims is public knowledge, but to construct that public knowledge as a secret. The effect is both to make his readers into privileged insiders and to create the queen's openly known secrets as objects of desire.

The terms of Puttenham's political apology are pressed into the service of literary criticism in *The Arte of English Poesie*, where the monarch's dark language becomes an explicitly poetic language. Such is the case in Puttenham's discussion of emblems, hieroglyphic poems that join enigmatic images with cryptic mottos, appearing on coins or the monarch's liveries. While emblems have a public significance, they work, Puttenham asserts, "by secret might." Their purpose is "to insinuat some secret, wittie, morall and braue purpose presented to the beholder, either to recreate his eye, or please his phantasie, or examine his iudgement or occupie his braine or to manage his will either by hope or by dread, euery of which respects be of no little moment to the interest and ornament of the ciuill life" (121). As an "ornament of the civil life," the emblem shares with the principal "poetical ornament," the gorgious, the ability to manipulate the effects of cloaking and revelation in order to produce a realm of interiorized meaning. By staging its own obscurity, the emblem manages the subject's will by keeping him — or in Mary's case, her — in a constant state of hope and dread about its possible significance. Hope and dread, the conventional affects of the Petrarchan lover, are here made to describe a level of advanced paranoia that the emblem induces, as each "beholder"

---

[28] Patricia Fumerton, *Cultural Aesthetics: Renaissance Literature and the Practice of Social Ornament* (Chicago: University of Chicago Press, 1991); Richard Rambuss, *Spenser's Secret Career* (Cambridge: Cambridge University Press, 1993).

is given the sense that the emblem is meant for his eyes, for her eyes, alone. As the subject attempts to penetrate the dark meanings of the emblem, the emblem penetrates the subject. Like the figure of "the gorgious," it both beguiles the eye and transfixes the conscience, creating a surface "so smooth and cleare as ye may see your face in it."

What the emblem signifies matters less than the way in which it signifies, producing a public, disciplinary effect by enlisting each subject as a private viewer and reader. Horace sees such a production of the private on behalf of the public as germane to the art of poetry: "In private sort the commen thing declare," he instructs the poet, in lines that Queen Elizabeth herself would translate into English: "General mattar shal be made thy private part."[29] This Horatian model of public knowledge made private informs what we might call Elizabeth's poetics of queenship, which Puttenham illustrates in both *The Arte of English Poesie* and "The Defence of the Honorable Sentence": it continually stages matters of public policy as the stuff of secrets.[30] This register is appropriate to the queen whose motto was "*video et taceo*," "I see and hold my tongue."[31] The queen who sees everything displays her omniscience by witholding expression of the full extent of her knowledge: but by calling attention to the hiddenness of that knowledge she delivers messages more piercing and arresting than she might by open proclamation. For Puttenham this power is concentrated in the queen's use of figurative language. The queen is the most important poet in English literary history for the same reason that allegory is the most important figure in *The Arte of English Poesie*: both use language to the greatest effect by withholding meaning.

III

Elizabeth's poetics of covertness is abetted by the textual practice of coterie manuscript circulation, the primary means of transmission for the queen's poetry. In the years around and after its composition in 1570,

---

[29] "The Art of Poetry," in Bradner, *Poems of Queen Elizabeth I*, 50.

[30] Such a strategy is similar to what Jonathan Goldberg calls "The trope of state secrets," by which James I effected "the transformation of privacy into public discourse"; *James I and the Politics of Poetry: Jonson, Shakespeare, Donne and their Contemporaries* (Baltimore: Johns Hopkins University Press, 1983), preface, xii.

[31] On the significance of this motto, see Mary Thomas Crane, " 'Video et Taceo': Elizabeth I and the Rhetoric of Counsel," *Studies in English Literature* 28 (1988): 1–15.

"The Doubt of Future Foes" appears to have been widely circulated, as attested by the eight manuscripts in which it survives today.[32] One such source, the Arundel Harington Manuscript, collects courtly poems along with scraps of letters and courtly gossip; in it, "The Doubt of Future Foes" is copied down in a careful hand and prefaced by a note, probably by Sir John Harington, which commends the poem to an unnamed woman:

> Good Madame,
>
> Herewith I commit a precious jewel, not for your ear, but your eye; and doubt not but you will rejoyce to wear it even in your heart: It is of her Highness own enditing, and doth witness, how much her wisdom and great learning doth outweigh even the perils of state, and how little all worldly dangers do work any change in her mynde. My Lady Wiloughby did covertly get it on her Majesties tablet, and had much hazard in so doing; for the Queen did find out the thief, and chid for spreading evil bruit of her writing such toyes, when other matters did so occupy her employment at this time; and was fearful of being thought too lightly of for so doing. But marvel not, good Madam, her Highness doth frame herself to all occasions, to all times, and all things, both in business, and pastime, as may witness this her sonnet.[33]

Creating a highly charged dialectic of hiddenness and exposure, Harington makes the poem's value coextensive with the restrictedness of its circulation. Its "covertness" reflects the privacy of its composition and circulation: the manuscript poem is "a precious jewel" which inhabits innermost places, such as the queen's private chamber or "Madame's "heart." Harington emphasizes the poem's privacy by staging its composition within what appears to be an almost exclusively feminine space, circumscribed by the queen, "my Lady Wiloughby," and the nameless "Madame," for whom Harington functions as a go-between.[34] By creating a private sphere of textual circulation that is also a female textual community, Harington's narrative invokes a set of conventions associated with the early modern female coterie.

---

[32] On the manuscripts of "The Doubt of Future Foes," see May, *The Elizabethan Courtier Poets*, 317–18 as well as the transcriptions in this volume.

[33] Ruth Hughey, ed., *The Arundel Harington Manuscript of Tudor Poetry*, 2 vols. (Columbus: Ohio State University Press, 1960), 1: 276–77; 2: 386–87.

[34] Harington dedicated his translation of Cicero's *De Amicitia* (London, 1550) to Katherine Willoughby, Duchess of Suffolk, who might be the "Lady Wiloughby" here.

Manuscript circulation among women of the upper classes appears to have been a fairly common and socially recognized practice, as Margaret Ezell establishes in her important work on the subject, and Arthur Marotti suggests that the manuscript medium appealed to women because its relatively private transmission did not violate early modern standards of female modesty.[35] But if the practice of manuscript production and circulation was associated with a specifically feminized space of privacy and enclosure in the Renaissance, it is also worth bearing in mind that the manuscript medium was far from an entirely "private" one but also had public uses, as Marotti and Harold Love have recently observed.[36] Modifying J. W. Saunder's famous observation that early modern poets feared "the stigma of print," Jonathan Crewe argues that we should see in these poets' uses of manuscript "neither a strong desire nor a capacity to limit their [texts'] circulation," so much as a calculated attempt to create an aura of "privileged insidedness" around the text and its readers.[37] The early modern coterie poet, argues Crewe, attempted "to hide and reveal the secret at the same time; to let the right outsiders become insiders."[38] If Crewe's insight offers us a way of reading the uses of manuscript in the period as part of a larger strategy of textual circulation, it stands to illuminate the different uses of privacy as they might have related to early modern women's writing. Rather than necessarily interpreting women's appar-

---

[35] Margaret J. M. Ezell, *The, Patriarch's Wife: Literary Evidence and the History of the Family* (Chapel Hill: University of North Carolina Press, 1987), especially chapter 3: "Women Writers: Patterns of Manuscript Circulation and Publication"; see also Ezell's "Elizabeth Delaval's Spiritual Heroine: Thoughts on Redefining Manuscript Texts by Early Women Writers," *English Manuscript Studies 1100–1700* 3 (1992): 216–37; Arthur Marotti, *Manuscript, Print, and the English Renaissance Lyric* (Ithaca, NY: Cornell University Press, 1995), 61; on the culturally defined "femininity" of manuscript, see Ann Baynes Coiro, "Writing in Service: Sexual Politics and Class Position in the Poetry of Aemilia Lanyer and Ben Jonson," *Criticism* 35 (1993): 359.

[36] Arthur F. Marotti, "The Transmission of Lyric Poetry and the Institutionalizing of Literature in the English Renaissance," in *Contending Kingdoms: Historical, Psychological, and Feminist Approaches to the Literature of Sixteenth-Century England and France*, ed. Marie-Rose Logan and Peter L. Rudnytsky (Detroit: Wayne State University Press, 1991); see also Harold Love, "Scribal Publication in Seventeenth-Century England," *Transactions of the Cambridge Bibliographical Society* 9 (1987): 130–54; and Richard B. Wollman, "The 'Press and the Fire': Print and Manuscript Culture in Donne's Circle," *Studies in English Literature* 33 (1993): 85–97.

[37] J. W. Saunders, "The Stigma of Print: A Note on the Social Bases of Tudor Poetry," *Essays In Criticism* 1 (1951): 139–64; Crewe, *Hidden Designs*, 78.

[38] Crewe, *Hidden Designs*, 78.

ent preference for manuscript as an attempt to hide their texts from circulation, we need to consider how manuscript could produce the appearance
of hiddenness in such a way as to promote circulation.

Such an analysis brings together an understanding of the calculated restrictedness of manuscript circulation on the one hand and the strategic
manipulation of public and private in Elizabethan discourses of secrecy on
the other to ask how the decorous privacy of women's writing allowed for
a wider influence than has been previously imagined. One example that illuminates the conjunction of these three terms is the early modern woman
writer Elizabeth Egerton.[39] Egerton wrote a number of poems in her lifetime, including occasional poetry, verse meditations on scripture, and
poems about and addressed to her family. These were all confined to
manuscript, and after her death her husband, John Egerton, wrote an epitaph praising his wife for her "modesty in concealing" her verse.[40] Yet
drawing attention to the poems' "concealment" also serves to publicize
them. In fact, at least three separate manuscripts of the poems currently
exist, which suggests that they were both circulated and recopied by readers outside the immediate Egerton household. The "modest concealment"
of Elizabeth Egerton's poems was thus apparently not inconsistent with
their circulation; indeed, it may well have played a significant part in it,
to the extent that their concealment becomes a marker of value and a
stimulant of readerly desire. We might identify this strategy as a "modesty
trope" that offered women writers a chance to stage the feminine privacy
and concealment of their verses while at the same time sending them into
circulation. Queen Elizabeth shows an awareness of such postures and conventions in her own poetry, which invokes the feminine and aristocratic
associations of manuscript in order to produce a kind of writing that
claims the highest privilege in its restrictedness at the same time that it
maintains an appearance of feminine modesty in its concealment. In this
way the queen's poetry represented a sphere of literary production in
which the privacy and enclosure of women's writing coincided with a
sphere of restricted circulation that was endowed with cultural prestige.[41]

---

[39] See Betty S. Travitsky, "Reconstructing the Still, Small Voice: The Occasional
Journal of Elizabeth Egerton," *Women's Studies* 19 (1991): 194; and "His Wife's Prayers
and Meditations: MS Egerton 607," in *The Renaissance Englishwoman in Print: Counterbal-
ancing the Canon*, ed. Anne M. Haselkorn and Betty S. Travitsky (Amherst: University
of Massachusetts Press, 1990).

[40] Cited by Travitsky, *Reconstructing the Still, Small Voice*, 245.

[41] My model of "restricted circulation" draws from Pierre Bourdieu's essay, "The

This interpretation is born out in Harington's narrative of the covert circulation of "The Doubt of Future Foes." In it, Elizabeth protests that the poem occupies a privatized space that she wants to distinguish from her public concerns, "the other matters that did so occupy her employment at this time." But what the poem reveals for Harington is not the exclusivity of the queen's privacy so much as the extensiveness of her art — her capacity to "frame herself to all occasions, to all times, and all things." As Harington observes, the queen's "privacy" is no less a "frame" than her public self-display. Indeed, her privacy is constructed retroactively through the narrative of the poem's exposure: it doesn't constitute a withdrawal from circulation so much as a way of representing limitation and restriction as markers of value that in turn promote circulation. This framing is central to what I have wanted to call Elizabeth's poetics of queenship; by framing it within the conventions of coterie poetry, Elizabeth's poem represents a topic of such public importance as the Queen of Scots affair as a secret more fitting to the private place of a lady's chamber.

By framing the queen's relationship with Mary as a private and not a public matter, the manuscript circulation of "The Doubt of Future Foes" supports Elizabeth's broader strategy for dealing with the Queen of Scots. The political dilemma that Mary posed was riven with paradox: once she entered England, Mary Stuart could be neither allowed to travel freely nor imprisoned outright, since both would directly threaten Elizabeth's security. Even after Mary was suspected of having plotted to overthrow her, Elizabeth was reluctant to punish her openly, since this could prompt retaliation from forces sympathetic to Mary both in England and in Catholic Europe. Instead of public suppression and punishment, the Queen of Scots required more covert management. In his study of Elizabethan secret services, Alan Haynes argues that it was largely the delicacy of the Queen of Scots affair that gave rise to a powerful domestic espionage network during Elizabeth's reign.[42] Given Mary's own increasingly daring circulation of

---

Market of Symbolic Goods," reprinted in *The Field of Cultural Production: Essays on Art and Literature*, ed. Randal Johnson (London: Polity Press, 1993).

[42] Alan Haynes, *Invisible Power: The Elizabethan Secret Services, 1570–1603* (Wolfeboro Falls, NH: Alan Sutton Publishing Inc., 1992). See also Alison Plowdon, *The Elizabethan Secret Service* (New York: St. Martin's, 1991), and John M. Archer, *Sovereignty and Intelligence: Spying and Court Culture in the English Renaissance* (Stanford: Stanford University Press, 1993).

letters in code to her allies, this network concentrated significant energies on the interception and interpretation of textual secrets.

Elizabeth's relationship with the Queen of Scots was played out in the circulation of texts. The two queens never met in the flesh and only communicated directly through the letters, poems, and tokens that circulated between them, which were coded by both the participants and outside observers as the private exchanges of affectionate women. Elizabeth herself encouraged this coding, and in so doing, she framed her relationship with the Queen of Scots within the female coterie conventions similar to those that Harinton represents. In a speech delivered to Parliament in 1586, after long equivocation, Elizabeth finally publicly admitted Mary's guilt and the necessity of her execution. In the speech, Elizabeth frames Mary's betrayal as a story of women's secret writing and its exposure:

> As it is not unknowne to some of my Lordes here (for now I will play the blabbe)[,] I secretlie wrote her a le[ter] upon the discou-[er]ye of her treasons, that if she would repent her throughlie of her evell course, confesse it and priuatlie acknoledge it by her l[et]res unto me, she neve[r] should be called for it into publique question, nether did I it of any minde to circumvente her, for then I knew as much as she could confesse, and so did I write.[43]

Once again the queen's relationship with Mary Queen of Scots is staged as a drama of female writing, distinguished by the "secrecy" and "privacy" of its texts, which are sharply distinguished from the "public question" before parliament as well as the inevitable, public scenes of trial and execution to come. The boundary between these realms is marked by the shame of exposure. Significantly, the queen locates her own representation of the scene of private female writing by "blabbing" it — to "blabb" is to make public what should be kept private. "Now I will play the blabb," Elizabeth announces to Parliament, and in so doing marks both herself and her speech as an unauthorized intrusion into this very public realm.

"Blabb," we might note, is an early modern term characterizing women's public speech as a sexually unbecoming activity, one that was used pointedly by other early modern women writers to describe their own writ-

---

[43] "A speech made by her ma[jes]tie tochinge the treasons of the Quene of Scotte," Inner Temple Library, Petyt MS 538 vol. 10, folio 6ᵛ.

ing and the shame it would incur through publication. As Lady Mary Wroth asks in *Urania*, "shall I turne blabb?"[44] Crafting herself as a "blabb" in her speech, the queen similarly draws attention to her own feminine modesty, her self-consciousness at the seeming impropriety of her public display. But while it affects a sincere fear of exposure, Elizabeth's use of the term "blabb" to describe her disclosure is another way in which Elizabeth "frames" herself and the topic of that speech. Her reference to the supposed impropriety of her public speech marks her communication with Mary as a moment of "private" confidence, but its effect is less to hide the scene of women's writing than to produce hiddenness as a public effect, thereby bracketing that scene within the supremely public medium of the speech to parliament.[45]

Elizabeth's description of this scene of female writing echoes Puttenham's and Harington's presentation of "The Doubt of Future Foes" — both in the particulars of its composition and circulation and in the vocabularies of concealment and disclosure that it wields. In writing "The Doubt of Future Foes," as Puttenham observes, the queen displays *that* she knows while masking *what* she knows: "to declare that she was nothing ignorant of those secret practices, though she had long with great wisdome and pacience dissembled it." In her own description of writing to Mary, Elizabeth similarly manipulates the appearances of knowledge and disclosure: as she puts it, "for then I knewe as much as she could confesse, and so did I write." By claiming to know in advance any secrets Mary might be hiding, Elizabeth attempts to produce an effect similar to that of Puttenham's emblem, which induces the reader "to examine his iudgement or occupie his braine or to manage his will either by hope or by dread." Wielding the appearance of knowledge while witholding its substance, Elizabeth hopes to entice Mary into making a full disclosure.

---

[44] On this example see Jeff Masten, " 'Shall I Turne Blabb?': Circulation, Gender, and Subjectivity in Mary Wroth's Sonnets," in *Reading Mary Wroth: Representing Alternatives in Early Modern England*, ed. Naomi J. Miller and Gary Waller (Knoxville: University of Tennessee Press, 1991).

[45] Allison Heisch notes that Elizabeth also carefully edited this speech for publication and in so doing "retained the section in which she plays 'the blabb,' plainly affecting not to know that her confidential interjection would find its way to a broad international audience." See "Queen Elizabeth I: Parliamentary Rhetoric and the Exercise of Power," *Signs* 1 (1975): 50.

IV

If only Mary had written to her, Elizabeth insists, her life would have been spared. During the nineteen years of her imprisonment, Mary in fact wrote Elizabeth frequently — sometimes in verse — expressing her desire to see her cousin, insisting upon her innocence, and protesting the conditions of her confinement. But in so doing, she not only refused Elizabeth the confession that was demanded, she also showed herself to be as skillful in the art of poetry and the poetics of queenship as her cousin, while engaging her in a textual struggle of the highest stakes. In Elizabeth's speech to Parliament, whose terms are echoed in Harington's description of the covert circulation of "The Doubt of Future Foes," the queen appeals to a model of women's writing as a private textual space, autonomous of political concerns. But the letters and poetry that circulated between Elizabeth and Mary demonstrate the ways in which both queens adapted poetic topoi to construct a language of female rulership.

On 1 September 1568, having fled Scotland and newly crossed England's border, Mary wrote to Elizabeth thus:

> I will beseach you to look upon and treat me as your relative and good friend. . . . entreating you not to let me be lost for want of a safe port; for like a vessel driven by all the winds, so am I, not knowing where to find a haven, unless, taking into your kind consideration my long voyage, you bring me into a safe harbour. . . . Receive me, then. . . . Do not ruin me, I beseech you, for it is my wish to devote my life and heart to you forever.[46]

The image of Mary as a lost vessel seems to have appealed to Elizabeth, for in a letter of 25 May 1569, she recycled it as a warning to the Queen of Scots about the dangers of her supposed alliance with the Duke of Anjou. Elizabeth writes, "The bark of your good fortune floats on a dangerous sea, where many contrary winds blow, and has need of all aid to obviate such evils, and conduct you safely into port."[47] As she will continue to do throughout their communication, Elizabeth displays an uncanny ability to pick up Mary's confessions of her own vulnerability and to repeat these back to her as threats.

---

[46] *The Letters of Mary, Queen of Scots*, ed. Agnes Strickland, 2 vols. (London, 1848), 1: 104–5.

[47] *Letters of Mary, Queen of Scots*, 1: 177.

"The Doubt of Future Foes" appears to respond in a similar vein to a poem that Mary sent Elizabeth in 1568, in testimony to her "affection," which concludes by repeating a by-now familiar image:

> Iay ueu la nef relascher par contraincte
> En haulte mer, proche d'entrer au port,
> Et le serain se conuertir en trouble
> Ainsi ie suis en soucy et en craincte
> Non pas de vous, mais quantes fois a tort
> Fortune rompt voille et cordage double?
>
> [I have seen a ship freed from constraint
> On the high sea, near to entering a port,
> And serene sky turned to storms:
> Likewise, I am troubled and in fear,
> Not because of you, but because Fortune
> Often wrongly rips sails and rigging.][48]

Echoing her letter, once again Mary compares her relation to Elizabeth to that of a ship unable to find a safe port. Mary's letter and poem, both of which stress her insecurity and desire, her "affection" as well as her "soucy" and "craincte," find in the ship a symbol of disappointed aspiration, as in the poem's opening stanza which claims: "Amer et doulx, change en mon coeur sans cesse, / Entre le doubte et l'espoir il m'oppresse" [Bitter and sweet, torments my heart without cease; / Between fear and hope it oppresses me].[49]

Mary finds in the Petrarchan ship a means of figuring her own fear and helplessness as effects of desire. This image is conspicuously taken from Petrarch's Canzone 132, "S'amor non è, che dunque è quel ch'io sento?" [If it is not love, what then is it that I feel?] and Canzone 189, "Passa la nava mia colma d'oblivio" [My ship laden with forgetfulness], which were similarly adapted by Chaucer, Wyatt, and Spenser.[50] But if these male poets

---

[48] My spelling and punctuation follow the manuscript of Mary's poem in British Library Cotton MS Calig. B.V., folio 316. The English translation is by Constance Jordan. See *The Paradise of Women: Writings by Englishwomen of the Renaissance*, ed. Betty S. Travitsky (New York: Columbia University Press, 1989), which also reprints a slightly modified French text of the poem, 198 and 262.

[49] Translation by Constance Jordan.

[50] Petrarch's lyrics are published in Italian and English in *Petrarch's Lyrics Poems*, trans. and ed. Robert Durling (Cambridge, MA: Harvard University Press, 1975), 270–71, 334–35. On the English influence of Petrarch's ship poems, see Thomas C. Stillinger,

take the Petrarchan ship as a figure for the male speaker's lovesickness, Mary makes lovesickness the explanation for her escape from Scotland: "l'affection de uous ueoir qui me presse."[51] Similarly, in her letters to Elizabeth, Mary repeats the argument that her flight to England has been motivated by her "affection:" "It is my wish to devote my life and heart to you forever," she testifies in her letter of 1 September 1568; and later, "I came to throw myself into your arms."[52]

Elizabeth repeats Mary's nautical language of desire and self-endangerment when she observes, "the bark of your good fortune floats on a dangerous sea;" her response, however, echoes Petrarch less than it does Horace's Ode 1.14, to the Ship of State:

> O navis, referent in mare to novi
> fluctus. O quid agis! fortiter occupa
> portum.

[O ship, new billows threaten to bear thee out to sea again. Beware! Haste valiantly to reach the haven!][53]

If Elizabeth accepts Mary's characterization of her as a safe harbor, she extends the imagery to comment on Mary's precarious political situation,

---

The Song of Troilus: Lyric Authority in the Medieval Book (Philadelphia: University of Pennsylvania Press, 1992).

[51] Another early modern woman poet in French, Catherine des Roches, makes use of the Petrarchan image in her "Son[n]ets de Sincero a Charite" (1578, 1579) to describe a man's lovesickness:

> Ma nef au gre des vens dedans l'onde pousee,
> Erroit de toutes parts quand vostre heureuse main,
> Piteuse de mon mal me retira soudain,
> En me sauvant des flotz de la mer courroucee.

[My ship, tossed at random among the waves, / Veered every way until your blessed hand / Pitying my suffering, suddenly released me, / Saving me from the waters of the wrathful sea.]

This text is cited and discussed by Ann Rosalind Jones in *The Currency of Eros: Women's Love Lyric in Europe, 1540–1620* (Bloomington: Indiana University Press, 1990), 66–67.

[52] *Letters of Mary Queen of Scots,* 1: 118; using similar topoi of love and courtship, Mary sends Elizabeth a heart-shaped jewel with a sonnet, and later complains to her: "I sent you my [heart] in a ring, and I have brought you the original, in order to tie the knot more firmly" (77).

[53] Horace, *Odes and Epodes,* trans. C. E. Bennett (Cambridge: Harvard University Press, 1988), 42–43; For a valuable discussion considering the relations between Petrarch and Horace in these poems, see Stillinger, *The Song of Troilus,* 196.

reinterpreting Mary's self-professed lovesickness as a sign of political instability and danger. Elizabeth further develops this politicized reading of the ship in "The Doubt of Future Foes," which offers what appears to be a direct rebuke to Mary's verses and the request for sanctuary that they advance. Elizabeth writes: "No forreigne bannisht vvight shall ancre in this port, / Our realme it brookes no strangers force, let them elsvvhere resort." Steeling her port against foreign ships and "strangers force," Elizabeth appears to assert the inviolability of her body politic against Mary's invasion.[54] The interpretive struggle that Mary and Elizabeth enact over the figure of the ship bears witness to each queen's attempt to gain the rhetorical upper hand through figurative poetry. Mary appropriates a Petrarchan language of lovesickness in order to explain her flight to England as motivated by her "affection" for her cousin. Elizabeth, on the other hand, picks up the image of the ship in order to cast Mary as a political liability and a potentially invading force.

Like the Ship of State, the allegory of the garden in "The Doubt of Future Foes" offers another popular figure of rulership. The queen's poem figures the state as a *hortus conclusus* in which the ruler attempts to cultivate peace by controlling disruptive forces of nature and rival gardens. Thus while "the daughter of debate" attempts to "sowe" discord, the legitimate ruler encourages "peace to growe." The ruler/ gardener's final act is to threaten to cut back the heads of unruly plants: "Our rusty svvorde vvith rest, shall first his edge employ / To polle their toppes that seeke, such change and gape for ioy." This allegory of gardening and rulership, as Frances Teague points out, is similarly adapted in Shakespeare's *Richard II*: "The natural metaphors, which compare treason to bad weather and traitors to barren plants, remind one of the garden scene in *Richard II*, particularly the Gardener's lines, 'Go thou and, like an executioner, / Cut off the heads of too-fast-growing sprays' (III.iv.34–35); the poem and the play have the same topos."[55] Like that more famous scene, Elizabeth's staging of the garden evokes an anecdote that would have been familiar to educated Renaissance readers. In Livy's *History*, Sextus, the son of the tyrant Tarquin the Proud, infiltrates the rival forces of the Gabians and sends a messenger to his father for further instruction:

---

[54] For a reading of Mary's position in "The Doubt of Future Foes" and contemporary literary works, see James Emerson Phillips, *Images of a Queen: Mary Stuart in Sixteenth-Century Literature* (Berkeley: University of California Press, 1964), esp. 81.

[55] Frances Teague, "Elizabeth I," in *Women Writers of the Renaissance and Reformation*, ed. Katharina M. Wilson (Athens: University of Georgia Press, 1987), 529.

To the messenger, presumably because his fidelity was not trusted, no verbal reply was given. The king, as though in deep thought, passed into the palace garden, followed by his son's messenger. The story goes that as he walked there, he silently cut off the heads of the highest poppies with his staff. The messenger, wearied of repeating his question and awaiting a reply, returned to Gabii thinking that his mission was a failure. He reported what he had himself said and what he had seen, remarking that whether through anger or hatred or an inborn arrogance the king had not uttered a single word. When Sextus realized what his father meant and what instructions he gave through his unspoken riddle, he destroyed the leading men of the city.[56]

Like Tarquin's gesture of "silently cut[ting] off the heads of the highest poppies," Elizabeth's "Doubt of Future Foes" offers a deadly message in a coded language. In so doing, the poem draws on an image that also directly engages the issue of communication itself and the circuits of privileged knowledge that it creates. "To this messenger, presumably because his fidelity was not trusted, no verbal reply was given," Livy recounts. In the anecdote's other manifestations — chiefly as told by Herodotus, Ovid, and Aristotle — the element that seizes chief significance is this scene of subverbal communication, which distinguishes between the father and son, whom the message's transmission includes, and the uncomprehending messenger, whom it excludes.[57] Elizabeth's manipulation of the gardening image similarly creates circles of insiders and outsiders by appealing to her reader to supply her missing meaning. To the knowing reader, the poem recounts not simply a scene of gardening but a grisly threat.

If Mary was the most knowing and hence the ideal recipient of "The Doubt of Future Foes," she was also capable of radically revising its meanings herself. The figure of the garden was a recurring motif in Mary's embroidery, to which she devoted herself in her captivity and with gifts of which, as J. E. Neale suggestively puts it, "she set siege to Elizabeth's heart."[58] Embroidery, a valued skill for Renaissance women, was one of Mary's few permitted forms of recreation, and she had time to produce a

---

[56] Livy, *History* (1.54), cited in H. J. Leon, "Classical Sources for the Garden Scene in *Richard II*," *Philological Quarterly* 29 (1950): 65.

[57] See Leon, "Classical Sources for the Garden Scene," 67–68.

[58] Neale, *Queen Elizabeth I*, 258; see Margaret Swain, *The Needlework of Mary, Queen of Scots* (New York: Van Nostrand Reinhold Co., 1973).

large quantity of it. But despite its association with female leisure, Mary's work demonstrates that embroidery could also be enlisted for more public purposes. According to William Camden, it was the discovery of some of Mary's embroidered "emblems" in particular that secured her conviction:

> Suspitions were layd hold on, as if there were a plot already layd to set her at liberty: and that, by occasion of certain *Emblems*[:] ... a scien graften into a stock, and bound about by bands, yet budding forth fresh, and written about, *Per vincula cresco*, that is to say, *Through bands I grow*. A palme tree pressed down, but rising up againe, with this sentence, *Ponderibus virtus innata resistit*, that is, *'Gainst weights doth inbred vertue strive.*[59]

The mottos themselves convey conventional expressions of piety and fortitude, familiar from contemporary emblem books. But in Camden's account they also signal rebellion on the highest order.

These emblems directly recall the figurative language of Elizabeth's "Doubt of Future Foes," which presents similar images: "The toppe of hope supposed, the roote of ruth vvil be, / And frutelesse all their graffed guiles, as shortly ye shall see." For Elizabeth, the political struggle for the crown is like planting upside down, placing the "toppe" where the "root" should be (to draw on the literal meaning of "the toppe of hope *supposed*," as *sub-ponere*, to place below). While the foes attempt to "sowe discorde," the speaker is self-assured that these efforts will be "fruteless" because they are "grafted" and unnatural. But Mary's emblems appear to interpret and answer these images in "The Doubt of Future Foes." Where Elizabeth imagines her enemies' plots to be "frutelesse" because "grafted," Mary's emblem of the "scien graften into a stock" envisions such grafting to be a source of fruition ("bound about by bands, yet budding forth fresh"). The battle over the tops of trees "supposed" (*sub-ponere*) is also refigured in Mary's emblem of the palm tree pressed down by weights ("*ponderibus*"), but springing back to its full height. As Camden notes, these emblems resonate with subversive potential; they suggest that the same mechanisms through which Mary is oppressed will be the very sources of her strength, like the bonds that enable the grafted plant to bud forth. Where Elizabeth figures her strength in punishment, Mary figures hers in being punished.

---

[59] William Camden, *Annales, or the History of the Most Renowned and Victorious Princesse Elizabeth, Late Queen of England*, 3rd ed. (London, 1635), 269.

Such is the message of an emblem of Mary's making that does survive. Between 1569 and 1571 in the early years of her captivity, Mary completed a work that has come to be known as the "Oxburgh Hanging." It was therefore made around the same time as the earliest manuscript of "The Doubt of Future Foes." The centerpiece of the hanging is a panel depicting a scene of gardening. In it, two trees are in fruit and along the base of their trunks winds a vine, half in fruit and half withered. Between them a hand with a blade extends from the sky, and above, a scroll displays the latin motto, *"Virescit Vulnere Virtus,"* "Virtue Flourishes through Wounding" (figure 2).[60]

Mary sent a copy of this emblem to Thomas, Duke of Norfolk, which was produced as evidence of treason at the trial that resulted in Norfolk's execution in 1571.[61] While Norfolk's examiners wondered whether the pruning knife was meant as a threat to wound Elizabeth, the emblem seems rather to embrace that wounding from the point of view of the threatened.[62] As such, it would appear to reverse the topoi wielded in "The Doubt of Future Foes:" "Our rusty sworde with rest, shall first his edge employ / To polle their toppes that seeke, such change and gape for joy." If Elizabeth proposes to "polle" the "toppes" of her enemies, Mary's

---

[60] The tapestry, on display at Oxburgh Hall in Norfolk and now owned by the Victoria and Albert Museum in London, is pictured and described by Francis de Zuleta in *Embroideries by Mary Stuart and Elizabeth Talbot at Oxburgh Hall, Norfolk* (Oxford: Oxford University Press, 1923), 8, and by Rozsika Parker in *The Subversive Stitch: Embroidery and the Making of the Feminine* (New York: Routledge, 1989), 11; on the Petrarchan resonance of the motto "virescit vulnere virtus," see Thomas Greene, *The Light in Troy: Imitation and Discovery in Renaissance Poetry* (New Haven: Yale University Press, 1982), 103.

[61] *The Tryal of Thomas Duke of Norfolk By His Peers* (London: 1709), 68; on the embroidery's significance in Norfolk's trial see also Neville Williams, *A Tudor Tragedy: Thomas Howard Fourth Duke of Norfolk* (London: Barrie Books Ltd., 1964), 236.

[62] Contemporary uses of the emblem favor this interpretation; Geoffrey Whitney's *A Choice of Emblemes*, for example, assigns the motto "Virecit Vulnere Virtus" to the image of a man trampling a plant, which is glossed thus:

> The Dockes (thoughe troden) growe, as it is dailie seene:
> So vertue, thought it longe bee hid, with woundinge waxeth greene.

Geoffrey Whitney, *A Choice of Emblemes* (1586), facs. ed. Henry Green (1866; repr. New York: G. Olms, 1971), 98; a similar emblem adorns the title page of Elizabeth Cary's *Tragedie of Mariam, the Faire Queene* of Jewry (London: Thomas Crede for Richard Hawkins, 1613), which features an image of a naked woman being scourged from above, accompanied by the motto, "Verita Verescit Vulnerae." While this appears to be the mark of the printer, Thomas Creede (whose initials are inscribed between the woman's feet), it also illustrates the gendered thematics of the drama.

Figure 2: The "Oxburgh Hanging," by Mary Queen of Scots.
Reproduced by permission of the Victoria and Albert Museum.

emblem suggests that such a wounding cut will only encourage more growth; as the gardener's wounding cut encourages plants to flourish, so does virtue flourish with wounding. If Mary is to fall victim to Elizabeth's blade, that blade will become the source of her fruition. Like the emblems in Camden's description, the "Oxburgh Hanging" produces a conspicuously covert code that demands to be deciphered. And the meanings that it encodes are threatening enough: it hints at the retributive forces that might gather to revenge Mary's "wounding," for example, which is not so empty a threat if we recall that the Spanish Armada was motivated by Mary's execution. But Mary's counter-threat is delivered in the medium as well as the message. The Queen of Scot's manipulation of figures through her embroidered emblems — the figure, after all, that Puttenham declared most suited to royal use — constitutes an effort to redefine her relation to Elizabeth with the very forms through which Elizabeth proclaimed her power.

To read both the "Oxburgh hanging" and "The Doubt of Future Foes" in light of Mary's trial and execution in 1587 is to be struck by the likelihood that both queens used poetic figures to write their own scripts in this historical drama. The suggestion that in 1570 Elizabeth already envisioned beheading Mary, the "daughter of debate," and declared as much in a poem is only slightly less shocking than the suggestion that around the same time Mary anticipated such a fate, and even dared it to come about — and did so, moreover, in an embroidery. But it is specifically the forms in which these threats and counter-threats were waged — through poetry and embroidery — that interest me here. Through her use of poetry Elizabeth attempts to reveal her mastery of the art of beautiful and false appearances. But instead of offering Elizabeth a confession and disclosing her secret guilt, Mary offers more figures. Mary's response to Elizabeth's poetics of queenship was to assert herself as a superior practitioner of both. The covert, figurative language of poetry thereby becomes a medium for producing female power on the highest level.

V

One modern reading of the position of the early modern women writers has followed Virginia Woolf's observation that they must have been "solitary great ladies who wrote without audience or criticism, for their own delight."[63] But Elizabeth I presents a striking example of how the early

---

[63] For a critical assessment of Woolf's influence on the field, see Margaret J. M.

modern woman writer's culturally enjoined privacy and enclosure could be cultivated and deployed to ends not normally associated with the "chaste, silent, and obedient" figure of popular conception.[64] Rather, Elizabeth's use of poetry suggests that the covert terms and restricted circulation associated with coterie manuscript poetry offered a means of manipulating the privacy that humanism famously demanded of women in order to produce the public effects on which the queen's authority as a monarch depended. Poems like "The Doubt of Future Foes" thereby offer us a chance to see how supposedly private women's writing could be manipulated to signify supreme cultural privilege, or to issue the deadliest of threats, or finally to uphold the execution of another woman. And, by extension, Mary's own manipulation of poetic topoi shows how proclaiming a position of piety and subjection — even in that most feminine of media, embroidery — could be taken as a threat so deep as to justify that execution. If these are not associations that we might easily make with what Puttenham calls "the arte of a ladies penne," a poem such as "The Doubt of Future Foes" productively challenges our accounts of female authorship and its representation in early modern England, as well as our understanding of the place of the female poet within "the art of English poetry" itself. What it reveals about Elizabeth I is two-pronged: first, that as a queen she framed herself as a poet, and second, that as a poet she framed herself as a woman.

Stanford University

Ezell, *Writing Women's Literary History* (Baltimore: The Johns Hopkins University Press, 1993).

[64] The famous phrase is from Suzanne W. Hull, *Chaste, Silent and Obedient: English Books for Women, 1475–1640* (San Marino, CA: Huntington Library, 1982).

CONSTANCE JORDAN

States of Blindness: Doubt, Justice, and Constancy in Elizabeth I's "Avec l'aveugler si estrange"

AT SOME POINT IN HER LONG REIGN as England's queen, Elizabeth I was moved to record her spiritual condition in two hundred and sixty nine lines of stanzaic French verse. Lacking a title, confused by awkward and unidiomatic diction, and without clear doctrinal references, Elizabeth's poem eludes explicit literary and theological categories. Its interest is primarily in what it conveys of the queen's sense of herself as a monarch and a Christian soul. From its place in the Cecil Papers, "Avecq l'aveugler si estrange" appears to have been written about 1590.[1] If this is in fact the

---

[1] The text of Elizabeth's poem is from *Elizabeth I: Autograph Compositions and Foreign Language Originals*, ed. Leah Marcus, Janel Mueller, and Mary Beth Rose (forthcoming, 2002). I have consulted the editors' translation, which is reprinted below, 255–77, but made adjustments when I thought it appropriate. The line numbers in the original texts are the same as those in the translation. All other quotations from Elizabeth's works are taken from this edition. I have also consulted the text and translation as represented by Steven W. May and Anne Lake Prescott: "The French Verses of Elizabeth I," *English Literary Renaissance* 24.1 (winter 1994): 9–43; their text shows some variants from the text of the Chicago edition. May and Prescott here regard Elizabeth's poem as a translation of a source hitherto unidentified (9, 11); the editors of the Chicago edition regard the poem as an original composition, as does May in an earlier comment on the work; Steven W. May, *The Elizabethan Courtier Poets: The Poems and their Contexts* (Columbia and London: University of Missouri Press, 1991), 318. Absent evidence that the poem is a translation and in light of verbal echoes to the literary context of relations between Elizabeth and Mary Queen of Scots, I have also assumed that it is an original work.

date of its composition, its account of a renewed confidence in a providential dispensation for the queen and the justice of her rule asks for a
reading that complements the events in her reign about that time. There
is considerable evidence that the poem reflects upon the queen's part in
the execution of Mary Queen of Scots.

Elizabeth's poetry has proved elusive in many ways. Some poems attributed to her have proved of uncertain authorship; with a few exceptions,
they appear to have been written quickly, for a particular occasion. Leah
Marcus describes the queen as "an accomplished graffiti artist — tossing
off hasty and topically loaded lines in odd, impromptu places."[2] Her
prayers, written in Greek, Latin, French, Italian, and Spanish, show her to
be a good linguist. It may be that they were intended to combine spiritual
with linguistic exercise; they were also demonstrations of a certain kind of
political power, one that sought to comprehend a wider sphere of influence than the one she possessed at home. "Avecq l'aveugler si estrange"
is, however, more than an exercise, more than a petition for enlightenment, more than a display of rhetorical finesse. It is rather the narrative of
a spiritual crisis and its resolution in the confidence of having done the
right thing. It moves from lamenting the unseeing ignorance that is occasioned by self-division, as the speaker's body and soul fail to cohere in a
union of flesh and spirit, to celebrating the visionary blindness of spiritual
peace. Intermediate reflections focus on justice, a meliorative form of
blindness. The scope of the speaker's reflections is essentially Pauline,
determined by a creative play between her earthly state of seeing through
a glass darkly and the enlightened state she finally attains. Looking beyond
the world's vicissitudes, she sees the supra-phenomenal world, whatever is
true, changeless, and thus redemptive. In short, having shattered the glass
of darkness, her vision is blinded by the light of heaven.

Between its descriptions of states of blindness, Elizabeth's poem takes
the form of a confession. It illustrates the speaker's lapse of faith and her
rejection of divine love with its correlative promise of grace. These depri-
vations threaten to annihilate all sense of herself. She implies that they
trouble her trust in her public persona, her role as queen regnant. As she
recovers her equanimity, she refers to her will,"volunte (sic)," as "absolu"

Other works by Elizabeth quoted or cited in this essay are also from the Chicago edition,
unless otherwise noted.

[2] Leah Marcus, "Queen Elizabeth I as Public and Private Poet: Notes toward a New
Edition," in this volume, 146.

and "ordinaire," terms that transpose ideas of her political power to her personal regimen (ll. 161-62). A danger to the eventual salvation of any Christian, despair was a sin that had further meaning for a monarch. The queen's state of spiritual health was bound up with the political health of her state. Her monarchic body was double, as the common lawyer Edmund Plowden had specified: it was both natural and politic, the body of a woman and the mystical body of the state over which she governed. In her official pronouncements, Elizabeth troped regularly on her identity as woman and "prince," her complex gender testifying to a range of affect to which no male monarch could lay claim.[3]

The burdensome and consequential life of her mystical body politic is registered throughout "Avecq l'aveugler si estrange." While the poem's status as royal speech makes a presumptive case for understanding its political and religious references, its imagery links it to a range of literary work occasioned by Elizabeth's relations with Mary Queen of Scots. This essay will suggest that Elizabeth is here arguing for the propriety of her own rule by drawing on a specific set of verbal cues that she finds in her earlier responses to Mary's presence in England, and that she regards this propriety as the reason she can expect her own salvation.[4]

I

Imperious, quick tempered, a clever wordsmith and a resourceful strategist, Elizabeth I is not known to have been much interested in profound or mystical religious experience. Rather, her prayers depict what might be called her lively faith, particularly as it informed her decisions as head of state. Historians have stressed her investment in religion as an instrument for maintaining the public order.[5] As Bacon famously observed, she

---

[3] As Janel Mueller notes, Elizabeth infused her body politic with the emotions animating her body natural: her life in both bodies "was replete with the mutual love between subjects and sovereign in which, from first to last, she constitutes her life and identity as Queen"; "Virtue and Virtuality: Gender in the Self-Representations of Queen Elizabeth I," in *Form and Reform in Renaissance England: Essays in Honor of Barbara Kiefer Lewalski*, ed. Amy Boesky and Mary Thomas Crane (Newark: University of Delaware Press, forthcoming). I am grateful to Janel Mueller for allowing me to consult this essay.

[4] Cf. May and Prescott, who argue that there is no basis for a political reading of this poem. They state that phrases illustrating an order of government are "clearly metaphors for the state of the well-governed soul; thus the source-text was not necessarily composed by a ruler" ("The French Verses," 12).

[5] See, for example, Patrick Collinson, *The Elizabethan Puritan Movement* (Oxford: Clarendon Press, 1990), 60; A. G. Dickens, *The English Reformation* (New York: Schoc-

sought a peaceful realm not doctrinal conformity:

> Her majesty not liking to make windows into men's hearts and se-
> cret thoughts, except the abundance of them did overflow into
> overt express acts and affirmations, tempered her law so, as it re-
> straineth only manifest disobedience in impugning and impeaching
> advisedly and ambitiously her majesty's supreme power, and main-
> taining and extolling a foreign jurisdiction.[6]

She herself was unwilling to renounce an interest in doctrine, however;
early in her reign she observed: "Indeed, I studied nothing else but divini-
ty till I came to the crown, and then I gave myself to the study of that
which was meet for government"; and later, in the same vein, she insisted: "I am supposed to have many studies, but most philosophical. ...
I hope God's Book hath not been my seldomest lectures" ("Speech 9, version 2, 'Queen Elizabeth's speech to a joint delegation of Lords and Commons, November 5, 1566'"; "Speech 16, 'Queen Elizabeth's speech at the
closing of Parliament, March 29, 1585,'" *Elizabeth I*, 96, 182). Clearly addressing the queen's spiritual condition, "Avecq l'aveugler si estrange" engages doctrine, although in an eclectic and unsystematic way. Its disclo-
sures do, in a sense, open a window into her heart, always admitting that
hers was no ordinary heart but one inhering in a body politic. These dis-
closures reveal how acutely she understood that the errors of a Christian,
even those of a queen regnant, could be resolved by terms that saw in
Christian doctrine the basis for a just rule.

   Elizabeth had not demanded nor would she in all likelihood have been
given the title her father had secured as "Head" of the English Church.
The Supremacy Bill of 1559 designated her its "Governor." Devised by
Parliament, the thirty-nine *Articles whereupon it was agreed by the Archbishoppes and Bishoppes of both provinces and the whole cleargie, in the Convocation holden at London in 1562*, stipulated precisely what the queen's role
should be. The thirty-seventh article told her:

> The Queenes Majestie hath the cheefe power in this Realm of
> England and other her dominions unto whom the cheefe govern-
> ment of all estates of this Realme, whether they be Ecclesiastical or

---

ken Books, 1964; repr. 1965), 294–95; Wallace T. MacCaffrey, *Queen Elizabeth and the
Making of Policy, 1572–1588* (Princeton: Princeton University Press), 27, 29, 31, 53, 76.
   [6] Quoted in William P. Haugaard, *Elizabeth and The English Reformation: The Struggle
for a Stable Settlement of Religion* (Cambridge: Cambridge University Press, 1968), 329–30.

Civile in all causes doth apparteyne and is not nor ought to be subject to any foraigne jurisdiction. We geve not to our princes the
ministering either of Gods word or of Sacramentes. . . . But that
only prerogative which we see to have ben geven always to all
godly Princes in holy Scriptures by God hymselfe, that is, that they
should rule all estates and degrees committed to theyre charge by
God whether they be Ecclesiasticall or Temporall and restrayne
with the civill sworde the stubburn and evylldoers.[7]

John Jewell, writing to establish the order of the Elizabethan church, had
at first insisted that the civil sword could touch the spiritual life of subjects.[8] By the 1570s, however, the queen's authority to rule in ecclesiastical matters having to do with the conduct of the clergy in their churches
and parishes (although not with points of doctrine) was being challenged
by godly clerics who claimed that she had exceeded her mandate in the
Articles. Their objections reveal the extent to which Elizabeth had to consider her limitations, her status as the head of a secular not a religious
order. As early as 1559, John Jewell, writing in a Puritan strain and somewhat against his later position as official defender of the Elizabethan
church, had testified with misgiving to the queen's willfulness in matters
of religion: "That little silver cross, of ill-omened origin, still maintains its
place in the Queen's chapel. Wretched me! This thing will soon be drawn
into a precedent."[9] Nicholas Throckmorton also worried about the power
of this very object: "I assure you . . . all that I can do doth not so much
further the cause as the cross and candlesticks in the Queen's Majesty's
chapel doth hinder it."[10] Her bishops later contended that in pursuing
her governorship, she was reaching beyond the terms proper to it and into
the spiritual sphere. The clerical practice of "prophesying," the explica-

---

[7] *Articles whereupon it was agreed by the Archbishoppes and Bishoppes of both provinces
and the whole cleargie in the Convocation holden at London in 1562* (London, 1571), Civ.
STC 10039.

[8] Cf. "The most ancient and Christian emperors and kings that ever were did busy
themselves with these [godly] matters. . . . Wherefore, if it were lawful for them to do
thus, being but civil magistrates and having the chief rule of commonweals, what offense
have our princes at this day made which may not have leave to do the like, being in the
like degree?" John Jewell, *An Apology of the Church of England*, ed. J. E. Booty (Ithaca,
NY: for The Folger Shakespeare Library by Cornell University Press, 1963), 119–20.

[9] The letter is to Peter Martyr. *The Zurich Letters*, ed. Hastings Robinson, 1st series
(Cambridge, 1842), 55; quoted in Jewell, *An Apology*, ix.

[10] P.R.O., S.P., 70/31, fol. 86r; quoted in Jewell, *An Apology*, x.

tion of points in theology to lay audiences, had worried the queen who saw in it a potential for schism and civil unrest. By 1576, she had taken steps to stop such "exercises," insisting on their "'utter suppression.'" Grindal, the Archbishop of Canterbury, demurred.

Having discovered scriptural precedent for such prophesying, Grindal wrote the queen that he could not obey her command: "I cannot with safe conscience, and without the offence of the majesty of God, give my assent to the suppressing of the said exercises. ... Bear with me, I beseech you, Madam, if I choose rather to offend your earthly majesty than to offend against the heavenly majesty of God." He asked her not "to pronounce so resolutely and peremptorily, *quasi ex auctoritate*," on religious matters: "Remember, Madam, that you are a mortal creature."[11] Although the remainder of the decade proved less contentious, as the bishops the queen came later to appoint were more willing (and had perhaps been instructed) to follow the *via media* that by definition ruled out the exercises the queen had opposed, the progress of puritan thinking and practices continued into the 1580s. In 1585, Elizabeth again had occasion to instruct her bishops to look into "private conventicles." She warned especially of those sponsored by merchants in the City: "expounding Scriptures and catechizing their servants and maids, in so much that I have heard how some of their maids have not sticked to control learned preachers and say that such a man taught otherwise in our house" ("Speech 15, 'Elizabeth's speech to Bishops and other clergy at Somerset Place, February 27, 1585,'" *Elizabeth I*, 179). These and other periods of conflict surrounding her governorship of the Church can hardly have failed to remind the queen of how complex a self she was, doubled and divided not once but twice. Her mortal being consisted of a body and soul; her soul (at least a part of it) had an immortal capacity. In her office as monarch, she was both natural and politic; as natural, she was mortal; as politic, she possessed a timeless aspect.

Throughout its argument, "Avecq l'aveugler si estrange"conveys how vividly the queen imagined herself as, first of all, a "mortal creature," as Grindal had suggested. She possessed an outer and phenomenal man, and

---

[11] Quoted in Collinson, *The Elizabethan Puritan Movement*, 191–95. Elizabeth twice referred to herself as "mortal" in her speeches. See "Speech 5, 'Queen Elizabeth's answer to the Commons' petition that she marry, January 28, 1563,'" *Elizabeth I: Collected Works*, ed. Leah S. Marcus, Janel Mueller, and Mary Beth Rose (Chicago: University of Chicago Press, 2000), 71 (hereafter cited as *Elizabeth I*); and "Speech 13, 'Queen Elizabeth's speech at the close of the parliamentary session, March 15, 1576,'" *Elizabeth I*, 170.

an inner and real (in the sense of eternal) man. Typically, she was the Christian of whom Erasmus said: "A man is than a certain monstruous beast compact togyther of partes ... of a soul, as of a certain goodly thing, and of a body, as it were a brute or dombe beast." Fashioned to come together in "blessed concorde," they had been separated by sin and existed only discordantly: "now they neither can be separate without very great turment and payne, neyther lyve joyned together without continual war." The condition of the Christian was therefore one of a spiritual combat coterminous with life itself, its end by the other "turment," death, to be both feared and desired.[12] But as queen regnant, Elizabeth was also a unique and exalted creature.

Her body natural found a figurative dimension in her body politic, distinct yet not to be divided from her body natural; it was a dimension that constantly both enhanced and compromised the actions of her purely human being. As she noted in her speech to Parliament in 1558: "I am but one body naturally considered, though by His permission a body politic to govern" ("Speech 1, 'Queen Elizabeth's first speech, Hatfield, November 20, 1558,'" *Elizabeth I*, 52). And it is this body politic whose attributes were extraordinary, mystical, and, as it were, immortal: "not subject to passions as the other is, not to Death. ... [At death] there is a separation of the two bodies and ... the body politic is transferred and conveyed over from the body natural now dead or now removed from the dignity royal to another body natural."[13] As a legal fiction, the queen's second body could make no claim to the salvation offered her mortal body, yet its

---

[12] Desiderius Erasmus, *Enchiridion militis christiani, which may be called in englyshe the hansome (sic) weapon of a chrysten knight* (London, 1548), Eiiiv. STC 10485.

[13] Edmund Plowden, "Willion v. Berkley," *The commentaries or reports* (London, 1761), 234. On the question of the gender of the queen's second body, see Constance Jordan, "Woman's Rule in Sixteenth-Century Political Thought," *Renaissance Quarterly* 40, 3 (1987): 421–51. This legal fiction made the operation of royal authority in the political sphere entirely consistent; it denied that royal authority in the political sphere could be qualified by a monarch's bodily or material defects. It did not rule out other and complementary understandings of the monarch that, in the case of Elizabeth, might picture her as the mother of her people, Astraea the goddess of Justice, and so forth. Elizabeth maintained the distinction between her masculine and feminine self when in her speeches she regularly referred to herself as a "prince," and occasionally as a "mother," "woman," or "queen." See Carole Levin, *The Heart and Stomach of a King: Elizabeth I and the Politics of Sex and Power* (Philadelphia: University of Pennsylvania Press, 1994), especially 121–48, who explores questions of Elizabeth's gender as both male and female, king and queen; see also Susan Frye, *Elizabeth I: The Competition for Representation* (New York and Oxford: Oxford University Press, 1993).

numinous power precisely evoked an already realized state of perfection: "this body . . . cannot be seen or handled, consisting of policy and government, and constituted for the direction of the people . . . [It] is utterly void of infancy, and old age, and other natural defects and imbecilities which the body natural is subject to" (Plowden, "Dutchy of Lancaster," *Commentaries*, 213). The looming presence of her body politic shadows Elizabeth's confession in interesting ways. Never precisely identified — the queen appears to speak only as a "mortal creature" — her "politic" voice is heard as an echo of the scriptural *dicta* shaping the role and character of the monarchy from the Psalms of David to Paul's Epistle to the Romans. Here the conflict she enters outstrips the terms of an ordinary salvation and engages others that reveal the outlines of her rule as monarch.

Elizabeth depicts the process by which she comes to understand her salvation in four stages. At first, she is a creature divided by sin and beset by darkness; next, she perceives the possibility of the dawn in a moment of what she calls the first degree of grace, "le primier degre de La grace" (ll. 51–52); then, she turns to the light aided by a "Second Secours" (l. 91); and finally, by a reflection upon her past and a recollection of its meaning, she is sealed by the last of graces, "La derniere de grace . . . y mettant tost son Cachet," in the confidence of salvation, "Salut" (ll. 250–54).[14] This final state is also one of a blinding or darkness, though now of a beneficent kind; in it, having harmonized the emotions within herself, "Metta ces temperementz avec si eguaL accord" (ll. 266–67), she is free from "l'inconstance" (l. 269). In its fullest realization, however, salvation remains outside time. Elizabeth ends her poem with a statement that readers have termed philosophical rather than religious;[15] her "Salut" is prefigured by a state in which she has simply transcended "l'inconstance."

The Erasmian duality I alluded to earlier haunts the first stage of this process. The speaker is two beings in one, "deux hommes en Un" (l. 13), and consequently suffers from a complete self-alienation:"en moy se vist/ rien qui fust en moy/Si Loing Je fus de moy" (ll. 8–10). The pathos of her condition is increased by her frustration, as her efforts to govern the kingdom of her self, "regner/En mon Royaulme" (ll. 19–20), are hindered by

---

[14] Elizabeth envisages three graces and implies that she subscribes to a doctrine in which each have a function. Christian doctrine generally allows for two kinds of grace; see below, note 22. Elizabeth may be conflating the graces of theology with those of art, though it is unclear what she might have sought to prove by doing so.

[15] May and Prescott note that the comparison of "the harmonized soul to a blind man has Stoic overtones" ("The French Verses," 43n26).

her shame, "honte" (l. 18), at not being able to do so. Erasmus derived his figure from Paul, who had enjoined the faithful "to laye downe ... the olde man, which is accordyng to the lustes of errour ... And to put on the newe man whiche after God is happen in righteousnesse,"[16] but Elizabeth will draw on the typically humanist reworking of these beings, who are reason and flesh, by referring to their relationship as a kind of government. In the words of Erasmus, the kingdom of her self mimics that of the commonwealth or "communaltye": reason is king, the lords are "Certayne gentyl affections," and the commoners are "vyle appetytes" (*Enchiridion*, Eiiiiv). Calvin's version of this relation is comparable: "Imagine," he asks, "that in the understanding minde sitteth reason, which like a lampe giveth light to all counsels, and like a queene governeth the will."[17] Elizabeth's failure to govern herself therefore entails an implied comparison with a more public failure to govern her people. The connection between the condition of the monarch and that of her realm is one she acknowledges in a prayer from 1563: she asks that here subjects "render to me the duty of a just obedience [to God] so that there will be a good and holy union between the head and the members, and that by this means all may know that on Thee alone depends the state of kingdoms and the government of nations."[18] Thus the self-alienation to which Elizabeth confesses in "Avecq l'aveugler si estrange" implies a more pervasive confusion whose ultimate threat is to the welfare of her people. The queen's dismay recalls her acutely conscious sense that she, a queen regnant, was open to public shame: "Princes, you know, stand upon stages so that their actions are viewed and beheld of all men; and I am sure my doings will come to the scanning of many fine wits, not only within the realm, but in foreign countries" ("Speech 17, 'Queen Elizabeth's first reply to the first parliamentary petitions urging the execution of Mary Queen of Scots, November 12, 1586,'" *Elizabeth I*, 189).[19]

---

[16] Ephesians, 4.22, 24; *The holy Byble, conteynyng the olde and newe Testament. Set foorth by aucthoritie, 1575* (London, 1575), STC 2114. I cite this edition of the so-called Bishops' Bible throughout this essay.

[17] John Calvin, *The Institution of the Christian Religion*, trans. Thomas Norton (London, 1578), Book II, Chapter 2, M5v. STC 4418.

[18] "Prayer 13, 'Prayer for the whole Kingdom and Body of the Church according the Their Estates and Members,'" *Elizabeth I*, 147. The original is in French.

[19] The image of her position on a public stage also appears in a description of her coronation: "The city of London [was] at that time a stage wherein was showed the wonderful spectacle of a noble-hearted princess toward her most loving people"; "Speech 2, 'Richard Mulcaster's account of Queen Elizabeth's speech and prayer during her

To the mortal woman, however, help comes from Christ in a moment of grace. Recovering from despair, Elizabeth pictures herself as a child learning to walk who still needs to be "half supported," "soustenait / Au demy" (ll. 34–35). Her knowledge is merely of "Les principles" (l. 48), and is registered as their clarification. Although the sun does not shine, the sky lightens: "Combien que Le Soleil n'aparuct (l. 58) / . . . Le Clair Jour se monstra" (l. 60), and her consciousness, like that dawn, is of a misery not quite past, "Le Songe qui me fascha/ . . . Sembla me tormenter" (ll. 68, 70). At this point, she begins to follow the language of Romans, at times recalling the terms in which Calvin discovered the meaning of that text.[20]

Central to Paul's text are metaphors of darkness, light, and degrees or kinds of light. Explaining Romans 1.20 — "his [God's] invisible thinges . . . through the creation of the worlde are seene" — Calvin states that ordinary vision (or reason) knows God in creation "cleere enough," but that this knowledge "differeth greatly from that knowledge [which] bringeth salvation."[21] The knowledge that brings salvation is the extraordinary light hoped for in the last verses of Romans: "Consyderyng the season . . . how that it is tyme that we should nowe awake out of sleepe. For nowe is our salvation nearer then when we beleeved. The nyght is past and the day is come nigh. Let us therefore cast away the deedes of darknesse, and let us put on the armour of light" (13.11, 12). For Calvin, this "Day" is not spiritual enlightenment but a foreshadowing of eternity. The eschatological turn of Paul's verse is important to Calvin: the "Day" celebrated is not "put for the light of faith . . . but for that brightnesse of the celestiall life whose beginnings are now seene in the gospel. The sonne is as by the spring of the day we gather that the full light of the sun is at hand,

---

passage through London to Westminster . . . January 14, 1559,'" *Elizabeth I*, 53.

[20] The echoes of Calvin's *Institutes* throughout this poem are faint, as far as I can tell; they do, however, suggest that Elizabeth is working within a Protestant tradition that embraced much of the spirit of Geneva though not necessarily its doctrine. Elizabeth translated into English the first chapter of the French text of the *Institutes*, which Calvin himself prepared and published in 1541. She titled it "How we should know God" and prefaced it with a dedicatory letter to Katherine Parr, which is dated 30 December 30 1545. This text is a sequel to the 1544 New Year's gift of the *Miroir* translation, and forms a companion piece to the 1545 New Year's gift to Henry of Elizabeth's trilingual translation of Katherine Parr's *Prayers or Meditations*. The shelfmark for the Calvin translation is Scottish Record Office, MS RH 13/78. I owe this reference to Janel Mueller. I am grateful to Lori Anne Ferrell for assistance in reading Calvin's *Institutes*.

[21] John Calvin, *A Commentarie upon the Epistle of Paul to the Romans*, trans. Christopher Rosdell (London, 1583), 1.20, B5. STC 4399.

even so as soone as God beginneth to call us, we gather that we ought to intend upon the comming of Christe" (*Commentarie*, Y8). Calvin sees the development in Romans as between a rational understanding of God's work and the pressing realization of an imminent redemption — a dawn and, as it were, a presentiment of full day. For the remainder of her poem and after the reception of the dawn, "l'aube" of the first grace, Elizabeth traces the pattern of her own experience of enlightenment in terms recalling those of Paul in Romans. To the extent that she describes her enlightenment as an event in eschatology rather than as a full knowledge of God in this life, she can, perhaps, be seen to have been affected by Calvin's interpretation of that epistle.

Memory is the faculty invoked next, in lines describing Elizabeth's struggle against the evils of the world, "[les] maulx de ce monde" (l. 94). She remembers her baptism; this reflection is consistent with her vision of a metaphoric light, a sun shining in the west as it had done in the east. The vision gives her an advantage. She acquires a second help: "Le Second Secours" (l. 91); that is, she receives what she later identifies as a second grace,[22] and finds that only the habit of sin remains in her, "La [sic] Coustume / me demeura du peche" (ll. 104–5), a habit that is set aside as soon as sin is recognized. Reflection again plays a part: She sees the state of her heart which *was* ruinous but is no more, where reason *was* scornful of it but does not need to be now. Her inner man, "mon homme au dedans" has returned to his center, "son Centre" (l. 118); he is protected by his past life which, now understood, no longer threatens him with the possibility of a misstep, a bad encounter or an encounter with evil, "La Vie passee / L'osta d'un male encountre" (ll. 119–20). Thus she is remade, "refaict," as a creature in whom disparate elements are unified, "tout bien Conjoinct" (l. 122). This action is celebrated by a commitment to spiritual combat. She arms herself for God: "J'enhanssas Le Countrepoint," a sentence that suggests two actions: she takes up a sword, she wields that sword for God (l. 125).[23] The sequence of these actions follows Romans

---

[22] Cf. Calvin: The first grace is "preventing" (i.e., prevenient); it is forthcoming when a "man of his own good motion proceeding naturally from him meriteth the first grace." The second grace follows when a man "being helpen by the first grace doth make himselfe worthye of eternall life"; *Commentarie*, 3.27, F4. Calvin does not, as Elizabeth will, comment on a third and final grace.

[23] Elizabeth had earlier alluded to the arms she needs for spiritual warfare: "May Thy Word, Lord, be . . . a corselet of righteousness for my breast, a helmet of salvation for my head, a sword of the Spirit for my right hand, a shield of faith for my left, and for my

6.6, 13. "Our olde man is crucified with hym also, that the body of sinne might utterly be destroyed," at which point the reader is told: "Neyther geve yey our members as instrumentes of unrighteousnesse unto sinne, but geve yourselves unto God ... and your members as instruments of righteousnesse unto God." These instruments of righteousness, termed "weapons" in the Geneva Bible, complement the "armour of light" that protects the faithful in 13.12.[24] Both instruments imply a continuing struggle with the evil of the world, an evil that were one a monarch one might need to acknowledge some part in creating. Having revived herself with the aid of the second grace, Elizabeth entertains a vision of her government as both good and problematic.

II

In many respects, Paul's Epistle to the Romans can be read as a directive to the "hygher powers" (13.1). Its apparently uncompromising endorsement of civil authority as ordained of God, its condemnation of those who would resist that authority as unholy — "whosoever therfore resysteth the power, resysteth the ordinance of God, and they that resyst, shall receyve to them selves damnation" (13.2) — served to shore up monarchic claims to an absolute power beyond what the prerogative had traditionally allowed, but also to relegate the divine ordination of that power to the office rather than the person of the monarch.[25] In any case, Paul provided

---

whole body the armor of God"; "Prayer 33, 'The Latin Prayer,' " *Elizabeth I*, 318.

[24] See also Ephesians 6.13, 17: "Wherefore take unto you the whole armour of God that ye may be able to resyst in the evyl day. . . . And take the helmet of salvation and the swoorde of the spirite whiche is the woorde of God."

[25] A representative text is John Ponet, *A Shorte Treatise of politike power*, 1556. Important to the definition of the monarch's powers as limited and inhering in the scope of her office are chapters entitled "Whether kinges, princes and other governours have anobsolute (sic) power and authoritie over their subjectes," "Whether kinges, princes and other politike governours be subjecte to Goddes lawes and the positive lawes of theyr countryes," and "In what thinges and how farre subjectes are bounden to obeie their princes and governours." See the facsimile edition in Winthrop S. Hudson, *John Ponet (1516–1556): Advocate of Limited Monarchy* (Chicago: University of Chicago Press, 1942), Biii–Cviv; Civv–Cviv considers Romans 13 specifically. John Colet interpreted these verses in their historical setting, as "a most prudent admonition to all the faithful in Rome," and noted that Paul was warning Christians, as yet a tiny community in Rome, that they could not hope to survive without complete obedience to the dictates of civil authority. John Colet, *An Exposition of St. Paul's Epistle to the Romans*, trans. J. H. Lupton (London, 1873), 91–92.

his readers with instructions on how they were to regard their political duties and allegiance. What is further remarkable is his framing of these instructions. Romans begins with questions to the Jew, the archetypal interpreter of the law, the figure of the judge and magistrate, the very embodiment of earthly command. Paul asks: "[thou] beleevest that thou thee selfe are a guide of the blynde, a lyght of them (which are) in darkenesse . . . a teacher of the unlearned . . . and of the trueth in the lawe. Thou therefore, whiche teachest another, teachest not thee self? (2.19–21). The question presupposed the moral axiom upon which Christian notions of government were based: she who rules others must first rule herself.[26] More important, perhaps: It raised a further question that, given the contentiousness of religious debate in late Tudor England, no monarch could afford to leave unanswered. As Aquinas had stated when commenting on Romans 13 but positing a political freedom to Christians derived from gospel, the subject must obey civil authority only when it is "derived from God" [*a deo descendit*].[27] This was a commonplace whose interpretation was to become increasingly vexed during the Reformation, but it always served, nonetheless, to convey a general warning to the "hygher powers" that they were not in and of themselves to rule absolutely, like gods. It was incumbent on the queen to regulate her official conduct by divine law and Christian norms; were she ignorant or dismissive of them, she could face legitimate threats to her rule.

The second phase of her reformation by the second grace shows Elizabeth, as if responding to Pauline dicta, as queen of herself and by inference of her people: "Je Vi mon regne bien gouverne/Par raison et non par degre / Je Vis trois Ames ressamblans / . . . L'une pour Commander / Et Les deux pour servir" (ll. 134–36; 139–40). The souls of this kingdom are

---

[26] Elizabeth had recourse to this figure, but with a different emphasis, when she called on the governor's political capacity to guarantee her spiritual health: "[I]nstructed with the help of Thy wisdom, may I . . . so rule others with the scepter that I may rule myself by Thy Word, managing the commonwealth so that the soul may rule the flesh, reason the soul, faith the reason, and Thy grace faith"; "Prayer 33, 'The Latin Prayer,'" *Elizabeth I*, 318.

[27] St. Thomas Aquinas, *Commentum in quatuor libros sententiarum magistri Petri Lombardi* in Thomas Aquinas, *Selected Political Writings*, ed. A. P. D'Entrèves, trans. J. G. Dawson (New York: Barnes and Noble, 1959), Book II, Distinction 44, Question 4, 183. With respect to the civil authority to collect tribute money, Aquinas states: "The children [of Christ] are free" [*ergo liberi sunt filii*], (that is, they can pay or not, according to their conscience), and cites Matthew 17.24–26. *Commentum*, Book II, Distinction 44, Question 2, 181.

reason, will, and the instincts or "Lourds Sentiments" (l. 146), a division
that recalls Erasmus's analysis of the soul as a tripartite government: the
monarchy, encompassing reason and the will by which it is made effective,
and the lords and commons as high and low feelings, respectively. Elizabeth sees the highest sphere of her self-government as a burning truth,
"Verite," and the whole as "nearly perfect": "Vi tout Le Gouvernement
/ Si Tout pres d'estre parfaict / Que me rendes Content" (ll. 158-60). Her
vision reveals the will (reformed by reason) giving orders both absolute and
ordinary: "Je vis La Volunte donner charge / Absolu et Ordinaire" (ll.
161-62); accordingly, her retinue (those actions and things her will controls) becomes "extraordinair" (l. 164). She imagines this ensemble, the
will and its retinue, as proceeding decorously toward a perfection that she
has already termed "tout pres d'estre parfaict": "Elle alla tout bellement"
(l. 165). The will she refers to is both spurred and bridled, moved by love
and controlled by reason: "Je Vis La part qui est l'esperon / Du Salut et La
bride" (ll. 166-67). This spur, "esperon," punningly conveys the hope,
l'esperance, of salvation, and is thus also a sign that the perfection perceived is desired but not yet attained. The action of the bridle is comparable to that of temperance, the virtue that allows one to function appropriately in time and thus the virtue made most explicit in history. Elizabeth
sees her longing for salvation as controlled by "Amour": love is the force
of the wind behind a sail that is given direction by the ship's helmsman.
An image of both divine and royal control, her ship of state makes way
through a temporal sea to an expected safety.[28]

Memory is again important. In a series of stanzas, Elizabeth encounters
"La Large histoire / De mon estre qui fust si Vain" (ll. 173-74). It is a history essential to her reformation and salvation. She dwells on it as if it
were not (and perhaps could not be) at that moment *sufficiently* condemnatory, as she experiences the burden, "Soing," of not having to bear
enough, "de n'en avoir de Soing asses" (ll. 194-95). Because her burden
is also her deliverance, she can only long for it to become more imposing.
This paradox introduces a sequence of others, generally focussed on the
mystery of the divine law's fulfillment in Christ's sacrifice. He becomes
her so that she may become him: "Je Vi comme il se fist moy / A se que

---

[28] Cf. "Beholde, we put byttes in the horses mouthes, that they may obey us, and we
turne about their whole body. Beholde also the shippes, whiche though they be so great,
and are dryven of fierce wyndes, yet are they turned about with a very smal helme,
whither so ever the lust of the governor wyl." The Epistle of James, 3. 3–4. As a monarch, Elizabeth was the governor of the ship of state.

Je me fis Luy" (ll. 209-10). Yet that event, although itself the promise of salvation, is also the consequence of an action of hers. To achieve that holy union, which follows her embrace of God, she must reject what is bestial and choose what is divine: "que se fust en mes mains / Prendre Le divinaL" (sic; ll. 219-20). Following this reflection, she considers the operation of divine justice throughout creation and particularly as directed to herself, a move that allows her to refer to her own civil justice.

Divine justice is at its most awesome in its creation of hell, "Le feu Evernel" (l. 227; i.e., Eternel), she states; but it is as much a warning as it is a punishment. In this sense, hell is providential. Elizabeth sees that its purpose is to exhort her, "pour m'exhorter," to keep her from itself: "Pour me garder de l'enfer" (ll. 229-29). In a sense, therefore, divine justice compromises the free will of choice, and its warnings serve as a precondition of choice. Calvin had observed that God's "providence ... in outwarde thinges doth bow and tourne the willes of men ... [T]heir choise is not so free, but that God's will beareth rule over the freedome thereof" (*The Institution*, II, 4, P5v). Like providence, divine justice is a form of circumscription; it limits the factors involved in choice and so instructs the chooser in the necessity of submission to its laws. The idea that the justice of punishment functions as a prophylaxis promoting salvation finds further scope in what is perhaps the most interesting stanza of "Avecq l'aveugler si estrange." It also reveals why Elizabeth saw that her Justice had to function apart from considerations of mercy:

> Je vi que quant ~~ma~~ la Justice
> > Alla forze et de discord
> Que a forse de ma malice
> > Cherchant misericorde
> Je la fais demander Justice.
> > Voyant cecy J'apperceu tel dessaing
> En moy de penitence
> > Que ~~pour alegerer telle paine~~ un moment de ceste paine
> Aligeroit L'eternal tourment. (ll. 231-39)

Elizabeth saw that when Justice, exiled from her kingdom by discord, was asked to grant mercy to malice, or the evil engendered by sin (her own or that of another), she (herself the principal exponent of Justice in her kingdom) insisted on Justice. In other words, she tells herself that she recalled Justice from exile and reinstituted it in her government — both her self-government and that of her people. The reason for her rigor is implied in the relation of Justice to Mercy: Justice is the *only* agency that can induce penitence, the requisite for salvation. Without a prior sentence from Justice, Mercy is irrelevant. A moment of the pain inflicted by the condemnation of Justice is an alleviation of eternal torment.

This reading, which adds a specific and historical reference to a stanza that has an obviously abstract and theological context, is further supported by a line in the stanza that Elizabeth wrote and then changed. Having first written "ma," she strikes it out and writes "la" (1. 231). Her emendation suggests that she regards Justice as the Lord's, but also, practically speaking, as the monarch's. Elizabeth's association of a divine with a civil justice here was not accidental.

She had regularly prayed for divine assistance in her administration of justice. But in the grand scheme of things, she saw mercy or pardon as coming from God. In a prayer published in a collection dated 1563, she asks:

> [T]rain me that I may be able to distinguish between good and evil, equity and iniquity, so as rightly to judge Thy people, justly to impose deserved punishments on those who do harm, mercifully to protect the innocent, freely to encourage those who are industrious, useful to the commonwealth. ... So that when Thou Thyself, the just Judge ... requirest an exact accounting, charge me not with badly administering my commonwealth and kingdom. But if by human thoughtlessness or infirmity Thy handmaid strays from the right in some thing, absolve me of it by Thy mercy.[29]

Later prayers ask for the same assistance: she holds the scepter "for the justice and equity of Thy people. ... May the mind of Thy handmaid be clear and just, her will sincere, her judgments fair and pious."[30] She wishes to deliver her people to a justice that conforms to their deserts, to give them judges — "true men who hate greediness and shun acceptation of persons" — so that they may be governed in "all equity and righteousness, the virtuous sustained in their justice and innocence, the wicked punished and chastised according to their faults" ("Prayer 13, 'Prayer for the whole Kingdom and Body of the Church according to their Estates

---

[29] "Prayer 9, 'Prayer for Wisdom in the Administration of the Kingdom,'" *Elizabeth I*, 143. The original is in Latin: see *Precationes Privatae, Regiae E.R. 1563* (London, 1563). STC7576.7.

[30] "Prayer 19, 'Third prayer, for the Administration of Justice,'" *Elizabeth I*, 154. The original is in Italian.

and Members,'" *Elizabeth I*, 147). In her administration of justice, "severity" is to be tempered by moderation and realized in equity, that is, a form of justice that takes account of circumstance and intention ("Prayer 33, 'The Latin Prayer,'" *Elizabeth I*, 318). In other words, her government will be just and equitable. If her people get mercy, it will be from God. "We confess," she acknowledges, "that mercy is in Thee alone" ("Prayer 4, 'A Collect,'" *Elizabeth I*, 137). She asks God to "regard neither my wickedness nor the deserts of my forebears or my people, for they are evil and infinite, but remember Thou Thy mercy."[31] Speeches in which Elizabeth explains her decision to execute Mary Queen of Scots illustrate more precisely how her vision of a recalled and reinstituted merciless Justice in "Avec l'aveugler si estrange" addresses her own very troubled role in that moment of crisis.

It was in that role that the queen's justice and equity were to be put most crucially and some would say cruelly to the test in 1586, when she had to decide whether or not to sign the death warrant of Mary Queen of Scots. Elizabeth reveals her vexation in two speeches. There was a case for pardon; the question was what its effect would be. The Act for the Queen's Safety (1585) provided that Mary would incur the death penalty even if she had had no hand in a plot favoring her but made by others.[32] Elizabeth understood that this Act committed her to the punish Mary's treason, but chose at first to see it as monitory: "so far from being intended to entrap her ... it was rather an admonition to warn the danger thereof." But once enacted, it became definitive: "[B]ut sith it is made, and in the force of law, I thought it good in that which might concern her to proceed according thereunto rather than by course of common law." In other words, the Act was law and once Mary's guilt was proved, her death sentence was inevitable. As Elizabeth declared: it has now "brought me into a narrow strait, that I must give direction for her death, which cannot be to me but a most grievous and irksome burden" ("A report," 193). Were she a private person, she would show mercy and pardon her cousin:

> [I]f ... that we were as two milkmaids with pails upon our arms; or that there were no more dependency upon us but mine own life were only in danger and not the whole estate of your religion and

---

[31] "Prayer 23, 'The Queen's Prayer'" *Elizabeth I*, 158. The original is in Latin.

[32] "Speech 17, version 2, '[Headed] A report of her majesty's most gracious answer ... at Richmond the twelfth day of November, 1586,'" *Elizabeth I*, 193n12.

well-doings; I protest ... I would most willingly pardon and remit
this offense. ("A report," 192)

As a queen regnant, however, her justice had to preserve the state and its
body politic. To this end, her counsellors reminded her of her duty. Warning her of the consequences of letting Mary go unpunished, the Lord
Chancellor insisted that "Mercy in this case would in the end prove cruelty against all ... Therefore to spare her is to spill us ... It would exceed-
ing grieve and wound the hearts of your loving subjects if they should see
so horrible a vice not condignly punished."[33] The case — against a
queen regnant — was nevertheless exceptional. It provided Elizabeth with
"just cause" to complain; for, as she said, it confounded much of her past
practice: "I ... have in my time pardoned so many rebels, winked at so
many treasons, and either not produced them or altogether slipped them
over with silence."[34] Why not skip over this queen's sedition too? But at
last the situation at hand permitted nothing better than a *quid pro quo*:
"Only my injurer's bane must be my life's surety ... [I]t is resolved that
my surety cannot be established without a Princess's end" ("The second
answer," 201). The queen's decision was consistent with the uncompromising justice that had been a feature of her self-representations earlier in
her reign, particularly when confronted with the threat of sedition by forces
identified with the Catholic cause and the desperate situation of Mary.

The work on the subject of sedition in which Elizabeth's rigorous justice is explained (and for which Elizabeth is perhaps best known) is the
poem entitled "The Doubt of Future Foes." Composed about 1571, it
"was doubtless written by Elizabeth in response to the threat posed by the
Catholic queen's flight into Protestant England in 1568 and its aftermath.[35] The imagery of this poem evokes aspects of the situation that
Elizabeth would be described nineteen years later in "Avecq l'aveugler si
etrange": the queen finds herself exiled from joy and threatened by falsehood in the absence of reason's rule. Especially important are stanzas

---

[33] *Cobbett's Complete Collection of State Trials and Proceedings for High Treason, etc.*, ed.
Thomas Bayly Howell (London, 1809), vol. 1: 1197. For this reference I am indebted to
Karen Cunningham.

[34] "Speech 18, version 2, [Headed] The second answer made by the queen's majesty
... to the second speech uttered in the names of the Lords and Commons ... , the 24th
day of November, 1586,' " *Elizabeth I*, 201.

[35] "Poem 5, 'The Doubt of Future Foes,' *Elizabeth I*, 133–34n1. See also the variants
of this poem in this volume.

clearly addressing Mary Queen of Scots, "The daughter of debate," and what would befall her should she attempt to foment sedition:

> The daughter of debate
> That discord aye doth sow
> Shall reap no gain where former rule
> Still peace hath taught to know.
>
> No foreign banished wight
> Shall anchor in this port:
> Our realm brooks no seditious sects —
> Let them elsewhere resort.
>
> My rusty sword through rest
> Shall first his edge employ
> To poll their tops who seek such change
> Or gape for future joy. (ll. 21–28)

The message is clear. It is, moreover, by way of a reply to a plea sent earlier to Elizabeth by Mary, who in 1568 represented herself as in need of a safe harbor — that is, a place in England. As Jennifer Summit has shown, "The Doubt" addresses the critical question of Mary's presence in Elizabeth's kingdom.[36] Mary herself had lodged her petition in verses describing her stormy predicament:

> J'ai vu la nef relacher par contrainte
> En haute mer, proche d'entrer au port,[37]
> Et le serain se convertir en trouble . . .

[I have seen a ship, close to the entry of a port, constrained to remain on the high seas, and the calm {sky} turned to storms . . .]

How dangerous was her situation Mary goes on to suggest by referring to "Fortune," who often rips the sails, *voile*, and the rigging, *cordage*, of ships

---

[36] Jennifer Summit," 'The Arte of a Ladies Penne': Elizabeth I and the Poetics of Queenship," *English Literary Renaissance* 26.2 (1996): 395–421, also included in this volume.

[37] The term *relâscher* means "to slacken"; *faire relâche à un port* means "to put in at a port." The poem therefore represents a specific nautical moment in which a ship headed for port is arrested just outside it by unfavorable winds. The text of Mary's poem is quoted from the MS of Mary's poem in British Library Cotton MS Calig. B.V., fol. 316; see the translation in this volume.

in peril on the sea. In such a predicament, a ship becomes completely un-seaworthy. Letters from the same year testify not only Mary's wish to enter England and explain her predicament to Elizabeth, but also her affection for the nautical trope of her poem:

> I will beseech you to look upon and treat me as your relative and good friend under this violent tempest of reports, entreating you not to let me be lost for want of a safe port, for like a vessel driven by all the winds, so am I, not knowing where to find a haven, un-less, taking into your kind consideration my long voyage, you bring me into a safe harbour.[38]

Elizabeth, resolute as ever, had answered in the same vein and without equivocation in a letter dated May 25, 1569, reminding Mary that she had threatened the throne of England by allying herself to France and promot-ing the Duke of Anjou as England's rightful monarch:

> I know not why they [the royal family of France] consider not that the bark of your good fortune floats on a dangerous sea, where many contrary winds blow, and has need of all aid to obviate such evils, and conduct you safely into port. And if so be they are able to serve you aught, still you can in honour deny the intention [of transferring her right to the English throne to the Duc d'Anjou]; for if this right abides in them, then to me pertains the wrong. (*Letters*, ed. Strickland, 1: 176–77)

"The Doubt" reveals not only that Elizabeth rejected Mary's plea, poeti-cally but emphatically, but also implies that were she, Mary, to venture to a port of the kind she desired, Elizabeth would treat her as seditious: Eliza-beth would sharpen her rusty sword and trim the tops of those, presumably Mary's allies, who dared revolution.[39] What Elizabeth offered was there-fore something less than nothing — it was in fact an outright warning to Mary not to seek for any security whatsoever.

Read as a further and arguably more conscientious reflection on her relations with Mary, and in light of her subsequent execution (though

---

[38] The letter is dated 1 September 1568, from Bolton castle. *Letters of Mary Queen of Scots*, ed. Agnes Strickland, 2 vols. (London, 1848), vol. 1: 104–5.

[39] The image is Livy's in his *History*, I.54. Readers should consult Summit's analysis of the horticultural imagery in "The Doubt" and its provenance in Mary's embroidery; Summit, " 'The Arte,' " 79–108 in this volume.

much after the fact), "Avecq l'aveugler si estrange" reworks the literal terms upon which Elizabeth had earlier constructed the pretext for what would become her decision to execute Mary. The poem written in 1590 transforms the nautical imagery of the queens' correspondence of 1569 so that it depicts Elizabeth's own ship of state, so unlike Mary's, as under the captaincy of divine love not human need or desire. Elizabeth's "Amour" hoists his sail and is well rewarded for his canvas — that is, his skill as governor is manifest in the ship's making way. Elizabeth also resorts to the dreadful figures of "The Doubt" later in "Avecq l'aveugler si estrange" when she alludes to herself as the "Countrepoint," the sword that she gives to God. In other words, although it is she who will poll tops, she will be acting as God's deputy. The action in which she delivers herself to God as his sword is therefore at one with her self-justification as the dispenser of justice. It is followed by the claim that her realm is now "bien gouverne par raison et non par degre": that is, she has dealt justly with all without respect to rank or blood.[40] The question to ask now is what factors could have caused Elizabeth specifically though allusively to comment on Mary's case in or around 1590, some three years after she ordered her execution. My answer is that for Elizabeth the case of Mary Queen of Scots, certainly of political importance, had also come to exemplify her own best exercise of a civil justice.

III

A king, Elizabeth had asserted when accounting for her relations with Mary in 1586, must have "justice, temperance, magnanimity, [and] judgement" ("Speech 18, version 2, The second answer," 204). Declining to

---

[40] In effect, she has dealt with Mary as Sidney's fictional king Euarchus dealt with his son and nephew, Pyrocles and Musidorus — who are princes of Macedonia but charged with crimes in Arcadia — although her reasoning is more draconian than that of Sidney's king. The issue there is whether such foreign princes are protected from arrest, trial, and judgment by the law of nations. Euarchus states that they are not, as that law protects only those who live up to the standards of behavior their rank requires. This is behavior that, quite independent of specific charges made against them at trial, the princes demonstrably failed to honor. Sir Philip Sidney, *The Countess of Pembroke's Arcadia (The Old Arcadia)*, ed. Katherine Duncan-Jones (London: Oxford University Press, 1985), 349. The argument made in favor of Elizabeth is less ambiguous: it is simply that the law of nations is a feature of diplomatic and international relations, and has no legal relevance to the business of maintaining social order within a particular kingdom.

comment on magnanimity,[41] she insisted that her justice had always been exemplary:

> [A]mongst my subjects I never knew a difference of person where right was one, nor never to my knowledge preferred for favor whom I thought not fit for worth; nor bent my ears to credit a tale that first was told me; nor was so rash to corrupt my judgment with my censure before I heard the cause. .... [T]his I dare boldly affirm: my verdict went ever with the truth of my knowledge. .... You will say that with me, I think. ("The second answer," 204)

There is no mention here of mercy or of the kind of circumstantial consideration given to cases allowing for equitable judgment. No difference, no favor — at least where "right" is at issue. In the interval between 1568 and 1586 Mary had asked Elizabeth to recognize the difference of her regal person; she had repeatedly addressed Elizabeth as her sister and cousin. She stated that they were in fact "equals," that therefore the English queen could not justifiably bring an action against the Scottish one — a claim clearly designed to establish a difference between Mary and other persons charged with sedition.[42] More important, perhaps, was a letter from James VI, written to Elizabeth just prior to Mary's execution, arguing the same point with an irony that made parlous Elizabeth's own position as head of state:

> What law of God can permit that justice shall strike upon them, whom he has appointed supreme dispensers of the same under him, whom he hath called Gods, and therefore subjected to the censure of none on earth, whose anointing by God cannot be defiled by man, unrevenged by the author thereof? — they being supreme and immediate lieutenants of God in heaven, cannot therefore be judged by their equals on earth.[43]

Were Elizabeth to defy this "law of God," James implied, she could be seen to defy the grounds upon which she herself ruled. There were, how-

---

[41] For these virtues and how Elizabeth understands them, see Mueller, "Virtue and Virtuality," 15–17.

[42] See 28 June 1568; 8 November 1582, *Letters*, ed. Strickland, 1: 84; 2: 40, respectively.

[43] 26 January 1586–87; *Letters*, ed. Strickland, 2: 232. Elizabeth's answer was conciliatory and equivocal; see 14 February 1586–87, 2: 273.

ever, obvious reasons to reject the Stuart distinction as specious. The divine right of a monarch could find judicial meaning only within his or her kingdom. To suggest that it conferred a universal right was to invoke the vague concept of a law of nations which, in itself, was less law than practice and had no court to maintain it.

The Stuart distinction was easily dismissed. A consideration of the effect of such a differentiated "equality" — in fact, an ironic inversion of an equality oblivious to difference — made the concept dangerous. Written soon after Mary's execution and in response to charges of "injustice," "cruelty," and "unprincely behaviour" against the queen, the anonymous *A Justification of Queene Elizabeth in Relacion to the Affaire of Mary Queene of Scots* declared that the Stuart argument from equality of divine right was irrelevant. What mattered was only the "force and authoritie to decide right" — that is, the judicial authority within a kingdom and enforced by its officers. Without this force and authority, and "for equalitie sake, of somme one sort or another, none or very few would fynd competent judges and take exception to the jurisdiction and so eskape all punishment and correction."[44] The courts would be incapacitated. In Mary's case, this understanding of equality meant that in the interest of securing the commonwealth the queen's public self had to dismiss the charity that her private self would have offered.

The final stanzas of "Avecq l'aveugle si estrange"establish that Elizabeth's vision of a "dessaing . . . de penitence" within her makes providential (and not reprehensible) the burden of imposing justice, both as God's Justice rules on her case and as she rules on others. On error generally, whether in the body natural or politic, Justice exacts a retribution that provokes a salutary "design" of penitence. That understood, the queen can rejoice in her condition: she sees herself so exalted, "Enhaulse," by her thinking, "deliberer" (ll. 243–44) that she finds herself within heaven's gates, pure soul and free of flesh. This is the condition conferred upon her by the last grace, "La derniere de graces," and it signals within her the concord of virtue with both nature and custom or habit. Made virtu-

---

[44] *A Justification of Queene Elizabeth in Relacion to the Affaire of Mary Queene of Scottes*, in *Accounts and Papers relating of Mary Queen of Scots*, ed. Allan J. Crosby and John Bruce, Camden Society Publications 93 (London, 1967), 119. *A Justification* describes the kinds of protest the queen received, the chief of which was that "her process was framed by authority of a private law of her Majesty's making"; 75. This text, like "Avecq l'aveugler si estrange," attempts to align the queen's justice with God's. In theory, it makes her justice at one with the justice enforced by positive law.

ous in her body or instincts and her will, the two faculties to be governed by her enlightened reason, she acquires a beneficent blindness to the disparate and discordant things of this world.

Described in philosophical rather than religious terms and recalling the language of law in the *Justification*, it is a condition repeatedly characterized by what Elizabeth calls the temperament of equality, "egualite" (sic): "[un] estre Si EgaL" "temperementz [en] si Egual accord" (ll. 261, 263, 266–67). The queen's pervasive and perfectly consistent harmony of the self is registered in the self-judgment that concludes her poem. She neither has nor could develop the habit of inconstancy, "habit [de]l'inconstance" (l. 269). On the one hand, she clearly dismisses vacillation between parts of herself that marked her first and strange blindness. Unified, she notes that she has achieved a self stabilized by her vision of the truth. On the other hand, I think, her claim becomes instrumental in the supraphenomenal world of the body politic, where she must adhere to the uncompromising dictates of justice. As any icon of Justice made obvious, that goddess was typically blind. By not seeing what was particular, contingent, or circumstantial, she rendered judgments that were supposed to be informed by the bare truth. The queen's blindness — a blindness uncannily strange — has thus been from its very outset providential, if providence is considered to work in ways that are beyond human reason. In this instance, what Elizabeth felt as a self-dividing despair was actually the harbinger of a wholeness: the imposing impartiality of her justice, itself justified by God's grace.

For Elizabeth finally to have expressed her salvation, "Salut," as the freedom from inconstancy, "l'inconstance," may strike the reader as a curious retreat from a spiritual to a moralized discourse. Having claimed she had entered the door of peace, acquired the seal of the third and final grace, the achievement of constancy seems the least and in a sense the most prosaic of virtues. Yet it is the principal characteristic of the virtue of justice.[45] Unlike the Virgin Mary, who intercedes for mercy in a heavenly cause, the virgin Astraea keeps faith with the right for the sake of people on earth. The actual phrase in which this claim is made, its negative formulation — that Elizabeth has lost the custom of being inconstant — is also characteristic of the poem's rhetorical design as a whole. It recalls her earlier vision of a "near perfection," and the characterization of

---

[45] Arthur Marotti notes that Elizabeth's motto was "Semper eadem"; *Manuscript, Print, and the English Renaissance Lyric* (Ithaca: Cornell University Press, 1995), 235.

her place as "within the door," or at the threshold of salvation. The end she sees and seeks is conveyed in terms of what she approaches but has not yet attained. Her journey is therefore asymptotic. Like the final vision of the new day in the last verses of Romans 13 — verses Calvin was careful to expound as eschatology — what she sees as her end is endlessly and always coming to her.

Claremont Graduate University

LEAH S. MARCUS

Queen Elizabeth I as Public and Private Poet:
Notes toward a New Edition

IN THE ART OF ENGLISH POESIE, (London, 1589), George Puttenham called Queen Elizabeth I "the most excellent Poet" of the age, who "easily surmounteth all the rest that have written before her time or since, for sense, sweetness and subtilty, be it in Ode, Elegy, Epigram, or any other kind of poem Heroic or Lyric, wherein it shall please her Majesty to employ her pen" (2, 51). Where have all these supposed masterpieces disappeared to? Or are we to assume, as the editors of Elizabeth's poems have until recently, that Puttenham's accolade was no more than painfully obvious flattery from a would-be courtier to the monarch to whom his volume was dedicated? In this paper I will suggest that we should take Puttenham's valuation seriously as a contemporary's view of her work and also as an assertion of the literary types she worked in. To borrow one of the queen's favorite allegorical depictions of herself in her correspondence with her French suitor the Duke of Alençon, Elizabeth as poet was a rock "assaulted by several storms and winds that blow from divers climes."[1] Most of the rock was submerged: there are only a small handful of poems that she suffered to be acknowledged as hers. Some of the rock has eroded fatally over time: the odes, elegies, and heroic verses Puttenham refers to

[1] Cited from letters of 17 January 1580, and June 1581, 245, 249–50 of *Elizabeth I: Collected Works*, ed. Leah S. Marcus, Janel Mueller, and Mary Beth Rose (Chicago: University of Chicago Press, 2000). Unless otherwise attributed, all of the writings by Elizabeth included in the present essay are cited from this edition, with modernized spelling and punctuation throughout.

have disappeared almost without a trace, except for the initial lines of a "Song" she wrote to celebrate the defeat of the Spanish Armada (about which more later). And like a rock at sea, Elizabeth's poetic production may often appear to be something other than it is — mere mist or cloud rather than solid substance. I will suggest here (albeit without much specificity) that some known but unattributed English and Latin verse of the period — as well as verses erroneously ascribed to other poets of the time — may well have been written by the queen.

In thinking about Renaissance authorship, we are accustomed to using metaphors drawn from the language of monarchy: the author has sole or sovereign authority over his text in much the same way that a ruler asserting prerogative powers claims sole or sovereign authority over an area of government. But in neither instance, as we post-Foucaultian critics have learned, is the authority as absolute as is usually claimed. An absolute monarch Renaissance-style could not boast Stalinesque totalitarian control over the mechanisms of state, but had relatively limited resources for enforcing royal edicts. Similarly, Renaissance authors had to contend with the vagaries of the manuscript system — which frequently practiced what Harold Love has called "serial composition," altering a manuscript even in the process of copying it — or with the vagaries of print, which could promise somewhat greater uniformity of copies, but still opened the would-be author to a host of institutional and market constraints that could alter the published form of a manuscript almost beyond recognition.[2] The "author as monarch" trope loses some of its éclat once we realize that the most celebrated English Renaissance monarch of all exerted very little control over her poetic materials except by withholding them from circulation.

For people outside the inner circles of the court, Queen Elizabeth as author/translator was publicly available for inspection in two places: Whitehall and Woodstock. A Moravian Protestant visitor to England, Zdeněk Brtnický z Valdštejina, whose title may be anglicized to Baron Waldstein, visited the royal palace of Whitehall in 1600. He was a fanatical recorder of inscriptions of all kinds, and described a room

> where the Queen keeps her books, some of which she wrote herself. Among them there was one which she dedicated to her father as follows:

---

[2] See the discussion in Harold Love, *Scribal Publication in Seventeenth-Century England* (Oxford: Clarendon Press, 1993).

A treshault et trespuissant et redouble Prince Henry 8 de ce nom Roy d'Angleterre, de France, et d'Irlande, defenseur de la foy, Elisabeth sa tres humble fille, rend salut et devot obedience.

The title-page of another book reads:

Colloque tresfamilier entre deux personnages c'est a sçavoir Aulus et Barbatus diviser ensemble des articles de nostre foy Chrestienne, extraict des oeuvres d'Erasmi de Roterodam.

We also saw here some prayers of Queen Catherine (the mother of Mary) which had been translated from English into Latin by Elizabeth.[3]

These "books" identified as Elizabeth's were doubtless all bound manuscript volumes translated rather than authored by Elizabeth, except for their letters dedicatory or other prefatory materials. The volume dedicated to Henry VIII may very well have been a manuscript copy of Elizabeth's trilingual translation of Queen Katherine Parr's *Prayers and Meditations*, which the girlish Elizabeth dedicated to her father as a New Year's gift on 30 December 1545. Beginning in 1544, Katherine Parr, the last wife of Henry VIII, had become strongly interested in the radical Protestantism wafting into England from the continent; she was also a strong ally and protector of Elizabeth herself. By translating Parr's work, Elizabeth not only performed a dutiful gesture towards her father and surrogate mother; she also asserted her own allegiance to Parr's new, radical brand of Protestantism. The prayers to which Baron Waldstein refers may have been a Latin copy of the meditations of Catherine Parr similar to the French one dedicated to Henry VIII that he had noted earlier — it is unlikely that Elizabeth would have kept available for public perusal in her library a volume of the translations of Henry's divorced and defiantly Catholic Queen Catherine of Aragon. Elizabeth's trilingual translation of Katherine Parr's *Prayers or Meditations*, as written out in Elizabeth's own fine italic hand, and bound and embroidered by herself, is still available to scholars in the British Library (Royal MS 7.D.X.), as are many other volumes from the royal library at Whitehall But the important thing for our purposes about these rather grandly titled volumes is that they were manuscript prose translations — not published and not poetry. Why was none of Elizabeth's poetry on display at Whitehall?

---

[3] G. W. Groos, trans., *The Diary of Baron Waldstein: A Traveler in Elizabethan England* (London: Thames and Hudson, 1981), 51.

There was one place in England where visitors could publicly peruse the queen's verses. After visiting Whitehall and other Westminster and London sights, Baron Waldstein eventually made his way to the Palace of Woodstock, outside Oxford, where Elizabeth had been held as a prisoner during the darkest days of her near-martyrdom under the reign of Mary Tudor. There, he toured the palace buildings, and found Elizabeth's writings on a wall:

> The thing above all to see in this palace is the room in which the present Queen Elizabeth was kept prisoner for a whole four years by order of her sister Mary. Even now one can read her verses in English, written on the wall in Elizabeth's own handwriting. They are as follows:
>
> > Oh Fortune, thy wresting wavering state
> > Hath fraught with cares my troubled wit,
> > Whose witness this present prison late
> > Could bear, where once was joy flown quite.
> > Thou causedst the guilty to be loosed
> > From lands where innocents were enclosed,
> > And caused the guiltless to be reserved,
> > And freed those that death had well deserved.
> > But all herein can be naught wrought;
> > So God grant to my foes as they have thought.
> >   Finis. Elizabetha a prisoner. 1555
> > Much suspected by me, but nothing proved can be.
>
> They say that she wrote other things too with a diamond on one of the windows, but those inscriptions no longer exist.[4]

What Waldstein appears to have done here is to have copied out two separate poems as though they were one. According to Paul Hentzner and Thomas Platter, other visitors from the Continent who had seen the verses at Woodstock a year or so before Waldstein, the princess's first ten-line poem on the perverse tendency of Fortune to wreak evil upon the innocent was written with charcoal on a windowframe or shutter (literally "fenestrae ligneae").[5] The line of verse written one line below "Finis.

---

[4] *Diary*, 117, 119.

[5] See Paul Hentzner, *Itinerarium* (Nuremberg, 1512), 144 (from which the Latin is quoted); and Hans Hecht, ed., *Thomas Platters des Jüngeren Englandfahrt im Jahre 1599* (Leipzig: Max Niemeyer Verlag, 1929), 121–22. Both of these versions were so badly gar-

Elizabetha a prisoner. 1555" had been long canonical by the time Waldstein saw it in 1600, having been printed first by John Foxe in his *Book of Martyrs* (1563) and then by Raphael Holinshed in his *Chronicles* (1587). Both Foxe and Holinshed print the line as a couplet and describe it as written by Elizabeth with "her diamond in a glass window," which may be where Waldstein got the idea that he was missing out on "other things" at Woodstock written with a diamond. As printed by Foxe and Holinshed, it is a two-line poem:

> Much suspected by me,
> Nothing proved can be.

This deceptively simple poem can be taken in at least two senses: much was suspected *of* Elizabeth by Mary Tudor's ministers as they interrogated her in hopes of linking her to one or another plot against Mary's crown; much was suspected *by* Elizabeth herself of others' nefarious plans for her destruction. But why is the couplet described in the printed authorities as written in glass while Baron Waldstein saw it written on a wall?

The queen's lodgings at Woodstock were, by the turn of the seventeenth century, an international Protestant shrine. It is significant that both Fox and Holinshed ascribe the verses written with a diamond to 1558, the tumultuous final year of Mary's reign and the eve of Elizabeth's accession, while modern editors and biographers date them more credibly but less dramatically to 1554–55, the time of Elizabeth's Woodstock imprisonment. This written witness to Elizabeth's sufferings under Catholicism was too important to be allowed to crumble away. We can speculate that in 1599 or thereabouts — between the visits by Hentzner and Platter and the visit recorded by Baron Waldstein — the originals of the two poems had decayed sufficiently that they were copied onto a wall of Elizabeth's prison-chamber one after another (which would explain Waldstein's copying of them as though they were a single poem) for the inspiration of Protestant visitors to the queen's Woodstock "shrine." But the precise language of the poems was by no means sacred: several words were likely altered in the process, because Waldstein's version of the poem differs in several instances from Platter's. Or was it, perhaps, the Continental visitors who were the creative copyists? In either case, the Woodstock poems were important to Elizabeth's contemporaries not so much because of their content or their skilled versification and neatness of expression, but be-

---

bled by the printer and/or transcriber that they can be reconstructed only conjecturally.

cause of their highly-charged symbolic status as monument for the beleaguered international community of Protestants.

Aside from the two lines printed by Foxe and Holinshed, Queen Elizabeth "authored" only one English poem — that is to say, there is only one poem that was not only printed as hers, but also uniformly assigned to her in manuscript collections — "The Doubt of Future Foes," sometimes known as "The Dread of Future Foes." I quote the first and last stanzas from the Folger Shakespeare Library copy (MS V.b.317, fol. 20v), which is the copytext for the poem in our edition of the writings of Queen Elizabeth I:

> The doubt of future foes
> Exiles my present joy
> And wit me warns to shun such snares
> As threatens mine annoy.
>
> For falsehood now doth flow
> And subjects' faith doth ebb,
> Which should not be if reason ruled
> Or wisdom weaved the web.
>
> . . . .
>
> No foreign banished wight
> Shall anchor in this port:
> Our realm brooks no seditious sects —
> Let them elsewhere resort.
>
> My rusty sword through rest
> Shall first his edge employ
> To poll[6] their tops who seek such change
> Or gape for future joy.
> Vivat Regina

This poem exists in numerous manuscript versions and at least one early printed text — George Puttenham gives it honored place in his *Art of English Poesie* as an example of the *"Gorgious,"* the *"last and principal figure of our poetical Ornament,"* which attires language "with copious & pleasant amplifications and much variety of sentences all running upon one point & to one intent" (206–7).

Nearly all of the manuscript versions I have seen attribute "The Doubt

---

[6] "Pull" in Folger; "poll" in all other manuscript versions.

of Future Foes" to Elizabeth in one way or another — either through her name at the bottom or her name in the title, as in the Folger copy and Bodley Rawlinson Poetical 108, both of which head the poem "Verses made by the Q[ueen's] Majesty." According to Puttenham, Elizabeth wrote the poem to declare to Mary Queen of Scots and to covert pro-Scottish factions in England who had been plotting in Mary's favor that Elizabeth "was nothing ignorant of those secret practises, though she had long with great wisdom and patience dissembled it" (207). One fairly late copy, from the miscellany of Robert Commaundre, chaplain to Sir Henry Sidney, is even more politically specific, heading the poem: "Certain verses made by the Queen's most excellent majesty against the rebels in the north parts of England and in Norfolk and other places of the realm, anno domini 1569 et 1570" (British Library Egerton MS 2642, fol. 237). The verses began appearing in manuscript miscellanies during the early 1570s — after the Northern Rebellion and the execution of the duke of Norfolk, who had plotted to wed Mary Queen of Scots and take over the government of England. But the poem took on new life after the 1587 execution of Mary Queen of Scots — the "daughter of debate" and "foreign wight" to which the poem darkly alludes — for yet another plot against Elizabeth's life, the Babington Plot uncovered in 1586.

Yet even these verses were apparently not willingly and openly circulated by Elizabeth herself. According to an anecdote from Sir John Harington, the queen's favorite and godson, "The Doubt of Future Foes" was put into circulation only against her majesty's wishes by one of the ladies of the court: "My Lady Willoughby did covertly get it on her majesty's tablet, and had much hazard in so doing; for the queen did find out the thief, and chid for spreading evil bruit of her writing such toys, when other matters did so occupy her employment at this time; and was fearful of being thought too lightly of for so doing."[7] Even though the poem had a clear political intent, the queen tried to pass it off — or so the anecdote goes — as a mere "toy." There are layers under layers of intentionality here: did she write it on her tablet for her own eyes only — to ease the inner burden of knowing her subjects' perfidy? Did she write it to be circulated, yet denied, as the anecdote of Lady Willoughby suggests? In the latter case, the apparent denial of authorship would be a ruse meant to increase the power and authority of the threat implied in the lyrics. Or, as the fact that manuscripts uniformly attribute the poem to her might suggest but the

---

[7] *Nugae Antiquae* (London, 1769), 58.

Willoughby anecdote denies, did Elizabeth write and promulgate "The Doubt of Future Foes" openly as a threat to her disobedient subjects during the Northern Rebellion and later?[8] It is noteworthy that the only poem by Elizabeth attributed to her uniformly in manuscripts and an early printed source alike is a poem whose occasion is political in the narrow and customary sense of the term.

This situation is in marked contrast to Elizabeth's translations and even some of her speeches, which were deliberately circulated in manuscript by the court, sometimes in beautifully tooled vellum binding, as a keepsake to her favorites or other notables. One such example is Bodleian Library MS 900, a manuscript book in a fine tooled and gilt limp vellum binding, which includes a copy of Elizabeth's Latin speech delivered at Oxford University, 28 September 1592, and other materials that perhaps relate to the same visit: Latin and English texts of "The Blessed Virgin Mary to the Messanians," which may reproduce part of an entertainment presented before the queen at Oxford, and Elizabeth's autograph English translation of Cicero's *Pro Marcello*. Some of the paper in this volume displays Elizabeth's own crown watermark. The volume was clearly meant for distribution to some highly favored courtier or university official, quite possibly one of the Oxford heads, since it ended up in the Bodleian. Similarly, the queen herself offered young Harington a manuscript copy of her 1576 speech in Parliament with the comment, "Boy Jack, I have made a clerk write fair my poor words for thine use, as it cannot be such striplings have entrance into parliament assembly as yet. Ponder them in thy hours of leisure and play with them till they enter thine understanding, so shalt thou hereafter, perchance, find some good fruits hereof when thy godmother is out of remembrance; and I do this because thy father was ready to serve and love us in trouble and thrall."[9] Again, as in the verses at Woodstock, these keepsake volumes appear to derive their value for recipients as much or more from their royal origin than from their contents.

Indeed, Elizabeth's translations were frequently rough and hasty: she did not do translation as a monarch in order to perform a service for her subjects by rendering Seneca or Boethius or Petrarch into polished English — she had courtiers of her own who were eager to perform such labors, or

---

[8] "The effect," as Jennifer Summit suggests, is to "create the Queen's openly-known secrets as objects of desire." See her essay in this volume, reprinted from *English Literary Renaissance* (1996): 395–422.

[9] *Nugae Antiquae*, Vol. 1 (London, 1804), 127–28.

could at least be drafted into doing so, as she apparently ordered Harington to translate Ariosto. No doubt she translated in part simply for pleasure and to keep her languages exercised, but the primary reason she translated, I would suggest, was in order to be publicly known to be translating. For Elizabeth I, translation was not the virtuous womanly service it might have been for some others, but a form of political assertion. It is no accident that she usually translated stoic texts, or texts expressing stoic sentiment. So, according to William Camden, her verse translation of Boethius' *Consolation of Philosophy* was made in the dark days after she heard the cataclysmic news of her ally Henry of Navarre's conversion to Catholicism so that he could accept the French crown as Henry IV. Very few of the keepsake volumes in which such work was sometimes released to her intimates appear to have survived. They do not, to my knowledge, include any of the queen's own poetry as opposed to verse or prose translation.[10]

Steven May has suggested that before the advent of the "Golden Age" of Elizabethan poetry under the inspiration of Sir Philip Sidney, the general attitude of the court was similar to Elizabeth's own as expressed in the anecdote reported by Harington: poetry, even politically important poetry, was mere trifling — not important enough to merit the monumentalization implied by careful copying, attribution, or (worse yet) publication.[11] Indeed, as late as 1589, we find Puttenham complaining that courtier-poets refuse outright to circulate their verses or circulate them only anonymously. This reticence was doubtless not motivated only by pride or social exclusiveness: if poems made as part of playful exchanges among courtiers in the relative intimacy of the Privy Chamber were made publicly available, they would perforce become the impetus for endless, heavy speculation about their intended meaning and political implications. Aside from "The doubt of future foes," such verse of Elizabeth's as has survived from the early decades of her reign has survived only because of the fortuitous durability of the surface on which it was recorded. The Woodstock poems were written on glass and wood, then copied to a wall. She wrote

---

[10] A possible exception may be Hatfield House MS CP, 147.150 (vol. 14: 326), a French manuscript in Elizabeth's hand, described by Steven May in *Courtier Poets* (note 11 below) as containing original French verses by the queen, but characterized later by May and Ann Prescott as a translation of an unknown original. See their transcription and translation in "The French Verses of Elizabeth I," *English Literary Renaissance* 24.1 (winter 1994): 9–43. Our edition of the writings of Elizabeth offers a new translation and describes these verses as an original poem rather than a translation.

[11] Steven W. May, *The Elizabethan Courtier Poets: The Poems and Their Contexts* (Columbia and London: University of Missouri Press, 1991), 41–68.

"No crooked leg" (somewhat incongruously) on the last leaf of her French
psalter, now at the Royal Library in Windsor Castle:

> No crooked leg, no blearèd eye
> No part deformèd out of kind
> Nor yet so ugly half can be
> As is the inward, suspicious mind.
> > Your loving mistress
> > Elizabeth R

In the queen's original, the lines of this epigram are all run together without line divisions — as if to express visually the crabbedness of mind about
which the poem complains. This may be the "obscure sentence" referred
to by lord Burghley as written by the queen in "a book at Windsor" when
she was "much offended with the earl of Leicester" in 1565.[12]

Similarly, the queen's moving Latin and English verses on the cares of
office, probably written during the 1570s, are known to us only because
they happened by chance to be written onto a blank space in a printed
book by the queen, answered by another courtier, Sir Thomas Heneage,
and copied by yet another hand into yet another printed book of 1570
that happened to end up in the Morgan Library (PML 7768), where the
verses were noticed by a modern scholar who was probably looking for
something else entirely. Here I cite only the second (English) half of the
poem, which translates the Latin of the first half:

> A hapless kind of life is this I wear:
> Much watch I dure, and weary, toiling days
> I serve the rout and all their follies bear;
> I suffer pride, and sup full hard assays;
> To others' will my life is all addressed,
> And no way so as might content me best.
> > This above was written in a book by the queen's
> > majesty.[13]

---

[12] William Murdin, ed., A Collection of State Papers Relating to Affairs in the Reign of
Queen Elizabeth from the Year 1571 to 1596, Vol. 2 (London: William Bowyer, 1759), 760.

[13] Cited from the Morgan Library copy of H[enry] B[ull]'s Christian Prayers and Holy
Meditations (London: for Henry Middleton, 1570; STC 4028), PML 7768, first flyleaf recto and second flyleaf recto. For further discussion, see May, Courtier Poets, 342–43.

It is not hard to imagine why the queen might want such a plaint to remain among her inner circle of courtiers. It should not surprise us that her poem and Heneage's consoling sonnet in response exist only in a single known manuscript copy. To flaunt such a statement by giving it public circulation would probably have appeared as odd to the court as publicly airing one's undergarments.

As Patricia Fumerton has noted in her fine discussion of the Elizabethan miniature, the queen and others of her court appear to have regarded these tiny portraits as somehow deeply private, self-revealing and therefore to be kept carefully concealed. The same is true, as Fumerton also suggests, of court verses. Sir William Browne's 1602 letter to the earl of Shrewsbury about the queen's handling of Cecil's picture in little perfectly captures the mingled concealment and bravado with which she tossed off her verses:

> I send your Lordship here inclosed some verses compounded by Mr. Secretary, who got Hales to frame a ditty unto it. The occasion was, as I hear, that the young Lady of Derby wearing about her neck, in her bosom, a picture which was in a dainty tablet, the queen, espying it, asked what fine jewel that was? The Lady Derby was curious to excuse the showing of it, but the queen wold have it, and, opening it, and finding it to be Mr. Secretary's, snatched it away and tied it upon her shoe, and walked long with it there; then she took it thence and pinned it on her elbow, and wore it sometimes there also; which Mr. Secretary, being told of, made these verses, and had Hales to sing them in his chamber. It was told her majesty that Mr. Secretary had rare music and songs; she would needs hear them, and so this ditty was sung which you see first written. More verses there be likewise, whereof some or all were likewise sung. I do boldly send these things to your lordship which I would not do to any else, for I hear they are very secret. Some of the verses argue that he repines not, though her majesty please to grace others, and contents himself with the favor he hath.[14]

---

[14] Cited from Lambeth Palace Library MS 3203 in Katherine Duncan-Jones, " 'Preserved Dainties': Late Elizabethan Poems by Sir Robert Cecil and the Earl of Clanricarde," *Bodleian Library Record* 14 (1992): 136–44. The citation is to 136, 138. I am indebted to Steven May for this reference. See also Patricia Fumerton, *Cultural Aesthetics: Renaissance Literature and the Practice of Social Ornament* (Chicago: University of Chicago Press, 1991), 66–110.

Characteristically for the period, although Sir William Browne's letter has survived, the accompanying verses apparently have not, though they exist in at least one other "secret" copy.[15] Given their secrecy, Shrewsbury may well have destroyed Browne's copy of the verses as soon as he had read them. Elizabeth's act of wearing Cecil's miniature in inappropriate places serves as an illustration of the comparable oddity of making courtier verses public. To the extent that they have surfaced, they seem to turn up, like the miniature worn on an elbow, only in almost comically marginal locations. Elizabeth was less a poet in our modern sense than an accomplished graffiti artist — tossing off hasty and topically loaded lines in odd, impromptu places, writing in total nonchalance about the verses' survival to posterity, interested only in the ephemeral social or political occasion at hand. Or so she went out of her way to portray herself.

"On Monsieur's Departure" may be an exception to this generalization. Like "The Doubt of Future Foes," it is a political poem uniformly attributed to Queen Elizabeth I in the three manuscript versions known to have survived. Its rather conventional but highly accomplished Petrarchanism expands into a fascinating set of enigmas if one imagines it as composed at the point of the Duc d'Alençon's final departure from England in 1582 after his unsuccessful but still pending courtship of the queen. The poem is cited here from British Library Stowe MS 962. fol. 231v, a bound manuscript volume from the early to mid seventeenth century entitled "Miscellaneous Poems," in which the royal verses are headed "Ely [for Elizabeth]: On Monsieur's Departure":

> I grieve and dare not show my discontent;
> I love and yet am forced to seem to hate;
> I do, and dare not say I ever meant;
> I seem stark mute, but inwardly do prate;
> I am and am not, freeze and yet am burned,
> Since from myself another self I turned.
>
> My care is like my shadow in the sun —
> Follows me flying, flies when I pursue it,
> Stands and lies by me, doth what I have done;
> His too familiar care doth make me rue it.
> No means I find to rid him from my breast
> Till by the end of things it be suppressed.

---

[15] See Duncan-Jones' discussion of Bodleian MS Don. C.54 (141).

> Some greater passions slide into my mind,
> For I am soft and made of melting snow;
> Or be more cruel, love, and so be kind:
> Let me or float, or sink, be high or low,
> Or let me live with some sweet content
> Or die, and so forget what love e'er meant.

Unfortunately, the provenance of this poem as we have it is suspect. The manuscript source most editors have used in transcribing the poem (Bodleian MS Tanner 76, fol. 94r) is dated by them 1601, but in error: that text is actually from the conspicuously late-seventeenth-century hand of Archbishop Sancroft's amanuensis, who was helping the archbishop to arrange antiquarian materials he had acquired from Tanner's earlier collection during the last decades of the seventeenth century. The manuscript volume's dating of 1601 refers not to the date of the collection itself, but to Sancroft's conjectural dating of the historical materials copied into the collection! The poem itself in this version is titled simply "Sonetto" and subscribed "*Eliz. Regina*"; it is reproduced below among Elizabeth's selected poems in the Bodleian Tanner version (Poem 3). By its placement within the antiquarian collection, Sancroft appears to have regarded its recipient as not Alençon, but the queen's later favorite the earl of Essex — many materials in the volume relate to Essex's trial and execution for treason in 1601. But the late date of this volume's arrangement makes its claim of an Essex connection for the poem less than fully persuasive. The poem more usually known as "On Monsieur's Departure" may indeed have been composed by Elizabeth, and may have been written on the occasion of the duke d'Alençon's departure from England, as two out of three manuscripts suggest through their headings, but it seems odd that "On Monsieur's Departure" does not survive in any sixteenth-century manuscript versions. All of the copies we have postdate Elizabeth's reign by a decade or more.

Are we dealing here with a case of royal authorship or with a spurious posthumous attribution? As Sir John Neale cautioned many long years ago, during the early and middle decades of the seventeenth century, Queen Elizabeth became an important cultural authority — oracle might be the more accurate term — on all subjects. Verses that had floated about anonymously may sometimes have been posthumously attributed to her as part of a growing seventeenth-century interest in antiquarianism and in the tidying up of manuscript collections through the determination of provenance and authorship. Of course, earlier, sixteenth-century copies of

the poem may well have existed at one time, and could still exist undis-
covered. But one thing is certain: "On Monsieur's Departure" was not an
"authorial" document of the queen's during her lifetime: it surely did not
circulate with anything approaching the currency of "The Doubt of Future
Foes," or at least a few early copies would have survived. Indeed, as Stev-
en May has suggested, the very fact that no manuscript copies survive
from the decades after the poem's creation, assuming that the poem does
indeed date from 1582, may suggest that she kept this poem truly private
during her lifetime; the distinction between "public" and "private" rests
entirely on whether or not the work in question was put into circulation.
The evidence for Elizabeth's authorship of "On Monsieur's Departure is
certainly strong enough that we should attribute the poem to her in modern editions. But we need to recognize that Elizabeth's "authorship" in
the sense of public acknowledgment of it was a posthumous construction.

The most common scenario was for Elizabeth's poems to circulate
anonymously, or at least without specific manuscript attribution. Previous
editors of Elizabeth's poetry have used a lack of manuscript attribution as
a reason for doubting royal authorship, as in the case of two of the most
graceful lyrics sometimes attributed to her: "When I was Fair and Young,"
and "Now Leave and Let Me Rest." That is particularly true of Leicester
Bradner's slim volume of *The Poems of Queen Elizabeth I*,[16] which has
been the standard edition from its publication to the present. Bradner
bases his characterization of Elizabeth's style upon the deliberately obscure
and gnomic "Doubt of Future Foes" and therefore posits Elizabeth as a
thoroughly "Drab" poet incapable of writing in the "Golden" manner of
Sir Philip Sidney and the best courtier poets during the 1580s and beyond.
Bradner doubts Elizabeth's authorship of "When I Was Fair and Young"
on grounds that the poem is too accomplished to be hers: "I do not believe that she could have turned out such a facile piece of ironical wit.
Her way of writing, as seen in her genuine poems, is more old-fashioned
and heavy-handed" (75–76n). Similarly, Bradner casts "Now Leave and
Let Me Rest" as a "doubtful" poem on the grounds that it was not attributed to Elizabeth by the family of Sir John Harington, in whose miscellany
it occurs: "Since the Haringtons were closely connected with her it is not
likely that the poem would remain anonymous in their collection in the
Arundel manuscript if she had really been the author" (77n). As I have
been trying to contend, just the opposite is true. The fact that graceful,

---

[16] Providence, RI: Brown University Press, 1964.

delicate lyrics were only sporadically attributed to Elizabeth in their manuscript sources is no sure reason for casting their authorship into doubt. Indeed, in several manuscript copies I have seen, the attribution to Elizabeth is heavily scored through — not necessarily because the attribution was incorrect, but because those who circulated her verses perceived even the correct attribution of them to the queen as faintly scandalous — a violation of secrecy. When it came to the writing of love poetry and other ephemeral occasional verse, Queen Elizabeth I took care never to acknowledge authorship. There are a handful of poems attributed to her that may be by others; conversely there may be many poems written by her that survive only anonymously.

An interesting case of the latter is an anonymous ditty published as a broadside in the 1640s (and perhaps earlier as well in editions that have not survived) as a dialogue between a shepherd and his love. Were it not for L. G. Black's transcription of a verse conversation between Sir Walter Ralegh and Elizabeth I and Peter Beal's cataloguing of the few contemporary manuscripts in which one or both poems has survived, we would never suspect that the anonymous popular broadside of the 1640s started out its career as a courtly *débat* between the queen of England and her "silly Pug." The broadside version generalizes the language so that the courtly origins of the verses are effaced, but is otherwise closely parallel to the extant sixteenth-century manuscripts of the two poems.

The debate was apparently started off by Ralegh, whose poem in the earl of Derby's copy at the British Library begins "Fortune hath taken away my love, / My life's joy and my soul's heaven above. / Fortune hath taken thee away, my princess, / My world's joy and my true fantasy's mistress."[17] Ralegh goes on for twenty more lines of lament, the final couplet of which repudiates Fortune entirely: "But love, farewell — though Fortune conquer thee, / No fortune base nor frail shall alter me." The occasion of this lament was no doubt the earl of Essex's rise to the status of royal favorite in 1587, which must have appeared to Ralegh a dire eclipse indeed. He had not learned, as Cecil claimed to have learned in 1602, to repine not, "though her majesty please to grace others," and to content "himself with the favor he hath." Elizabeth responds to Ralegh in a considerably more colloquial, down-to-earth vein than Ralegh's poem to her. I quote the poem's first twelve lines as they were copied into a mis-

---

[17] BL Additional MS 63742, fol. 116r; a bound volume in contemporary limp vellum described in the catalogue as "Letters of Henry, 4th Earl of Derby."

cellany of the period at the Inner Temple Library, then (characteristically) scored through, but not to the point of illegibility:

> Ah, silly Pug, wert thou so sore afraid?
> Mourn not, my Wat, nor be thou so dismayed.
> It passeth fickle Fortune's power and skill
> To force my heart to think thee any ill.
> No Fortune base, thou sayst, shall alter thee?
> And may so blind a witch so conquer me?
> No, no, my Pug, though Fortune were not blind,
> Assure thyself she could not rule my mind.
> Fortune, I know, sometimes doth conquer kings,
> And rules and reigns on earth and earthly things,
> But never think Fortune can bear the sway
> If virtue watch, and will her not obey. ....[18]

Fortune may conquer kings, but not queens, she argues, deftly parrying Pug's self-pitying lament with an implicit accusation of over presumption.[19] In this verse exchange, Elizabeth is unnamed as the author, but the margin of the manuscript identifies the poem as "per reginam" and she is easily recognizable through the pet name she attaches to Ralegh as well as through the ease and authority with which she assumes the posture of the queen. Her authorship of the reply to Ralegh is also confirmed by Puttenham, who cites one of Elizabeth's couplets on fortune from the poem as an example of "*sententia,* or the sage sayer" (197).

In the "Reply to Ralegh" Elizabeth is highly effective as a poet and debater — arguably more effective than Sir Walter Ralegh himself, who usually earns far higher marks than she for artistry. Nevertheless, the queen's identity is established largely through inference. This was surely not the only exchange of verses between the queen and the favorite. Thomas Fuller recounts a story that, if accurate, depicts yet another instance of the writing of courtly graffiti:

---

[18] Inner Temple Library MS Petyt 538, Vol. 10; for other manuscript copies see L. G. Black, "A Lost Poem by Queen Elizabeth I," *Times Literary Supplement,* 23 May 1968, 535.

[19] For discussion of the poem, see May, *Courtier Poets,* 342–43; Black; and Margaret Downs-Gamble's nearly completed book on Renaissance verse conversations, based in part on her dissertation, "John Donne's Monstrous Body," University of Texas, 1993.

When Ralegh had newly come to court, desire for the queen's favor
made him write in a glass window, obvious to the queen's eye,
> "Fain would I climb, yet fear I to fall."

Her majesty, either espying or being shown it, did under-write,
> "If thy heart fails thee, climb not at all."[20]

Ironically, when it came to idle "toys" like courtly occasional verses, the
queen was no more an "author" in the Foucaultian sense of the term than
her basely born subject, Ralegh. Many of Ralegh's verses also circulated
anonymously, and the canon of his work is equally vexed in terms of certain attribution, as we would expect of a courtier poet of the period. But
Ralegh has been turned into an "author" through a series of scholarly editions, while Elizabeth has not. Arthur Marotti has powerfully characterized
Elizabethan courtly love poetry as itself political — maneuvering in an
elaborate courtship ritual in which the queen and her signs of favor were
the endlessly deferred prizes.[21] Yet when it comes to the attribution of
authorship, manuscript culture would appear to have differentiated clearly
between such courtly "toys" and more explicitly political verses. Even the
poetry of a revered and powerful queen was not preserved with any particular meticulousness unless it happened to resonate powerfully with national priorities and crises.

How many other unattributed lyrics of the period might be Elizabeth's
as well? We may never find the odes, elegies, and heroic verses attributed
to her by Puttenham. Many may have been in Latin rather than English,
like the poem she surely should be credited with in response to the Holy
Roman Emperor's poet laureate, Paul Melissus, who had frequently written
verse praises of her. Both his poem and Elizabeth's response were published in Nuremberg by Melissus himself in a 1580 volume of his verses,
P. Melissi Mele sive Odae . . . Epigrammata. Melissus' epigram stated that he
dedicated all of his books to Elizabeth and, indeed, placed his whole self
beneath the yoke of royal servitude as her slave. Elizabeth responded (characteristically) with thanks for the poetry but a denial of the poet's proposed role of servitude as base and unfitting: "What king would shame to
cherish / A poet who, from demigods, makes us gods?"[22] Of course it is

---

[20] Thomas Fuller, *The History of the Worthies of England* (London, 1662), 261.

[21] Arthur Marotti, " 'Love is not love': Elizabethan Sonnet Sequences and the Social
Order," *English Literary History* 49 (1982): 396–428.

[22] See also James E. Phillips, "Elizabeth I as a Latin Poet: An Epigram on Paul Melissus," *Renaissance News* 16 (1963): 289–98.

quite possible that such a poem would be touched up before publication by its recipient, but it is doubtful that Melissus would have invented it altogether. We know he met Elizabeth I personally in England in 1585, when he visited as part of a delegation of German Protestant princes seeking aid from Elizabeth for their efforts to help Henry of Navarre in France; and that may not have been his first visit. Yet once more, the poem to be given public notice is the poem with a specific political agenda: Elizabeth always took care to preserve her friendship with her German allies even when (as was with the case with the duke of Württemberg during the 1590s) they somewhat wore out their welcome. Bradner doubts the attribution to Elizabeth on grounds that she is not otherwise known to have composed Latin poetry, but the verse exchange with Heneage, discovered since Bradner's edition was published, provides an example of Latin epigram sufficiently like the "Reply to Melissus" that we should accept the attribution. What is not sought will surely never be found: if we counter Bradner's assumption with the assertion that Queen Elizabeth was an English and neo-Latin epigrammatist of considerable skill, we will at least leave open the possibility that more of her verses will surface.

Another political poem in English, lost to literary scholars until recently rediscovered by Steven May, was a "Song" composed by the queen in celebration of the English victory in 1588 over the Spanish Armada. During the nineteenth century, the single known manuscript of this "Song" was in the possession of John Henry Gurney, esquire, of Keswick Hall, Norfolk, at which time it was still bound into a manuscript volume containing various materials of the period collected by the noted seventeenth-century antiquary Sir Henry Spelman. The queen's "Song" on the Armada victory was surveyed along with the rest of Gurney's collection by members of the Historical Manuscripts Commission (12th Report, Appendix 9, fol. 160), but the commissioners saw fit to publish only its first two lines. Had the item been a letter by Elizabeth rather than a poem, they would, according to their usual practice, have printed it in its entirety! In 1936, the Gurney manuscript volume was broken into its component parts and sold piece by piece at auction. Appropriately enough, the queen's poem made its way into the Caird Library of the National Maritime Museum, Greenwich, where it has reposed quietly and almost unnoticed until now.

In its own time, the poem was rather more highly regarded. According to the heading of the Caird Library manuscript, it was "A song made by her majesty, and sung before her at her coming from Whitehall to Paul's through Fleet Street in anno domini 1588" and a marginal note further specifies that it was "sung in December after the scattering of the Spanish

Navy." Here is the first of its three stanzas:

> Look and bow down Thine ear, O Lord;
> From Thy bright sphere, behold and see
> Thy handmaid and Thy handiwork
> Amongst Thy priests, offering to Thee.
> Zeal be incense, reaching the skies;
> Myself and scepter, sacrifice.

In this simple but very powerful poem, available in its full text in *Elizabeth I: Collected Works*, Elizabeth publicly offers herself as a sacrifice of thanksgiving in the ancient Hebraic manner. Indeed, the rest of the poem goes on to draw an extended parallel between the English, threatened by Spanish invasion but miraculously saved by the waves that scattered Philip II's fleet, and the ancient Israelites in exodus from Egypt, miraculously saved by the waves across the Red Sea that scattered Pharaoh's army.

In the case of Elizabeth's victory "Song," despite the very public venue of its performance in 1588, the queen as a poet has, yet once more, maddeningly but predictably, receded into invisibility while the queen as translator and prose-writer is amply evident in contemporaneous manuscript collections. Queen Elizabeth I "authored" proclamations and speeches; she conducted her rule, in her own words, like other "princes," set on a stage, "in the sight and view of all the world duly observed."[23] She wrote poetry — perhaps just as prolifically and often as well as other highly competent courtier poets of the period both Drab and Golden — but in a voice that remains nearly anonymous.

Vanderbilt University

---

[23] Cited from our transcription with modernized spelling and punctuation of Elizabeth's first speech on the execution of Mary Queen of Scots, 12 November, 1586, BL Lansdowne MS 94, Art. 35A, fols. 84ʳ–85ʳ.

SANDRA J. BELL

Kingcraft and Poetry:
James VI's Cultural Policy

MUCH CONTEMPORARY RENAISSANCE CRITICISM focuses on the relationship of poetry and politics in the court of Elizabeth, and occasionally the
interest extends to the court of her successor, James I. Jonathan Goldberg's *James I and the Politics of Literature: Jonson, Shakespeare, Donne, and
Their Contemporaries* (1983) discusses James's self-representations in the
king's political language, and how these representations are played out by
a number of poets in his reign. A number of other critics examine James's
relationship to drama, especially the plays of Shakespeare and the Jacobean masques.[1] Other studies examine poetry and patronage in their relationship to the development, support, and subversion of monarchical ide-

---

[1] For James and Jacobean drama and masques, see, for instance: Richard Levin, "The
King James Version of *Measure for Measure*," *CLIO* 3 (1974): 111–63; Stephen Orgel,
"The Royal Theatre and the Role of King," in *Patronage in the Renaissance*, ed. Guy
Fitch Lytle and Stephen Orgel (Princeton: Princeton University Press, 1981), 261–73;
George Walton Williams, "*Macbeth*: King James's Play," *SoAR* 47 (1982): 12–21; Jona-
than Goldberg, *James I and the Politics of Literature: Jonson, Shakespeare, Donne, and Their
Contemporaries* (Baltimore: Johns Hopkins University Press, 1983); Catherine F. Siegel,
"Hands off the Hothouses: Shakespeare's Advice to the King," *Journal of Popular Culture*
20 (1986): 81–88; Theodore B. Leinwand, "Conservative Fools in James's Court and
Shakespeare's Plays," *Shakespeare Studies* 19 (1987): 218–37; Douglas F. Rutledge, "The
Structural Parallel Between Rituals of Reversal, Jacobean Political Theory and *Measure
for Measure*," *Iowa State Journal of Research* 62 (1988): 421–41; Jerzy Limon, *The Masque
of Stuart Culture* (Newark: University of Delaware Press, 1990). For an extensive list, see
Susanne Collier's "Recent Studies in James VI and I" bibliography in *English Literary
Renaissance* (1993): 509–19.

ologies, and follow Stephen Greenblatt's "poetics of culture" — "the collective making of distinct cultural practices and [the] inquiry into the relations among these practices": the exchange between society and its representations.[2] Along with the poets' representations, James's own tracts and speeches are examined not only to uncover what the king claims are a monarch's rights and obligations, but also to discuss the rhetoric of his policies and his self-representations. But despite the interest in James I, these studies almost completely omit the thirty-six years James spent as king of Scotland prior to his arrival in England, and the poetry he wrote there.[3]

James VI began his personal reign at a time when the Scottish monarchy was under increasing scrutiny, and poetry was one of the earliest means by which the king attempted to establish his own monarchical power. James wrote three collections of verse; two were published during

---

[2] "Circulation of Social Energy," in *Shakespearean Negotiations* (Berkeley: University of California Press, 1988), 5. See also Greenblatt's "Towards a Poetics of Culture," in *The New Historicism*, ed. H. Aram Veeser (New York: Routledge, Chapman and Hall, 1989), 1–14.

[3] There are a few studies of James VI's poetry. R. D. S. Jack examines some of James VI's court poets, but for James's own writings, see Jack's "James VI and Renaissance Poetic Theory," *English* 16 (1967): 208–11; "Poetry under King James VI" in *The History of Scottish Literature*, Vol. 1, *Origins to 1660*, ed. R. D. S. Jack (Aberdeen: Aberdeen University Press, 1988), 125–40. See also: Emery Jones, " 'Othello', 'Lepanto' and the Cyprus Wars," *Scottish Literary Studies* 21 (1968): 47–52; Helena Mennie Shire, *Song, Dance and Poetry of the Court of Scotland under King James VI* (Cambridge: Cambridge University Press, 1969); Richard M. Clewett, Jr., "James VI of Scotland and his Literary Circle," *Aevum* 47 (1973): 441–54; J. Derrick McClure, " 'O Phoenix Escossois': James VI as Poet," in *A Day Estivall*, ed. Alisoun Gardner-Medwin and Janet Hadley Williams (Aberdeen: Aberdeen University Press, 1990), 96–111; and "Translation and Transcreation in the Castalian Period," *Studies in Scottish Literature* 26 (1991): 185–98; Kevin Sharpe, "Private Conscience and Public Duty in the Writings of King James VI and I," in *Public Duty and Private Conscience in Seventeenth Century England*, ed. J. Morrill, P. Slack and D. Woolf (Oxford: Oxford University Press, 1993), 77–100; Kevin Sharpe, "The King's Writ: Royal Authors and Royal Authority in Early Modern England," in *Culture and Politics in Early Stuart England*, ed. Kevin Sharpe and Peter Lake (London: Macmillan, 1994), 117–38. For an exceptional historical survey of James VI and I, see Jenny Wormald's studies. See also my "Writing the Monarch: James VI and *Lepanto*, "in *Other Voices, Other Views: Expanding the Canon in English Renaissance Studies*, ed. Mary Silcox, Helen Ostovich, and Graham Roebuck (Newark: University of Delaware Press, 1999), which examines James's long historical poem in the political context of its 1591 publication date; Peter C. Herman, "Best of Poets, Best of Kings": King James VI/I and the Scene of Monarchical Verse," in *Royal Subjects: Essays on the Writings of James VI/I*, ed. Daniel Fischlin and Mark Fortier (Detroit: Wayne State University Press, forthcoming), and Robert Appelbaum's essay, "War and Peace in *The Lepanto*," in this volume.

his Scottish reign, and the first contained a treatise on Scottish poetics.[4] Through his treatise and verse, the king made himself the subject of his own poetic discourse. James endeavoured to mythologize his authority within the Scottish cultural consciousness, and to shape the expression of his court poets with poetic laws and patronage.[5] At this time, James also established a circle of court poets known as the Castalian Band.[6] In this essay, I will address the issue of monarchical self-representation through poetry — James's early cultural policy in Scotland — and will examine his first collection, *The Essayes of A Prentise, in the Divine Art of Poesie*, published in 1584. I posit that James consciously adopted a cultural policy in response to a specific set of historical conditions;[7] to suggest the importance of the king's involvement in poetry at this time, I will first provide a brief outline of the political and poetical circumstances leading up to his first publication.

Growing Opposition

James's first collection of poetry, *The Essayes of a Prentise, in the Divine Art of Poesie*, was published in 1584, an important year in the development of the king's reign. The monarchy in Scotland had been under increasing scrutiny for a number of decades. The Reformation — firmly established by Parliament in August 1560 — wished to limit the monarch's power; state-

---

[4] The third collection, *All the kings short poesis that are not printed*, was edited and arranged, as if for publication, by Prince Charles, the Groom of the Chamber Thomas Carey, and James himself. James Craigie notes that this collection may have been intended for publication along with the 1616 *Works*, but it remained unpublished until 1911. All three collections, and uncollected verse, are found in James Craigie's two volumes of James's verse: *The Poems of King James VI of Scotland* (Edinburgh and London: Blackwood, 1955, 1958).

[5] Kevin Sharpe makes a similar claim in "The King's Writ: Royal Authors and Royal Authority in Early Modern England": "James's writings, through representation and self-presentation, attempt to reaffirm and reauthorise paradigms that sustained his divine right; and to control the arena of interpretation and discourse" (*Culture and Politics*, 131).

[6] Priscilla Bawcutt argued convincingly at the Ninth International Conference on Medieval and Renaissance Scottish Language and Literature that "Castalian Band" is a recent, rather than sixteenth-century, naming.

[7] "[M]onarchs endeavoured in the new circumstances they confronted to re-establish their authority by a reassertion of their interpretive power over rival voices"; Kevin Sharpe, "The King's Writ," 118. Though Sharpe refers here specifically to James I's patronage of the new authorized translation of the Bible, this statement is applicable to much more of the king's work; Sharpe later examines James's *Lepanto* and his *Furies* in some detail.

ments curtailing James's religious jurisdiction were supported by political theorists such as John Mair (Major) and Hector Boece, who diminished the monarch's control over the state also.[8] George Buchanan, James's tutor until the king reached the age of thirteen, also drew on these theorists for two works which vindicate the right of the people to overthrow unsatisfactory monarchs: De Jure Regni apud Scotos Dialogus (1579) and his History of Scotland (1583).[9] Buchanan also wrote four plays which portrayed the consequences of tyranny, and dedicated these to King James.[10] A growing and fervent religious and political Reformation increasingly questioned the extent of the monarch's authority, and even Scotland's need for a monarch at all.

For some years before 1584, there had not been a strong, centralized monarchy to counter such an attack. Too many controversies surrounded James's mother Mary (r. 1561–1567); her perceived indifference to her political duties, her attachment to court musician David Riccio, her apparent complicity in the death of her husband Darnley, and her overhasty marriage to the murderer Bothwell three months later, combined with her Ro-

---

[8] In the 1520s, John Mair (Major), a theologian and historian, assigned the monarch "a role subordinate to and contained by the state"; Jenny Wormald, "James VI and I, Basilikon Doron and The Trew Law of Free Monarchies: the Scottish Context and the English Translation," The Mental World of the Jacobean Court, ed. Linda Levy Peck (Cambridge: Cambridge University Press, 1991), 40. Supreme power would be invested in the community. In 1526, Hector Boece used mythical sources to fabricate a Scottish history in which a line of forty tyrannical kings were deposed by the people ("James VI and I," 40).

[9] In his De Jure Regni, Buchanan asserted that "the constitution of Scotland was such as to justify the deposition of any king if the majority of the Scottish people found him unsatisfactory"; Maurice Lee, Jr., Great Britain's Solomon: James VI and I in His Three Kingdoms (Urbana: University of Illinois Press, 1990), 34. Wormald clarifies that "the people" are "in practice the aristocracy"; Court, Kirk and Community: Scotland 1470–1625 (London: Edward Arnold, 1981), 146. See also Arthur H. Williamson, who states that Buchanan "drastically demoted the king, while making the check against royal authority an ongoing process," in Scottish National Consciousness in the Age of James VI: The Apocalypse, the Union and the Shaping of Scotland's Public Culture (Edinburgh: John Donald, 1979), 10. De Jure Regni went through three editions in three years.

[10] David Norbrook notes that "the drama that Buchanan most loved, that of classical Greece, had been produced in a democracy"; Poetry and Politics in the English Renaissance (London: Routledge & Kegan Paul, 1984), 94. Interestingly, Baptistes, a play published in 1577, was Englished in 1642 as "Tyrannical-Government Anatomised: or, A Discource Concerning Evil Counsellors," and "in 1643 the House of Commons ordered a translation of his [Buchanan's] work as part of the campaign to justify their rebellion" (Poetry and Politics, 94).

man Catholicism to provide ample reasons for her deposition.[11] The monarchy was further weakened by the series of regents who ruled in James's minority, and the shifting alliances under these temporary governors.[12] The many coups during James's minority showed the extent to which kidnapping and the literal possession of the king's body was used to authorise the nobility's political transactions.[13] The increasing strength of the Reformers from 1560 on, the disastrous reign of Mary, Queen of Scots, and James's minority worked to weaken the position of the monarchy, and to sever the connection between monarch and nation.

Scottish Reformers voiced their concerns not only from the pulpit and in prose tracts, but also in poetry; these Reformation satires are largely concerned with the government of the commonwealth. Scotland had a long tradition of satire which questioned religious and political authorities, with writers such as William Dunbar (?1456–?1513) and David Lyndsay (c.1486–1555).[14] During the early 1560s, Scotland saw a flood of Reformation satires which turned from the general criticism of court and church

[11] The Darnley-Bothwell-Mary triangle begins to sound similar to that of Old Hamlet-Claudius-Gertrude in Shakespeare's *Hamlet*. For background information on Mary, see: James Emerson Phillips, *Images of a Queen: Mary Stuart in Sixteenth-Century Literature* (Berkeley: University of California Press, 1964); Antonia Fraser, *Mary Queen of Scots* (London: Weidenfeld and Nicolson, 1969); Donald Gordonson, *Mary Queen of Scots* (London: English Universities Press, 1974); and Jenny Wormald, *Mary Queen of Scots: A Study in Failure* (London: George Philip, 1988).

[12] James's regents were: Lord James Stewart, Earl of Moray (1568–1570); James's grandfather Matthew Stewart, Earl of Lennox (1570–1571); John Earskine, Earl of Mar (1571–1572); and James, Earl of Morton (1572–1578).

[13] "Between the formal end of the regency of the earl of Morton in March 1578 and the overturn of the regime of the earl of Arran in September 1585 there were at least six such coups which were more or less successful and one which failed"; Maurice Lee, Jr., *Government by Pen: Scotland under James VI and I* (Urbana: University of Illinois Press, 1980), 4. There were attempts to kidnap James as late as 1600 (the Gowrie conspiracy).

[14] While critics differ on Lyndsay's position as a Reformation writer, the poet's works were amenable to the Reformers' cause; Edinburgh printer and bookseller Henry Charteris produced a collection of his works in 1568 — the year after James's accession — and the preface emphasises Lyndsay's connection to the Reformers: Charteris prayed that God would "rais and steir up mony David Lyndesayis, yat [that] will continuallie admonische baith Prince and pepill of thair dewtie and vocatioun"; *Sir David Lyndesay's Works*, ed. Jack Nichols, 2 vols. (Early English Text Society, 1871), 1: 4. For further discussion of Charteris's preface, see Gregory Kratzmann, "Sixteenth-Century Secular Poetry," in *The History of Scottish Literature*, Vol. 1, *Origins to 1660*, 105–24. For a survey of Lyndsay's life and works, and the courts of James IV and V, see Carol Edington, *Court and Culture in Renaissance Scotland: Sir David Lindsay of the Mount* (Amherst: University of Massachusetts Press, 1994).

of such early writers to specific and often vitriolic attacks on Mary.[15] An excerpt from a poem by Robert Sempill, the most prolific of the Reformation satirists, exemplifies their direct and condemnatory nature:

> Than sen that bowdin[swollen], bludy beist Bothwell
>   Hes trayterously in myrk[darkness] put downe our
>   King,
> His wyfe the Quene syne[thereupon] rauyssit[ravished]
>   to him sell,
>   In fylthie lust, throw cullour of wedding;
> Thocht sho, bewitcheit, wald in ruttery[lechery] ring,
>   The Nobillis sould nether of thir[them] enduire —
> That lowne[scoundrel] to leif, nor hir to be his huire.
>
> And gif[if] the poysone in hir hart be sonkin,
>   That sho will not consent he puneist be,
> Gif with his fylthie lust sho be sa dronkin
>   That sho forzet office and honestie,
> Than man[must] hir Nobillis of necessitie
>   Cut of hir force quhill[while] tresoun be reuengeit,
> And this confusioun in ane ordour changeit.
>   (Cranstoun, *Satirical Poems*, 1: VII 113–26)

For the good of the commonwealth, the poet claims that Mary's power must be wrested from her; as another of Sempill's poems points out, this could mean deposition: "Zea, thocht[though] it were ane King for to depose,/ For certaine crymis, I think the subiectis may/ . . . Rather than lat ane haill countrie decay."[16] Sempill unites the criticism of the monarch developed by Reformation religious and political thought, with the Scottish tradition of flyting alliteration and invective. The flyting was a genre of competition, used primarily for advancing rival claims to positions at court.[17] The Scottish Reformers appropriated this traditional form for

---

[15] The satires in James Cranstoun's two-volume collection are from the years 1565 to 1584; *Satirical Poems of the Time of the Reformation* (Edinburgh: Blackwood, 1891/93; New York: Scottish Text Society, 1974). The following poem by Sempill is from this collection.

[16] "Ane Declaratioun of the Lordis iust quarrell," in Cranstoun, *Satirical Poems*, 1: 155–56.

[17] The flyting genre, a Scottish genre itself influenced by Italian examples, was occasionally used in England also. John Skelton's four-part flyting against courtier Christopher Garnesche in August 1514 was written at the request of the king and is the first example of the flyting genre in English; Skelton drew on the Scottish "Flyting of Dunbar and

their own political purposes: competing poets became competing political and religious parties, and political ideas subversive of the monarch's authority were naturalized and nationalized through their incorporation into a traditional, Scottish poetic genre.

The publication of these Reformation satires as broadsides made them immediately available to a wide audience: they were "set up under Silence of Nycht in diverse publict Places" to be read and copied.[18] An Act of Parliament in 1567 — the year of James's accession — attempted to put a stop to such broadsides with threats of imprisonment; the satires were treated with the seriousness of an incitement to rebellion. As James acquired more of the government from his regents, he took further steps to lead Scotland away from such subversive poetic practices and oppositional political ideas. Through patronage, but also through his own poetic practice, the king developed a cultural policy to strengthen his position as king of Scotland.

Kingcraft and Poetry

The publication of *The Essayes of a Prentise* in 1584 was part of a larger movement by both James and Parliament to reestablish the authority of the monarch, and to identify the monarch once more with the Scottish nation. In 1584, Parliament passed two Acts: the first " 'perpetuallie confirmis the royall power and auctoritie over all statis alsweill spirituall as temporall'," and the second promised "the full rigour of the law against any who uttered calumnies 'to the dishonour hurt or preiudice of his hienes his parentis and progenitouris'."[19] The final publication date for any of the Reformation satires in Cranstoun's collection is also 1584,[20] which implies that such Acts — in the case of the Reformation satires at least — were successful. This was also the year that James recalled Bu-

---

Kennedy" which had been published in 1508. See Nan Cooke Carpenter, *John Skelton* (New York: Twayne, 1967). For more information on the flyting genre, see Priscilla Bawcutt, "The Art of Flyting," *Scottish Literary Journal* 10.2 (1979): 5–24.

[18] From an Act of Parliament of April 1567, which threatened punishment to the writer, printer and reader of these broadsides (in Cranstoun, *Satirical Poems*, 1: lvii–lviii).

[19] Quoted in Wormald, "James VI and I," 44n8.

[20] "Every poetical broadsheet of Scottish origin belonging to the Reformation period, known to exist . . . is included in this collection" (*Satirical Poems*, 1: x).

chanan's controversial *De Jure Regni* and *History*. It is not coincidental, then, that James's own publication appears in this specific year.

James had also recently escaped from ten months of house arrest after a successful coup known as the "Ruthven Raid": in August 1582, the Scottish Protestant lords kidnapped the king and banished James's French and Roman Catholic favourite, Esme Stuart, who died in France shortly thereafter. This corresponded with the disbanding of the court poets, the Castalian Band — at least one of whom was openly Catholic and had connections with Esme Stuart.[21] The Castalians regrouped shortly after James's escape in 1583, and also began publishing in 1584. The development of a court poetry, along with the king's own involvement in poetry and his publication of his *Essayes* at this time, are part of James's larger strategy of strengthening both the monarchy and his personal rule.

The poems in the *Essayes* are markedly different from those of the Reformation satires, and reveal James turning Scottish poets in a new direction which supported his authority. The general design of the collection and the variety of styles and subject matter, all contribute to a poetry which avoids the direct confrontational style of the Reformation broadsides. James's position as monarch also ensured a very different presentation and reception. Unlike the single sheet broadsides, "set up under Silence of Nycht," the king's collection is one hundred and twenty eight bound pages, printed by Huguenot refugee Thomas Vautroullier "Cvm Privilegio Regali."[22] The collection is an official, formal and commanding publication, itself an indication of the king's new independence and control at the beginning of his reign.

Near the end of the *Essayes* is "Ane Schort Treatise, conteining some revlis[rules] and cautelis[devices] to be obseruit and eschewit in Scottish Poesie," what Helena Mennie Shire calls "the manifesto of the new poet-

---

[21] Alexander Montgomerie was a distant relative of Lennox and a supporter of Mary. For information on this poet, see Helena Mennie Shire, "Alexander Montgomerie: The oppositione of the courte to conscience. 'Court and Conscience walis not weill'," *Studies in Scottish Literature* 3 (1966): 144–50 and *Song, Dance and Poetry of the Court of Scotland under King James VI*. See also a number of studies by R. D. S. Jack: "Montgomerie and the pirates," *Studies in Scottish Literature* 5.2 (1968): 133–36; "The Lyrics of Alexander Montgomerie," *Review of English Studies* 20 (1969): 168–81; "The Theme of Fortune in the Verse of Alexander Montgomerie," *Scottish Literary Journal* 10 (1983): 25–44; and *Alexander Montgomerie* (Edinburgh: Scottish Academic Press, 1985).

[22] James's *Essayes* are found in Craigie, *Poems of King James VI of Scotland*, 1: 1–96. Bibliographical information is found in 1: lxxi–lxxxii.

ry of Renaissance Scotland."[23] It is the first (and perhaps only) treatise on Scottish poetry ever written, and outlines the new styles and subject matter of his Renaissance. Some critics fault James for his limited description of poetry, and much of the "Treatise" accumulates material also discussed in Ronsard, du Bellay, Ascham, and perhaps Puttenham, Gascoigne and Buchanan.[24] While some see the derivative nature of the "Treatise" negatively, as a comment on the king's lack of originality, the incorporation of such material shows James's determination to draw Scottish poetry into the mainstream of European poetry and civility.

The "Treatise" consists of an introductory quatrain, a preface to the reader, two sonnets, and eight short chapters outlining the proper use of a variety of stanza forms, rhythms, rhymes, and tropes, depending on the occasion. James's purpose, however, goes beyond aesthetics. Like George Puttenham, he uses a book on poetics as a political vehicle, but where Puttenham describes politics from the position of a courtier, James writes form the position of a monarch. James's poetic rules are a means to mould not only the poetry, but the poets themselves, into law-abiding, civilized subjects. The "Preface to the Reader" explains why James feels the need for a treatise on Scottish poetry. He gives "tua caussis": the first states that "lyke as the tyme is changeit [], sa is the ordour of Poesie changeit" (1: 67). Earlier, the Reformers had presented their satires as part of the natural progression of national poetic practices by using the vernacular, the familiar genres of satire and flyting, and the wide-reaching format of the broadside. James now proffers his own Renaissance as the culmination of Scottish poetry: "quhait[what] I speik of Poesie now, I speik of it, as being come to mannis age and perfectioun, quhair[where] as then, it was bot in the infancie and chyldheid" (1: 67). James connects himself to Scotland through his participation in, and perfection of, the country's developing literature; the nation and the king reach "mannis age" together.

James's second reason for writing the "Treatise" further connects the monarch to the nation: James states that "there hes neuer ane of thame written in our language" (1: 67). Here he expresses a certain pride in the

---

[23] Helena Mennie Shire, *Song, Dance and Poetry of the Court of Scotland under King James VI*, 98.

[24] For some examinations of James's "Treatise" and his use of other treatises, see Craigie, *Poems of King James VI of Scotland*, 1: xxviii–lxiv and notes on pages 306–14. See also R. D. S. Jack, "James VI and Renaissance Poetic Theory," in *English* 16 (1967): 208–11; and "Poetry under King James VI," in *The History of Scottish Literature*. Vol. 1. *Origins to 1660*, 125–27.

Scottish vernacular, and further differentiates himself from his mother Mary, who also used poetry for significant political ends, but whose poetic language was French. This national pride appears in the king's political treatise, *Basilikon Doron,* in an interestingly anti-humanist section on writing: James advises Henry "to write in your owne language: for there is nothing left to be saide in Greeke and Latine alreadie . . . and besides that, it best becommeth a King to purifie and make famous his owne tongue" (48). In the "Treatise," James notes that English "is lykest to our language," but states that "we differ from thame in sindrie [separate] reulis of Poesie, as ze will find be experience" (1: 67).[25] James wishes not only to legitimize the use of the vernacular, but also to connect himself as king with the nation through the nation's language. Also, by both joining the Scottish vernacular to and separating it from the English, James attempts to balance a movement to union with a movement to sovereignty — a balancing act which continued even into his reign in England.

James wished to change the form of Scottish poetry from the narrative, ballad-like structure of the Reformation satires to a variety of complex stanza forms, rhymes and metres used in European poetry. The "Treatise" outlines the general move to more imaginative, fictional topics dressed in "speciall ornamentis to verse" (Chapter IIII; 1: 77), very different from the Reformation poets' "factual" lists of people, places and problems, with their emphasis on content over style.[26] In Chapter VIII, James provides a list of verse forms for various topics, drawn from continental and English authors, though the examples used to illustrate the forms are from Scottish authors (often himself and Alexander Montgomerie). Scots and the Scottish vernacular, he shows, are equally capable of competing with European and English poetry.

---

[25] For example, Jack notes that between 1580 and 1630, over seven hundred Scottish sonnets were composed, and he marks the distinction between the English and Scottish use of this form. The four main differences are: shorter sonnet sequences (often four or five sonnets); a broader thematic range; preference for French rather than Italian sources; and an ababbcbccdcdee rhyme scheme (later used by Spenser). "Poetry," 127.

[26] Gregory Kratzmann sees the Reformers unadorned statements of political belief as embodying a Calvinist aesthetic, which permits writers "to articulate moral lessons without pretence at entertainment or adornment" ("Sixteenth-Century Secular Poetry," in *The History of Scottish Literature,* 111). Cranstoun goes so far as to say that there is "an almost total absence of poetic feeling" (*Satirical Poems,* 1: xi) in these satires. The Reformation satires themselves valued political over literary merit: one poet asked the Lords "To mark the sentence rather nor the style" (*Satirical Poems,* 1: VI, line 14). However, the direct, unencumbered style — the aesthetics of plainness — was part of the political nature of the satires.

James also hoped to change the nature of political poetry. As the king states in the "Preface," quoted above, "lyke as the tyme is changeit . . . sa is the ordour of Poesie changeit" (1: 67); one change is the "Treatise'"s insistence on decorum, and the hierarchy implied therein is one means by which the king's authority is to be reinforced. Chapters III and IIII provide a standard explanation of decorum: the poet's choice and ordering of words, and of comparisons and epithets, should be "proper for the subiect" (1: 77). High and grave matters demand "heich, pithie, and learnit wordis" (1: 76); invective and derogatory terms, like those found in the Reformation satires (for example the one previously quoted), are not suitable for descriptions of the heads of nations.[27] The poetical flourish of such a basic rhetorical strategy as decorum becomes one means of establishing the hierarchy of monarch and subject.

Not only rhetorical decisions, but choices of topic indicate the subjects' obedience. Chapter VII of the "Treatise" ostensibly deals with invention, but James includes a warning to those poets who might, like their Reformation counterparts, wish to write about politics.

Ze man also be war of wryting any thing of materis of commoun weill, or vther sic[such] graue [] subiectis (except Metaphorically, of manifest treuth opinly knawin, zit[yet] nochtwithstanding vsing it very seindil[seldom]) because nocht onely ze essay nocht zour awin[own] Inuentioun, as I spak before, bot lykewayis they are to graue materis for a Poet to mell in. (1: 79)

Here James objects to historical or political topics because they are not imaginative or fictional enough. As well, his insistence on the gravity of matters of the commonwealth — and that poets should not "mell" or meddle in such matters — implies that politics is not the natural or proper realm of the poet.[28]

James's concern with the subversive potential of poetry comes directly from the Scottish context of Reformation satires, but also corresponds with contemporary discussions of specific poetic genres, notably the pastoral.

---

[27] The satirists might argue that there was no breach of decorum, since the monarchs themselves had become base.

[28] Alexander Montgomerie, the chief poet of the Castalian Band, appears to refer to this section of James's "Treatise" in a poem written to fellow Castalian Robert Hudson. "With mightie maters mynd I not to mell, / As copping courts, or comonwelthis, or kings . . ."; *The Poems of Alexander Montgomerie*, ed. James Cranstoun (Edinburgh, 1887), XXVI, lines 1–2. Ironically, this poem was written after Montgomerie had lost James's favor, perhaps because of his political/religious connections.

Puttenham, in his *The Arte of English Poesie* (1589), claims that the eclogue was devised "not of purpose to counterfait or represent the rusticall manner of loues and communication: but vnder the vaile of homely persons, and in rude speeches to insinuate and glaunce at greater matters" (Book I, Chapter XVIII).[29] Sir Philip Sidney's *An Apology for Poetry* (1586) reiterates this idea: "sometimes, under the pretty tales of wolves and sheep, [the poet] can include the whole considerations of wrongdoing and patience."[30] Interestingly, at the same time James warns against meddling with matters of the commonwealth, he appears to sanction the "metaphorical" or figurative discussion of politics, as long as it is clear what is being discussed.[31]

Annabel Patterson's phrase "functional ambiguity" — an indeterminacy of language acknowledged by both writer and reader — is clearly applicable to James's statement; the king is not concerned with simply censoring poetical-political material, but wishes to avoid direct confrontation by using encodings known to all readers.[32] While figurative language did separate the new Renaissance poetry from the direct criticism of the Reformation satires, it also opened poems and poets to possible misunderstandings. Keys were not always "opinly knawin," and audiences separated from original intentions and contexts could easily miss the point. The majority

---

[29] Quoted from the edition by Gladys Doidge Willcock and Alice Walker (Cambridge: Cambridge University Press, 1936), 38. I have regulated the long s in my quotation.

[30] *An Apology for Poetry*, ed. Geoffrey Shepherd (London: Thomas Nelson, 1965), 116. Annabel Patterson discusses Sidney's representation of this idea in his *Arcadia*; *Censorship and Interpretation: The Conditions of Writing and Reading in Early Modern England* (Madison: University of Wisconsin Press, 1984), 24–43.

Henry Wotton's statement on architecture in 1624 complements this theory of poetic influence; Wotton claims that architecture "had also a secret and strong Influence, even into the advancement of the Monarchie, by continuall representation of vertuous examples; so as in the point the ART became a piece of State" (quoted in Goldberg, *Politics*, 34).

[31] Jonathan Goldberg notes that while this section limits the poet, the parenthetical addition "reinvest[s] him with power anew. James returns to the poet the power of language that allows him to go beyond mere representation"; *James I and the Politics of Literature*, 19–20. Goldberg further comments that James's own verse is non-political and stylistically limited. However, any verse written by a king is potentially political, and in his rendering of the psalms alone James used twenty-eight stanza forms (Craigie, *Satirical Poems*, 2: xx). This first collection under discussion is itself highly diverse and political.

[32] "[T]he indeterminacy inveterate to language was fully and knowingly exploited by authors and readers alike . . . authors who build ambiguity into their works have no control over what happens to them later"; Patterson, *Censorship and Interpretation*, 18.

of the "Treatise" is thus spent outlining different poetic codes and their purposes.

James's poems themselves provide examples of how to approach grave political matters metaphorically — to avoid and to engage politics simultaneously — and of the kinds of topics suitable for his court poets.[33] The *Essayes* opens with twelve sonnets, iconic representations of gods and detailed descriptions of the poetical landscapes they influence. The sonnet form and the classical content of these poems draw the vernacular into the European poetical mainstream, and are part of James's desire to improve his own and Scotland's standing in European circles. While these sonnets are unrelated to topical Scottish politics, and are a clear if somewhat sterile example of James focusing on non-topical issues, they are nonetheless political in their very omission of topical politics. Thus, at the beginning of his collection, James shows how to avoid the Reformers' brand of oppositional politics with its emphasis on civil turmoil, and how to embrace a more benign political poetry, which reveals Scotland as a peaceable, European nation.

These introductory sonnets are most interesting in that they contain James's belief in the ability of language to represent the writer's thoughts transparently. As he states in *Basilikon Doron*, "your writes will remaine as true pictures of your minde" (47), and in these sonnets James hopes his intent, shaped by the poems, will be directly and clearly transmitted to the reader. The fourth sonnet will suffice as an example:

> And graunt I may so viuely put in verse
> The Sommer, when I lyke theirof to treat:
> As when in writ I do theirof reherse,
> Let Readers think they fele the burning heat,
> And graithly see the earth, for lacke of weit[wet],
> With withering drouth and Sunne so gaigged[cracked] all,
> As for the grasse on feild, the dust in steit
> Doth ryse and flee aloft, long or it fall.

---

[33] J. Derrick McClure considers James's poems "as poems and not as outcomes of events in his personal history or evidence regarding his thought or character"; " 'O Phoenix Escossois': James VI as Poet," 98. While McClure comments insightfully on James's use of rhetorical techniques, his avoidance of historical and biographical contexts is limiting. James's *Lepanto* (published 1591), for example, becomes simply "a thoroughly good and enjoyable poem" (106). Compare Emery Jones, who dismisses the aesthetics of poetry to focus on *Lepanto*'s historical content: "The poem is hardly of much interest in its own right"; " 'Othello', 'Lepanto' and the Cyprus Wars," 47.

> Yea, let them think, they heare the song and call,
> Which Floras wingde musicians maks to sound.
> And that to taste, and smell, beleue they shall
> Delicious fruictis, whilks in that tyme abound.
> And shortly, all their senses so bereaued,
> As eyes and earis, and all may be deceaued.
>   (Craigie 1: 10)

Like the other eleven sonnets, this poem insists on the mimetic ability of language. The persuasive power of poetry is also evident; poetry works on the senses of the readers to shape their perception of the world.[34] James claims a powerful political potential for poetry: poetic language provides the king with the peaceable and almost magical, mystical means to enter the readers' consciousness — to "bereaue" and "deceaue" their senses — and so to shape readers into obedient subjects. The poem's subject matter combines with the aesthetic capabilities of verse to create a persuasive political rhetoric.

The opening sonnets in the *Essayes* are followed by a translation of Salust Du Bartas's *L'Uranie*, just one of the translations James made of Du Bartas's poems.[35] "The Vranie" outlines why and how poets should separate sacred from secular affairs. The poet's role is not to write the "praise vntrewe of Kings" (l. 22), but to forego writing about the court at all and concentrate on general spiritual matters. Unlike the Reformers, for whom the spiritual is highly political, James attempts to posit a distinction between the two. As James states: "Platos common wealth did pack / None of these Poets . . . / Whose pleasaunt words betraied the publick corse" (1: 27, ll. 161-62, 164), and for the king, the use of the spiritual estate to question his authority makes the Reformation satirists betrayers of the commonwealth. It is the writer of holy verses that avoid political hostility who will reap the rewards of patronage: "Echone your verse for oracles wolde take, / And great men of their counsell wolde you make" (183-84).[36] The king's role as patron, along with his own poetic examples,

---

[34] The reader is mentioned in all but the last sonnet: "Let readers think" sings like a refrain throughout.

[35] James also translated *The Furies* (1591) and parts of the second day of "La Premiere Sepmaine" and "Eden." James encouraged other members of his court to translate the French poet and commissioned poet and musician Thomas Hudson's version of *Judith* (1584).

[36] It is interesting to note James's translation, which here slightly but significantly alters the original. For line 184 just cited, the hopeful Du Bartas wrote: "Et les grands

would help to direct other Scottish poets to more profitable and less politically troublesome subject matter, especially in the spiritual realm.[37]

While the move towards more general spiritual topics draws poets from more topical political issues, James's choice of Du Bartas clearly has a politics of its own. The translation of French authors was frequently practised in Scotland, and so the king keeps his Renaissance within a traditional cultural framework; however, James promotes "the diuine and Illuster Poete" (1: 16) over those whose political views are antagonistic to the monarchy. For example, Pierre Ronsard, favored by the court's chief poet Alexander Montgomerie, questioned Henry II's claim to divine right, and sympathized with Mary, Queen of Scots.[38] Importantly, Du Bartas supported a strong centralized authority, as James states in *The Trew Law of Free Monarchies*: "... as the diuine Poet DV BARTAS sayth, Better it were to suffer some disorder in the estate, and some spots in the Commonwealth, then in pretending to reforme, vtterly [to] ouerthrow the Republicke" (66–67). Translation is a means to incorporate Du Bartas's belief in the monarchy into the Scottish language and culture. Politics, then, is behind James's preference for Du Bartas, and for the spiritual rather than the amorous or satiric poetry of France.

"The Vranie" is also interesting for its presentation of the power of poetry and of the relationship of author to reader. Poetry so works on the senses and emotions, that the author's words can shape the mind of the reader:

> For as into the wax the seals imprent
> Is lyke a seale, right so the Poet gent[raised aloft? gently?],
> Doeth graue so viue in vs his passions strange,
> As maks the reader, halfe in author change.
> For verses force is sic, that softly slydes
> Throw secret poris, and in our sences bydes. ...
>   (1: 27, ll. 153–58)

---

commettroient en vos main leurs affaires" (1: 28); the wary James does not give quite this much control to his poets.

[37] For an account of English poets' movement to spiritual verse around 1603 — inspired by James's interest in spiritual poetry — see James Doelman, "The Accession of King James I and English Religious Poetry," *Studies in English Literature* 34.1 (1994): 19–40.

[38] Ronsard had been a page in the train of Madelene, wife of King James V, and had visited Scotland twice. He was also Mary's poetic tutor in her minority in France. See Jack, *Alexander Montgomerie*, 4.

Poetry has such persuasive power that the reader's understanding begins to correspond to the author's, or in this case, the subject's understanding begins to correspond to the king's. The "Uranie," like the introductory twelve sonnets, emphasises the ability of poetry to "imprent" the author's desire onto the passive, receptive reader. The belief in such unique power — power that works on the minute level of "secret poris" and senses — helps to explain why James needs to prescribe (or proscribe) specific topics, and why he chooses to use the medium of poetry in the first place.

Despite the apparent passivity of the readers in the above section, they have an essential role in creating meaning, as James also notes in the opening sonnets; it is perhaps for this reason that James continually appends letters and prefaces to limit his audience to "beloved" readers.[39] The monarch's position as poet works in two opposite but complementary ways; on the one hand he can persuade and shape his readers into "docile" subjects, but on the other hand, he is reliant on these subjects' "correct" interpretation of the metaphorical keys to poetry, of monarchical desire. The relationship between author and reader thus affects the relationship between king and subject; the difficulty of interpretation and, as Richard Helgerson points out, print itself, can problematize the monarch's use of the poetic medium as a tool of social control.[40] James therefore needs to be as careful as possible to limit difficulties in interpretation and audience with his choice of subject matter, its presentation and its reception.

James's "Paraphrasticall Translation Ovt of the Poete Lvcan," like his translation of Du Bartas, has a clear political agenda. In his *Pharsalia*, Lucan supports the republic over the monarchical tyranny of Caesar, and

---

[39] For example, see the introductory quatrain to the "Treatise" (1: 66):

> To ignorants obdurde, quhair vvilfull errour lyis,
> Nor zit to curious folks, quhilks carping dois deiect thee,
> Nor zit to learned men, quha thinks thame onelie vvyis,
> But to the docile bairns of knavvledge I direct thee.

[40] Helgerson notes that one's image in print is "liable to hostile interpretation and even rejection," and that while it gives the writer-king authority, it also empowers the reader-subject: "print fixes the author and frees the reader"; "Milton Reads the King's Book: Print, Performance, and the Making of a Bourgeois Idol," *Criticism* 29.1 (winter 1987): 6. See also David Scott Kastan's "Proud Majesty Made a Subject: Shakespeare and the Spectacle of Rule," *Shakespeare Quarterly* 37.4 (1986): 462: "Representation thus undermines rather than confirms authority, denying it its presumptive dignity by subjecting it to common view." Kastan focusses on drama and spectacle, but his comments are equally applicable to written text.

would thus appear to be antithetical to James's interests.[41] However, by omitting Lucan's criticism and satire of absolute monarchies, and by isolating and expanding a small speech in which Caesar addressed his troops on the occasion of a mutiny and emphasized the power of the prince, James *redefines* Lucan.[42] In James's "paraphrastical translation," the poem is introduced with six lines from Lucan, and is followed by five stanzas that expand Lucan's primary metaphor on the nature of the relationship of the ocean and the rivers. James's fourth stanza makes clear the parallel relationship of the king and the subject. The first and fourth of James's stanzas will suffice to illustrate the main comparison:

> If all the floods amongst them wold conclude
> To stay their course from running in the see:
> And by that means wold thinke for to delude
> The *Ocean*, who sould impaired be,
> As they supposde, beleuing if that he
> Did lack their floods, he should decresse him sell:
> Yet if we like the veritie to wye,
> It pairs him nothing: as I shall you tell.
> . . . . . .
> So euen siclike: Though subiects do coniure
> For to rebell against their Prince and King:
> By leauing him although they hope to smure[suffocate]
> That grace, wherewith God maks him for to ring.
> Though by his gifts he shaw him selfe bening[benign],
> To help their need, and make them thereby gaine:
> Yet lacke of them no harme to him doth bring,
> VVhen they to rewe their folie shalbe faine. (1: 62–63)

Subjects are to the king as rivers are to the ocean; they can neither give to nor take away from the source. The relationship, as James describes it in *The Trew Law*, is not a contractual one; "the power flowes alwaies from him selfe [the king]," while the people "are alwaies subiect vnto him, and

---

[41] David Quint states that Lucan's *Pharsalia* is the epic of a defeated people "whose resistance contains the germ of a broader republican or anti-monarchial politics; *Epic and Empire: Politics and Generic Form from Virgil to Milton* (Princeton: Princeton University Press, 1993), 8.

[42] James is hailed as Caesar in a number of the dedicatory sonnets to this collection and to *His Maiesties Poeticall Exercises at vacant houres* (1591). The section of Lucan James uses heads the king's paraphrase, and is from *Pharsalia* v, 335–40.

naked of all authoritie on their part" (McIlwain 63, 69).[43] The king does
not need his subjects, but gives to them because he is "bening." James reworks the politics of this verse translation through his choice of passage,
and as he advises in his "Schort Treatise," the meaning of the extended
nature metaphor is made "opinly knawin" by an allegorical key. James redefines and rewrites Lucan to produce monarch-centered verse, and thus
again moves Scottish verse away from the oppositional poetry of the Reformation satires.[44]

In "Ane Metaphorical Invention of a Tragedie Called Phoenix,"
"metaphorical" again appears to mean allegorical. Two introductory verses
— the same verse in two different shapes — help to explain the key to the
poem's encoded subject, although Craigie claims that no one connected it
to the Duke fo Lennox until 1859 (1: 304n5). It is difficult to see how anyone could misread the author's intent, however; the first introductory
poem, in the shape of a diamond column or urn,[45] is reformed in the
second poem into an acrostic whose first and last letters spell "Esme
Stewart Dw[v]ike."

E   If Echo help, that both together w   E
(S   ince cause there be) may now lament with teari   S
M   y murnefull yearis. Ye furies als with hi   M
E   uen Pluto grim, who dwels in dark, that h   E
S   ince cheif we se him to you all that beari   S
T   he style men fearis of Dirae: I reques   T
E   che greizlie ghest, that dwells beneth the S   E
W ith all yon three, whose hairis ar snaiks full ble   W

---

[43] James redefines the basis of the contractual relationship of king and subject so that
it loses its contractuality; the inferior party cannot break that contract. See Wormald,
"Context and Translation," 45.

[44] And the Castalian poets appeared ready to follow James's example. The dedicatory
sonnet of Alexander Montgomerie to this collection repeats James's ocean metaphor:
"Can Fountainis small the Ocean sea incresse? / No, they augment the greater nocht a
quheit[whit]: / Bot they them selues appears to grow the lesse" (1: 5, ll. 10–12).

[45] The poem is introduced as "A Columne of 18 lynes seruing for a Preface to the
Tragedie ensuying." The first line is of one syllable, the second two, and so increases to
twelve syllables, when the lines begin to decrease to one syllable again; the last four lines
— the base of the column — are of three, five, seven, and nine syllables. In the acrostic
poem, there is a complex internal rhyme instead of end rhyme; the final word of each
line rhymes with a word in the middle of the following line.

A nd all you crew, assist me in thir tw   A
R epeit and sha my Tragedie full nei   R
T he chance fell heir. Then secoundlie is bes   T
D euils void of rest, ye moue all that it rei   D
W ith me, indeid, lyke dolour thame to gri   V
I then will liv', in lesser greif therebi   I
K ythe[appear] heir and trie, your force ay bent and quic K
E xcell in sik lyke ill, and murne with m   E
    From Delphos syne Apollo cum with speid,
    Whose shining light my cairs wil dim in deid. (1: 44)

As in the introductory sonnets to the whole collection, this verse calls on the gods to assist the poet in moving his audience to sympathy, in this case, to persuade his subjects to sympathize with the king's interpretation of a recent political event: the expulsion of James's distant relative and favorite, the French Catholic Esme Stewart, Duke of Lennox, by the Protestant lords in the Ruthven Raid of 1582.[46]

The poem itself is an allegory of warring birds, an idea the king borrows from David Lyndsay, who "did complaine of old / His *Papyngo*, her death and sudden end" (ll. 24-25); the female phoenix apparently represents Esme, and birds of prey the Ruthven lords. The following two stanzas record the Ruthven's growing suspicion of Lennox, and Lennox's connection to James:

    Thir were the rauening fowls, whome of I spak
    Before, the whilks[which] (as I already shew)
    Was wount into her presence to hald bak
    Their crueltie, from simple ones, that flew
    With her, ay whill Inuy all feare withdrew.
    Thir ware, the Rauen, the Stainchell, and the Gled,
    With other kynds, whome in this malice bred.
    . . . . . .
    When she could find none other saue refuge
    From these their bitter straiks, she fled at last
    To me (as if she wolde wishe me to iudge
    The wrong they did her) yet they followed fast
    Till she betuix my leggs her selfe did cast.

---

[46] At line 262, James notes the bird's name "doeth end in X"; this could refer to both "phoenix" and "Lennox."

> For sauing her from these, which her opprest,
> Whose hote pursute, her suffred not to rest.
>   (141–47, 162–68)[47]

Not even the king could change the historical events, however, and the phoenix, like Esme, is driven from the land to die on foreign shores. But the use of the mythical bird does allow James to recapture the victory from the Ruthvens; Esme was reborn in the figure of his son — "this worme of Phoenix ashe" (272) — Ludovick Stewart, whom James invited to Scotland late in 1583.[48] The poetic trope of the phoenix restored control to the king; the monarch, like the phoenix, would be continually reborn.

James's successful (perhaps too successful) encoding of this recent and volatile political event raises doubts as to the benefits of metaphorical or allegorical poetry which James advocated — perhaps in reference to this poem — in his poetical treatise. The "Phoenix" avoids the direct mention of political topics, which made the Reformation satires so subversive, but such an allegory also makes it difficult for James to convey to the reader his intentions.[49] While a short excerpt of the "Phoenix" is included in Robert Allot's compilation *England's Parnassus* (1600) in the section entitled "Poetical Comparison," there is no indication of what that comparison might be.[50] The lack of contemporary critical comment could indicate that the king was now able to state his preferences for favorites and councillors without reprisal (though the need for "indirect" figurative language might question this); it could also indicate that James's poem raised either little concern, or little interest, or that — despite the two introductory verses to the poem — the "metaphorical invention" was not understood. In the end, the subject's inability or unwillingness to understand or react to James's poem emphasized that despite the king's skill or intent, the interpretive power lay always in the hands of his subjects.

---

[47] Craigie claims that the three birds named "probably stand for the Earls of Angus, Gowrie and Mar" (*Poems of King James VI of Scotland*, 1: 306n).

[48] Ludovick "was at one received into favour and proved to be one of James's most loyal and devoted servants among the Scottish nobility" (Craigie, *Poems of King James VI of Scotland*, 1: 304n).

[49] Craigie notes that this has been read as a poem about James's mother, Mary, and about kingship, although these interpretations are from criticisms of 1802 and 1933 respectively (*Poems of King James VI of Scotland*, 1: 304n).

[50] Craigie, *Poems of King James VI of Scotland*, 1: 281, Appendix B.

Conclusion

James's *Essayes* appeared at a time when the king was making a concerted effort to separate himself from the turmoil of his mother's reign, to end concern over the state of the monarchy in Scotland, and to establish his own personal government. James's involvement in poetry — both his own writing and his patronage of the Castalian Band — forestalled the flood of critical Reformation satires, and created a court poetry that supported rather than questioned the monarchy. Through his use of the Scottish vernacular and Scottish poetic traditions, James attempted to collapse the growing difference between monarch and nation; he incorporated himself as poet and king into the country's changing cultural consciousness, and established the monarch as an essential element in the development of Scotland as a civilized and sovereign nation.

James's use of the poetic medium was not, however, without its difficulties. Publication — print — allowed the king to retain a sense of separateness and mystery, but it also opened James to scrutiny and criticism; the king as poet was available to anyone who could read. A substantial and official publication such as the *Essayes* might have evoked more respect than the sub-literary genres of hastily printed broadsides, but it also narrowed the king's audience considerably; the king's collection waas not meant for the masses, but for the literate court members who had the power to influence the common people. And James's preference for figurative language, while it sanctioned the writing of non-controversial political verse, could not close down the oppositional voices of poets and readers who employed and interpreted such "metaphorical" verse. Finally, James's role as poet also complicated his position as king; the poet's reliance on the understanding and acceptance of the "beloved" reader foregrounded that the authority of the monarch was equally dependent on the agreement and willingness of his subjects. No matter what the claims of James's translation of Lucan, or the king's later *Trew Law of Free Monarchies*, the relationship of monarch and subject was, in the end, a contractual one.

Despite all of the possible limitations and difficulties of the written text, James recognised the need for representation, and that self-representation provided more control than circumscribing other poets with "revlis and cautelis to be obseruit and eschewit." James continued to write poetry in his Scottish reign, publishing a second collection in 1591, *His Maiesties Poeticall Exercises at vacant houres*. This collection comprised two poems: a translation of Du Bartas' *Furies*, and James's own heroic *Lepanto*, a poem outlining the victory of the Catholic league against the Turks in the naval war of 1571. This latter poem was one of James's most popular, and in addition to a French translation by Du Bartas, there were translations into Latin, Dutch and German; the poem was also republished in London in 1603.[51]

Like *Basilikon Doron*, *Lepanto* introduced James to his English subjects in 1603, who responded with nothing (it seems) but praise for James's poetic skill:

> Is any penne so rich in poetrie,
> As to pourtray thy matchlesse Maiestie?
> Can mortall wight conceit thy worthines,
> Which fills the world's capacious hollowness?
> Lo then the man which the *Lepanto* writ;
> Or he, or els on earth is no man fitt.
>   (Craigie 1: 276, Appendix A, m)

If *Lepanto*'s content — the poem praised a Catholic general — caused any concern for its English audience, it was not recorded. The very act of writing poetry was — at the promising beginning of James's English reign — more important than the poetry that was written. However, as the title and the preface to this second collection indicate, the increasing pressure of governmental affairs left only "vacant houres" for James to write: "Yea, scarslie but at stollen moments, haue I the leasure to blenk upon any paper ...,"[52] and by the time James became king of England, his poetry-writing days were essentially over.

James entwined his role as poet with his role as king through his cultural policy in Scotland, and it is as a poet-king that he entered his English reign. As Ben Jonson wrote in an epigram to James, "How, best of Kings, do'st thou a scepter beare!/ How, best of Poets, do'st thou laurell weare!"[53] For many of his Scottish and English subjects, the two callings

---

[51] For an extended discussion of *Lepanto*, see Robert Appelbaum's chapter in this collection. My "Writing the Monarch: King James VI and *Lepanto*" also examines this poem and its reception at length. James also wrote a third collection of poetry that was not published, although the poems — many of which are dedicated to individuals — most certainly circulated in manuscript.

[52] This prefatory letter to the reader also states: "my burden is so great and continuall, without anie intermission, that when my ingyne and age could, my affaires and fasherie will not permit mee, to re-mark the wrong orthography committed by the copiars of my vnlegible and ragged hand ..." (Craigie, *Poems of King James VI of Scotland*, 1: 98).

[53] Quoted in Craigie, *Poems of King James VI of Scotland*, 1: 278. This is one of 27 commendatory contemporary comments on James's verse included in Appendix A.

of king and poet together defined James. In England, his increasing role as patron rather than poet may have obviated the stigmas attached to the writing and publication of verse, but no longer would the king have such direct control over the production of his own representations as he did at the beginning of his reign in Scotland.

University of New Brunswick

ROBERT APPELBAUM

War and Peace
in *The Lepanto*[1]

WAR AND PEACE. The topos antedates Tolstoy's novel by over 2000 years, and one of its common uses, as in Tolstoy too on occasion, is the way in which, as terms of rhetoric and representation, war and peace interpenetrate, or even become one another.

> [M]uch remains
> To conquer still; peace hath her victories
> No less renownd than warr,

writes Milton in a sonnet "To Lord General Cromwell," capitalizing on one of the many traditional variations on the theme: peace can be a lot like war in that, although it is the opposite of war, it may demand militant vigilance, and may even have its own "victories."[2] Imaginative and historical literatures perhaps incline to tell tales of war because, even if peace is sometimes militant, wars give the teller more to tell. But it is not much of a stretch to suppose that many tales of war, going back to the first epics, are in fact tales about peace: tales about where peace comes from, how it operates, and what it ultimately means. Such in any case is the state of affairs, I'd like to propose, concerning one of James VI and I's most significant accomplishments as a poet, his *The Lepanto*, first pub-

---

[1] This essay first appeared in *Modern Philology* 97.3 (2000): 333–63, and it is reprinted with the kind permission of the editors.

[2] *The Riverside Milton*, ed. Roy Flannagan (Boston: Houghton Mifflin, 1998), 291.

lished in 1591 and probably written in 1585.[3] But if *The Lepanto* is a tale about peace, it tells its story in a complicated way, including as it does not only the representation of what appeared to be a glorious military victory but also an implicit argument about the justice of just wars. It even participates in a European-wide effort to depict the Battle of Lepanto as a glorious victory, in spite of evidence to the effect that the battle was neither unambiguously heroic nor unambiguously triumphant. (In fact, although the allied Christian forces certainly won a battle over the Ottoman armada in 1571, virtually wiping out the enemy fleet, they were very possibly on their way that day toward losing a century-long war.) Moreover, the great hero of the battle and of James's poem, Don Juan of Austria, continued after Lepanto to make a name for himself in military expeditions where not the hated Turk but thousands of Christians were defeated and killed. So James's situation as a poet in this case, again, was highly complicated. My intention here, however, isn't so much to resolve the complexities entailed in James's poem as to underscore them, and to raise questions about what it might mean for someone like James — who was among other things, a man of peace — to write a heroic poem about someone else's victory (apparent or real) in someone else's war. Along the way I intend to raise questions about what it might have meant for a monarch to be writing heroic verse in the first place, doing so after the fashion not of great kings but of great poets writing in the service of great kings. And I also want to consider the problem of what it may have meant in general for any poet of the Renaissance to have turned a single day's fighting — for the Battle of Lepanto lasted no more than a day — into an exemplary story of quasi-epic proportions. But I am mainly concerned with the meaning of war and peace in *The Lepanto*, and how (and why) James uses one to serve as an example of (or for) the other.

A large part of what is at issue here is what may be called James's "self-professions." There were many such self-professions over the course of James's career, and they weren't always innocent of controversy. Styling himself "King of Great Britain," for example, at a time when the ruling elite in England had little desire to see England absorbed into a larger political entity — that was a "self-profession" concerning what was indeed

---

[3] James Craigie, Introduction, *The Poems of James VI of Scotland*, 2 vols., ed. James Craigie (Edinburgh: Blackwood, 1955–58), 1: xlviii and passim. For an assessment of James's accomplishments as a poet see both Craigie's introductory remarks in both volumes and G. P. V. Akrigg, "The Literary Achievement of King James I," *University of Toronto Quarterly* 44 (1975): 115–29.

called the "style," the official designation of the man, which caused a
great deal of unrest among a politically powerful segment of the popula-
tion, and provoked some of James's most long-abiding opposition in Parliament.[4] But at least two self-professions held up over time, thanks in large
part to the machinery of state mythology that James obdurately supported.
One was that James was a Solomon among kings, a ruler of superlative
learning, wisdom, and justice. The second, related self-profession was
James's identity as a peacemaker. "The first ... of the blessings, which
God hath joyntly with my Person sent unto you," James told Parliament
in his inaugural address of 1604, "is outward Peace: that is, peace abroad
with all forreine neighbours: for I thank God I may justly say, that never
since I was a king, I either received wrong of any other Christian Prince
of State, or did wrong to any: I have ever, I praise God, yet kept Peace
and amitie with all. ..."[5] Moreover, the "second great blessing," as he
went on to say, was "peace within," peace that is between Scotland and
England, now united in his person and rule after centuries of division, and
even between the English houses of Lancaster and York, both of which
were peacefully united in his own blood as they had been in the Tudor
monarchs before him.[6]

Beati pacifici, blessed are the peacemakers, had been adapted by James
as his motto — another form of "self-profession" — soon upon arriving in
England; and James frequently saw to it that the iconography of Peace
should be associated with his reign, whether in ceremonies like court
masques or in printed matter, such as the frontispieces to the books published under his name. This particular self-profession wasn't adopted without some ambivalence, to be sure. "I know not," James wrote, "by what
fortune the dicton of *Pacificus* was added to my title at my coming to England, that of the lion, expressing true fortitude, having been my dicton
before."[7] There was something suspiciously unmanly or cowardly about
being called a peacemaker from which James wanted to deflect attention.
It was better to be known as a lion, a man of fortitude. Lingering long
into the seventeenth century, as James himself well knew, were the tradi-

---

[4] Bruce Galloway, *The Union of England and Scotland 1603–1608* (Edinburgh: John
Donald, 1986).

[5] James VI and I, *Political Writings*, ed. Johann P. Sommerville (Cambridge: Cambridge University Press, 1984), 133.

[6] *Political Writings*, 136.

[7] Quoted in Harris D. Willson, *King James VI and I* (New York: Henry Holt, 1956),
272.

tional timocratic, masculinist values of aristocratic warrior culture, as well as the metaphorically belligerent values of Christian militancy, both of which, whether alone or in combination, would often enough explode into genuine belligerence between individuals, factions, and nations.[8] And as James let the public know by the publication of his *Basilicon Doron*, he did not intend his taste for non-aggression to mean that he would never be aggressive in the interest of his nation: "a honourable and just warre," he wrote, "is more tollerable, then a dishonouable and disadvantageous peace."[9] However, James could also own up to his reputation as a peacemaker, and claim his new motto as his just desert. "I am not ashamed of this addition," he added concerning his new "dicton." "For King Solomon was a figure of Christ in that he was a king of peace. The greatest gift that our Saviour gave his apostles immediately before his ascension was that he left His peace with them."[10]

The principle of "peacemaking" or, as we say today, "pacifism,"[11] lay at the heart of James's foreign and domestic policies, and increasingly became the byword of his personal mythology. James hadn't only established

---

[8] See Steven Marx, "Shakespeare's Pacifism," *Renaissance Quarterly* 45.1 (1992): 49–95. "Militancy" as both metaphor and reality, with worldly as well as spiritual implications, is emphasized as a cause of aggression and revolution in Michael Walzer, *The Revolution of the Saints: A Study in the Origin of Radical Politics* (Cambridge, MA: Harvard University Press, 1965), esp. 268–99.

[9] *Political Writings*, 33.

[10] Quoted in Willson, *King James VI and I*, 272.

[11] In his remarkable essay, "Just Wars and Evil Empires: Erasmus and the Turks," Ronald G. Musto appeals to the difference between a "peacemaker" and a "pacifist," and warns against the anachronism implied in the latter term. "The labels 'pacificism' and 'pacifist,' " he writes, "are meaningless in any context other than that of the internationalists of the early twentieth century by and for whom they were first coined." (198) "Peacemaker," by contrast, is a word as old as the Bible, and better describes the activism in pursuit of peace that has often been exemplified in both pre-modern and modern Christian societies (*Renaissance Society and Culture: Essays in Honor of Eugene F. Rice, Jr.*, ed. John Monfasani and Ronald G. Musto [New York: Italica Press, 1991], 197–216). However, in his comprehensive study, *The Catholic Peace Tradition* (Maryknoll, NY: Orbis Books, 1986), while providing a good deal of historical and multilingual context for an understanding of the terms "peace," "peacemaking," and the more recent "pacifism," Musto frequently finds it difficult to describe even ancient movements without occasional recourse to the words "pacifism" and "pacifist." And so I find it here. The meaning of the terms is clear enough in their general sense, and can be applied as fairly to early leaders of the Christian Church as to conscientious objectors in the twentieth century: a "pacifist" philosophy, sentiment, or discourse is one which favors non-violent means for the resolution of disputes and/or, correlatively, supports a condition of peace among peoples and nations as a positive value outweighing other values. See Musto, *The Catholic Peace Tradition*, 9–14.

a pacific government; peace was also to be, he was proud to say, his particular *legacy* — that profession of the self that should survive beyond the self, that "apparance of perpetuity or long continuance" that James understood to be attached to his person.[12] Peacemaking was to be a legacy through which James's progeny would carry on the conduct of government, and continue the work of bestowing "blessings" on the Christian world, at home and abroad. Domestically he was sustaining a kind of sublime order, and passing it on peacefully through the body of his son.[13] In international affairs he was following a policy which on at least one occasion he referred to as the *via regia*, a démarche among the competing states and factions of Europe, moderating their hostilities with the calculated sagacity of an independent negotiator.[14] "O happy moderator, blessed Father," Thomas Middleton wrote in a paean to the king called *The Peace-maker*, which some have believed to have been written by James himself, so closely does it follow James's own program of self-professed pacifism — "O happy moderator, blessed father, not Father of thy country alone, but Father of all thy neighbors countries about thee."[15] In point of fact the Thirty Years War was about to break out; but James still had hopes of resolving the conflicts through fatherly diplomacy. "Peace is the passage from life to life," Middleton wrote, summoning his readers to an admiration of his king; "come then to the factory of Peace, thou that desirest to have life: behold the substitute of Peace on earth, displaying the flag of Peace, *Beati pacifici*."[16]

The business of professing oneself a man of peace could be complicated, however. Peace for whom? For everyone? And by what means? Any means necessary? How does honor fit into the picture? How does the existence of evil? How does national sovereignty? How does religious rivalry?

---

[12] *Political Writings*, 137.

[13] The "sublimity" of James's state mythology is discussed at some length by Robert Appelbaum in *Literature and Utopian Politics in Seventeenth-Century England* (Cambridge: Cambridge University Press, 2001), chaps. 1–2.

[14] *Letters of King James VI and I*, ed. G. P. V. Akrigg (Berkeley: University of California Press), 284.

[15] Thomas Middleton, *The Peacemaker*, in *Works*, ed. A. H. Bullen, 8 vols. (London, 1886), 8: 327. On the authorship of the pamphlet see Rhodes Dunlap, "James I, Bacon, Middleton, and the Making of *The Peace-Maker*," in *Studies in the Renaissance Drama*, ed. Josephine W. Bennett et al. (New York: New York University Press, 1959), 82–93. Dunlap shows the work to have indeed been by Middleton, but to have incorporated material Bacon had earlier sketched out at the king's direction.

[16] Middleton, 8: 326.

And what does peace look like when one has it, anyway? How does one express peace, or represent peace?

Consider for a moment a pair of famous paintings meant to represent the making of peace by James VI and I, the two major end panels to Rubens's ceiling at the Banqueting House at Whitehall. They are part of a group of works that comprise the single greatest monument to the pacifistic aspirations of James's reign — in politics, in culture, in religion. The paintings are solemnly, even sublimely eulogistic. But they can be puzzling too.[17]

In one of the main panels James is shown active in life, seated on his throne, conferring a union upon Scotland and England (*The Union of Scotland and England*); in another he is shown bestowing blessings that come from a realm's being at peace with itself (*The Benefits of Government*). In the latter picture, indeed, we see James presiding over a scene where the Goddess of Peace is "hastening, reassuringly, into the arms of Plenty," and Minerva is beating back an assault by War.[18] But the particular power of Rubens's images is the sense in them not of beatitude, or the accomplishment of political harmony, but of exertion, of tremulous energy and effort. There is nothing peaceful about Rubens's allegories of peace. In *The Benefits of Government*, though Plenty is reaching to the arms of Peace and

---

[17] In my account of the paintings I am collapsing the findings of a number of scholars, to whom I am greatly beholden: Per Palme, *The Triumph of Peace: A Study of the Whitehall Banqueting House* (Stockholm: Almqvist & Wiksell, 1956). C. V. Wedgwood, *The World of Rubens 1557–1640* (New York: Time-Life, 1967), and Wedgwood, *The Political Career of Peter Paul Rubens* (London: Thames and Hudson, 1975); Roy Strong, *Britannia Triumphans: Inigo Jones, Rubens and Whitehall Palace* (London: Thames and Hudson, 1980); Christopher White, *Peter Paul Rubens: Man and Artist* (New Haven: Yale University Press, 1987); J. Newman, "Inigo Jones and the Politics of Architecture," in *Culture and Politics in Early Stuart England*, ed. Kevin Sharpe and Peter Lake (Stanford: Stanford University Press, 1993), 229–56; Lisa Rosenthal, "The Banqueting House Ceiling: Two Newly-discovered Projects," *Apollo* 139 (1994): 29–34, and Rosenthal, "Manhood and Statehood: Rubens's construction of heroic virtue," in *Oxford Art Journal* 16.1 (1993): 92–111. It is Roy Strong who argues for Inigo Jones's role in the making of the paintings, Palme and then Rosenthal who argue for early sketches for the paintings in consultation with James's agents well before James's death and the actual finalization of the commission.

As for the political complexities of James's, Charles's, and Rubens's involvements in diplomatic efforts to end the Thirty Years War, see Willson, *King James VI and I*, chapter 15; Maurice Lee, *Great Britain's Solomon* (Urbana: University of Illinois Press, 1990), 261–98; Simon Schama, "Peter Paul Rubens's Europe," *New Yorker* (5 May 1997), 206ff.

[18] Palme, *The Triumph of Peace*, 241

Minerva is beating back War, the gestures are incomplete. Peace and Plenty have *not yet* embraced. War has *not yet* been cast off from the vicinity of the King and his seat of government. And James is shown to be directing the affairs of state with a somewhat frantic and ambiguous if biblically majestic and commanding gesture. The benefits of government aren't yet realized in this picture; they are in the process of being realized; James is shown belligerently commanding the pacification of the realm.

The Union of Scotland and England portrays what is in some ways a still more disturbing picture. A seated but forward-leaning and gesturing James faces the spectacle of two women, Scotland and England, fighting over an infant, the naked Charles. The Goddess Britannia is attempting to crown the infant, but the two women seem to be contending over which of them will get to keep the child, each woman pulling on one of the infant's arms and one woman even trying to grab the crown out of Britannia's hands. Like Solomon passing judgment between the two women claiming the same child, King James is expressing a decision, pointing a dagger toward the child. So far as James's legacy is the theme of the picture, the picture implies that James is giving his son Charles to both kingdoms, providing for both his son and his kingdoms with the wisdom of Solomon. But it is unclear what decision is actually being rendered in this particular scene; perhaps James is threatening, like Solomon, to cut the child in half. In the biblical story the threat to cut the child in half reveals which woman is more worthy to be the child's mother and will get to keep him. But if James is supposed to be leaving a legacy of the unification of Scotland and England, the biblical allegory nevertheless suggests that the kingdoms cannot be united, that one mother country and not the other is going to have possession of the next king, except perhaps so far as James will impose a decision upon them.

The political and moral complexities of Rubens's allegory can be construed in a variety of ways, interpreted with regard to Rubens's own political and moral purposes as well as to those of James or Charles or either of their advisers, including Inigo Jones, all of whom played a role in the design of the ceiling; and it is difficult to settle on a single intention. Even the one sure instance of pacification in James's reign, the de facto union of England and Scotland, is represented with some mystery. For if James had ever promised an infant son to the realms of England and Scotland alike it was Henry the elder brother, not Charles — Henry the more popular and the more militarily inclined of the two brothers, whose place in the English imagination, after his death in 1613, Charles was never able to take.[19] As it has often been remarked about the court masques which in a certain sense the Rubens paintings supplanted, the productions in question were intended to be not only representational but also representative, not only mimetic but also exemplary. Only, *of what* these paintings were to serve as an example, or *for what* policies and modes of behavior these paintings were to serve as examples, it is never easy to say. The pull of competing impulses lodged in Rubens's vision for the ceilings, the moving drama of these allegories about a legacy of peace, all but overpowers the architectonic unity of their execution. And those impulses derive not only from Rubens's own complex reading of the artistic and ideological project set before him and the drama which he knew better than anyone else to invest in an intrinsically stagnant scene, but of complexities inherent to the project itself — to the various masters it was designed to serve, to the political tensions it was compelled to respond to, and in general to the perplexities of war and peace and of leadership and government for which the paintings were to propose a kind of solution.

Now *The Lepanto* would seem to present a much *simpler* situation, with regard both to its production and its interpretation. *The Lepanto* tells the straightforward story of Don Juan of Austria's leadership in the naval battle of 1571, when in a single day of fighting a Christian fleet of 208 galleys, sailing under the flag of a "Holy League" organized by Pope Pius V, the Spanish monarchy, and the Venetian republic, won a total victory over a rival Turkish fleet, capturing 180 out of 274 Turkish ships, freeing more than 12,000 Christian galley slaves, killing over 25,000 Turkish fighters and taking about another 15,000 Turkish fighters into captivity as slaves.[20] The battle was already famous when James put his hand to it — the subject of chronicles in Spanish, Italian, and Latin, two or three brief works in Italian and Latin having been James's primary sources. (James could not read Spanish, and did not own any books in that lan-

---

[19] Roy Strong's suggestion, that the child James is pointing to neither Henry nor Charles but Great Britain itself, is ingenious, but perhaps too ingenious. In any case, to the extent that the painting shows James bestowing the union of Scotland and England on a child who is about to be crowned, the painting cannot help suggesting the alternative idea that this child must also represent a real son, Charles or Henry or both.

[20] Jack Beeching, *The Galleys at Lepanto* (London: Hutchinson, 1982), 220–21. The variety of figures given for battle losses by different historians is discussed in Michael G. Paulson and Tamara Alvarez-Detrell, *Lepanto: Fact, Fiction, and Fantasy; with a Critical Edition of Luis Vélez de Guevara's "El águila del agua," a play in three acts* (Lanham: University Press of America, 1986), 27–28.

guage.)[21] Thus the exercise that James set before himself would seem to
have been of the most commonplace kind: take a story of adventure and
heroic victory and turn it into suitable verse. Nor was the exercise without
a good deal of precedent. Heroic verse, the stepchild of epic, was among
the more popular and esteemed forms of verse in the sixteenth century,
and James does not fail to acknowledge Virgil and Homer as his chief masters and models. A young man with artistic aspirations, who had already
tried his hand at translations and lyrical poems, could scarcely pick a more
suitable genre or subject matter to put his hand to — especially, again, a
young poet who was also a king. Here if anywhere was a subject matter
and a mode of representation entirely fit for a king.

There was only one problem, or pair of related problems, it seemed.
The hero of this poem was "a forraine Papist bastard," as James confesses
in his Preface, written after some of his readers had already seen a manuscript version of the poem.[22] Don Juan of Austria's Roman Catholicism
and illegitimacy alike exposed James's work to reproach; moreover, Juan's
next (and last) great military adventure had been a devastatingly successful
Spanish expedition against Protestant forces in the Netherlands. Yet James
had a ready if somewhat unusual answer for his detractors. The poem, he
wrote, was actually "an argument, *a minore ad majus*, largely intreated by
a Poeticke comparison, beeing to the writing hereof mooved, by the stirring uppe of the league and cruell persecution of the Protestants in all
countries ..." (198). In other words, the story of the Pope Pius's Holy
League of 1571 fending off a Turkish military operation under the leadership of Don Juan was an allegory for the Protestants' conflicts with the
French Catholic League which had been "stirring up cruell persecution"
since 1576 and especially now in 1585, when James finds himself
"mooved" to write his epic. (This Catholic League in France — whose
leaders had been affiliated with Mary Queen of Scots, James's own
mother! — was bent upon keeping the Protestant Henry of Navarre from

---

[21] Craigie, Introduction, *Poems of James VI of Scotland*, vol. 1: lix–lx.

[22] *The Battle of Lepanto* in *Poems of James VI of Scotland*, ed. Craigie, 1: 198. Future
citations will be included in the text, the Preface by page number and the verse itself by
line number. I will be following the "English" version of the text that Craigie reproduces, that is the actual work as printed by the Englishman Robert Waldegrave, who altered James's manuscript Scots spelling and rearranged the verse from fourteeners to a
ballad form, with alternating lines of eight and six syllables. Here as elsewhere, I have silently changed "u" to "v" and "i" to "j" where appropriate, and disregarded the printer's practice of capitalizing as well as italicizing proper names. A modernized version is
available at the back of this volume.

the French throne in the likely event that the Catholic Henry III should die without leaving any male heirs. The League may also have had the more ambitious goal of eradicating Protestantism in France altogether, but that it was persecuting Protestants "in all countries," or even really in France, was an exaggeration.[23]) What James *represented*, then, a victory of Catholics over Turks, was a dark conceit intended actually to be *representative* of the cause of Protestants against its persecution by Catholics. An example of holy war was meant to be exemplary of resistance to holy war.

As for the second part of objection, that his poem makes a hero out of a foreign bastard, to this too James had a curious but ready answer. His poem, he writes, isn't obsequious or biographically oriented; unlike Virgil or Homer, he has not "penned the whole Poeme" in the praise of a single hero, but only brought the hero in when the narrative situation warranted him to do so. Moreover, although the poem has some good things to say about Don Juan (whom James calls "Don-Joan"), "what ever praise I have given to *Don-Joan* it is neither in accounting him as first or second cause of that victory, but only as a particular man, when he falls in my way, to speak the truth of him. For as it becomes not the honour of my estate, like an hireling, to pen the praise of any man: So it becomes it far lesse the highness of my rancke and calling, to spare for the feare of favour of whomseover living, to speake or write the truth of anie" (200). If, on the one hand, the poem is an allegory, and means something very different from what it may seem to mean, on the other hand the poem is a historically truthful representation, and a historical figure truly praiseworthy in life will be represented in the same way in the historical account of his life. A king must be magnanimous in questions like this. It is the king's way; in fact, it is even the king's prerogative, since, unlike a "hireling" poet, a king owes praise to no one.

James's answers are both logical and plausible. A Renaissance king of the type that James frequently claimed to be was indeed free to praise any man.[24] And there was not a little poetical justice in using the Turkish

---

[23] *The New Cambridge Modern History*, Volume 3, ed. R. B. Wernham (Cambridge: Cambridge University Press, 1979), 292–306; Robert J. Knecht, *The French Wars of Religion, 1559–1598* (London: Longman, 1989).

[24] See Kevin Sharpe, "The King's Writ: Royal Authors and Royal Authority in Early Modern England," in *Culture and Politics in Early Stuart England*, 117–38; and Sharpe, "Private Conscience and Public Duty in the Writings of James VI and I," in *Public Duty and Private Conscience in Seventeenth Century England*, ed. J. Morrill, P. Slack, and D. Woolf (Oxford: Oxford University Press, 1993), 77–100.

enemy in one story to stand for the Catholic enemy in another: the implied irony, that Catholics were related to Protestants as Turks were related to Christians, lent a bitter edge to James's assertion that the Catholic League in France was a thing to be abhorred. But the crossing of the
historical and the allegorical in James's poem is still a curious, even puzzling phenomena. In order to condemn Catholic persecution he chooses to
tell the story of Catholicism's own greatest recent campaign against persecution. In order to respond to a case of mass victimization, James chooses
a story with a heroic individual leading an army of heroes. And more: in
responding to a condition of religious persecution the poem tells the story
of war and indeed of a glorious, total military victory, as if war were in
fact a solution to the problem of persecution. But the suggestion that
James is glorifying war violates what we seem to know about James's commitment to peacemaking and pacifism.

It may be suggested that what we know about James's pacifism in 1604
or 1619 need not have any bearing on the young king's attitudes towards
war in the 1580s. However, most of what we know about the king suggests
that he experienced a lifelong aversion to violence, and the poem itself
expresses distaste for violence too, even as it celebrates a violent victory.[25] We also know that the French writers whom he was most fond of
studying and imitating during the 1580s, figures like Ronsard and especially du Bartas, were themselves noted for their pacifistic leanings.[26]
Ronsard had written a famous "Ode au Roy Henry II sur la paix faitte
entre luy et le roy d'angleterre, l'an 1550," and an even more famous "Exhortation pour la paix" in 1558, which inspired a whole generation of
peace poems in France, an exhortation beginning

> Non, ne combatez pas, vivez en amitié,
> Chrestiens, changez vostre ire avecques la pitié,
> Changez á la douceur les rancunes ameres,
> Et ne trempez vos dars dans le sang de vos freres. . . .[27]

---

[25] Willson, *King James VI and I*, 273–74; Akrigg, Introduction, *Letters of James VI and I*, 3–5.

[26] On the pacifist tradition in French poetry see James Hutton, *Themes of Peace in Renaissance Poetry*, ed. Ita Guerlac (Ithaca, NY: Cornell University Press, 1984), esp. 80–168.

[27] Pierre Ronsard, *Oeuvres Complètes*, ed. Jean Céard, Daniel Mènager, and Michel Simonin, 2 vols. (Paris: Gallimard, 1993), 2: 807.

As for du Bartas, James's favorite poet, du Bartas had written a "Hymn to Peace" in 1580; and his popular collections, the first and second *Sepmaines*, parts of which James translated for publication, contained a great deal of pacifist sentiment too.[28]

Just as important, James was also familiar at an early age with Erasmian humanism, which propounded an unmistakably pacifist message. "Peace, praised by the voices of the gods and men, ... the fountain, parent, nourisher, augmenter, and defender of all things, that [either] the air hath or the earth," Erasmus wrote in his *Complaint of Peace*. "All Christian men's letters and books, whether thou read the Old or the New Testament, do sound nothing but peace and amity."[29] In his *Education of a Christian Prince*, one of the models for James's own *Basilicon Doron*, Erasmus had insisted that the "arts of peace" were considerably more important to any Christian Prince than the "arts of war," although many Christian princes of the time seemed to think it the other way around, and he asserted that "Christ himself and Peter and Paul everywhere teach the opposite" of war.[30]

So the production and publication of *The Lepanto* recalls many of the kinds of interpretive complexities presented more overtly (and perhaps deliberately) in Rubens's Whitehall paintings. A man of peace is writing a poem about war. In writing about war he is writing about his desire for a certain kind of peace, although hinting (perhaps!) that a military solution is called for. In writing about war, moreover, the author is deliberately coopting the mythology, or at least the history, of those he may be claiming to be his enemies. The effect of the poem on its literal level is unambiguous: an epochal victory at sea through the wise and valorous leadership of Don Juan, the Papist bastard, is commemorated and celebrated in the language of a Christian epic. "At last the joyfull tidings" of the victory came to the Venetians, the poet writes at the conclusion of his narrative. "Sing

---

[28] "Ventuese ambition," the section entitled "La Decadence" begins, for example,

> Chaud fuzil de la guerre,
> Helas! combien de sang tu verses sur la terre.
> O sceptres, ô bandeaux, ô throsnes haut montz,
> Combien de trahisons, cruels, vous enfantez!

The Works of Guillaume De Salluste Sieur Du Bartas, 3 vols., ed. Urban Tigner Holmes, Jr. et al. (Chapel Hil: University of North Carolina Press, 1940), 3: 442.

[29] Erasmus, *Complaint of Peace*, ed. William James Hirten, repr. of 1559 translation (New York: Scholar's Facsimile, 1946), 25.

[30] Desiderius Erasmus, *The Education of a Christian Prince*, trans. Lester K. Born (New York: Columbia University Press, 1936), 251.

praise to God both young and olde." (ll. 873, 881) But the allegorical implications of the victory of Lepanto are something of a challenge to deci-
pher, and, even when deciphered, something of a challenge to accept.
James is adopting a Spanish and Italian story for the sake of a diverse audience in Scotland and abroad; the poem was soon published in several
European languages including Latin, and none other than du Bartas himself did the king the honor of translating the poem into French. James is
writing, moreover, as a Protestant partisan, the ruling monarch of a Protestant nation with close diplomatic ties to both Protestant and non-Protes-
tant nations (especially France, his mother's birthplace, where James was
in close contact with both Protestant and Catholic partisans, as well as
the still-Catholic court), and as a man already ambitious (in the years contemporary with the imprisonment and assassination of his mother) to succeed to the throne of an even greater Protestant nation. But James was already partial to pacifism rather than militarism, and as soon as he acceded
to that Protestant throne he would sign a peace treaty with Spain, which
had been England's bitterest enemy for several decades, bringing new op-
portunities for economic expansion to England while alienating its allies
in France and Venice — and giving away England's military and political
advantages over Spain, according to many observers then and now.
Whether in life or in art, the *via regia* seems to have been a field strewn
with perils. Or, to change the metaphor, it seems to have involved a kind
of distribution of good will and ill, of signs favorable and unfavorable, of
political capital credited and debited, where one's intentions might be
held at quite a distance from one's actions, and one might ever find oneself inhabiting the drama of resolving conflict rather than experiencing
the condition of resolution itself.

   In *The Lepanto*, the end result is an always interesting epic in miniature, where a variety of narrative impulses are allowed to collide for sometimes clear and sometimes obscure purposes. Catholicism, Protestantism,
war, peace, God's grace, and even Turkish infidels are all by terms celebrated within the context of a heroic episode of the near past, a sea battle
of unprecedented violence, about which many of James's contemporary
readers had to have been ambivalent, and about which James, by his own
confession, had to have been ambivalent as well. But that is not to say
that there is no orderliness to James's poem. The poem adheres to the
Aristotelian principle of the unity of action quite well; and if it involves
itself in unresolvable complexities regarding authorial intention, genre,
allegory, and the ideologies of war and peace, it does so in pursuit of a sustained poetic effect and a sustained (if somewhat paradoxical) version of

the ethic of humanist pacifism. Let us consider these complexities one by one.

1. The ambiguity of authorial intention

The ambiguity of authorial voicing in the poem is in fact deliberate, and follows from James's understanding of the nature of poetic inspiration, although it raises difficulties for the king on a political level. It is not the case that James is speaking in the poem simply "as himself," whatever that might mean to those who believe it is possible for authors to speak as themselves. Here as in other writings of his early years, including his *Paraphrase of the Revelation*, where James writes as a theologian contributing to biblical exegesis, James takes note of the dualities coincident with the writing of scholarly and poetic texts. In his official writings in his capacity as a king — in proclamations and speeches to the Parliament, for example — James would be less concerned about this particular complexity. Speaking *as* king, by virtue of his power as a king, in his capacity as "speaking law," James assumes a kind of monological unity between the meaning and the force of his words.[31] But in his imaginative and scholarly writings James makes it clear that he is not writing in his official capacity as king, or not *only* in that capacity, and the meaning and force of his words are for that reason not necessarily the same. On the contrary, as soon as any of what may be called James's "literary" writings is released to the public (those writings where James writes as either a poet or a man of letters), a rift threatens to develop between the author and his text, between what the author has supposed himself to mean and what the public will actually receive the text to mean.

Skill had a great deal to do with this rift. Whatever he may assume about the rhetorical force of his official pronouncements, when James writes as a scholar or poet he can be quite humble about his ability to express himself as well as he would like. Writing about his admiration for the poems of du Bartas, for example, James complains that though "I was moved by the oft reading & perusing of them, with a restles and lofty de-

---

[31] See Jonathan Goldberg, *James I and the Politics of Literature* (Stanford: Stanford University Press, 1989), for an extended discussion of this issue, along with Kevin Sharpe, "Private Conscience and Public Duty in the Writings of James VI and I," esp. 89. As will be seen, I differ from both Goldberg and Sharpe by arguing that James's poetry operated under separate rules from James's other discourses, and by finding a kind of "dialogical" principle, in Bahktin's sense, struggling to operate in the former.

sire, to preas and attaine to the like vertue, ... God, by nature hathe refused me the like lofty and quick ingyne, and ... my dull *Muse*, age and
Fortune, had refused my the lyke skill and learning."[32] This humility
topos today immediately elicits a cynical reaction; but there is no reason
to think that James wasn't being sincere.[33] He was well aware of what
may have been his limits as a poet and scholar, and aware, perhaps more
importantly, that poetry and scholarship answered to standards which were
independent of the social status of the writer and the ethical force that
social status might in other contexts contribute to one's language. In a
very early poem, for example, he noted a difference between a "thought"
kept to himself and a "word" passed on to a public, and advised himself
to find ways of invention that would best preserve his intentions:

> Since thought is free, thinke what thou will
> O troubled hart, to ease thy paine.
> Thought, unrevealed, can doe no euill;
> Bot words past out, cummes not againe.
>   Be cairfull aye for to invent
>   The waye to gett thy owen intent.[34]

James seems to have been especially sensitive to the difference between intention and invention when it came to literary writing; and to the extent
that he hoped to excel as a poet he expected to compete on an equal foot-
ing with other poets, according to the relatively autonomous standards of
poetic discourse. If a king was a "speaking law," a poet-king was, at bot-

---

[32] Craigie, *Poems*, 1: 16.

[33] The sincerity of James's sincerity is discussed at some length in Sharpe, "Private
Conscience and Public Duty."

[34] Craigie, *Poems* 2: 132; quoted in Akrigg, *Letters*, 6. This poem contains an interestingly ambiguous continuation which differs in one significant word in its English and
Scots versions. The English version says:

> To pleas thy selfe with thy concaite
> And lett none knowe what thou does meane
> Houpe ay at last, though it be late
> To thy intent for to attaine.

The Scots version, by contrast, renders "play" instead of "pleas":

> To play thy self with thy awin consait
> and lat nane knaw quhat thow does mene ... (2: 133)

In either case, the point is again being raised that the poet can fail to communicate his
meaning to his audience, but whether he fails while endeavoring too selfishly to "please"
himself or to "play" himself is an interesting question.

tom, only a poet. In fact, it was precisely the autonomy of literary writing, such as it was, that attracted him to experimenting with it, since it allowed him to try on other identities and speak in other capacities than those the office of monarchy imposed upon him.

But apart from the problem of the limits of a writer's skill, then, James recognized that rifts could open between literary discourse and authorial intention precisely because literary discourse had its own rules, and was articulated on its own plane of communication. He was very much attracted to the idea of divine inspiration as he had learned it from du Bartas, among others, and seems to have deduced from it the principle that literary production often involved a form of split subjectivity, where the poet, so long as he was inspired, was no longer quite "himself" when he wrote, but rather "parted" from himself, removed to a different plane of existence. In his translation of *The Uranie*, for example, James can be found writing a line like, "All art is learned by art, this art alone / It is a heavenly gift," suggesting very strongly that poetry is an autonomous domain of practice, falling under the head of the divine rather than the human but in any case following its own laws. Or again:

> For man from man must wholly parted be
> If with his age, his verse do well agree.
> Amongst our hands, he must his witts resing,
> A holy trance to highest heaven him bring
> For even as humane fury maks the man
> Les than the man: So heavenly fury can
> Make man pas man, and wander in a holy mist.[35]

In his translation of du Bartas's *The Furies*,[36] James even adds an original "Translator's Invocation" where, in much the spirit of du Bartas,

---

[35] Craigie, *Poems*, 23–25, ll. 85–86 and 113–20.

[36] Craigie, *Poems*, 112, ll. 6–12:

> O now inflame my sacred Muse to sing
>   Unto the Lord of Lords.
> O now inflame my furious Spreit,
>   That furiously I may
> These Furies (mankinds plagues allace!)
>   With furious Pen display.

The lines anticipate du Bartas's own invocation in *The Furies*, where du Bartas asks the Holy Spirit to "Change me, and cast me over again," in order to put him in a fit condition to poeticize about the strife of man against nature and himself (*Poems*, 114, l. 25).

James alludes to the split subjectivity that he will have to exemplify if he is going to be moved into expressing the violent and inherently repellent material that a poem on "the furies" — the divine punishments of man — necessarily involves. Sometimes in parting from himself the poet descends from himself; that's where he finds himself capable of writing about violence and cruelty. As for *The Lepanto*, this poem too opens with an invocation of the muse, calling upon the Holy Spirit to "inflame" the author's pen "above my skill" (17–24). At one point, while the woes of Venice on the eve of the formation of the Holy League are being recounted, the poet even invokes the muse to stop the current strain of inspiration and move on to something else: "O stay my Muse, thou goes too farre." The poet claims that the mourning he has been caused to write about will with "trikling teares so fill my penne / That it will write no more" (181–84).

So if James writes a poem about the Battle of Lepanto while sitting as the King of Scotland, and eventually allows the poem to be issued in print under his name, he understands that the force of his language, such as it is, stems primarily from the language itself and whatever flame of expressivity divine inspiration and poetic alterity may have contributed to it. The poet is not to be attended to simply as the man (the king) he is; he is to be attended to as a poet, in some sense "apart" from himself, speaking by way of divine inspiration and aspiring to the skills appropriate to poetic invention. And the poem itself, by the same token, is not to be confused with other forms of discourse where the force of the king's language operates under the rules of political discourse; it is to be attended to as a poem, according to the conventions, ambitions, and limits of verse. Only, even if a poem is a poem and the poet a poet, the original problem of intention and invention is never entirely resolved. For as James is also well aware, so far as James the king takes responsibility for the authorship of a poem, he is not simply a poet; he is a poet in whom readers are interested in so far as he is both a poet *and* a king. And the poem then is *not* simply a poem, since the construal or misconstrual of the poem reflects back on the king who wrote it and the foreign and domestic policies he represents. "It falls out often," he begins in his Preface to *Lepanto*, speaking in his voice as king and repeating his ideas about invention and intention, "that the effects of mens action comes cleane contrairie to the intent of the Authour. The same finde I by experience (beloved Reader) in my Poëme of *Lepanto*" (198). The danger, moreover, is as much political as it is literary. If the poem is misunderstood as a poem, it is also misunderstood as an act of meaning for which a king has taken responsibility in his political capacity as king. The poem itself, of course, on its own terms, is *already*

political, since it is a parable about war and peace and religious persecution, and misconstrual may have a variety of unwanted political effects.

The problem is not readily soluble. For his part, James prefers that his
poems speak for themselves, saying that adding a "Commentarie" to a
poem, telling his readers what the poem is supposed to mean, is a kind of
"reproach of the skillfull learnedness of the Reader," and a thing he
would rather avoid lest he make the work "more displeasant" to the
reader (198). But what then? And how, again, is the allegory of the poem
to be construed? In the end, we find the poem related to its royal author
in much the same as the Whitehall ceilings are related to the king. The
poems, like the ceilings, both *refer* to the royal author and stem from him:
he *wrote* the poems (albeit in consultation with various sources and with
long and short term political goals in mind, both domestically and interna-
tionally); he *promoted* the allegories of the ceilings (albeit, again, in consultation with a number of others, and, again, with a varied political program
in mind.) And yet the poems, like the ceilings, are meant to speak for
themselves. It is the artistic image that we see, and that allows us to look
backward (but only so far) to read the royal intention behind it. On the
one hand, the artistic image is representative of royal intention; it speaks
for the king, and on behalf of the king. On the other hand, the artistic
image is also separate from royal intention, obeying its own laws, speaking
in its own voice: and it is this image, with its own laws and its own voice,
James tells us, that he wants his "skillfull" readers to construe.

2. The choice of epic

In fact, so far as the poem operates as an epic, it functions as a kind of
unambiguous (if not unambivalent) statement, such that the kinds of mis-
construals James said his poem had suffered from ought not to have been
anticipated, except so far as his readers were guilty of negligence or incom-
petence (an accusation which James specifically and politely wishes not to
level against his readers.) The dark conceit attached to the epic may work
against the epic in many ways. But the epic itself is plainly visible. It de-
termines the shape and tone of the poem; it establishes the logic of its plot
and the affective force of its results. In choosing to cast his story as an
epic, James has made a number of decisions about what the events of Lepanto must have meant. On a literal level, James has chosen to say, the
battle conveys a heroic, epic meaning, and conveys it with few surprises.

Epic, as David Quint has recently re-defined it, and especially that "epic of winners" of which *The Lepanto* is certainly an example, tells a story of warfare and of a power capable of bringing warfare to a meaningful conclusion. It "tells of a power able to end the indeterminacy of war and to emerge victorious, showing that the struggle had all along been leading up to its victory"; the epic thus imposes upon its material a specific "narrative teleology" where a certain kind of justice is shown to operate in history and ultimately prevail.[37] And thus, the Christian navy in James's poem is shown to have been destined to win the battle by divine decree; it is shown to have fought the battle for a divine cause, as argued by Christ himself in heaven as well as by a heavenly messenger on earth who stirs the Venetians and other Christians into action; and it is shown to have fought the battle both valiantly and fairly, thanks in part to the heroism and leadership of an individual rising to the occasion of greatness. This conventional, epic end result is unmistakable; God's purpose has prevailed, and God's purpose is precisely that teleological rationale which has operated from beginning to end in the battle, ultimately revealing itself in full with the phenomenal victory of the Christians over the Turks. James even goes so far in following epic tradition to show the Turks as having been worthy opponents of the Christian soldiers, although he also shows that their predations on Christian civilization were the aggravating cause of the battle. When the battle is about to get underway the Turkish leader Ali Basha visits all his host "With bold and manly face," and exhorts his men to action in the language worthy of a classic epic hero (518). But in the end, whatever their worthiness as opponents, the Turks finally manifest that "confusion and disorder" that Quint finds common to the losers of epic battles, "so that victory over them may be ascribed as a triumph of reason and meaning."[38] Courageous to the end, the Turks finally lose their battle-sense and turn back in confusion, as many versions of the story would concur, when in the heat of the fight their general Ali Basha is beheaded, and Don Juan displays his head on a mast for all to see, "At sight whereof, the faithlesse Host / Were all so sore agast, / That all amas'd gave back at once" (839–41). And thus the poet, having noted the swift victory over a suddenly distracted army, can end his poem "Exhorting all you Christians true / Your courage up to bend" (1020–21). The poem has provided an example of epic victory, and made it serve the usual ends of

---

[37] David Quint, *Epic and Empire: Politics and Generic Form from Virgil to Milton* (Princeton: Princeton University Press, 1993), 45.

[38] Quint, *Epic and Empire*, 46.

epic victory, the enemy scattered in confusion, the victor boldly vaunting his monopoly on meaning, holding the severed head of Ali Basha aloft. The teleological legitimacy of a political regime and its place in history has been elucidated and confirmed, and the subjects of that regime have been accordingly consoled.

And yet, as it must also be stressed, there was nothing in the actual chain of events involving the battle that was in and of itself of "epic" significance. I am turning here from the poem's version of events to consider for a moment the actual history of Lepanto, as James's own Preface warrants the reader to do; and I am trying to point out that there was no pattern in the actual events such that it should of necessity have been interpreted as an epic or short quasi-epic heroic poem. Why should there have been such a pattern in the events? That in 1571 the Venetians and their allies were provoked into a retaliatory strike against the Ottoman Empire there can be no question. Relations between Muslims and Christians had of course been a complicated affair for centuries, involving both collaborative and adversarial arrangements, as well as a good deal of mutual indifference in many cases. But in the sixteenth century, as the major Christian states were vying amongst themselves for international hegemony, so the Ottoman state was vying for international hegemony too, and the latter was the single strongest power in the Mediterranean basin.[39] The Ottoman state was clearly expansionist in its foreign policy, as were its rival Christian states, and clashes (as well as alliances) were all but inevitable. But when, in any case, in violation of certain treaties, though not entirely without provocation, the Ottomans wrested Cyprus from Venetian control at a great cost of Christian and Muslim lives, it was not unreasonable for men like Pius V and Philip II to infer that not only Venetian hegemony but the survival of the Christian states altogether was at risk. (At risk over the long term, it should be added: certainly there was no immediate danger that Christianity was going to be exterminated, only that the political hegemony of its states in the Mediterranean was in danger of serious attenuation.) The result was the forming of the Holy League, organized by Pius V to defend the common interests of the Roman Catholic states

---

[39] See Paul Coles, *The Ottoman Impact on Europe* (London: Thames and Hudson, 1968); Ferdinand Braudel, *The Mediterranean and the Mediterranean World in the Age of Philip II*, trans. Sian Reynolds, 2 vols. (New York: Harper & Row, 1972); Bernard Lewis, *Islam and the West* (Oxford: Oxford University Press, 1993); and Lewis, *Cultures in Conflict: Christians, Muslims, and Jews in the Age of Discovery* (New York: Oxford University Press, 1995).

against the Ottoman Empire, and in the first place to retaliate for the Turkish reconquest of Cyprus.

Although the immediate results of the Holy League's first offensive naval expedition was their total victory over the Turkish fleet, however, it was not entirely clear what that total victory meant. One standard reading of the event, which was not unknown even in the sixteenth century — Michel de Montaigne, for one, having expressed it[40] — was that it didn't mean much at all. Lepanto, it has often been said, was more a "moral" or "symbolic" victory than a real one, as would have been evident to an impartial judge within a few years after the event.[41] By 1572 — that is, within a year after losing the great battle — the Ottomans had already rebuilt their navy, and were making new incursions on the Spanish protectorate of Tunis, overtaking the town for good in 1574. In 1573 the Venetians, working independently of the League, negotiated a separate peace with the Ottomans, ceding Cyprus and a large indemnity in return for the reestablishment of trade. Far from being a decisive victory in the campaign of Christianity against the infidel, the battle was a temporary triumph in a sequence of events which ended in a loss of territory, wealth, and prestige for Spain, Venice, and the Christian confederacy alike, and an early dissolution of the confederacy itself. "This victory seemed to open the door to the wildest hopes," Ferdinand Braudel writes. "But in the immediate aftermath of the battle, it had no strategic consequences." Indeed, "Historians have joined in an impressively unanimous chorus to say that Lepanto was a great spectacle, a glorious one even, but in the end leading nowhere."[42]

Nevertheless, from the outset there was a drive to see in the Battle of Lepanto a historical moment of larger, even monumental significance, leading well beyond itself. And it was to this drive to monumentalize the meaning of the Battle that we find a contribution being made ... by the young King of Scotland. Indeed, James's *Lepanto* is one of the first extant attempts to transform the Battle into a subject of heroic poetry, and it was one of the first to use the model of the classic epic as the key frame for re-

---

[40] Michel de Montaigne, "We Should Meddle Soberly With Judging Divine Ordinance," in *The Complete Essays of Montaigne*, trans. Donald Frame (Stanford: Stanford University Press, 1958), 158.

[41] *New Cambridge Modern History, Volume II: The Counter-Reformation and Price Revolution*, ed. R. Wernham (Cambridge: Cambridge University Press, 1979), 252–53; 353–54. Also see Bernard Lewis, *Islam and the West*, 18.

[42] Braudel, *The Mediterranean and the Mediterranean World in the Age of Philip II*, 2: 1103.

constructing the story. Apart from a few attempts in Spanish, apparently unknown to James, to use the epic model in representing the battle, other writers in other places framed their narrative of events in rather different terms.

On the Iberian peninsula, apart from the relatively obscure epics by Latino (1572), Corte Real (1578) and Rufo (1582), and a canto in the second part of Ercilla's well-known *La Araucana* (1578), Lepanto most predominantly became the subject of popular ballads, written in the key of conventional romance.[43] In this balladry Don Juan takes the place of many another knight fighting against infidels out of chivalrous motives, but the infidels too are understood in terms of the chivalric code. For all its journalistic realism and dramatic intensity, *La Araucana*, too, is not without a strong admixture of chivalric ideology, as the Turks momentarily take the place of South Americans, standing for the savagely noble enemy against which the Christian knight (albeit aboard ship, rather than on foot or horse) may put his honor to the test. An educated court poet and cleric in Spain, on the other hand, writing at about the same time as James VI and I, wrote a heroic poem on Lepanto which recalled episodes not from chivalric romances or Homer and Virgil but from Judges, Chronicles, and Kings. In his *Canción en Albanza de la Divin Majestad por la Victoria del Señor Don Juan*, Fernando de Herrera (d. 1597) reconstructs the story as a "hymn" celebrating the power of a jealous God, a "God of Battles," who overcame His enemies in the field, His "wrath" having "swallowed them up, as fire does the dry chaff."[44] In this account of events the Turk is by no means the worthy opponent that James and other epicists makes him out to be, or even the hated but chivalrous enemy of the ballads. On the

---

[43] Juan Latino, *Austriadis libri duo* (Granada, 1573); Hieronymo Corte Real, *Felicissima concedida del cielo al señor don Juan d'Austria, en el golfo de Lepánto de la pederasa armada Othomana* (Lisbon, 1578); Juan Rufo, *La Austriada*, in *Poemas épicos*, ed. D. Cayetano Rosell (Madrid: Impr. De los Suceseros de Hernando, 1925) 2: 1–136; Alonso de Ercilla Y Zúñiga, *La Araucana*, English Translation *The Araucaniad*, trans. Charles Maxwell Lancaster and Paul Thomas Manchester (Nashville: Vanderbilt University Press, 1945); Manuel da Costa Fontes, "Dona Maria and Batalha de Lepanto: Two Rare Luso-American Ballads," in *Portuguese and Brazilian Oral Traditions in Verse Form*, ed. Joanne B. Armistead et al. (Los Angeles: University of Southern California Press, 1976), 148–57; Juan de Mendano, *Silva de Varios Romances Recopliados por Juan de Mendano* (Granada, 1588; Madrid: Editorial Castalia, 1966). For discussion of the heroic poems in Spanish and Latin see Michael Murrin, *History and Warfare in Renaissance Epic* (Chicago: University of Chicago Press, 1994), esp. 182–96.

[44] Fernando de Herrera, *Canción en Albanza de la Divin Majestad*, in *Renaissance and Baroque Poetry of Spain*, Bilingual Edition, ed. and trans. Elias L. River (New York: Dell, 1966), 113–14.

contrary, he is a "proud Tyrant" driven by "impious madness" to oppress the people of God and defy God himself. "Where is these men's God?" the Grand Sultan demands, noting his power over people throughout the Mediterranean. "*¿Dónde el Dios déstos está?*" "Who is he hiding from? "*¿De quién se esconde?*"[45] The Sultan calls a council where he and his Levantine allies decide to "make a great lake of [Christian] blood," "destroy them as a nation, together with the name of their Christ," and "feast our eyes upon their death."[46] The victory against these Satanic Asiatics, explained with little concern for narrative details, is wholly God's. "Today the eyes and grandeur of the proud man were humiliated, and You alone, Lord, were exalted; for your day is come." "*Tu día es legado.*"[47] In fact, in this hymn on "Don Juan's victory" Don Juan is never mentioned by name; he is only the "Christian prince" through whom God demonstrates his power.

Later on, in the seventeenth century, the heroic model would become a standard form for representing the event.[48] But at a time nearer to the battle itself there was no particular reason for viewing it that way, and only a few attempted to do so. In *Don Quixote*, Cervantes, who had himself participated in the battle, is rather tragicomically Machiavellian than heroic in his assessment of Lepanto, and comes close to presenting the same judgment on the event as our modern historian Braudel would ultimately adopt. The novelist has his character "The Captive" explain the event as a trial of military valor, where a number of men were able to prove their worthiness as soldiers, and "the world and all the nations learnt how wrong they were in supposing that the Turks were invincible on the sea." In a single day "the insolent pride of the Ottoman was broken for ever."[49] Long term strategy with regard to the Ottoman Empire was thus revised, and real long term success against it made more cer-

---

[45] Herrera, *Canción*, 116.

[46] Herrera, *Canción*, 116–17.

[47] Herrera, *Canción*, 118–19.

[48] Paulson and Alvarez-Detrell, *Lepanto: Fact, Fiction, and Fantasy.*

[49] Miguel de Cervantes Saavedra, *The Adventures of Don Quixote*, trans. J. M. Cohen (Harmondsworth: Penguin, 1950), 348. Thus Braudel argues too, suggesting that the "moral" or "symbolic" victory at Lepanto had real long term effects, it having marked "the end of a period of profound depression, the end of a genuine inferiority complex on the part of Christendom and a no less real Turkish supremacy." Braudel, *Mediterranean*, 2: 1103. On Cervantes's "tragicomic" approach to Lepanto see Stanislav Zimic, "Un Eco de Lepanto en la Ironia Cervantina," in *Romance Notes* 12 (1970): 174–76.

tain, because Christian soldiers had learned that they were pretty tough, and could beat the Turks if and when they resolved to do so. But this vision of the Battle as a definitive test of manliness, leading toward a greater resolve to fight in the future, is not quite a "heroic" vision in a literary sense; unlike the spokesmen of conventional heroic verse, Cervantes's Captive dissociates military valor from other manly virtues, and his story has nothing to say about the inevitable triumph of virtue in general over vice, whether in this life or the next. On the contrary, the Captive carries his story of Lepanto over to the defeat of the apparently virtuous Christians at Tunis, and holds up as an example of valor the fact that during the Turkish siege of their fortress the Christian knights were slaughtered to the man.

The vision of the event among the Venetians soon afterwards, although in a much different key, wasn't heroic in a conventional sense either. On the contrary, in the immediate aftermath of the battle Venetians inclined toward construing the event eschatologically. Absorbing the meaning of Lepanto into traditional millenarian and Joachimite doctrine, Venetians saw the victory of the Turks not so much as the "day of God," as Herrera had done, or even as a day of destructive Christian manliness, as Cervantes was inclined to think of it, but as a day, earlier forecast by Italian prophets, when the tide of history would turn and the Byzantine Empire — Venice's father kingdom — would soon be a restored.[50] The Venetian stake in this battle was evidently very different from what the Spanish, the Papal, or for that matter the Scottish Court might imagine it to be: the Venetians looked eastward to their future in a way that had become incomprehensible to the Western European powers since the end of the Crusades, and their discourse of Lepanto reflected that fact and even encouraged it.

James's *Lepanto*, then, has to be seen as a certain kind of reading of events, in spite of all the counter-evidence that history could provide or counter-examples that other literary works could present; it has to be seen as a certain kind of contribution to the *mythos* of Lepanto, where heroic, epic models are caused to predominate, and where the events are refashioned, then, into a parable of epic heroism. Epic heroism is what the poem shows the battle to be an example *of*; the head of the enemy is displayed and the story is over. And clearly, then, heroism is what the poem

---

[50] Letizia Pierozzi, "La vittoria di Lepanto nell'escatologia e nella profezia," *Rinascimento: Rivista dell'Istituto Nazionale di Studi sul Rinascimento* 34 (1994): 317–63.

is trying to be an example *for*. On this level of meaning *The Lepanto* is unambiguous.

But that still leaves us far away from James's claims that the poem is actually an allegory about the persecution of Protestants; much less does it help resolve the conflict between James's apparent pacifism and the poem's apparent glorification of war.

3. Allegorical attenuations

James's dark conceit, however, is hinted at throughout the poem — sometimes heavy-handedly, yet often with considerable ambiguity too — even as on a literal level the poem continues to glorify the victory of the Holy League over the Turks. At the conclusion of the poem, for example, where a "Chorus Angelorum" sings a hymn "Exhorting all you Christians true / Your courage up to bend," we also learn that there is an important difference between "all Christians true" and those Christians who "serv'd not right" their God, and whom God aided anyway, since he "doth love his name / So well" (1022-24). We find out that God "doth the bodie better love," that is the bodie of Christians true, than those Christians who are only the "shadow" of true Christians (1027-28). And yet those Christians whose fortunes the poem has been documenting, the members of the Pope's Holy League fighting against the Turk — those Christians are the "shadow" Christians whom God loves less than others. Evidently they are shadow Christians both in the sense that they are mere shadows, Christians in name only, and in that their story is but a shadow of the story of "true Christians," that is the Protestants, members of the church of true believers. This idea is suggested from the beginning. In the opening scene, for example, a council in heaven between God, Satan, and Christ, with obvious allusions to the opening scene of Job, Christ complains that Satan has "inflamde" the "maddest mindes" of the "faithles Turkes" "Against them all that doe professe / My name with fervent fayth" (51-56). To profess the "name" of Christianity is important in itself, Christ implies. And God the Father agrees. "All christians serves [sic] my Sonne," he proclaims, "though not / Aright in everie thing." And he will now put an end to the Turks' oppression of "these Christians" so that it will be seen that "of my holie hallowed name / The force is great and blest" (79-84).

In this epic, evidently, the young poet is already trying to walk the *via regia*: he is at once condemning Catholics and acknowledging their ties to

Protestants, allowing them a merited heroism while stipulating that theirs is but a shadow of Protestant heroism, and indeed their faith but a shadow of Christian faith. "I could wish from my heart," James said in 1604, "that it would please God to make me one of the members of such a generall Christian union in Religion, as laying wilfulnesse on both hands, we might meete in the middest" — although of course he can't, because of "the newe and grosse Corruptions of theirs," which they refuse to renounce.[51] "I protest to God," he wrote in a letter to Robert Cecil in 1603, "I reverence their church as our mother church, although clogged with many infirmities and corruptions. ... I only wish that such order might be taken as the land might be purged of such great flocks of them that daily diverts the souls of many from the sincerity of the gospel."[52] On the one hand the Catholics of Venice, Spain, and the Papal States are members of a "mother church" and "serve" the Christian God and His purposes on earth.[53] On the other hand, they serve God poorly. They are but shadows of what James thought of as the "Trew, Ancient, Catholike and Apostolike faith, grounded upon the Scriptures and expresse word of God."[54] And they can be dangerous. James never had any illusions but that the catholic ambitions of members of the Catholic Church represented a danger to the equally catholic ambitions of Protestants, as well as to the independent national hegemonies of Protestant rulers. So the Catholics "shadow" the Protestants in various ways, for good and ill. Finally, however, by way of what from this distance seems to be a stunningly unconvincing piece of chop-logic, what the Battle of Lepanto is supposed to communicate in this poem is an ostensibly unambiguous moral lesson: if God will do so much for his "shadow" Christians, concerned as He is merely to preserve "the name" of Christianity, think what he will do for the real Christians! Think what he will do for Protestants threatened by Catholic persecution! "Then though the Antichristian sect / Against you do conjure," the poem concludes, addressing its Protestant audience (as Catholics can be "Antichristians" as well as worthy "shadows" in James's political theology),

---

[51] James, *Political Writings*, 140.

[52] James, *Letters*, 205.

[53] Venice, of course, was admired by Protestants for its independence from Rome, and for its own nascent proto-Protestant practices on an ecclesiastical and theological level. But it was officially Roman Catholic, and Roman Catholic in most of its religious practices, all the same.

[54] James, *Political Writings*, 140.

> He doth the bodie better love
> > Then shadow be ye sure:
> Do ye resist with confidence,
> > That God shall be your stay
> And turne it to your comfort, and
> > His glory now and ay. (1025–32)

This bit of sophistry, along with the dark conceit supporting it, is what the poem's early detractors overlooked. It is what James had to use his authorial and kingly authority in a Preface to impose upon the reading of the text, even though he preferred and indeed insisted that readers discover the meaning on their own. The situation is not perhaps all that different from that more famous and nearly contemporary epic, *The Fairie Queene*, where again a story drawn from epic convention, dwelling on violence and requiring the glorification of aggression to make its case, is nevertheless being positioned by its author as a post-epic, Protestant allegory, where Christian rather than timocratic militancy is ultimately being extolled, and where the idea of real warfare as opposed to metaphoric warfare is at the very least problematic.[55] But leaving aside the question of Spenser and *The Fairie Queene*, in what way does James suppose that his reader is now to "resist" the incursions of Catholicism? And how does learning about the Battle of Lepanto according to heroic models of discourse teach the reader to resist them?

It may incidentally be observed, as earlier indicated, that even if James glorifies the battle, he nevertheless expresses distaste for the violence it involves. In the beginning of the poem he characterizes his subject matter as "a cruell Martiall warre, / A bloodie battel bolde, / Long doubtsome fight, with slaughter huge / And wounded manifolde" (5–9). There is little delight in violence in this language, and not much awe of it either, although there is a strain of a conventional teaser here too: get ready, the storyteller tells his readers, for a gory tale. In any case, as he begins to describe the actual battle the poet pauses, longer than seems entirely necessary, to excuse himself for presuming to write about an event he hasn't seen, and meanwhile registering perhaps some hesitancy at the task before him of imagining the violence and suffering of war. As it becomes necessary to tell the story of war the poet doesn't stint from grisly details, to be sure,

---

[55] On ideology and representation of warfare in Spenser see Murrin, *History and Warfare*, 136–37; and Richard Mallette, *Spenser and the Discourse of Reformation England* (Lincoln: University of Nebraska Press, 1997), 143–68.

but he emphasizes three interesting things, which attenuate the militarism of the poem: he emphasizes, first of all, the horror of warfare, especially so far as this was in particular a battle where gunfire and cannonade played major roles in the combat, and even the "Fishes were astonisht all, /To heare such hideous sound" (617–18); secondly, he emphasizes the almost mechanical valor of the soldiers on both sides, all of whom were willing to fight to the end; and thirdly, he emphasizes how close the battle had been, the tide not turning until Don Juan finally captured the galley of Ali Basha. James is uninterested in military strategy or in the finer points of combat which led to the Christian victory. He is mainly concerned with the tableau of combat as a whole, the vast spectacle of warfare, a spectacle of blood and smoke and unrelenting fury. Many things are "cruell," "hideous," "horrible," and "bloodie" in this battle:

> The Azure Skie was dim'd with Smoke
>   The dinne that did abound,
> Like Thunder rearding rumling rave
>   With roares the highest Heaven,
> And pearst with pith the glistering vaults
>   Of all the Planets seaven:
> The piteous plaints, the hideous howles,
>   The greevous cries and mones,
> Of millions wounded sundrie waies,
>   But dying all at ones,
> Conjoynd with former horrible sound,
>   Distemperd all the aire,
> And made the Seas for terrour shake
>   With braying every where. (619–32)

As James claimed, although the victory belongs to Don Juan, the action does not revolve around him; and when he finally appears in the decisive encounter with Ali Basha it is against the backdrop of other Christians fighting similar fights, and other Christians similarly poised now at the brink of success, now at the brink of failure, and not able to tell how the combat is going for either side.

It would be over-reading the text to see in James's depiction of combat a kind of anti-war propaganda. Observations of the horror of war are also part of the epic tradition, and can be used not to diminish but to highlight genuine acts of heroism. But when the "Spanish Prince" finally "did hazard" battle with Ali Basha, in James's account, there was nothing particularly noteworthy about his comportment, and indeed "Ali-Basha proov'd so well, / With his assisters brave," that initially Don Juan was beaten back. Only when he was "boldned with spite, / And vernisht red with shame" did Don Juan lead his men back into the fray, this time success-fully. He fought to save his honor; but so did everyone else. And as it hap-pened, an anonymous "Macedonian soldier . . . / Great honour for to win" was the one to accomplish the decisive act of severing Ali's head from his body (820-30).[56] So, skipping over a great many details which to a mili-tary historian would tell the real story of how the battle turned out the way it did, from the complex characters of the participants (note, for example, how mechanically Don Juan's motives are characterized: he is "red with shame" and "boldned with spite") to the convergence of tac-tics, firepower, manpower, and luck — skipping over all this, the poem shows that victory, simply, is won. Honor is won. The head of Ali Basha is displayed. And there is no celebration of heroism per se. In fact, the battle is no sooner won than the scene immediately shifts to reports of the victory among the citizens of Venice, who sing a hymn in praise not of any particular heroes or of heroism but of the grace of God.

Perhaps the "shadowing" of the Christians in this story extends to the attenuation of their individuality and moral vigor. But to the extent that their heroism is compromised they provide poor models for the kind of vigorous faith James is evoking for Protestants. Indeed it is not impossible that when James exhorts his true Christians to "resist with confidence," he is supposing that passive resistance may be a serious option. And if he is supposing that a more active resistance might be necessary, it is not im-possible that what he really means is that Protestants should wait with patience for their opportunity to resist; they should wait until the Anti-christ presents Protestants with an opportunity for alliance and victory the way the Turk presented the members of the Holy League with such an op-portunity. In other words, they should wait until the occasion arises for undertaking a "just war."

4. The just war

"Let first the justnesse of your cause be your greatest strength" in the con-duct of war, James advises his son.[57] And what was meant by a "just

---

[56] As Beeching and others tell it, the man who beheaded Ali Basha was actually a galley slave.

[57] James, *Political Writings*, 32.

cause" for war was by then fairly clear.[58] Apart from the *jus in bello*, rules
for the just conduct of war (and James has a good deal to say on that particular subject to his son) there was also a *jus ad bellum*, rules for the justice of going to war (about which James actually says little to his son, as if
assuming that his son will know a just cause for war when he sees one.)
The *jus ad bellum*, as handed down by a tradition with which James was familiar, can be distilled into four conditions: accordingly, a government is
justified in going to war (1) when the sovereignty of the government is certain, (2) when the government or its people has suffered a wrong at the
hands of another sovereign government, (3) when warfare is the only
means left to redress the grievance and assert the rights of the injured
party, and (4) when the war is conducted with the "right intent: the restoration of peace."[59] The application of this doctrine was of course open
to debate. If, for example, Spanish ships are attacked by Turkish or English pirates, does the government of Spain have the right to wage war
against the government of Turkey or England, or only to defend itself
against pirates? Or if Spanish colonists in the New World are attacked by
Native Americans, exactly what is the status, by turn, of the injured party,
of the injuring party, and of the injury? Which party, in fact, is which?[60]
One thing that the doctrine seemed specifically to prohibit was aggressive
war — war waged for the sake of territory, wealth, or private motives like
vengeance and fame. But even this specific prohibition was subject to several interpretations. In the context of his disputes with the Spanish over
the Thirty Years War and the stalled negotiations for settlement by marriage, Bacon reminded James that a just war, a defensive war, sometimes
had to be waged preemptively, and therefore offensively. "Neither is the
opinion of some of the schoolmen to be received," he wrote in his *Essays*,
referring specifically to Aquinas, "that 'a war cannot justly be made but
upon a precedent injury or provocation.' For there is not question but a
just fear of an imminent danger, though there be no blow given, is a law-

---

[58] On the "just war" tradition see James Turner Johnson, *Ideology, Reason, and the Limitation of War: Secular and Religious Concepts 1200–1740* (Princeton: Princeton University Press, 1975); Frederick H. Russell, *The Just War in the Middle Ages* (Cambridge: Cam-
bridge University Press, 1975); and Ronald G. Musto, *The Catholic Peace Tradition*.

[59] Musto, *The Catholic Peace Tradition*, 104.

[60] This last was a topic of particular concern to Victoria and Suarez. See James B.
Scott, *Spanish Origins of International Law* (Oxford: Oxford University Press, 1934) which
includes translations of some of Francisco Victoria's most important works on just war
theory, including *De jure belli*, and *De Indis*.

ful cause of war."[61] Moreover, the very ethic of personal and national honor (an ethic to which James, as we have seen, also subscribed, even if he preferred to subscribe to it non-aggressively) demanded the exercise of a kind of Machiavellian *virtù*, a militancy not only in defense of one's integrity but positively, as an expression of integrity. "No nation which doth not directly profess arms," Bacon continued, "may look to have greatness fall into their mouths. And on the other side, it is a most certain oracle of time, that those states that continue long in that profession (as the Romans and the Turks principally have done) do wonder."[62] Much depended, ultimately, on what it was that one reckoned "peace" to be.

In this context, pacifism cannot be equated with passivity,[63] and it is noteworthy that James himself understood peacemaking to be an aggressive act, even if what it aggressively formed were bonds of "firm and unchangeable friendship" and strict mutual "obligations."[64] Even Erasmus had recognized this.[65] The right of a nation to make war was intimately connected to the right of the nation to exist as a sovereign state and the right of its legitimate rulers to enforce the law within the borders of the state.[66] And so in *The Lepanto* James is careful to show that the battle was fought fairly, in keeping with rules of *jus in bello*, and, more importantly, in keeping with the strictest rules of the just cause for going to war, the *jus ad bellum*. It is likely out of respect for the rules *jus in bello*, as well out of respect for the conventions of epic conflict, that James has his combatants fight on predominantly equal terms, with equal valor on both sides. In James's version of events, the Battle of Lepanto was an *honorable* battle; that is, it was fought in keeping with codes of honor.[67] (The same could not be said, for example, of Herrera's version, where there is nothing honorable about the Turkish opponents to the Christians, and where

---

[61] Francis Bacon, " Of Empire," in *Francis Bacon*, ed. Brian Vickers (Oxford: Oxford University Press, 1990), 377; Bacon is referring to the *Summa Theologica*, 2.40.1.

[62] Francis Bacon, 401. Also see Francis Bacon, *Advertisement Touching a Holy War* (1622) in *Works*, ed. James Spedding, Robert Leslie Ellis, and Douglas Denn Heath, 14 vols. (London: Brown and Taggard, 1858–74), 13: 171–228; and Bacon, *Considerations Touching a War with Spain* (1624), in *Certain Miscellany* (London, 1629).

[63] See Musto, *The Catholic Peace Tradition*, 9.

[64] James, *Letters*, 384.

[65] See *On the War Against the Turks*, in *The Erasmus Reader*, ed. Erika Rummel (Toronto: University of Toronto Press, 1990), 318–33.

[66] *On the War Against the Turks*, 319, 322.

[67] This may also be a reason why James neglects to mention the fact that the Christian forces may have had a technological and strategic advantage in the battle.

the victory itself expresses God's justice to the almost total *exclusion* of human effort and the honor that might be attached to it.) But again, the rules of *jus ad bellum* require a war to be fought not only honorably but strictly with the "right intent." And James makes it clear that the Christian forces had the "right intent" from the beginning.

Il faudrait des dieux, Rousseau once said about the need for a supramundane principle if one wanted to warrant human law absolutely.[68] And in a similar vein, when, with poetic license, following both epic convention and biblical precedent, James opens *The Lepanto* with a council of the gods — God the Father, the Son, and Satan — the poet deliberately moves the cause for war out of the realm of strictly human motives. "Even if there are some [wars] which might be called 'just,'" Erasmus had remarked in *The Education of a Christian Prince*, "yet as human affairs are now, I know not whether there could be found any of this sort — that is, the motive for which was not ambition, wrath, ferocity, lust, or greed."[69] But by putting the cause of the war in the hands of the gods (and ultimately God) James removes the Erasmian objection. It is Christ who accuses the Turks with unjustly persecuting Christians, having been motivated to it by Satan, and it is Satan who admits to this meddling in human affairs through Turkish imperialism, saying that the Christians deserve the grief that Turks are causing them. God settles the matter. "No more shall now these Christians be / With Infidels opprest" (81–82). And God proceeds then to incite the Christians "to revenge of wrongs the Turks / Have done ..." (91–92), but to incite them to respond to their situation as a reasonable, rational response to a difficult impasse. In fact, he has the Archangel Gabriel descend to Venice, where he causes the word to spread around (in rather democratic fashion, it may be noted, James here deferring to Venice's republican government) that the Venetians have tolerated oppression at the hands of the Turks too long, and it is God's will for them finally to take up arms. "They kill our Knights, they brash our forts, / They never let us never rest" (123–24). The Duke and the Senate, motivated by the people, meet and agree:

> The Towne was driven into this time,
>> In such a piteous strait
> By Mahometists, that they had els
>> Given over all debait;

[68] Hannah Arendt, *On Revolution* (Harmondsworth: Penguin, 1963), 183.
[69] *The Education of a Christian Prince*, 252.

> The turke had conquest Cyprus Ile,
>   And all their lands that lay
> Without the bounds of Italie,
>   Almost whole I say. (141-48)

Though one may of course disagree with James's assessment of the Venetians' situation, the assessment itself conforms entirely to those conditions which need to be fulfilled if a just war is to be waged. The sovereignty of the Venetian government is certain; its people have suffered a wrong, indeed a series of wrongs, at the hands of another sovereign government; warfare is shown to be the only means left to redress the grievance; and the war is conducted with the intent of restoring peace. The Venetians have had their lands usurped, their men killed, their "rest" disturbed. They fight, with divine authority, but also having been unambiguously provoked into it, only to recover what is already theirs. And what is theirs, what belongs to the Venetians, in sum, is peace.

As Aquinas had long before put it, peace is not just "concord" (*concordium*) but "ordered concord" (*ordinatum*). It is a "tranquility of order" (*tranquillitas ordinis*), a co-ordination of parts into the kind of unified whole knit by the "amity" and "obligations" James often discussed. But in that case, being a positive value, an active rather than a passive condition, peace is inherently, albeit paradoxically, aggressive. Peace isn't the mere absence of conflict but rather a condition of harmony actively enforced and actively expressed. And peace, therefore, can readily become a cause and justification of war.[70] In fact, according to the idea of "right intent," peace is the only justification of war.

It is clear that in the course of constructing his poem about the Battle of Lepanto James was adhering to the main thrust of that doctrine, including those features of it that were, as I am analyzing it, paradoxical. (It will be recalled that in his later years Bacon wrote to dissuade him of one of Aquinas's ideas on the subject of war, as if James had in fact openly discussed Aquinas's doctrine with his advisers and familiars.) If James's poem dwells on the details of a "a bloodie battel bolde," it also dwells on a vision of Venetian society — republican, communitarian, sovereign, God-loving, with its canals and palaces "a wondrous sight" to see, but under seige (102). It is this vision of the Venetian peace (even if it is only a

---

[70] St. Thomas Aquinas, *Summa Theologica*, 11-11, q. 29, art. 1, ad. 1; quoted and translated with valuable commentary in John K. Ryan, *Modern War and Basic Ethics* (Washington, DC: Catholic University Press of America, 1933), 13.

"shadow" peace with respect to its observance of the principles of "true Christianity," and perhaps something of a shadow too in its embrace of republican rather than regal government) that provides the pretext for the Battle of Lepanto; it is only for the sake of that peace that war is waged and victory celebrated. When the war is over, the Venetians draw together to thank God for what is in effect their *tranquillitas ordinis*.

James's sensitivity to the idea that war must only be fought for the sake of restoring peace may been a factor allowing him to celebrate a war whose long term effects were negligible. He was probably well aware of the fact that the Christians gained no land by waging their war against the Turks, not even getting Cyprus back. What they got back — in reality as in the poem — was peace and only peace, (and yet a peace with honor too, since the Christians had proven themselves by beating the Turkish fleet), a peace asserting the right of Venetian Christians to be themselves and thus to be let alone and prosper. When it came time for the Venetians to enjoy the benefits of peace, which is to say when it came time for them to hasten into the arms of plenty, they simply signed a treaty (neither ignominiously nor disadvantageously from a point of view like James's — James also probably being favorably disposed toward the Venetians because they practiced a kind of renegade, proto-Protestant Catholicism) swearing off aggression in return for trade. But of course, it is before this final embrace of plenty, as in the scene dramatized by Rubens about the benefits of government, that James has his heroic poem come to an end. The rewards are deferred. If some narrative threads are brought to completion, others are left open, as if to leave the reader in a condition of unsatisfied desire, a condition of hopefulness and resolve, perhaps, but first of all a condition of want.

§

In a sense, a non-militant "restoration of peace" was all James ever really wanted for the Protestant cause itself. Militant though he may have been in his conviction that Protestantism was the true church, and destined to overcome the predations of the Antichrist, he mainly wanted Protestants to be let alone. ("I only wish that such order might be taken as the land might be purged of such great flocks of them that daily diverts the souls of many from the sincerity of the gospel.")[71] Protestantism would spread of

---

[71] See above, note 55.

its own accord, so long as individuals were allowed — and also not "diverted from" — a pursuit of the "sincerity of the gospel." Not by any means a true ecumenist or internationalist (as Kevin Sharpe seems to claim him to be) James believed in the peace of nations as a condition for evangelical militancy, the apostolic catholicism of the Protestant church. But of course, believers in the Protestant faith (and for James, it is important to remember, this was one faith, admitting of no schisms or sects, though it allowed for some theological dispute), if not in harmony with Roman Catholics, were not necessarily in conflict with them either. The latter were shadows of the former, and might some day rejoin themselves to the former. Only, when Catholics behaved with suffecent belligerence to disturb the peace of Protestantism, preventing their pursuit of the gospel, then Protestants had a just cause to "resist," so long as they resisted fairly. And in any case, in James's politics the integrity of the state as a secular entity, over and above any evangelical or catholicizing purposes that might be attached to it, is an end in itself. It too demands peace, and is in fact a condition of peace, and needs to be let alone, even if its rulers are wicked and its people heretical.[72] The peace of a sovereign state, though it may conflict with the peace of the church of true believers, is a rival value, a rival peace, and hence a rival cause for aggression.

It was convenient for the young poet-king that the story of Lepanto involved a struggle with the one enemy that no one in his audience would have trouble reviling. Even Erasmus recognized that a war against the Ottoman Empire might on some occasion be necessary; and when Ronsard called upon Christians to embrace one another as brothers, he added without irony that those who needed an outlet for aggression could go fight against the Turks.[73] So if the Ottoman Empire isn't turned by James into an evil and impious empire, it is still deployed by him as a sign of that opposition to peace which a lover of peace may be forced to resist, that Other which can only be allowed to spread itself so far, lest peace be turned into oppression. Peace was always *local* for James, even if its locality, the true church, was sometimes mobile, and in principle powerfully expansive. And so the love for the victories of peace might naturally lead to an enthusiastic engagement with the paradoxical languages of war, with its cruel and bloody victories, and its unambiguous celebrations of meaning.

---

[72] See Jenny Wormald, " 'Basilikon Doron' and 'The Trew Law of Free Monarchies,' " in *The Mental World of the Jacobean Court*, ed. Linda Levy Peck (Cambridge: Cambridge University Press, 1991).

[73] *On the War Against the Turks*, 333.

And it might do so even though, or rather because of the fact that it is hard to get poems about war to mean what they really mean. James leaves us staring up at the ceiling of a painted room, wondering at its richly puzzling ambiguities, remembering others who may have wondered there before us, waiting for a final decision, a final coming of meaning, to be imposed upon us. And that too, a great waiting for meaning in the interests of both war and peace, may be one of the things the poem is trying to mean.

University of San Diego

PART II

Figure 3: "Pastime with Good Company," from the Henry VIII manuscript.
Reproduced by permission of The British Library,
MS. Add. 31922, f14ᵛ–15ʳ, 18ᵛ.

HENRY VIII[1]

PASTIME WITH GOOD COMPANY
(The King's Ballad)

Pastime with good company
I love and shall until I die.
Grudge who likes, but none deny;[2]
So God be pleased, thus live will I.[3]
   For my pastance:[4]   5
   Hunt, sing, and dance.

---

[1] Henry's English lyrics of more than one line are here presented, slightly modernized and silently emended. All of Henry VIII's lyrics known to date are best found collected, with others, in the *Henry VIII Manuscript* (London, BL Add. MS 31.922), a document of ca. 1522 reflecting the lyrical tastes of Henry's early court. Fully edited texts of all the lyrics in the MS — those of Henry VIII and others — are available in *The Lyrics of the Henry VIII Manuscript*, ed. R. G. Siemens (currently being prepared for publication by the Renaissance English Text Society); transcriptions of and settings for the lyrics of this manuscript are also available in John Stevens' works, *Music and Poetry in the Early Tudor Court* (London: Methuen and Co., 1961) and *Music at the Court of Henry VIII* (London: Stainer and Bell, 1962).

[2] This line has been paraphrased as "let grudge whosoever will, none shall refuse (it to me)." Margaret of Austria, regent of the Netherlands, employed a motto containing a similar sentiment, "Groigne qui groigne et vive Burgoigne," as did Anne Boleyn ("Ainsi sera, groigne qui groigne"); a lyric attributed to Wyatt, "If yt ware not," has as the first line of its burden "Grudge on who liste, this ys my lott" (ca. 1530). For a discussion of the relationship among the three, see R. G. Siemens, "Thomas Wyatt, Anne Boleyn, and Henry VIII's Lyric," *Notes and Queries* n.s. 44 (1997): 26–27.

[3] In two readings found in London BL Add. MS 5, 665 (141^v–142^r, voices 2 and 3), this phrase reads "this life."

[4] Pastime.

My heart is set!
All goodly sport
For my comfort.
Who shall me let?[5]   10

Youth must have some dalliance,
Of good or ill some pastance.
Company I think then best —
All thoughts and fancies to digest.
    For idleness   15
    Is chief mistress
    Of vices all.
    Then who can say
    But mirth and play
    Is best of all?   20

Company with honesty
Is virtue — vices to flee.
Company is good and ill,
But every man has his free will.
    The best ensue.   25
    The worst eschew.
    My mind shall be.
    Virtue to use.
    Vice to refuse.
    Thus shall I use me!   30

ALAS, WHAT SHALL I DO FOR LOVE?

Alas, what shall I do for love?
For love, alas, what shall I do,
Since now so kind
I do you find,
To keep you me unto?   5
Alas!

---

[5] Hinder, prevent.

Oh, my heart

Oh, my heart and, oh, my heart,
My heart it is so sore,
Since I must from my love depart,
And know no cause wherefore.

The time of youth is to be spent

The time of youth is to be spent,
But vice in it should be forfent.[6]
Pastimes there be I note truly
Which one may use and vice deny.
And they be[7] pleasant to God and man: 5
Those should we covet[8] when we can —
As feats of arms, and such other
Whereby activeness one may utter.[9]
Comparisons in them may lawfully be set,
For, thereby, courage[10] is surely out fet.[11]   10
Virtue it is, then, youth for to spend
In good disports which it does fend.[12]

---

[6] Forbidden.

[7] If they be.

[8] Desire, be inclined or drawn to.

[9] Vanquish, conquer, or overcome.

[10] Spirit, vitality, vigour, lustiness, and so forth. It is used in two different, though related, senses in the lyrics of the Henry VIII MS: one — relating to confidence, boldness, bravery, and valour — is the dominant sense here; another — relating to sexual vigour and inclination, the desire to love, the amorous spirit — is found more prominently in Henry's "Though That Men Do Call it Dotage," where the two are set in close relation, via the practices of courtly love (ll. 2, 13).

[11] Fetched out of it, gained.

[12] Support.

ALAC! ALAC! WHAT SHALL I DO?[13]
(Henry VIII)

Alac! Alac! What shall I do?
For care is cast in to my heart
And true love locked thereto.

HEY NONNY NONNY, NONNY NONNY NO!
(Unattributed)

Hey nonny nonny, nonny nonny no!
Hey nonny nonny, nonny nonny no!

This other day
   I heard a maid
   Right piteously complain.   5
She said always,
   Without denay,[14]
   Her heart was full of pain.

She said, alas,
   Without trespass,   10
   Her dear heart was untrue.
In every place,
   I know he has
   Forsaken me for a new.

Since he, untrue,   15
   Has chosen a new
   And thinks with her to rest

---

[13] Ringler suggests that the text of "Alac! Alac!" is probably incomplete and, as Stevens has noted, the peculiar layout in the manuscript suggests that this song and that which follows it in the manuscript, the unattributed "Hey Nonny Nonny, Nonny Nonny No!" (36'), are quite closely related. The original numbering of "Hey Nonny" in the manuscript corresponds with the number given to "Alac! Alac!" in the table of contents (2'). In consideration of this, and the fact that the matter of each song is complementary, the songs are here presented together. See William A. Ringler Jr., *Bibliography and Index of English Verse in Manuscript 1501–1558* (London: Mansell, 1992) 51.

[14] Denying.

And will not rue,
    And I so true:
    Wherefore, my heart will burst.   20

And now I may,
    In no manner away,
    Obtain that I do sue.
So ever and aye
    Without denay,   25
    My own sweet heart, adieu.

Adieu, darling.
    Adieu, sweeting.
    Adieu, all my welfare.
Adieu, all things   30
    To good pertaining.
    Christ keep you from care.

Adieu, full sweet.
    Adieu, right mate[15]
    To be a lady's peer.   35
With tears wet,
    And eyes replete,[16]
    She said, adieu, my dear.

Adieu, farewell.
    Adieu, la belle.   40
    Adieu, both friend and foe.
I cannot tell
    Where I shall dwell,
    My heart it greaves me so.

She had not said   45
    But, at abraid,[17]
    Her dear heart was full near

---

[15] Suitable companion.
[16] Full of tears.
[17] Suddenly, unaware, as if awakened.

And said good maid,
    Be not dismayed,
    My love, my darling dear.   50

In arms he hent[18]
    That lady gent
    In voiding[19] care and moan.
The day they spent
    To their intent   55
    In wilderness,[20] alone.

GREEN GROWS THE HOLLY

Green grows the holly.
    So does the ivy.
Though winter's blasts blow ever so high,
    Green grows the holly.

As the holly grows green   5
    And never changes hue,
So I am — ever have been —
    unto my lady true.

Ever the holly grows green
    With ivy all alone,   10
When flowers cannot be seen
    And greenwood leaves be gone.

Now unto my lady
    Promise to her I make:
From all other, only   15
    to her, I me betake.[21]

---

[18] Held, took hold of.
[19] Removing, eliminating.
[20] The countryside, but the term also has threatening connotations.
[21] Entrust, commit, give in charge.

Adieu, my own lady.
   Adieu, my special
Who has my heart truly,
   Be sure, and ever shall.   20

WHOSO THAT WILL ALL FEATS OBTAIN

Whoso that will all feats obtain[22]
In love he must be without disdain.
For love enforces all noble kind,[23]
And disdain discourages all gentle[24] mind.
Wherefore, to love and be not loved   5
Is worse than death? Let it be proved!
Love encourages, and makes one bold;
Disdain abates and makes him cold.
Love is given to God and man —
To woman also, I think the same.   10
But disdain is vice, and should be refused,
Yet nevertheless it is too much used.
Great pity it were, love for to compel[25]
With disdain, both false and subtle.

IF LOVE NOW REIGNED AS IT HAS BEEN

If love now reigned as it has been
And were rewarded as it has seen,[26]
Noble men then would surely ensearch[27]
All ways whereby they might it reach.

---

[22] Whosoever will show himself fully valorous.

[23] Strengthens all those of a noble nature, as well as all those natures (i.e., people) that are noble; *kind*: Birth, origin, descent, but especially the character or quality derived from birth or native constitution.

[24] Of noble birth, blood, or family; also courteous, polite, but with a sense of belonging to the aristocracy.

[25] Be constrained.

[26] And were rewarded as it had been since; alternatively, and were rewarded as it is evident it should be.

[27] Search it out.

But envy reigns with such disdain   5
And causes lovers outwardly to refrain,
Which puts them to more and more
Inwardly, most grievous and sore:
The fault in whom I cannot set,
But let them tell who love does get.   10
To lovers I put now sure this case:
Which of their loves does get them grace?[28]
And unto them which do it know
Better than do I, I think it so.

WHERETO SHOULD I EXPRESS

Whereto should I express
        My inward heaviness?
No mirth can make me fain,[29]
        'Till that we meet again.

Do way, dear heart, not so.   5
        Let no thought you dismay.
Though you now part me from,
        We shall meet when we may.

When I remember me
        Of your most gentle mind,   10
It may in no way agree
        That I should be unkind.

The daisy delectable,
        The violet waning and blue,
You are not variable —   15
        I love you and no more.

---

[28] One answer to this riddle, if we acknowledge the very real world of the court in the courtly love tradition, is "the king."

[29] Glad, rejoiced, well-pleased, but there is also the common pun on "feign," meaning pretend. "Feign" is also a common verb for describing the act of writing fictions.

I make you fast and sure;
   It is to me great pain
Thus long to endure
   'Till that we meet again.   20

THOUGH THAT MEN DO CALL IT DOTAGE

Though that men do call it dotage,
Who loves not wants courage.[30]
And whosoever may love get
From Venus surely he must it fetch, [31]
Or else from her which is her heir,   5
And she to him must seem most fair.
When eye and mind do both agree
There is no help! — there must it be!
The eye does look and represent,
But mind affirms with full consent.   10
Thus am I fixed without grudge:
My eye with heart does me so judge.
Love maintains all noble courage;
Who love disdains is all of the village.[32]
Such lovers, though they take pain,   15
It were pity they should obtain.
For often times where they do sue
They hinder lovers that would be true.
For whoso loves should love but one.
Change whoso will, I will be none.   20

---

[30] Sexual vigor and inclination, the desire to love, the amorous spirit.

[31] From lines 4–10, Henry puts forward a neo-platonic theory of love's reception by the lover akin to that outlined by Cardinal Pietro Bembo in the fourth book of Baldassare Castiglione's The Book of the Courtier (trans. Charles Singleton [New York: Anchor, 1959], 337 ff.). According to Cardinal Bembo, love is received from Venus, or the woman who is heir to Venus, and the object of love is perceived to be fair by the lover both visually and mentally/emotionally — first appreciated by the eye, and then by the mind and heart.

[32] Villainage, peasantry, not of courtly circles.

DEPARTURE IS MY CHIEF PAIN

Departure is my chief pain.
I trust right well to return again.

WITHOUT DISCORD

Without discord,
And both accord,
   Now let us be.
Both hearts alone
To set in one,   5
   Best seems me.
For when one soul
Is in the dole
   Of love's pain,
Then help must have   10
Himself to save
   And love to obtain.

Wherefore now we
That lovers be
   Let us now pray: 15
Once love sure
For to procure
   Without denay.[33]
Where love so sues
There no heart rues,   20
   But condescends.
If contrary,
What remedy?
   God it amend.[34]

---

[33] Deny.
[34] MS "amen"; amend, but also in the sense of "answer our prayer"; cf., in this context of prayer.

Though some say that youth rules me

Though some say that youth rules me,
    I trust in age to tarry.
God and my right,[35] and my duty,
    From them shall I never vary,
    Though some say that youth rules me.   5

I pray you all that aged be
    How well did you your youth carry?
I think some worse of each degree.
    Therein a wager lay dare I,
    Though some say that youth rules me.   10

Pastimes of youth some time among —[36]
    None can say but necessary.
I hurt no man, I do no wrong,
    I love true where I did marry,
    Though some say that youth rules me.   15

Then soon discuss that hence we must.[37]
    Pray we to God and Saint Mary
That all amend, and here an end.
    Thus says the king, the eighth Harry,
    Though some say that youth rules me.   20

Whoso that will for grace sue

Whoso that will for grace sue,
His intent must needs be true,
And love her in heart and deed,
Else it were pity that he should speed.[38]
    Many one says that love is ill,   5
    But those be they which know no skill.

---

[35] Henry's royal motto was "Dieu et mon droit."
[36] I.e., "to be sometimes engaged in pastimes of youth."
[37] Drive away, dispel, disperse, scatter; *that hence*: That which.
[38] Succeed.

Or else, because they may not obtain,
They would that others should it disdain.
But love is a thing given by God:
In that, therefore, can be none odd,   10
    But perfect in deed, and between two.
    Wherefore, then, should we it eschew?

LUSTY YOUTH SHOULD US ENSUE

Lusty Youth should us ensue.[39]
His merry heart shall sure all rue.
For whatsoever they do him tell
It is not for him, we know it well.

For they would have him his liberty refrain,   5
And all merry company for to disdain.
But I will not do whatsoever they say,
But follow his mind in all that we may.

How should Youth himself best use?
But all disdainers for to refuse.   10
Youth has as chief assurance
Honest mirth with virtue's pastance.[40]

For in them[41] consists great honour,
Though that disdainers would therein put error.
For they do sue to get them grace,   15
All only riches to purchase.

With good order, counsel, and equity,
Good Lord grant us our mansion to be.
For without their good guidance
Youth should fall in great mischance.   20

---

[39] Imitate.

[40] Likely the pastimes noted in Henry's "The Time of Youth Is to Be Spent," the "feats of arms" (l. 7) and other "good disports" (l. 12); see also l. 24.

[41] Honest mirth, etc.

For Youth is frail and prompt to do
As well vices as virtues to ensue.
Wherefore by these he must be guided,
And virtue's pastance must therein be used.

Now unto God this prayer we make,   25
That this rude play may well betake
And that we may our faults amend
And bliss obtain at our last end. Amen.

edited by Ray G. Siemens, Malaspina-University College

The writynges and letters found in the sayd casket, which are auowit to be written with the Scottishe Quenis awne hand.

Certaine French Sonnettes written by the quene of Scottes to Bothwell, befoir hir mariage with him, and
(as it is sayd) quhile hir husband lyuit,
But certainly befoir his diuorce from
hys wife as the wordes tham selues
shew , befoir quhom she here prefer-
reth hir selfe in deseruing to be belo-
ued of Bothwell.

O *Dieux ayez de moy compassion,*
   Et m'enseignez quelle preuue certain
Ie puis donner qui ne luy semble vain
De mon amour & ferme affection.
Las n'est il pas ia en possession
Du corps, du cœur qui ne refuse paine
Ny deshonneur, en la vie incertaine,
Offense de parentz, ne pire affliction?
Pour luy tous mes amis i'estime moins que
Et de mes ennemis ie veux esperer bien. (rien,
I'ay hazardé pour luy & nom & conscience:
Ie veux pour luy au monde renoncer :
Ie veux mourir pour luy auancer.
Que reste il plus pour prouuer ma constance?

Q.iiij.   Entre

Figure 4: First page of the Casket Sonnets, from George Buchanan,
*Ane Detectioun of the Duinges of Marie, Quene of Scottes,
Touchand the Murder of Hir Husband* (1571).
Reproduced by permission of The Huntington Library,
San Marino, California.

MARY STUART[1]

QUATRAIN WRITTEN IN THE MASS BOOK BELONGING TO HER AUNT ANNE OF LORRAINE, DUCHESS OF AERSCHOT, 1559

Si ce lieu est pour écrire ordonné
Ce qu'il vous plaît avoir en souvenance,
Je vous requiers que lieu me soit donné
Et que nul temps m'en ôte l'ordonnance.
Reine de France Marie

[If this place is ordered for writing
That which it pleases you to have in remembrance,
I require of you that this place be given me
And that no time take away the ordering from me.][2]

VERSES WRITTEN IN 1582[3]

Celui vraiment n'a point de courtoisie
Qui en bon lieu ne montre son savoir;
Etant requis d'écrire en poésie,
Il vaudrait mieux du tout n'en point avoir.

---

[1] Unless otherwise noted, the translations are by Peter C. Herman.

[2] Translation by Lisa Hopkins.

[3] Calendar of the state papers relating to Scotland and Mary, Queen of Scots 1547–1603 preserved in the Public Record Office , ed. J. D. Mackie (Edinburgh: H.M.S.O., 1969), vol. 13: 31. See also Robin Bell's edition of Mary's poems, *Bittersweet Within My Heart* (San Francisco: Chronicle Books, 1992), 93.

[A man is lacking in civility
If, when time calls, he fails to show his wit
And when the occasion merits poetry
He would far rather have no part of it.]

Les dieux, les cieux, la mort et la haine et l'envie
Sont sourds, irés, cruels, animés contre moi.
Prier, souffrir, pleurer, à chacun être amie,
Sont les remèdes seuls qu'en tant d'ennuis je vois.

[The Gods, the heavens, death, and hate rail on;
They are deaf, angry, cruel, marshalled against me.
To pray, weep, suffer, be a friend to everyone
Are the only cures for the many woes I see.][4]

SONNETS TO BOTHWELL[5]

I

O dieux, ayez de moi compassion,
Et m'enseignez quelle preuve certaine
Je puis donner qui ne lui semble vaine
De mon amour et ferme affection.
Las n'est-il pas déjà en possession
Du corps, du coeur qui ne refuse peine
Ni déshonneur en la vie incertaine,
Offense des parents,[6] ni pire affliction?
Pour lui tous mes amis j'estime moins que rien
Et de mes enemies je veux espérer bien.
J'ai hasardé pour lui et nom et conscience.
Je veux pour lui au monde renoncer:
Je veux mourir pour lui avancer.
Que reste il plus pour prouver ma constance?

[O you gods, have mercy on me

---

[4] 1582; translation by Lisa Hopkins.
[5] 1567?; first published in 1571.
[6] In A *Dictionarie of the French and English Tongues* (London, 1611), Randle Cotgrave defines "parent" as "a kinsman, cousin, allie," which suggests that Mary's phrase, "offense des parents," refers to her political allies as well as her family.

and show me what certain proof
I can give that will not seem vain to him
of my love and firm affection.
Alas, does he not already possess
this body, this heart, which does not reject pain
or dishonor, in this uncertain life,
offense to family, or worse affliction?
For him I value all my friends as less than nothing
And of my enemies I hope well.
I have risked for him fame and conscience:
I would for him renounce the world:
I would die to advance him.
What is left to prove my constancy?]

II

Entre ses mains et en son plein pouvoir
Je mets mons fils, mon honneur et ma vie,
Mon pays, mes sujets, mon âme assujettie
Et toute à lui, et n'ai autre vouloir
Pour mon objet que, sans le décevoir,
Suivre je veux, malgré tout l'ennui
Qu'issir en peut. Car je n'ai autre envie
Que, de ma foi, lui faire appercevoir
Que, pour tempête ou bonace qu'il fasse,
Jamais ne veux changer demeure ou place.
Bref, je ferai de ma foi telle preuve,
Qu'il connaîtra sans feinte ma constance,
Non par mes pleurs ou feinte obéissance,
Commes autres ont fait, mais par divers épreuves.

[Into his hands and his absolute power
I place my son, my honor and my life,
My country, my subjects, my subjected soul
Are all for him, and I have no other desire
For my object than, without deceipt,
To follow him, despite all the suffering
That may follow. Because I have no other wish
But to make him perceive that my faithfulness,
Whatever storm or good weather that comes,

Will never change its house or place.
In short, I will so prove my faith
That he will know my constancy to be unfeigned,
Not by my tears or feigned obedience, not
As some other have done, but by various deeds.]

III[7]

Elle, pour son honneur, vous doit obéissance.
Moi, vous obéissant, j'en puis recevoir blâme,
N'etant, à mon regret, comme elle, votre femme.
Et si n'aura pourtant en ce point préeminence
Pour son profit elle use de constance,
Car ce n'est peu d'honneur d'être de vos biens dame.
Et moi, pour vous aimer j'en puis recevoir blâme.
Et ne lui veut céder en toute l'observance.
Elle, de votre mal n'a l'apprehénsion.
Moi, j'ai nul repos tant je crains l'apparence.
Par l'avis des parents, elle eut votre accointance.
Moi, malgré tous les miens, vous porte affection
Et de sa loyauté prenez ferme assurance.

[She, for her honor, owes you obedience
I, in obeying you, can receive only blame,
not being, to my regret, like her, your wife.
And even so, she will not surpass me in this point.
She uses her constancy for her own benefit,
Because there is no small honor in being mistress of your wealth.
And me, because I love you, I get only blame.
And I will not cede to her or lag in any observance.
She has no idea about your danger;
Me, I cannot rest for fear of what might happen.
She, through her family, made your acquaintance.
Me, despite all of mine, bring you love
And yet you place your firm trust in her loyalty.]

---

[7] This poem has thirteen lines. Unaccountably, Robin Bell adds a line so that the poem becomes a conventional, fourteen line sonnet (*Bittersweet Within My Heart*, 32, l. 13 in this version).

IV

Par vous, mon coeur, et par votre alliance
Elle a remis sa maison en honneur
Elle a joui par vous la grandeur
Dont tous les siens n'ont nulle assurance
De vous, mon bien, elle a eu la constance,
Et a gagné pour un temps votre coeur.
Par vous elle a eu plaisir et bonheur,
Et par vous a reçu honneur et réverence,
Et n'a perdu sinon la jouissance
D'un fâcheux sot qu'elle aimait chèrement
Je ne la plains d'aimer donce ardemment
Celui qui n'a en sens, ni en vaillance,
En beauté, en bonté, ni en constance,
Point de seconde. Je vis en cette foi.

[Through you, my love, and through your marriage,
She restored honor to her house.
She enjoyed through you such greatness
Of which her family never had assurance.
From you, my love, she has had constancy
And for a while won your heart.
From you she had pleasure and good fortune,
And from you she received honor and reverence;
And she lost nothing but the pleasures
Of a tiresome fool she once loved dearly.
I don't blame her for loving so ardently
One who in wisdom nor bravery,
In beauty, generosity, or in constancy
Is second to none. I live in that faith.]

V

Quand vous l'aimiez, elle usait de froideur,
Si vous soufriez pour l'amour passion
Qui vient d'aimer de trop d'affection,
Son doigt montrait la tristesse de coeur,
N'ayant plaisir de votre grande ardeur.
En ses habits, montrait sans fiction
Qu'elle n'avait peur qu'imperfection

Peut l'effacer hors de ce loyal coeur.
De votre mort je ne vis la peur
Que méritait tel mari et seigneur.
Somme de vous elle a eu tout son bien
Et n'a prisé ni jamais estimé
Un si grand heur sinon puisqu'il n'est sien
Et maintenant dit l'avoir tant aimé.

[When you made love to her, she lay frigid
So that you suffered a passionate love for her
That comes from loving with too much emotion,
Her hand showed her heart's discontent,
Taking no pleasure in your great ardor.
In her clothes, she showed without fiction
That she never feared that poor taste
Would erase love from a loyal heart.
I did not see the fear of your death
That such a husband and lord would deserve
In sum, she has had all her wealth from you,
And she never prized, nor ever valued
This great fortune, since it is not hers by right.
And now she says she loved you best of all!]

VI

Et maintenant elle commence à voir
Qu'elle était bien de mauvais jugement
De n'estimer l'amour d'un tel amant
Et voudrait bien mon ami décevoir
Par les écrits tout fardés de savoir
Qui pourtant n'est en son esprit croissant
Ains[8] empruntés de quelque auteur éluissant,
A fait très bien un envoi sans l'avoir
Et toutefois ses paroles fardées,
Ses pleurs, ses plaintes remplies de fictions,
Et ses hauts cris et lamentations,
Ont tant gagné que par vous sont gardées

---

[8] Ainsi.

Ses lettres écrites auxquelles vous donnez foi
Et si[9] l'aimez et croyez plus que moi.

[And now she starts to see
That she had very bad judgment
Not to value the love of such a lover;
And she would now deceive my beloved
Through writings all painted with learning,
Which could not have come from her mind
But cribbed from some dazzling author.
She crafted well a letter without having the brains.
And yet her filched words,
Her tears, her plaints filled with fictions,
And her great cries and laments,
Have so won you that you keep
Her letters and believe them.
And so you love and believe her more than me.]

VII

Vous las croyez, las[10] trop je l'aperçois
Et vous doutez de ma ferme constance,
O mon seul bien et ma seul espérance,
Et ne vous puis assurer de ma foi
Vous m'estimez légère qui le voy,
Et si[11] n'avez en moi nulle assurance
Et soupçonner mon coeur sans apparence
Vous défiant à trop grand tort de moi.
Vous ignorez l'amour que je vous porte,
Vous soupçonnez qu'autre amour me transporte,
Vous estimez mes paroles du vent,
Vous dépeignez de cire mon las coeur,
Vous me pensez femme sans jugement.
Et tout cela augmente mon ardeur.

[You believe her, alas, too well I see you do
And you doubt my firm constancy,

---

[9] Ainsi.
[10] Helas.
[11] Ainsi.

O my sole wealth and my sole hope.
And I cannot make you sure of my faith.
I see that you judge me light,
And so you do not have any confidence in me
And you distrust my heart without any evidence,
Your distrust does me great wrong
You do not realize the love I bear for you.
You suspect that some other love transports me.
You consider my words mere wind.
You think my heart malleable as wax.
You think me a woman without judgment.
And all this increases my passion.]

VIII[12]

Mon amour croît et plus en plus croîtra
Tant que je vivrai et tiendra à grandeur,
Tant seulement d'avoir part en ce coeur
Vers qui enfin amour paraîtra
Si très à clair que jamais n'en doutera.
Pour lui je veux rechercher la grandeur
Et ferai tant qu'en vrai connaîtra
Que je n'ai bien, heur, ni contentement,
Qu'a l'obéir et servir loyalement.
Pour lui j'attends toute bonne fortune.
Pour lui je veux garder santé et vie.
Pour lui tout vertu de suivre j'ai envie,
Et sans changer me trouvera toute une.[13]

[My love grows and will grow more and more
So long as I will live, and I will hold it a great happiness
To have only a part in that heart,
To which finally my love will appear
So clearly that he will never suspect it.
For him I wish to search for honor

---

[12] This poem also has thirteen lines, and Bell once more adds a line, this time line 6 in his version.

[13] While the assertion of constancy is a Petrarchan trope, it is possible that Mary is also echoing Elizabeth I's motto, *semper eadem*, always the same.

And will do so much that he will truly know
That I have no wealth, happiness, or contentment,
Other than to obey him and to serve him loyally.
For him I await good fortune.
For him I wish to keep good health and long life.
For him I wish to follow each virtue
And he will find me always without change.]

IX

Pour lui aussi j'ai jeté mainte larme.
Premier, quand il se fit de ce corps possesseur,
Duquel alors il'n'avait pas le coeur.
Puis me donna une autre dure alarme
Quand il versa de son sange mainte dragme,[14]
Dont de grief il me vint laisser douleur,
Qui m'en pensa ôter la vie et frayeur
De perdre las[15] le seul rempart qui m'arme.
Pour lui depuis j'ai méprisé l'honneur
Ce qui nous peut seul pourvoir de bonheur.
Pour lui j'ai hasardé grandeur et conscience.
Pour lui tous mes parents j'ai quitté et amis,
Et tous autres respects sont à part mis.
Brief de vous seul je cherche l'alliance.

[For him I cry so many tears.
First, when he made himself possessor of the body
Of which he did not have the heart.
Then he gave me another hard shock
When he spilled some of his blood
That out of grief I thought to ease the pain
By thinking to end my life and never fear again
To lose, alas, the one wall that supports me.
For him I have scorned honor,
Which alone can bring us happiness.
For him I have gambled rank and conscience.

---

[14] Cotgrave construes this word as "A dramme; the eighth part of an ounce, or three scruples; also, a handful of" (Dictionarie of the French and English Tongues).
[15] Helas.

For him I have left all family and friends,
And all other concerns I have let go.
In short, I have sought to marry you alone.]

X

De vous je dis seul soutien de ma vie
Tant seulement je cherche m'assurer,
Et si[16] ose de moi tant présumer
De vous gagner malgré tout l'envie.
Car c'est le seul désir de votre chère amie,
De vous servir et loyalement aimer,
Et tous malheur moins que rien estimer
Et votre volonté de la mienne suivre.
Vous connaîtrez avec obéissance
De mon loyal devoir n'omettant la science
A quoi j'étudierai pour toujours vous complaire,
Sans aimer rien que vous, sous la sujétion
De qui je veux, sans nulle fiction,
Vivre et mourir et à ce j'obtempère.[17]

[Of you, I say, the sole support of my life,
I only seek an assured commitment
And yet I dare presume so much of myself
To win you in spite of all envy.
Because the sole desire of your dear lover
Is to loyally serve and love you
And to consider all misfortunes less than nothing,
And for my will to follow yours.
By this, you will know the obedience
In my loyal devotion, never forgetting
Always to study how best to please you,
Loving no-one but you, under the subjection
Of the one whom I, with no fiction,
Live and die for, and obey.]

---

[16] Ainsi.

[17] Cotgrave defines "obtemperer" as "obey, doe the will . . . be at the commaund of"
(*Dictionarie of the French and English Tongues*).

XI

Mon coeur, mon sang, mon âme, et mon souci,
Las,[18] vous m'avez promis qu'aurions ce plaisir
De deviser avec vous à loisir,
Toute la nuit où je languis ici,
Ayant le coeur d'extrême peur transi,
Pour voir absent le but de mon désir.
Crainte d'oubli un coup me vient à saisir
Et l'autrefois je crains que rendurci
Soit contre moi votre aimable coeur
Par quelque dit d'un méchant rapporteur.
Un autre fois je crains quelque aventure
Qui par chemin détourne mon amant,
Par un fâcheux et nouveau accident.
Dieu détourne tout malheureux augure.

[My heart, my blood, my soul and my care,
Alas, you promised me that I would have the pleasure
To talk with you at leisure
The whole night, where I languish here,
My heart transfixed by extreme fear
For you, absent, the end of all my desire.
Fear of forgetting seizes me with a shock
And other times I fear that your loving heart
Is made hard against me
By the saying of some lying gossip.
Another time I fear that some chance
Along the way has turned back my lover
By some troublesome and new accident.
God prevent any unhappy omens!]

XII

Ne vous voyant selon qu'avez promis
J'ai mis la main au papier pour écrire
D'un différent que je voulu transcrire.
Je ne sais pas quel sera votre avis

---

[18] Helas.

Mais, je sais bien qui mieux aimer saura,
Vous direz bien qui plus y gagnera.

[Not seeing you, as you had promised,
I have put my hand to paper to write
About a dispute that I would write about.
I do not know what will be your opinion,
But I know well which one of us knows better how to love,
You may tell who will win the most.
[unfinished]]

SONNET TO ELIZABETH[19]

Une seul penser qui me profite et nuit
Amer et doux, change en mon coeur sans cesse,
Entre le doubte et l'espoir il m'oppresse
Tant que la paix et le repos me fuient.
Donc, chère soeur, si cette carte suit
L'affection de vous voir qui me presse,
C'est que je vis en peine et en tristesse,
Si promptement l'effect ne s'en ensuit.
J'ai vu la nef relâcher par contrainte
En haute mer proche d'entrer au port,
Et le serein se convertir en trouble.
Ainsi je suis en souci et en crainte,
Non pas de vous mais quant aux fois à tort
Fortune rompe voile et cordage double.

[A single thought that haunts me, day and night,
Bitter and sweet, torments my heart, without cease,
Between fear and hope it oppresses me
So that peace and rest flee me.
So, dear sister, if this paper reveals
The desire to see you that oppresses me,
That is because I live in pain and sadness,
So long as my suit is not quickly granted.

---

[19] 1568; Elizabeth responded to Mary's poem with "Doubt of Future Foes." The original is in the British Library, Caligula BV, fol. 316. I have consulted Constance Jordan's private translation of this poem.

I have seen a ship freed from constraint
On the high seas, near to entering a port,
And the calm sea turned to storms:
Likewise, I am troubled and in fear,
Not because of you, but because Fortune,
Often wrongly rips sails and rigging.]

FROM G[EORGE] B[UCHANAN],
Ane Detectioun of the Duinges of Marie, Quene of Scottes,
Touchand the Murder of Hir Husband. . . .[20]

Certaine French Sonnettes written by the quene of Scottes to Bothwell,
befoir hir mariage with him, and (as it is sayd) quhile hir husband lyuit,[21]
But certainly befoir[22] his divorce from hys wife as the wordes tham
selves[23] shew, befoir quhom she here prefereth hir selfe in deserving to
be beloved of Bothwell.[24]

O Dieux ayez de moy compassion,
Et m'enseignez quelle preuve certain
Je puis donner qui ne luy semble vain
De mon amour & ferme affection.
Las[25] n'est il pas ja en possession
Du corps, du coeur qui ne refuse paine
Ny deshonneur,[26] en la vie incertaine,
Offense de parentz, ne pire affliction?
Pour luy tous mes amis j'estime moins que rien
Et de mes ennemis je veux esperer bien.
J'ay hazardé pour luy & nom & conscience:
Je veux pour luy au monde renoncer:

---

[20] 1571; sig. Q.iiii.–S.i.; The compositor for Buchanan's book used italics for the
French and black letter type for the Anglo-Scots (see the illustration). I have silently
adopted the modern usage of i/j and u/v.

[21] Lived.

[22] Before.

[23] Themselves.

[24] This introductory headnote appeared before Mary's sonnets in Buchanan's *Ane
Detectioun*.

[25] Alas, or "Helas."

[26] Dishonneur.

Je veux mourir pour luy avancer.
Que reste il plus pour prouver[27] ma constance?

Entre ses mains & en son plein pouvoir
Je metz mon filz, mon honneur, & ma vie,
Mon pais, mes subjectz, mon ame assubjectie
Est tout à luy, & n'ay autre voulloir
Pour mon object que sans le decevoir
Suivre je veux malgré tout l'envie
Qu'issir en peult, car je n'ay autre envie
Que de ma foy, luy faire appercevoir
Que pour tempeste ou bonnace qui face
Jamais ne veux changer demeure ou place.
Brief je feray de ma foy telle preuve,
Qu'il cognoistra sans fainte ma constance,
Non par mes pleurs ou fainte obeyssance,
Comme autres ont fait, mais par divers espreuve.

Elle pour son honneur vous doibt obeyssance
Moy vous obeyssant j'en puis recevoir blasme,
N'estát, à mon regret, comme elle vostre femme.
Et si n'aura pour tant en ce point préeminence.
Pour son profit elle use de constance,
Car ce n'est peu d'honneur d'estre de voz biens dame
Et moy pour vous aymer j'en puis recevoir blasme
Et ne luy veux ceder en toute l'observance
Elle de vostre mal n'a l'apprehension
Moy je n'ay nul repos tant je crains l'apparence
Par l'advis des parentz elle eut vostre accointance
Moy malgré tous les miens vous porte affection
Et de sa loyauté prenez ferme asseurance.

Par vous mon coeur & par vostre alliance
Elle à remis sa maison en honneur
Elle à jouy par vous la grandeur
Dont tous les siens n'ayent nul asseurance
De vous mon bien elle à eu la constance,

---

[27] Preuver.

Et à gaigné pour un temps vostre coeur.
Par vous elle à eu plaisir en bon heur,
Et pour vous à receu honneur & reverence,
Et n'a perdu sinon la jouyssance
D'un fascheux sot qu'elle aymoit cherement
Je ne la playns d'aymer donc ardamment,
Celuy qui n'a en sens, ny en vaillance,
En beauté, en bonté, ny en constance
Point de seconde. Je vis en ceste[28] foy.

Quant[29] vous l'aimiez elle usoit de froideur.
Sy vous souffriez pour s'amour passion
Qui vient d'aymer de trop d'affection,
Son doig[30] monstroit, la tristesse de coeur
N'ayant plaisir de vostre grand ardeur
En ses habitz monstroit sans fiction
Qu'êlle n'avoit paour[31] qu'imperfection
Peust[32] l'effacer hors de ce loyal coeur.
De vostre mort je ne vis la peaur
Que meritoit tel mary & seigneur.
Somme de vous elle à eu tout son bien
Et n'à prisé ny jamais estimé
Un si grand heur si non puis qui'l n'est sien
Et maintenant dit l'avoir tant ayme.

Et maintenant elle commence à voir
Qu'elle estoit bien de mauvais jugement
De n'estimer l'amour d'un tel amant
Et voudroit bien mon amy decevoir,
Par les escriptz tout fardez de sçavoir
Qui pourtant n'est on son esprit croissant
Ains emprunté de quelque autheur eluissant,[33]

---

[28] c'est.
[29] Quand.
[30] doigt.
[31] peur.
[32] peult.
[33] auteur luissant.

A faint tresbien[34] un envoy sans l'avoir
Et toutefois ses parolles fardez,
Ses pleurs, ses plaincts remplis de fictions,
Et ses hautz cris & lamentations
Ont tant gaigné qui par vous sont gardez
Ses lettres escriptes ausquelz vous donnez foy
Et si l'aymez & croyez plus que moy.

Vous la croyez, las[35] trop je l'apperçoy
Et vous doutez de ma ferme constance,
O mon seul bien & mon seul esperance,
Et ne vous puis asseurer de ma foy
Vous m'estimez legier qui le voy,
Et si n'avez en moy nul asseurance
Et soupçonnez mon coeur sans apparence
Vous deffiant[36] à trop grand tort de moy.
Vous ignorez l'amour que je vous porte,
Vous soupçonnez qu'autre amour me transporte,
Vous estimez mes parolles du vent,
Vous depeignez de cire mon las coeur,
Vous me pensez femme sans jugement.
Et tout cela augmente mon ardeur.

Mon amour croist & plus en plus croistra
Tant que je vivray, & tiendray à grandheur,
Tant seulement d'avoir part en ce coeur
Vers qui en fin mon amour paroistra
Sy tres à clair que jamais n'en doutra.
Pour luy je veux recercher la grandeur,
Et feray tant qu'en vray cognoistra,
Que je n'ay bien, heur, ne contentement,
Qu'à l'obeyr & servir loyaument.
Pour luy jattendz[37] toute bonne fortune.
Pour luy je veux garder santé & vie.

---

[34] Fait tres bien.
[35] Alas, or helas.
[36] Meffiant.
[37] j'attendz.

Pour luy tout vertu de suyvre j'ay envie,
Et sans changer me trouvera tout une.

Pour luy aussi je jette mainte larme.
Premier quand il se fist de ce corps possesseur,
Duquel alors il n'avoit pas le coeur.
Puis me donna un autre dur alarme,
Quand il versa de son sang mainte dragme,[38]
Dont de grief il me vint lesser doleur,
Qui m'en pensa oster la vie, & frayeur
De perdre las le seul rempar qui m'arme.
Pour luy depuis j'ay[39] mesprisé l'honneur
Ce qui nous peult seul pourvoir de bonheur.
Pour luy j'ay hazardè grandur & consience.
Pour luy tous mes parentz j'ay quité, & amis,
Et tous autres respectz sont apart mis.
Brief de vous seul je cerche[40] l'alliance.

De vous je dis seul soustien de ma vie
Tant seulement je cerche[41] m'asseurer,
Et si ose de moy tant presumer
De vous gaigner maugré toute l'envie.
Car c'est le seul desir de vostre chere amie,
De vous servir & loyaument aymer,
Et tous malheurs moins que riens estimer,
Et vostre volunté de la mien suivre.
Vous cognoistrez avecques obeyssance
De mon loyal devoir n'omettant lascience[42]
A quoy j'estudiray pour toujiours vous complaire
Sans aymer rien que vous, soubz la subjection,
De qui je veux sans nulle fiction
Vivre & mourir & à ce j'obtempere

---

[38] drasme.
[39] "Jay" in the original, but since the compositor usually has "j'ay," I assume "jay" is an error.
[40] Cherche.
[41] Cherche.
[42] la science.

Mon coeur, mon sang, mone ame, & mon soucy,
Las, vous m'avez promis qu'aurons ce plaisir
De deviser avecques vous à loysir,
Toute la nuict,[43] ou je languis icy,
Ayant le coeur d'extreme paour transy,
Pour voir absent le but de mon desir
Crainte d'oublir un coup me vient à saisir:
Et l'autre fois je crains que rendurcie
Soit contre moy vostre amiable coeur
Par quelque dit d'un meschant rapporteur.
Un autre fois je crains quelque aventure
Qui par chemin detourne mon amant,
Par un fascheux & nouveau accident.
Dieu detourne toute malheureux augure

Ne vous voyant selon qu'avez promis
J'ay mis la main au papier pour escrire
D'un different que je voulu transcrire.
Je ne scay pas quel sera vostre advis
Mais je scay bien qui mieux aymer scaura,
Vous diriez bien que plus y gaignera.

[O Goddis have of me compassioun,
And schew quhat [44]certain profe
I may geif,[45] which shall nat seem to him vaine,
Of my love and fervent affectioun.
Helas, is he nat alredy in possessioun
Of my bodie, of hart, that refusis no payne,
Nor dishonour in the life uncertaine,
Offenc offrendes,[46] nor worse afflictioun,
For him I esteme al my frends les then nathing,
And I will have gude hope of my enemies.
I have put in hasard for him both fame & conscience,

---

[43] Nuit.
[44] What.
[45] Give.
[46] Offense of friends.

I will die to set him forwart.
Qhat remayneth to gief proof of my constancie?

In his handis[47] and in his full power,
I put my sonne, my honour, and my lyif,
My contry, my subjects, my soule al subdewit,[48]
To him, and has none other will
For my scope, quhilk[49] without deceit,
I will folow in spite of all envie
That may ensue: For I haif na other desire,
But to make him perceive my faythfulnes,
For storme or fayre wedder[50] that may come,
Never will it chainge dwelling, or place.
Shortly I sall geif of my trueth sic profe,[51]
That he sall know my constancie without fiction,
Not by my weping, or faynit[52] obedience,
As other have done: but by other experience.

She for hyr honour oweth you obedience:
I in obaying you may receive dishonour,
Nat being (to my displesure) your wife as she.
And yit in this poynt she shall have na preheminence.
Sche useth constancy for hyr awin profite:
For it is na little honour to be maistres of your goodes,
And I for luifing[53] of you may receive blame,
And will nat be overcumme by hyr in loyall observaunce.
Sche has no apprehension of your evyll,[54]
I feare so all appearing evill that I can have na reste:
Sche had your acqueintance by consent of hyr friendes,
I against al thair will have borne you affection.

---

[47] Hands.
[48] Subdued.
[49] Which.
[50] Weather.
[51] Shortly I shall give of my truth such proof. . . .
[52] Feigned.
[53] Loving.
[54] Meaning, the evil threatening you.

And nat the lesse (my hart) you doubt of my constance,
And of hir fathfulness you haif firme assurance.

By you (my hart) and by your aliance[55]
Sche hath restored hyr house unto honour,
By you she is become to that greitnes,
Of quhilk[56] hyr friendis had never assurance,
Of you (my wealth) sche got the acquentance,
And hath conquest the same time your hart.
By you sche hath pleasure and good lucke,
And by you hath received honour & reverence,
And hath nat lost, but the rejoysance[57]
Of one unpleasant foole, qhhilk she louit deirly.[58]
Than I moane hyr nat to love ardently
Him that hath none in wit, in manhead,
In beauty, in bounty, in truth, nor in constancy,
Any second: I lief[59] in the beleif.

Quhen[60] you lovit hyr she usit coldnesse,
Gif[61] you suffrith for hir luif passioun,
That commith of so greit affectioun of luif,
Hyr sadness schew the tristesse of hyr hart,
Taking na pleasure of your vehement burning,
In hyr clothing she schew unfaynitly,[62]
That sche had na feir,[63] that imperfection
Could deface hyr out of that true hart.
I did not see in hyr the feir of your death,
That was worthy of sic[64] husband and Lord.
Schortly she hath of you all hyr wealth.

---

[55] Alliance.
[56] Which.
[57] Rejoicing, or enjoyment.
[58] Which she loved dearly.
[59] Live.
[60] When.
[61] So that you suffered for her [a] love passion . . .
[62] Unfeignedly.
[63] Fear.
[64] Such a husband.

And hath never weyit nor estemit[65]
One so greit hap, but sins it was nat hirs,
And now she saith that she loueth him so well.

And now sche beginneth to see
That she was of veray evill jugement,
To esteeme the love of sic ane lover,[66]
And wald[67] fayne deceive my love,
By writinges and paintit learning,
Quhuk nat the lesse did not breid in hir braine,[68]
But borrowit from sum feate[69] authour,
To fayne one [letter] and haif none.
And for all that hyr payntit wordis,
Hyr teares, hyr plaintes full of dissimulation,
And hyr hye cryes and lamentations
Hath won that poynt, that you keip in store,
Hir letters and writinges, to quhilk you geif trust,[70]
Ye, and lovest and belevist hyr more than me.

You beleve hir (helas) I perceive it to[71] well,
And callist in doubt my firme constancie
(O mine onely wealth, and my onely hope)
And I can not assure you of my truth.
I see that you esteeme me light,
And be no way assurit of me,
And doost suspect (my hart) without any appearing cause,
Discrediting me wrangously.[72]
You do nat knaw the love I beare to you.
You suspect that other love transporteth me.
You thinke my wordes be but wind:

---

[65] Weighed or esteemed.
[66] Such a lover.
[67] Would.
[68] "Which not the less did not breed in her brain," meaning, which did not originate in her mind.
[69] Accomplished.
[70] To which you give trust.
[71] Too.
[72] Terribly, without cause.

You paint my wery heart,[73] as it were of waxe,
You imagine me an woman without jugement.
And all that encreaseth my burning.

My love increaseth and more and more wil increase,
So lang as I shall lief,[74] and I shall holde for ane greit felicitie
To have onely pairt in that hart,
To the quhilk at length my love sall appeare,[75]
So clearely, that he sall never doubt.
For him I will strive against wan weard,[76]
For him I will recerfe greitnes,[77]
And sall do so mikle[78] that he shall know
That I haif no wealth, hap,[79] nor contentation,
But to obay, and serve him truely.
For him I attend all gude fortune.
For him I will conserve health and life,
For him I desire to ensew courage,[80]
And he shall ever finde me unchangeable.

For him also I powred[81] out many tearis,
First quhen he made himselfe possessor of thys body.
Of the quhilk[82] then he had nat the hart.
After he did geve me one other hard charge,
Quhen he bled of his blud[83] great quantitie,
Through the great sorrow of the quhilk came to me that dolour,
That almost caryit away my life, and the feire
To lefe the onely strength that armit me.
For him since I haif despisit honour,

---

[73] Weary, but possibly a mistranslation for "very."
[74] So long as I shall live.
[75] To the which at length my love shall appear.
[76] Bad fortune.
[77] Receive greatness.
[78] Shall do so much.
[79] Happiness.
[80] Literally, "ensue courage, " or "follow courage," meaning to be virtuous.
[81] Poured.
[82] Which.
[83] Blood.

The thing onely that bringeth felicitie.
For him I haif[84] hazardit greitness & conscience,
For him I haif forsaken all kin and friendes,
And set aside all other respectes,
Schortly, I seke the aliance of you onely.

Of you I say onely upholder of my life,
I onely seke to be asseurit,[85]
Ye and dare presume so much of my selfe,
To win you in spite of all envy:
For that is the onely desire of your deir love;
To serve and love you truely,
And to esteme all wan hap lesse then nathyng,
And to follow your wyll wyth myne,
You shall knaw wyth obedience,
Not forgetting the knawlege of my real deuty,[86]
The quhilke[87] I shall study to the fine[88] that may ever please you.
Lovyng nothyng but you, in the subjectioun
Of quhome I will without any fictioun,
Live and die, and this I consent.[89]

My hart, my bloud, my soule, my care,
Helas you had promist that I should have that pleasure.
To devise[90] wyth you at leysure.
All the night quhair[91] I lye and languishe here.
My hart beyng overset[92] wyth extreme feare
Being absent the butte[93] of my desire.
Feare of forgetting sometyme taketh me,
And other tymes I feare that lovesum hart,

---

[84] Have.
[85] Assured.
[86] Duty.
[87] Which.
[88] Goal, end.
[89] I.e., to this I consent.
[90] To plan, or plot.
[91] Where.
[92] Overcome.
[93] End, or goal.

Be not hardenit agaynst me
By sum saying of ane wickit reporter,[94]
Other tymes I feare sum aventure,[95]
That by the way should turne abacke my love
By sum troublous and new accident.
God turne abacke all unhappy augure.

Not seing[96] you as you had promist,
I put my hand to the paper to write,
Of ane differens that I have willit copye.[97]
I can not tell what shalbe your jugement,
But I knaw well quho can best love,
You may tell who shall winne maist.[98]

---

[94] Of a wicked reporter, i.e., by slanderous gossip.

[95] Adventure, bad luck.

[96] Seeing.

[97] Of a difference I will copy, meaning, of a dispute that I will write about.

[98] Most.

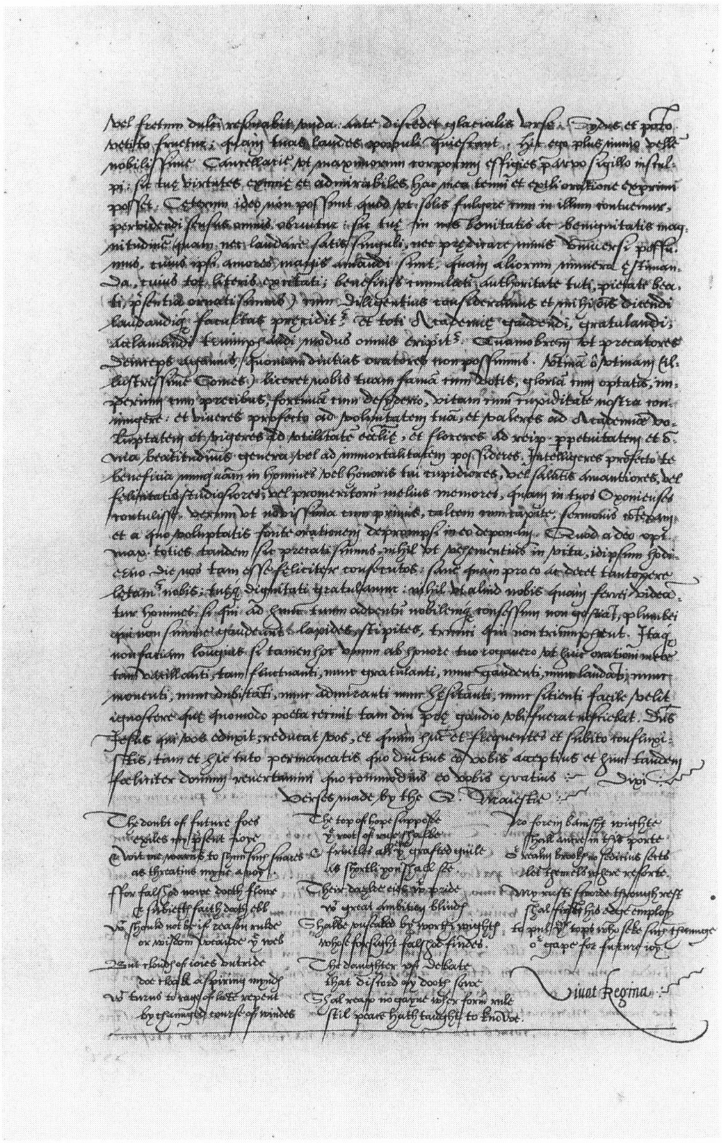

Figure 5: "The Doubt of Future Foes," from V.b. 317, fol. 20ᵛ.
Reproduced by permission of the Folger Shakespeare Library.

ELIZABETH I[1]

1. WRITTEN ON A WINDOW FRAME AT WOODSTOCK[2]

O Fortune, thy wresting, wavering state
Hath fraught with cares my troubled wit,
Whose witness this present prison late
Could bear, where once was joy flown quite.
Thou causedst the guilty to be loosed
From lands where innocents were enclosed,
And caused the guiltless to be reserved,
And freed those that death had well deserved.
But all herein can be naught wrought,
So God grant to my foes as they have thought.
    Finis. Elisabetha the prisoner, 1555
Much suspected by me, but nothing proved can be.

---

[1] Except for the variants of "The Doubt of Future Foes," Elizabeth's poetry and the notes are excerpted from *Elizabeth I: Collected Works*, ed. Leah S. Marcus, Janel Mueller, and Mary Beth Rose (Chicago: University of Chicago Press, 2000). I am grateful to Alan Thomas of the University of Chicago Press for his help and for granting permission to reprint this material.

[2] Ca. 1555. The poem is as copied in 1600 by the Moravian magnate Zdeněk Brtnický z Valdštejina, or Baron Waldstein, and reproduced in G. W. Groos, trans., *The Diary of Baron Waldstein: A Traveller in Elizabethan England* (London: Thames & Hudson, 1981), 117, 119. The poem was also copied in 1598 by Paul Hentzner, *Itinerarium* (Nuremberg, 1612), 44–45; and in 1599 by Thomas Platter, as reproduced in Hans Hecht, ed., *Thomas Platters des Jüngeren Englandfahrt im Jahre 1599* (Leipzig: Max Niemeyer Verlag, 1929), 121–22. Platter and Hentzner's versions are so garbled that they can only be restored conjecturally, and modern versions of these texts derive from eighteenth-century attempts at reconstruction.

2. Written with a Diamond[3]

In her imprisonment at Woodstock, these verses she wrote with her diamond in a glass window:

> Much suspected by me,
> Nothing proved can be.
>   *Quod*[4] Elizabeth the prisoner

3. On Monsieur's Departure[5]

I grieve and dare not show my discontent;
I love, and yet am forced to seem to hate;
I do, yet dare not say I ever meant;
I seem stark mute, but inwardly do prate.
    I am, and not; I freeze and yet am burned,
    Since from myself another self I turned.[6]

My care is like my shadow in the sun —
Follows me flying, flies when I pursue it,
Stands, and lies by me, doth what I have done;
His too familiar care doth make me rue it.
    No means I find to rid him from my breast,
    Till by the end of things it be suppressed.

Some gentler passion slide into my mind,
For I am soft, and made of melting snow;
Or be more cruel, Love, and so be kind.
Let me or float or sink, be high or low;

---

[3] Ca. 1555. This poem is published in John Foxe, *Acts and Monuments of These Latter and Perilous Days* (London, 1563), 1714, and Raphael Holinshed, *The Third Volume of Chronicles* (London, 1587), 1158. The version reproduced here comes from Foxe, and although the wording of the introductory sentence is different, both say Elizabeth wrote the poem in 1558, the tumultuous final year of Mary's reign and the eve of Elizabeth's accession.

[4] Said.

[5] Ca. 1582; Bodleian MS Tanner 76, fol. 94[r].

[6] Cf. Petrarch, *Rime Sparse*, 71, 76, 79.

Or let me live with some more sweet content,
Or die, and so forget what love e'er meant.
  Elizabetha Regina

4. Verse Exchange between Sir Walter Ralegh and Elizabeth[7]

Ralegh to Elizabeth

Fortune hath taken away my love,
My life's joy and my soul's heaven above.
Fortune hath taken thee away, my princess,
My world's joy and my true fantasy's mistress.

Fortune hath taken thee away from me;
Fortune hath taken all by taking thee.
Dead to all joys, I only live to woe:
So is Fortune become my fantasy's foe.

In vain, my eyes, in vain ye waste your tears;
In vain, my sights, the smoke of my despairs,
In vain you search the earth and heaven above.
In vain you search, for Fortune keeps my love.

Then will I leave my love in Fortune's hand;
Then will I leave my love in worldlings' band,
And only love the sorrows due to me —
Sorrow, henceforth, that shall my Princess be —

---

[7] Ca. 1587. Ralegh's poem to Elizabeth is transcribed from BL MS Additional 63742, fol. 116ʳ, a volume bound in limp vellum and described as "Letters of Henry, fourth Earl of Derby," (1531–1593). Other MS copies are listed in Peter Beal, *Index of English Literary Manuscripts*, Vol. 1, part 2 (London: Mansell, 1980), 388–89. For discussion of the verse exchange, which was occasioned by the Earl of Essex's rapid rise to favor in 1587 and Ralegh's consequent loss of status (at least in his own eyes), see L. G. Black, "A Lost Poem by Queen Elizabeth I," *Times Literary Supplement*, 23 May 1968: 535. Black transcribes another MS of Ralegh's poem from a verse miscellany in Archbishop Marsh's Library, Dublin (MS Z. 3. 5.21, fol. 30ʳ). The text of Elizabeth's answer is transcribed from Inner Temple Library MS Petyt 538, Vol. 10, fol. 3ʳ, which identifies the poem in the margin as "*per reginam* / Walter Rawley," but strikes through both the identification and the poem itself.

And only joy that Fortune conquers kings.
Fortune, that rules the earth and earthly things,
Hath taken my love in spite of virtue's might:
So blind a goddess did never virtue right.

With wisdom's eyes had but blind Fortune seen,
Then had my love, my love forever been.
But love, farewell — though Fortune conquer thee,
No fortune base nor frail shall alter me.

Elizabeth to Ralegh

Ah, silly Pug,[8] wert thou so sore afraid?
Mourn not, my Wat, nor be thou so dismayed.
It passeth fickle Fortune's power and skill
To force my heart to think thee any ill.
No Fortune base, thou sayest shall alter thee?
And may so blind a witch so conquer me?
No, no, my Pug, though Fortune were not blind,
Assure thyself she could not rule my mind.
Fortune, I know, sometimes doth conquer kings,
And rules and reigns on earth and earthly things,
But never think Fortune can bear the sway
If Virtue watch and will her not obey.
Ne chose I thee by fickle Fortune's rede,[9]
Ne she shall force me alter with such speed
But if to try this mistress' jest with thee.
Pull up thy heart, suppress thy brackish tears,
Torment thee not, but put away thy fears.
Dead to all joys and living unto woe,
Slain quite by her that ne'er gave wise men blow,
Revive again and live without all dread,
The less afraid, the better thou shalt speed.

---

[8] Elizabeth's nickname for Ralegh.
[9] Judgment.

5. ELIZABETH'S FRENCH VERSES

[Twenty-seven stanzas in French, composed circa 1590][10]

With the blinding so strange,
    So contrary to my name,[11]
    Although every evil deceives me
By this share in being man,
I recognized how foolish
This being in which I was born —
    So much was it lost from all
That appeared in me then —
    Nothing that was mine
So far was I from me.   10

    However much I resist evil,
Being a little awakened,
I saw my two men[12] in one
    And in the end I was most sure,
In seeing that it was one there.
    Of myself I had a wish
Then to put myself to the proof
    But for shame that I felt,
Not finding myself to reign
    In my kingdom, I hold back.   20

---

[10] The source for this poem is Hatfield House, Cecil Papers 147, fols. 207^r–213^r, an untitled and mostly unrhymed stanzaic poem in Elizabeth's late, loosely cursive italic hand. Steven May and Anne Lake Prescott published a transcription of the poem and a prose translation in "The French Verses of Elizabeth I," *English Literary Renaissance* 24.1 (winter 1994): 9–43. While May and Prescott now are of the opinion that this poem is a fragmentary translation into French from some unknown original, barring the discovery of such an original we find no features of the manuscript to invalidate our assumption that this poem is a complete, original composition by Elizabeth.

[11] According to William Camden, "Elizabeth" means "Peace of the Lord or Quiet rest of the Lord, the which England hath found verified in the most honored name of our late sovereign," *Remains of a Greater Work concerning Britain* (London: G. E. for Simon Waterson, 1605) (STC 4521), 79.

[12] See Ephesians 4:22, 24 and Colossians 3:9–10: Christ remakes the "old man" of sin into the "new man" of grace.

When I found myself so lost,
    I thought to depart from evil,
But when I strive to make the change
    I find myself so crippled
That it was not possible to change.
Then it gave me so much sorrow —
    Seeing evil strive so much
And its vigor being such
    That I, wanting to prove my strength —
It made proof of my weakness.   30

    Help was not lacking to me
As I tried to stand up alone,
But He who helped me
At the beginning would hold me up;
    Halfway, He let go of me,
He did not let up on his pains,
    Ever, in holding me up,
Without otherwise giving His help,
    Whereby I myself could help
My own weakness.   40

    Like the child who does not walk
But leans forward to go further,
If he who leads it is wise
    And takes care where it goes,
Little by little he will hurry it along —
    Just so, He who led me
Drew me along like a child;
He taught me fundamentals;
    The remainder that I did not learn
He was keeping for one who was capable.[13]   50

    I arrive at the first degree
Of grace, which begins

---

[13] An alternative reading might be "keeping for when I was capable": cf. 2 Corinthians 3:1–2, which compares the newly converted to "babes in Christ" fed with milk and not yet with the meat of the Word.

Where he is who is well bound
(If he does not lose his head)
     Thinks himself well placed.
There the light shone brightly;
     The shadows vanished away.
Although the sun did not appear,
     Where the heaven opened wide
     The clear day dawned.   60

Seeing myself, who at dawn
     Begin to understand myself,
It was time then for me to depart,
     But not in such sort
That I did not know how to govern well.
     Little by little I remembered
(For I was so sad)
     That the dream that grieved me —
The dream that was past —
     Seemed to torment me.   70

     As a shepherd who has slept
The night in his hut
     When the morning comes,
Gets up, half asleep,
     And goes to the mountain,
And blowing on his hands
     Staggers about and wakes up,
So the soul that was dead
     In desires only too futile
Found that it was watchful.   80

As far as the abyss of heaven
     I saw the air serene
And remembering my baptism,
 I acknowledged that so far
I was always from myself;
 I saw the sun, in its appearance
So lovely and so shining,
 That like what it was in the East,

So much light in one instant
    It showed in the West.   90

Now the Second Help
    Began to uphold me,
From whom I knew how to prevail
    Over the evils of this world
Without danger of destroying myself.
    From my evil I thought myself cured
But not so much without pain
    That this much was in my power:
To tread as well by the crooked path
    As by the level one.   100

Remembering God in dream,
    Looking on high
I found myself so advanced
    That in me only the habit
Of sin remained;
    And I turned myself from sin,
And my soul was ready to flee
    The evil that I apprehended,
But it was killed so soon —
    Just as soon as the evil appeared.[14]   110

Thus newly made,
    I saw the state of my heart,
Which was so ruinous
    That reason, seated in my soul,
Was most scornful of it.
    Created as from nothing,
I saw my inner man[15]

---

[14] An alternative reading of the reversible correlative conjunction in these two lines ("tôt ... tantôt" in French) would be, following May and Prescott, "But as soon as this was killed / Just so soon the evil reappeared." We have preferred the more positive reading because of its better fit with the opening line of the next stanza.

[15] Literally in French the "man within," but we use the typically Pauline vocabulary; see, for example, Ephesians 3:6, "His Spirit in the inner man."

So reduced from thence into its center[16]
That his life, being past,
    Rid him of a bad encounter.   120

Ceasing to be a stranger,
    I was remade in a moment
With all well conjoined.
    For Him who is the best
I raised up the sword;
For He who created me,
    Who is well pleased with all,
Furnished me in divers sorts:
    To begin with, He made me,
And then He converted me.   130

Being advanced so high,
    As I said, and transformed
Into my ordained rank,
    I saw my realm well governed
By reason and not by degree.
    I saw three similar souls
Set in operation,
    Each in his office:
One to command,
And two to serve.[17]   140

Soon I saw Fantasy
    Panting like a child,
But Reason did not allow it
    For the good of the other part,
Which bypassed the dispute.
    I saw the same dull feelings
Without wanting to have them,

---

[16] Center of the heart; an alternative reading, adopted by May and Prescott, would interpret it as the center of the man.

[17] The "three souls much alike" are, as the following stanzas indicate, the tripartite soul of Reason, Will, and Fantasy or Imagination.

And found that, according to their habits,
  They were seeking only
  Their first motions.   150

I saw the highest sphere
  Of the soul that governed
And, as it seemed to me,
  Inside it burned,
And outside was shadowed.
There I saw the Understanding,
  Having Truth for its object,
And I saw the whole government
  So very near to perfect,
That it brought me contentment.   160

I saw the Will give responsibility,
  Absolute and ordinary,
By which her retinue increased
  To something extraordinary;
She went along very gently.
I saw the part that is the spur
  Of Salvation, and the bridle;
I saw Love, who hoisted his sail
  Of desire, who for a farthing
  Went his way, well paid for his canvas.[18]   170

I saw, besides, exalted Memory,
  The treasury of human good,
Where I found the extended story
  Of my being, which was so vain
That it existed only to give glory.
  That sufficed to make me remember
My iniquitous evil, sent away
  Since my soul has agreed

---

[18] The imagery in lines 166–70 takes the same sequence as James 3:2–4, a series of reflections on sins of the tongue: "If any man offend not in word, the same is a perfect man, and able also to bridle the whole body. Behold we put bits in the horses' mouths, that they may obey us, and we turn about their whole body. . . . Behold also the ships, . . . driven of fierce winds, yet turned about . . . whithersoever the governor listeth."

That, remembering its past,
　　It would correct its present,   180

Its past, and what is to come —
　　All laid out before it.
And of having been inconstant
　　I have just given it an account,
Whom it did not make constant.
　　There returns to my awareness
What it is and what it was.
　　All of this, in my presence, put
On me, who retained the handling;
　　It put itself in its dwelling place.   190

Regret for my fault
Delivered me from sin,
　　For it afflicted me so
That this alone was my care —
　　That I did not have care enough;
Knowing better, that in joy
　　I had to suffer,
I turned myself to so many tears
　　That a thousand times my comfort
Renewed my pains.   200

To increase the grief
Of my foolish past,
　　Contemplating my Creator,
I remembered the making
　　Of me, a sad sinner;
I saw that God redeemed me,
　　Being cruel against Him,
And considering well who He was,
　　I saw how He made Himself me,
　　So that I would make myself Him.   210

I saw that when He formed me
　　He gave me no state at all,
But placed in my hand

What I myself took,
What contented me most —
    Which could be bestial,
Or otherwise human,
    Or which was angelical —
And that it was in my hands
    To take the divine.   220

I saw His high providence
    Where all is done that happens,
Who never gave me counsel
    That was not for the good.
From my own knowledge
    I saw the cause why He wished
To make the fire everlasting —
    And it was to exhort me,
To keep me from hell
    That I might gain paradise.   230

I saw that when Justice
    Went away, compelled by Discord,
That compelled by my Malice,
    Seeking Mercy,
I made her ask for Justice.
    Seeing this, I perceived such an intent
Of penitence in me
    That one moment of this pain
Would alleviate eternal torment.

I fled so high to convert,   240
    And was so much helped by God,
That soon to the highest degree
    In my firm deliberation
I saw that I was exalted
    Such that, inside the door, I find myself —
So much in peace and so exalted,
    The war so far given over,
That the flesh fell dead
    That the soul might keep itself alive.

The last of graces   250
    Is the same that confirms all,
After the second and the first.
    And there soon putting its seal[19]
Left me in this sort:
    Left me in such salvation,
Placed me in such state,
    And within me made accord —
Virtue with nature,
    And custom with virtue.[20]

Like the blind man who in all that happens   260
    Maintains such equilibrium
And comports himself such
    And his being so equal,
Neither stirs itself up nor grieves,
    Just so the soul in its substance
Has placed these temperings
    With such equal accord
That in herself she neither has nor could
    Wear inconstancy for a garment.[21]

6. VARIANTS OF "THE DOUBT OF FUTURE FOES"

Starting in 1569, Elizabeth's "The Doubt of Future Foes" circulated in several manuscript variants, and versions of the poem were published in George Puttenham's *The Arte of English Poesie* (1589, although probably

---

[19] The "seal" of salvation, 2 Corinthians 1:22; Ephesians 1:14; and 4:20; and Revelation 7:3–8.

[20] This inward accord in the state of salvation is markedly Stoic in its triple conjunction of virtue, nature, and custom (or law). According to Diogenes Laertius, Zeno taught that virtue was life in agreement with nature, and Chrysippus further held that such life in agreement with nature was lived "by the law common to all things, that is to say, the right reason which pervades all things, and is identical with God, Lord and ruler of all that is," *Lives of Eminent Philosophers*, trans. R. D. Hickes (Cambridge, MA: Harvard University Press, 1925), vol. 2: 195, 197.

[21] Immediately below the last line of this stanza, at the bottom of a recto page, Elizabeth has written two capital S's with transverse strokes through them: this notation pointedly signals the end of her text.

written twenty years earlier) and Henry Harington's *Nugae Antiquae* (1769).[22] While presumably all versions descend from the manuscript putatively copied by Lady Willoughby (see the letter below from John Harington that Henry Harington reproduced in the *Nugae*), the copies in the verse miscellanies and the printed texts differ significantly in their diction, grammar, and line length, e.g., the variant readings (or corrections) included by whoever copied the poem into the Bodleian Digby manuscript. Rather than choosing to privilege one text over all others and relegating the variants to the decent obscurity of a footnote, I have decided to "unedit" Elizabeth's poem and to present eight versions roughly in the order of their appearance. The versions in Folger Manuscript V.b. 317, the Arundel Harington Manuscript, and Bodleian Rawlinson Poetical 108 date from the 1570s, after, as Marcus writes in her essay in this volume, "the Northern Rebellion and the execution of the duke of Norfolk, who had plotted to wed Mary Queen of Scots and take over the government of England."[23] Bodleian Digby 138, British Museum Harleian 6933, and British Museum Harleian 7392, on the other hand, are probably later, and so the impetus for the poem's appearance in these miscellanies may have been the Babington Plot and the subsequent execution of Mary, Queen of Scots.[24] Ironically, the version that is, according to the narrative it presents, the earliest, appeared last: the Harington letter.

By providing different versions of the same poem, I hope to illustrate the problematics of editing early modern texts (how do you decide which manuscript has more authority than another? Is an eighteenth century published version ostensibly copied from Elizabeth's autograph manuscript preferable to a manuscript copy dating from the 1570s?) as well as to open up the possibility of studying this poem in relation to the material conditions surrounding its transmission and publication.[25] In order to give a better sense of the variations within the poems, I have not modernized

---

[22] Leicester Bradner, *The Poems of Elizabeth I* (Providence, RI: Brown University Press, 1964), 72; Steven May, *The Elizabethan Courtier Poets: The Poems and Their Contexts* (Columbia: University of Missouri Press, 1991), 47–48.

[23] Leah S. Marcus, "Queen Elizabeth I as Public and Private Poet: Notes toward a New Edition," 141.

[24] Marcus, "Queen Elizabeth I," 141. I am grateful to Leah S. Marcus for her help with dating the manuscripts.

[25] See Leah S. Marcus, *Unediting the Renaissance: Shakespeare, Marlowe, Milton* (New York: Routledge, 1996) and H. R. Woudhuysen, *Sir Philip Sidney and the Circulation of Manuscripts 1558–1640* (Oxford: Clarendon Press, 1996).

spelling or grammar; square brackets, though, indicate an expanded con-
traction.

Peter C. Herman

1. From *Folger Manuscript V.b. 317, fol. 20v* [26]

The doubt of future foes
    Exiles my p[re]sent joy
& wit me warns to shun such snares
    As threatis mine anoy.

ffor falshod nowe dooth flowe
    & subjectes faith dooth ebb
W[hich] should not be if reason ruled
    Or wisdom weavde y[e] web.

But cloudes of joies untried
    Doe cloak aspiring myndes
W[hich] turn to rage of late repent
    By chaunged course of windes.

The top of hope supposde
    y[e] root of rue shalbe
& fruitles all y[eire] grafted guile,
    as shortli you shall see.

Their dazled eies w[ith] pride,
    w[hich] great ambition blindes,
Shalbe unsealed by worthi wights
    whose forsight falshod findes.

---

[26] Transcription by Leah S. Marcus, who informs me that Elizabeth's poem rests
among historical documents, some dealing with the Northern Rebellion, which suggests
that the copyist regarded "The Doubt of Future Foes" as belonging to the realm of the
political rather than the aesthetic. Note how the copyist crams the poem into the available space at the bottom of the page (figure 5), which makes for an interesting contrast
with the careful treatment given to Henry's "Pastime with Good Company" (figure 3).

The daughter of debate
    That discord ay dooth sowe
Shal reap no gayne wher form[er] rule
    still peace hath taught to knowe.

No forein banisht wighte
    shall ancre in this porte
O[ur] realm brooks no sedicious sects
    let them elswhere resorte.

My rusti sworde through rest
    shall first his edge employ
To pul[27] y[eir] tops who seke such chaunge
    O[ur] gape for future joy.

    Vivat Regina

2. From Bodleian Rawlinson Poetical 108, fol. 44v [28]

"Verses made by the Quenes Maieste"

The dowbt off future foes exiles my p[r]sent ioye
    and wytte me warnes to shunne suche snares as threate[n] mine anoye
ffor falshode nowe doth flowe & subiects faithe dothe ebbe
    W[ch] shuldnot be yf reason rulde or wisdome weaued the webbe
but clowdes of ioyes untyed do cloke aspirynge mynds
    W[ch] turnes to raige of late report bi chaunged course of windes
The toppe of hope supp[o]st the roote upreard shalbe
    & fruitles all there grafted guile, as shortlye yo[u] shall see
The dayseled eyes with w[th] pride, w[ch] greate ambition blyndes
    Shalbe unseelde bi wo[r]thie wyghts, whose foresight falshode finds
The dawghter off debatte, y[t] discord aye doye sowe
    shall reape no gayne, where form[er] rule styll peace hathe taught to
        know
no fforene banished wight shall ancore in this port

---

[27] Prune.
[28] Transcribed by Jennifer Summit.

o[ur] realme brokes not seditious sects, lett them els where resort
My rustye sword throwghe rest shall first his eydge imploye
    to powle there toppes y^t sekes suche chaunge or gape for future ioye;

3. From George Puttenham, The Arte of English Poesie (London, 1589)[29]

From Book 3, chapter 20, "Exargasia, or The Gorgious," which Puttenham writes is "The last and principall figure of our poeticall Ornament":

I finde none example [in English meetre] that euer I could see, so well
maintayning this figure in English meetre as that ditty of her Maiesties
owne making passing sweete and harmonicall, which figure beyng as his
very originall name purporteth the most bewtiful [and gorgious] of all
others, it asketh in reason to be reserued for a last complement, and desci-
phred by the arte of a ladies penne, her selfe beyng the most glorious and
bewtifull, or rather bewtie of Queenes: and this was th'action [the occa-
sion], our soveraigne Lady perceiving how by the Sc. Q.[30] residence within this realme at so great libertie and ease, as were skarce worthy of so
great and dangerous a prysoner, bred secret factions among her people, and
made many of her nobilitie incline to favour her party: many of them de-
sirous of innovation in the state: some of them aspiring to greater fortunes
by her libertie and life. The Queene our soveraigne Lady to declare that
she was nothing ignorant in those secret favours, though she had long
with great wisdome and pacience dissembled it, writeth this ditty most
sweet and sententious, not hiding from all such aspiring minds the daunger
of their ambition and disloyaltie,[31] which afterward fell out most truly by
th'exemplary chastisement of sundry persons, who in favour of the said Sc.
Q. derogating from her Majestie, sought to interrupt the quiet of the
Realme by many evill and undutifull practizes. The ditty is as followeth.

The doubt of future foes, exiles my present joy,
And wit me warnes to shun such snares as threaten mine annoy.

---

[29] The Arte of English Poesie, facs. repr. (Kent, OH: Kent State University Press, 1970), 254–55.

[30] The Scottish Queene, i.e., Mary, Queen of Scots.

[31] Cf. Puttenham's claim that Elizabeth wrote "Doubt of Future Foes" to reassure her friends and warn her enemies with Sir John Harington's anecdote below, in which the poem enters circulation through a highly staged "accident."

For falshood now doth flow, and subject faith doth ebbe,
Which would not be, if reason rul'd or wisdome weu'd the webbe.
But clowdes of tois vntried, do cloake aspiring mindes,
Which turne to raigne of late repent, by course of changed windes.
The toppe of hope supposed, the roote of ruth will be,
And fruteless all their graffed guiles, as shortly ye shall see.
Then dazeld eyes with pride, which great ambition blinds,
Shalbe unseeld by worthy wights, whose foresight falsehood finds.
The daughter of debate, that eke discord doth sowe
Shal reap no gaine where formor rule hath taught stil peace to growe.
No forreine bannisht wigh shal ancre in this port,
Our realme it brookes no strangers force, let them elswhere resort.
Our rusty sword with rest, shall first his edge employ,
To polle their toppes that seeke, such change and gape for ioy.

4. From the Arundel Harington Manuscript[32]

The dread of future foes exyle my present Ioy
And wit mee warns to shunne soche snares as thretten myne annoy
ffor fallshood now doth flow and subiects fayth doth ebbe
which shold not bee yf reason rewld or Wydsome wove the webbe./
But clowds of Ioys vntried, doth cloke aspiring minds
Which turne to rage of late report, by chaunged course of minds
The topps of hope suppose, the roote of Rue shalbee./
and fruteles of their graffed guile as shortlie yow shall see
The dazeled eyes with pride, with great ambition blynde
shalbe vnsealld by worthie wights, whose foresight falshood fyndes
The daughter of Debate, that discord ay doth sow
Shall reape no gaine where former rule, still peace hath taught to know
No fforrain banisht wight, shall ankor in this Port
Our Realm brooks no seditious sects, Let them elswhere resort
My Rustie sword through rest, shall first his edge imploy

---

[32] From *The Arundel Harington Manuscript of Tudor Poetry*, ed. Ruth Hughey (Columbus: Ohio State University Press, 1960), 276–77. As the name suggests, the Harington Arundel manuscript belonged to the Harington family, and many of the poems are in Sir John Harington's own hand. Elizabeth's poem, however, is written in two hands; the identity of the first is unknown, but the second, starting on line 4, might be that of Sir John Harington's secretary (Hughey, vol. 2: 386).

To poll the topps that seekes such chaunge or gapes for further Ioy.

        ffinis

            Elizabetha

            Regina./[33]

5. *From Bodleian Digby 138, fol. 159r* [34]

E Reg

              foes
1.   The dowte of future <u>force</u>
        exiles my presente joye
        And wytt me warnes, to shonne suche snares
        as threten myne Anoye

2.   Ffor fallsehode nowe dothe flowe
        and subiectes faythe dothe ebb,
        wch shulde not be yf reson ruled
        or wysdome weved the webb.

              joyes
3.   But cloudes of <u>toyes</u> untryed

---

[33] Earlier in the collection, we find this poem by Edward Dyer, which might answer Elizabeth's poem in the same way that Ralegh answers Marlowe's "The Passionate Shepherd," as it deals with the same subject — ambition — and echoes Elizabeth's arborial imagery:

> The lowest tree haue toppes, ye ant her gaule,
>   ye flye her splene & littell sparkes ther heate
> And heare caste shadowes thoghe they be but smale
>   And bees have stinges although they be not greate
>   Seas have ther shours & and so haue shollowe springes
>   & love is love in beggers and in kinges
> Wher waters smothest run depe are the fordes
>   the diall stures yet none p[er]ceve it move
> The firmest faythe is in the fewest wordes
>   & turtles cannot singe, & yet they love
>   Trewe hartes have eies & eares, noe tonges to speake
>   they heare & see, and sighe, & then they breake.

(Arundel Harington Manuscript, 238)

[34] Transcribed by Jennifer Summit.

doe cloake Aspyrynge myndes
wch turne to <u>reyne</u> of late report
By changed course of wyndes

            joy
4.   The toppe of <u>hope</u> supposed
         the roote of <u>rule</u> shall be
         and frutelesse all there grafted guyle
         as shortlye yow shall see

5.   There dasled yes[35] wth pryde
         wch grete Ambytyon blyndes
         shalbe unseled by woorthye wyttes
         whoes forsyghtes falshode ffyndes

6.   The daughter of debate
         that dyscord aye did sowe
         shall reape no gayne wher fo^rm[er] rule
         Still peace hathe taughte to knowe

7.   No forreygne bannyshed wyeghts
         shall Anker yn thys porte
         Our rallme brookes not sedytyous sectes
         Lett them ellse where resorte

8.   Our rustye swordes throughe reste
         shall fyrste hys edge employe
         to polle there toppes yt seaks suche chainge
         or gapes for future ioyes.

6. *From British Museum Harleian 7392, fol. 27v* [36]

The doubte of future foes, exiles my present Joy,

                                        mine
And wit me warnes to shun such snares, as threten ˄ annoy.

---

[35] Their dazzled eyes.
[36] Transcribed by Jennifer Summit.

Ffor falshood now doth flow, and subiectes fayth doth ebbe,
W^ch should not be, if reason rulde or wisdom wevde ye Webbe.
But clowdes of toyes untryde, do cloke aspiringe mindes,
W^ch turne to rayne of late report, By chaunged course of windes.
The Top of hope suppozd, ye roote of ruthe shalbe,
And fruitles all ye grafted guiles, as shortly you shall see.
Their dazeled Eyes wth Pride, wch great Ambition blindes,
Shalbe unseald of worthy wittes, whose foresight falsehood finds.
The daughter of debate, y^t discord eake doth sowe.
Shal reap no gaine, wher former rule, still peace hath taught to knowe.
No forrayn bannisht wight, shall anker in this porte,
Our realme brookes no seditious sectes, let them else where resorte.
Our Rusty Sword throw rest, shall firste hys Edge employ:
To powle their toppes, y^t seeke suche change, or gape for future Joy

      FINIS EL.

7. From British Museum Harleian 6933, fol. 8^r [37]

The following Ditty on the Factions raised by the Q. of Scots while Prisoner in England,[38] was composed by Q. Elizabeth and was printed not
long after, if not before, the beheading of the said Scots Queen.

The doubt of future Foes, exiles my present Joy.
And Wit me warns, to shun such snares, as threaten my Anoy.
For Falshood now doth flow, and subject Faith doth Ebb,
Which woud not be, if Reason ruld, or wisdom weavd the Web.
But clouds of Toys untryd, do cloak aspring Minds,
Which turn to rain of late Report, by course of changed Winds.
The top of Hope supposed, the Root of Ruth will be,
And fruitless all their grafted Guiles, as shortly ye shall see.
Then dazzled Eyes with Pride, which great Ambition blinds,
Shall be unseeld by worthy Wights, whose foresight Falsehood finds.
The <u>daughter of Debate</u>, that eke Discorde doth sow,
Shall reap no Gain, where former Rule, hath taught Peace still to grow
No foreign banishd Wight, shall ancre in this Port,

---

[37] Transcribed by Jennifer Summit.
[38] The copyist is incorrect, as the occasion of the poem was the Northern Rebellion.

Our Realm, it brooks no strangers force, let them elswhere resort.
Our rusty sword with Rest, shall first his Edge employ

                                         lawless
To poll their Tops that seek such change, and gape for ⌃ Joy.

8. *From Henry Harington*, Nugae Antiquae (*London, 1769*), *vol. 1: 58–59*

[The letter is probably by Sir John Harington)

Good Madam,

Herewith I commit a precious jewel, not for your ear, but your eye; and doubt not but you will rejoyce to wear it even in your heart: It is of her Highness own editing, and doth witness, how much her wisdom and great learning doth outweigh even the perils of state, and how little all wordly dangers do work no change in her mynde. My Lady Wiloughby did covertly get it on her Majesties tablet, and had much hazard in so doing; for the Queen did find out the thief, and chid for spreading evil bruit of her writing such toyes, when other matters did so occupy her employment at this time; and was fearful of being though too lightly of for so doing.[39] But marvel not, good Madam, her Highness doth frame herself to all occasions, to all times, and all things, both in business, and pastime, as may witness this her sonnet:

                   I.
        The dread of future foes
        Exyles my present joye,
And wit me warns to shunne such snares,
        As thretten myne annoye.

                 II.
        For falsehood now doth flowe,
        And subjects faith doth ebbe;
Which should not be if reason rul'd,
        Or wisdome wove the webbe.

---

[39] Cf. Puttenham's version of the poem's original distribution above.

III.

But clouds of joys untry'd
Doth cloke aspyring mynds;
Which turn to rage of late report,
By course of changed kindes.

IV.

The toppes of hope suppose,
The roote of rue shall be:
And fruitless of their grafted guyle,
As shortlie all shall see.

V.

The dazzeled eyes with pride,
And great ambitions blynde,
Shall be unseal'd by worthy wyghts,
Whose foresighte falshood fyndes.

VI.

The daughter of debate,
That discord aye doth sowe,
Shall reape no gain where former rule
Still Peace hathe taughte to flowe.

VII.

No forrain banyshed wyght
Shall ankor in this port;
Our realme brookes no seditious sects,
Let them elsewhere resort.

VIII.

My rustie sworde through reste,
Shall firste his edge imploy;
Poll the toppes that seek such change,
Or gape for such like joye.

Now tell me, if this be not worthie your commendation, and then pray for
the Poet. I will do myself the honor of your Lord's company to Cambridge
as he doth so kindlie proffer, and there send what other matters are working.

HIS

MAIESTIES

LEPANTO,

Or,

HEROICALL SONG,

being part of his Poeticall exercises
at vacant houres.

Imprinted at London by Simon Stafford,
and Henry Hooke,
1603.

Figure 6: Title page of King James VI, *The Lepanto* (1603).
Reproduced by permission of the The Huntington Library,
San Marino, California.

JAMES VI/I

THE TWELVE SONNETS OF INVOCATIONS TO THE GODS[1]

1.

First Jove, as greatest God above the rest,
Grant thou to me a part of my desire,
That when in verse of thee I write my best
This only thing I earnestly require,
That thou my vein poetic so inspire,
As they may surely think, all that it read,
When I describe thy might and thundering fire,
That they do see thy self in very deed
From heaven thy greatest thunders for to lead,
And syne[2] upon the Giants[3] heads to fall,
Or coming to thy Semele[4] with speed
In thunders least, at her request and call.

---

[1] From *The Essayes of a Prentise, in the Divine Art of Poesie* (Edinburgh, 1584). Edited and modernized by Peter C. Herman.

[2] Soon.

[3] The Titans who rebelled against Jove's rule. The mythographical tradition usually treats them as archetypal rebels.

[4] A daughter of Cadmus and mother of Bacchus (Dionysus). She died when, at her request, Jove appeared before her in his full majesty.

Or throwing Phaeton[5] down from heaven to eard,[6]
With threatening thunders, making monstrous reard.[7]

2.

Apollo next, assist me in a part,
Since unto Jove thou second art in might,
That when I do describe thy shining cart,
The readers may esteem it in their sight.
And grant me als,[8] thou world's ô only light,
That when I like[9] for subject to devise
To write, how as before thy countenance bright
The years do stand, with seasons double twice,
That so I may describe the very guise
Thus by thy help, of years wherein we live.
As readers syne may say, here surely lies,
Of seasons four, the glass and picture vive.[10]

Grant als, that so I may my verse warp,
As thou may play them syne upon thy harp.

3.

And first, ô Phoebus, when I do descrive[11]
The Springtime sprouter of the herbs and flowers,
Whomewith in rank none of the four do strive,
But nearest thee do stand all times and hours.
Grant readers may esteem, they see the showers,
Whose balmy drops so softly does [sic] distill,
Which watery clouds in measure such down pours,
As makes the herbs, and very earth to smell

---

[5] Son of Apollo who, having obtained his father's permission to drive the chariot of the sun, lost control and was killed by Jove to prevent him setting the earth on fire.

[6] Earth.

[7] Roar.

[8] Also.

[9] Look.

[10] Lifelike, lively.

[11] Describe. I have retained the original spelling so as to preserve the rhyme.

With savors sweet, fra time that once thy sell[12]
The vapors softly sucks with smiling cheer,
While syn in clouds are keeped close and well,
While vehement Winter come in time of year.
>   Grant, when I like the springtime to display,
>   That readers think they see the spring alway.

4.

And grant I may so vively[13] put in verse
The summer, when I like thereof to treat.
As when in writ I do thereof rehearse,
Let readers think they feel the burning heat,
And graithly[14] see the earth, for lack of wet,
With withering drought and sun so gaigged[15] all,
As for the grass on field, the dust in street
Doth rise and flee aloft, long ere it fall.
Yea, let them think, they hear the song and call,
Which Flora's winged musicians makes [sic] to sound.
And that to taste, and smell, believe they shall
Delicious fruits, which in that time abound.
>   And shortly, all their sense so bereaved,
>   As eyes and ears, and all may be deceived.

5.

Or when I like my pen for to employ
Of fertile harvest in the description true,
Let readers think they instantly convoy[16]
The busy shearers for to reap their due,
By cutting ripest corns with hooks anew,
Which corns their heavy heads did downward bow,
Else seeking earth again, from whence they grow,

---

[12] From the time that once thy self, i.e., from the time that you yourself softly soak up the vapours with your smiling cheer which then are kept close in clouds, while winter comes in its time of year. . . .

[13] Lively.

[14] Exactly.

[15] Cracked.

[16] Accompany.

And unto Ceres[17] do their service vow.
Let readers also surely think and trow,[18]
They see the painful vigneron[19] pull the grapes,
First tramping them, and after pressing now
The greenest clusters gathered into heaps.
      Let them the harvest so vive to them appear,
      As if they saw both corns and clusters near.

6.

But let them think, in very dead they fall,
When as I do the winter's storms unfold,
The bitter frosts, which waters does [sic] congeal
In winter season, by a piercing cold.
And that they hear the whiddering[20] Boreas bold,[21]
With hideous hurling, rolling rocks from high.
Or let them think they see god Saturn old,
Whose hoary hair, overcovering earth, makes fly
The little birds in flocks, fra[22] time they see
The earth and all with storms of snow overclad.
Yea, let them think they hear the birds that die,
Make piteous moan, that Saturn's hairs[23] are spread.
      Apollo, grant thir[24] foresaid suits of mine,
      All five I say, that thou may crown me syne.

7.

And I do describe the ocean's force,
Grant syne, ô Neptune, God of seas profound,
That readers think on leeboard, and on dworce,[25]
And how the seas overflowed this massive round.

---

[17] Goddess of the harvest.
[18] Believe.
[19] Winemaker, vintner.
[20] Withering, blustering.
[21] The north wind.
[22] From.
[23] I.e., Saturn's "hoary" hairs.
[24] These.
[25] Starboard.

Yea, let them think they hear a stormy sound,
Which threatens wind, and darkness come at hand.
And water in their ships syne to abound,
By weltring waves, like highest towers on land.
Then let them think their ship now low on sand,
Now climbs and skips to top of raging seas,
Now down to hell, when shipmen many not stand,
But lifts their hands to pray thee for some ease.
      Syne let them think thy trident doth it calm,
      Which makes it clear and smooth like glass or alme.[26]

8.

And grant the like when as the swimming sort
Of all thy subjects scaled I list declare,
As Triton, monster with manly port,
Who drowned the Trojan trumpeter most rare,[27]
As mermaids wise, who weeps [sic] in weather fair,
And marvelous monks, I mean, monks of the sea.[28]
But what of monsters, when I look and stare
On wondrous heaps of subjects serving thee?
As whales so huge,and sea eels rare, that be
Mile longs [sic], in crawling cruikis[29] of sixty pace.
And dolphins, seahorse, selchs[30] with oxen eye,
And merswines,[31] pertrikes[32] als of the fish's race.
      In short, no fowl doth fly, nor beast doth go,
      But thou hast fishes like to them and mo.[33]

---

[26] Alum.

[27] Misenus. Triton drowned him after he challenged to god to a contest, of exactly what Vergil does not specify. See *Aeneid* 6: 160–74.

[28] Monkfish, but given James's militant Protestantism at this time (see his preface to the *Lepanto,* he probably also means a degree of anti-fraternal satire.

[29] Coils.

[30] Seals.

[31] Porpoises.

[32] Sole.

[33] More.

9.

O dreadful Pluto,[34] brother third to Jove,
With Proserpine,thy wife, the queen of Hell,[35]
My suit to you is, when I like to loave[36]
The joys that do in Elise[37] field excel.
Or when I like great tragedies to tell,
Or flyte,[38] or mourn my fate, or write with fear
The plagues ye do send forth with Dirae[39] fell.
Let readers think that both they see and hear
Alecto threatening Turnus' sister dear,[40]
And hear Celaenos wings, with Harpies all,
And see dog Cerberus rage with hideous bear,[41]
And all that did Aeneas once befall.
        When as he past through all those dungeons dim,
        The foresaid fields syne visited by him.[42]

10.[43]

O furious Mars, thou warlike soldier bold,
And hardy Pallas, goddess stout and grave.
Let readers think, when combats manifold
I do describe, they see two champions brave,
With armies huge approaching to resave[44]
Thy will, with clouds of dust in the air.
Syne fifers, drums, and trumpets clear do crave

---

[34] God of the underworld.

[35] Daughter of Ceres and Jupiter. Pluto seized her as she was gathering flowers and carried her away to Hades.

[36] Praise.

[37] Elysium.

[38] A form of satiric verse.

[39] The Dirae or Harpies are spirits of revenge.

[40] The nymph, Iuturna. See the *Aeneid* 12: 843–86.

[41] Roar.

[42] The reference is to Aeneas' visit to the underworld, *Aeneid* 6: 268–899.

[43] This poems makes an interesting comparison with James's actual practice in the *Lepanto*.

[44] Receive.

The pell-mell choke [sic] with larum[45] loud alwhere,[46]
Then nothing heard but guns, and rattling fair
Of spears, and clincking swords with glance so clear,
As if they fought in skies, then wrangles there
Men killed, unkilled, while Parcas breath reteir.[47]
>   There lies the vanquished wailing sore his chance,
>   Here lies the victor, ruing else the dance.

11.

And at your hands I earnestly do crave,
O fecund[48] Mercury, with the Muses nine,
That for conducting guide I may you have,
Aswell unto my pen, as my engine.[49]
Let readers think thy eloquence divine,
O Mercury, in my poems doth appear,
And that Parnassus flowing fountain fine
Into my works doth shine like crystal clear.
O Muses, let them think that they do hear
Your voices all into my verse resound.
And that your virtues singular and seir[50]
May wholly all in them be also found.
>   Of all that may the perfect poem make,
>   I pray you let my verses have no lack.

12.

In short, you all forenamed gods, I pray
For to concur with one accord and will,
That all my works may perfect be alway,
Which if ye do, then swear I for to fill
My works immortal with your praises still.
I shall your names eternal ever sing,
I shall tread down the grass on Parnass hill

---

[45] Alarums.
[46] Everywhere.
[47] Take away.
[48] Eloquent.
[49] Native talent, imagination.
[50] Various.

By making with your names the world to ring.
I shall your names from all oblivion bring.
I lofty Vergil shall to life restore,
My subjects all shall be of heavenly thing,
How to delate[51] the gods immortals gloir.[52]
Essay me once, and if ye find me swerve,
Then think, I do not graces such deserve.

A PARAPHRASTICALL TRANSLATION OUT OF THE POËTE LUCAN

Caesaris an cursus vestrae sentire putatis
Damnum posse fugae? Veluti si cuncta minentur
Flumina, quos miscent pelago, subducere fontes:
Non magis ablatis unquam decreverit aequor,
Quam nunc crescit aquis. An vos momenta putatis
Ulla dedisse mihi?

Lucan, *Pharsalia* Bk. V. 335-40

If all the floods amongst them would conclude
To stay their course from running in the sea,
And by that means would think for to delude
The ocean, who would impaired be,
As they supposed, believing if that he
Did lack their floods, he should decrease him sell,[53]
Yet if we like the verity to why,
It pairs[54] him nothing, as I shall you tell.

For out of him they are augmented all,
And most part creat[ed],[55] as ye shall persave,[56]   10

---

[51] Relate, spread about.
[52] Glory.
[53] Himself.
[54] Impairs.
[55] Created.
[56] Persuade.

For when the sun doth souk[57] the vapors small
Forth of the seas, whilks[58] them contain and have,
A part in wind, in wet and rain the lave
He render dois, [59]which doth augment their strands.
Of Neptune's wool a coat syne they him weave,
By hurling to him fast out ower[60] the lands.

When all is done, do to him what they can
None can persave[61] that they do swell him mair.[62]
I put the case then that they never ran,
Yet not the less that could him nowise pair.[63]   20
What needs he then to count it, or to care,
Except their follies would the more be shawin?[64]
Sen[65] though they stay, it harms him not a hair,
What gain they, though they had their course withdrawn.

So even siclike.[66] Though subjects do conjure
For to rebel against their Prince and King
By leaving him, although they hope to smure[67]
That grace, wherewith God makes him for to ring,
Though by his gifts he shaw[68] himself bening,[69]
To help their need, and make them thereby gain.   30
Yet lack of them no harm to him doth bring,
When they to rue their folly shall be faine.

---

[57] Sink.
[58] Which.
[59] Does.
[60] Over.
[61] Persuade.
[62] Swell him more.
[63] Impair.
[64] Shown.
[65] Since.
[66] Suchlike.
[67] Smear, harm, also to suffocate.
[68] Show.
[69] Kindly, benign.

L'ENVOY

Then floods run on your wanted course of old,
Which God by nature duly has provided,
For though ye stay, as I before have told,
And cast in doubt which God hath else decided,
To be conjoined, by you to be divided
To kythe[70] your spite, & do the deep no skaith,[71]
Far better were in other ilk confided,
Ye Floods, thou Deep, which were your duties baith.[72]

---

[70] Reveal, make known.
[71] Harm.
[72] Both.

PREFACE TO THE 1603 EDITION OF *THE LEPANTO*[1]

The Author's Preface To The Reader

It falls out often that the effects of men's actions comes clean contrary to the intent of the Author. The same find I by experience (beloved Reader) in my poem of *Lepanto*. For although till now it have not been imprinted, yet being out to the public view of many, by a great sort of stolen copies, purchased (in truth) without my knowledge or consent,[2] it hath for lack of a preface been in some things misconstrued by sundry, which I of very purpose thinking to have omitted, for that the writing thereof might have tended, in my opinion, to some reproach of the skillful learnedness of the reader, as if his brains could not have conceived so uncurious[3] a work without some manner of commentary, and so have made the work more displeasant unto him. It hath by the contrary fallen out that the lack thereof hath made it the more displeasant to some through their mistaking a part of the meaning thereof. And for that I know, the special thing misliked in it is that I should seem far contrary to my degree and religion, like a mercenary poet, to pen a work, *ex professo*,[4] in praise of a foreign Papist bastard. I will by setting down the nature and order of the poem resolve the ignorant of their error, and make the other sort inexcusable of their captiousness.

The nature then of this poem is an argument, *à minore ad majus*,[5] largely intreated by a poetic comparison, being to the writing hereof moved by the stirring up of the league and cruel persecution of the Protestants in all countries, at the very first raging whereof I compiled this poem, as the exhortation to the persecuted in the hindmost eight lines thereof doth plainly testify, being both begun and ended in the same summer wherein the league was published in France. The order of the cantique[6] is this: First, a poetic preface, declaring the matter I treat of, wherein I name not Don Joan, neither literally nor any ways by description, which I behooved to have done, if I had penned the whole poem in

---

[1] Modernized and edited by Peter C. Herman.

[2] In fact, there is no evidence that James's epic circulated in manuscript, either with his permission or without it.

[3] So artless, so simple a work.

[4] Literally, "from authority."

[5] From the lesser to the major, from small to large.

[6] Cantos.

his praise, as Virgil, *Arma virumque cano*, & Homer, *Dic mihi musa virum*,[7]
of whose imitation I had not been ashamed if so my purpose had been
framed. Next follows my invocation to the true God only, and not to all
the he and she–Saints, for whose vain honors Don Joan fought in all his
wars. Next after my invocation, follows the poetic history of my comparison, wherein following forth the ground of a true history (as Virgil or
Homer did) like a painter shadowing with umbers a portrait else drawn in
gross, for giving it greater vividness, so I eke,[8] or pair to the circumstances of the actions as the rules of the poetic art will permit. Which historic
comparison continues 'til the song of the Angels, in the which I compare
and apply the former comparison to our present estate, taking occasion
thereupon to speak somewhat of our religion. Lastly, the epilogue of the
whole in the last eight lines, declares fully my intent in the whole, and
explains so fully my comparison and argument, from the more to the less,
as I cannot without shameful repetition speak any more thereof. And in a
word: whatsoever praise I have given to Don Joan in this poem, it is
neither in accompting[9] him as first or second cause of that victory, but
only as of a particular man, when he falls in my way, to speak the truth of
him. For as it becomes not the honor of my estate, like an hireling, to pen
the praise of any man, becomes it far less the highness of my rank and
calling to spare for the fear of favor of whomsoever living to speak or write
the truth of any. And thus craving pardon (beloved reader) for this long-
some apology (being driven thereto not by nature, but by necessity) I bid
you heartily farewell.

---

[7] The first words of Virgil's *Aeneid* and Homer's *Iliad*, the former praising Aeneas, the
latter, Achilles.

[8] Also.

[9] Accounting.

THE LEPANTO[1]
by King James VI/I

I sing a wondrous work of God,
    I sing his mercies great,
I sing his justice herewithall
    Powered from his holy seat.
To wit, a cruel martial war,
    A bloody battle bold,
Long doubtsome fight, with slaughter huge
    And wounded manifold.
Which fought was in Lepanto's gulf
    Betwixt the baptized race   10
And circumcised turbaned Turks
    Rencounting[2] in that place.
O only God, I pray thee thrice,
    Thrice one in persons three,
Alike Eternal, like of might,
    Although distinct ye be.
I pray thee, Father, through thy Son,
    Thy word immortal still,
The great archangel of records
    And worker of thy will,   20
To make thy holy Spright[3] my muse,
    And eke my pen inflame
Above my skill to write this work
    To magnify thy name.
Into the turning still of times,
    I err, no time can be,
Where was and is, and times to come,
    Confounded are all three.
I mean before great God in Heaven,
    (for sun and moon divides   30

---

[1] This poem was reprinted in 1603 in England under the title, *His Majesties Lepanto, or, Heroicall Song, being part of his Poeticall Exercises at Vacant Hours,* and this book included a French translation of James's epic. A Latin version appeared in 1604. Edited and modernized by Peter C. Herman.

[2] Meeting.

[3] Spirit.

The times in Earth by hours and days,
     And season still that slides).
Yet man, whom man must understand,
     Must speak into this case,
As man, our flesh will not permit,
     We heavenly things embrace.
Then, as I else began to say,
     One day it did fall out,
As glorious God in glistering throne,
     With angels round about   40
Did sit, and Christ at his right hand,
     That crafty Satan came,
Deceiver, liar, hating man,
     And God's most sacred name.
This old abuser stood into
     The presence of the Lord,
Then, in this manner, Christ accused
     The sower of discord:
"I know thou from that city comes,
     Constantinople great,   50
Where thou hast by thy malice
     The faithless Turks to fret.
Thou hast inflamed their maddest minds
     With raging fire of wrath
Against them all that do profess
     My name with fervent faith.
How long, ô Father, shall they thus
     Quite underfoot be tread,
By faithless folks, who executes [sic]
     What in this snake is bred."   60
Then Satan answered: "Faith?" quoth he,
     "Their faith is too too small,
They strive, methink, on either part,
     Who farthest back can fall.
Hast though not given them in my hands,
     Even both the sides I say,
That I as best doth seem to me,
     May use them every way?"
Then Jehovah, whose nod doth make,
     The heavens and mountains quake,   70

Whose smallest wrath the centers makes [sic],
    Of all the earth to shake,
Whose word did make the world of nought,
    And whose approving sign
Did establish all, even as we see,
    By force of voice divine.
This God began, from thundering throat,
    Grave words of weight to bring:
"All Christians serves [sic] my Son, though not
    Aright in every thing.   80
No more shall now these Christians be
    With infidels oppressed,
So of my holy hallowed name
    The force is great and blessed.
Desist, ô tempter. Gabriel, come
    O thou Archangel true,
Whom I have oft in message sent
    To realms and towns anew.
Go quickly hence to Venice town,
    And put into their minds   90
To take revenge of wrongs the Turks
    Have done in sundry kinds."
No whistling wind with such a speed,
    From hills can hurl o'er heugh[4]
As he whose thought doth furnish speed,
    His thought was speed aneugh[5]
This town it stands with the sea,
    Five miles or thereabout,
Upon no isle nor ground, the sea
    Runs all the streets throughout.   100
Who stood upon the steeplehead
    Should see a wondrous sight,
A town to stand without a ground,
    Her ground is made by slight:
Strong timber props dug in the sea
    Do bear her up by art,

---

[4] Valley.
[5] Enough.

An isle is all her marketplace,
     A large and spacious part,
A duke with senate joined doth rule,
     Saint Mark is patron chief,   110
Ilk[6] year they wed the sea with rings
     To be their sure relief.
The angel then arrived into
     This artificial town,[7]
And changed in likeness of a man,
     He walks both up and down,
While time he met some man of spright,[8]
     And then began to say,
"What do we all? Methink we sleep!
     Are we not day by day   120
By cruel Turks and infidels
     Most spitefully oppressed?
They kill our knights, they brash our forts,
     They let us never rest!
Go to, go to, once make a proof:
     No more let us desist,
To bold attempts God gives success,
     If once assay we list."[9]
With this he goes away, this man
     Unto another tells   130
The purpose whereunto they both
     Agree among them sels.[10]
This other to another tells,
     And so from hand to hand
It spreads and goes, and all that heard
     It, necessary it fand.[11]
And last of all, it comes unto
     The Duke and Senate's ear,

---

[6] Each.
[7] Venice exists through art, through human intervention, not naturally.
[8] Spirit.
[9] If once we try.
[10] Selves.
[11] Found.

Who found it good, and followed forth
      The same as ye shall hear.   140
The town was driven into this time,
      In such a piteous straight
By Mahometists, that they had else
      Given over all debate:
The Turk had conquest Cyprus Isle,
      And all their lands that lay
Without the bounds of Italy,
      Almost the whole I say.
And they for last refuge of all,
      Have moved each Christian King   150
To make their churches pray for their
      Relief in everything.
The town with piteous plaints did call
      Upon the Lord of might,
With praying still and fasting oft,
      And groaning all the night,
Was nothing heard but sobs and sighs,
      Was nothing seen but tears,
Yea, sorrow drave the bravest men
      With mourning to their biers.   160
The women swouned[12] for sorrow oft,
      The babe for woe did weep,
To see the mother giving milk
      Such doleful gesture keep.
Young men and maids within the town
      Were aye arrayed in black,
Each ev'n the sun was sooner hid
      Then erst, the night to make.
No Venus then, nor Cupid false
      Durst kyth[13] or once appeare,   170
For pale Distress had banished them,
      By sad and sorry cheer.

---

[12] Swooned.
[13] Show up.

As seas did compass them about,
     As seas the streets did rin,[14]
So seas of tears did ever flow,
     The houses all within.
As seas within were joined with howls,
     So seas without did raire,[15]
Their careful cries to Heaven did mount,
     Resounding in the air.   180
O stay, my Muse, thou goes too far,
     Show where we left before,
Lest trickling tears so fill my pen
     That it will write no more.
Then Venice being in this state,
     When Gabriel there was sent,
His speeches spread abroad, made town
     And senate both so bent
To take revenge, as they implored
     The Christian princes aid,   190
Of forces such as easily
     They might have spared and made.
At last, support was granted them,
     The holy league was passed,
Als[16] long to stand, as 'twixt the Turks
     And Christians war should last.
It was agreed that into March,
     Or April every year,
The army should on eastern seas
     Convene from far and near.   200
Thus bent upon their enterprise,
     The principals did convene,
Into Messina to consult,
     What order should have been

---

[14] Ring.
[15] Rear.
[16] Also.

Observed in all their army great.
       There Don Joan d'Austria[17] came,
Their general great, and Venier[18] als
       Came there in Venice name.
From Genes[19] Andrea Doree[20] came
       And Rome Colonne[21] sent,   210
When they with others many days
       Had into counsel spent,
In end Ascagnio de la Corne,[22]
       A martial man and wise,
His counsel gave, as ye shall hear,
       Upon their enterprise:
"Three causes be (ô chieftains brave)
       That should a general let[23]
On Fortune's light uncertain wheel
       The victory to set.   220
First, if the loss may harm him more,
       Than winning can avail.
As if his realm he do defend
       From them that it assail.
The next is when the contrary host
       Is able to divide
For sickness sore or famine great,
       Then best is to abide.
The third and last, it is in case
       His forces be too small,   230
Then better far is to delay,
       Than for to perish all.

---

[17] Don John (Juan) of Austria (1545–78), Spanish military commander and illegitimate son of Charles V. In 1576, he was appointed governor of the Netherlands.

[18] Sebastain Venerio (1496–1578), Venetian governor of Candia.

[19] Genoa.

[20] Gian Andrea Doria (b. 1540), heir and great nephew of Andrea Doria, ruler of Genoa.

[21] Marc Antonio Colonna (1535–84), head of the Roman house of Colonna.

[22] Ascanio della Corgna (1514–3 December 1571), architect, engineer, and noted military strategist, who died of wounds suffered at the Battle of Lepanto.

[23] Prevent.

But since of these two former points
    We need not stand in doubt,
Then though we leese,[24] we may defend
    Our countries round about.
As to the last, this army is
    So awful strong and fair,
And furnished so with necessaries
    Through your foreseeing care,   240
That nought doth rest but courage bold.
    Then since your state is such,
With trust in God assay your chance,
    Good cause availeth much.
But specially take heed to this,
    That ere ye make away,
Ye order all concerning war,
    Into their due array.
For if while that ye see your foes,
    Ye shall continue all,   250
Then shall their sudden sight with fear
    Your bravest spreights appall,
Each one command a sundry thing,
    Astonished of the case,
And every simple soldat[25] shall
    Usurp his captain's place."
This counsel so contents them all,
    That every man departs,
With whispering much, and so resolves
    With bold magnanime[26] hearts.   260
Their preparations being made,
    They all upon a day,
Their biting anchors gladly weighed,
    And made them for the way.
The Grecian fleet, for Helen's cause
    That Neptune's town[27] did sack,

---

[24] Lose.
[25] Soldier.
[26] Magnanimous.
[27] Troy.

In brave array, or glistering arms,
     No match to them could mak.[28]
There came eight thousand Spaniards brave,
     From hot and barren Spain,   270
Good order keepers, cold in fight,
     With proud disdainful brain.
From pleasant fertile Italy,
     There came twelve thousand als,
With subtle sprights bent to revenge,
     By crafty means and false.
Three thousand Almans also came,
     From countries cold and wide,
These money men with awful cheer
     The choke will dourly bide.   280
From divers parts did also come,
     Three thousand venturers brave,
All voluntaries of conscience moved,
     And would no wages have.
Armed galleys twice a hundred and eight
     Six ships all wondrous great,
And five and twenty loadened ships
     With baggage and with meat.
With forty other little barks
     And pretty galents[29] small,   290
Of these aforesaid was compound
     The Christian navy all.
This cloud of galleys thus began
     On Neptune's back to row,
And in the ships the mariners
     Did skip from toe to toe.
With willing minds they hailed the ties,
     And hoist the flaffing[30] sails,
And strongest tows, from highest masts,
     With force and practic[31] hails.   300

---

[28] Make.
[29] Galleons.
[30] Flapping.
[31] Practiced.

The foreseats[32] loathsomely did row,
    In galleys 'gainst their will,
Whom galley masters oft did beat,
    And threaten ever still.
The foaming seas did bullor[33] up,
    The risking oars did rashe,[34]
The soldats pieces for to clang
    Did showers of shots delashe.[35]
But as the Devil is ready bent
    Good works to hinder aye,   310
So sowed he in this navy strife,
    Their good success to stay.
Yet did the wisdoms of the Chiefs
    And of the general most,
Compound all quarrels and debates
    That were into that host,
Preferring wisely, as they ought,
    The honor of the Lord
Unto their own, the public cause
    To private men's discord.   320
The feathered fame of wondrous speed
    That doth delight to flee
On tops of houses prattling all
    That she can hear or see,
Part true, part false: this monster strange
    Among the Turks did tell,
That divers Christian princes joined,
    Resolved with them to mell.[36]
Then spies were sent abroad, who told
    The matter as it stood,   330
Except in arithmetic (as
    It seemed) they were not good,

---

[32] Galley slaves.
[33] Boil, make a roaring noise.
[34] To cut or slash.
[35] Discharge.
[36] Fight.

For they did count their number to
     Be less than was indeed,
Which did into the great Turk's mind
     A great disdaining breed.
A perilous thing, as ever came
     Into a chieftain's brain,
To set at nought his foes (though small)
     By lighleing[37] disdain.   340
Then Selim sent a navy out,
     Who wandered without rest,
While time into Lepanto's gulf
     They all their anchors kest.[38]
In season when with sharpest hooks
     The busy shearer's cow[39]
The fruitful yellow locks of gold,
     That do on Ceres grow,
And when the strongest trees for weight
     Of birth do downward bow   350
Their heavy heads, whose colored knops[40]
     In shower's rains ripely now,
And husband-men with woodbind crowns
     To twice-borne Bacchus dance,
Whose pleasant poison sweet in taste,
     Doth cast them in a trance.
Into this riping season sure,
     The Christian host I say
Were all assembled for to make
     Them ready for the way.   360
But or they from Messina came,
     The vines were standing bare,
Trees void of fruit and Ceres polde,[41]
     And lacking all her hair.

---

[37] Lying.
[38] Cast.
[39] Cut.
[40] Buds.
[41] Bald.

But when that leaves with rattling falls
     In banks of withered boughs,
And careful laborers do begin
     To yoke the painful ploughs
The navies near to other drew,
     And Venier (sent before)   370
Gave false alarum, sending word,
     The Turks had skowped[42] the score.
That fifty galleys quite were fled,
     This word he sent express,
To make the Christians willingly
     To battle them address,
As so they did, and entered all,
     (Moved by that samin[43] flight).
Into Lepanto's gulf, and there
     Prepared them for the fight.   380
While this was doing here on earth,
     Great God who creates all,
(With wakrife[44] eye preordoning[45]
     Whatever doth befall),
Was sitting in his pompous throne,
     In highest heaven above,
And gloriously accompanied
     With Justice and with Love.
The one hath smiling countenance,
     The other frowning cheer,   390
The one to mercy still persuades
     Him as a father dear,
The other for to power his plagues
     Upon repining sin,
And fill the fields with woeful cries,
     The houses all with din,
But yet the Lord so temperates them,
     That both do brook their place,

---

[42] To bound or skip.
[43] Same.
[44] Wakeful, vigilant.
[45] Preordaining.

For Justice whiles obtains her will,
    But evermore doth grace.   400
Jehovah als hath balances
    Wherewith he weighs aright
The greatest and the heaviest sins,
    With smaller faults and light,
These grace did move him for to take,
    And so he weighed in heaven,
The Christian faults with faithless Turks,
    The balance stood not even,
But swayed upon the faithless side.
    And then, with awful face,   410
Frowned God of Hosts, the whirling heavens
    For fear did tremble apace,
The staiest[46] mountains shuddered all,
    The grounds of earth did shake,
The seas did bray, and Pluto's realm
    For horror cold did quake.
How soon Aurora's joyful face,
    Had shed the shady night,
And made the shivering larks to sing
    For gladness of the light,   420
And Phoebe with inconstant face,
    In seas had gone to rest,
And Phoebus chasing vapors moist,
    The sky made blue celest.
The general of the Christian host
    Upon his galley mast,
The bloody sign of furious Mars
    Made to be fixed fast.
Then, as into a spacious town
    At breaking of the day,   430
The busy workmen do prepare
    Their worklumes[47] every way,
The wright doth sharp his hacking axe,
    The smith his grinding file,

---

[46] Stateliest.
[47] Tools.

Glass-makers beats [sic] their fire that burns
      Continual not a while,
The painter mixes colors vive,[48]
      The printer letters sets,
The mason clinks on marble stones,
      Which hardly dressed he gets.   440
Even so, how soon this warrior world
      With earnest eyes did see
Yon sign of war, they all prepared
      To win or else to die.
Here hagbutters[49] prepared with speed
      A number of bullets round,
There cannoners, their cannons steeled
      To make destroying sound,
Here knights did dight their burnished brands,
      There archers bows did bend,   450
The armorers on corselets knocks [sic],
      And harness hard did mend,
The fierie[50] mariners at once
      Makes all their tackling clear
And whispering din, and cries confused,
      Preparing here and there.
As busy bees within their hives
      With murmuring ever still,
Are earnest upon their fruitful work
      Their empty holes to fill.   460
The flags and ensigns were displayed,
      At Zephyr's will to wave,
Each painted in the colors clear
      Of every owner brave.
But all this time in careful mind,
      The general ever rolled,
What manner of array would best
      Fit such an army bold,

---

[48] Lively.
[49] An early type of rifle.
[50] Nimble.

To pance[51] on this it pained him more,
    This more did trouble his breast,   470
Than cannons, corselets, bullets, tackle,
    And swords, and bows, the rest,
And at the last, with ripe advice
    Of chieftains sage and grave,
He shed in three in crescent's form
    This martial army brave.
The general in the battle was,
    And Colonne undertook
The right wing with the force of Genes,[52]
    The left did Venier brook.   480
When this was done, the Spanish prince
    did row about them all,
And on the names of special men
    With loving speech did call,
Remembering them how righteous was
    Their quarrel, and how good,
Immortal praise, and infinite gains,
    To conquer with their blood,
And that the glory of God in earth,
    Into their manhead stands,   490
Through just relief of Christian souls
    From cruel Pagans' hands.
But if the enemy triumphed
    Of them and of their fame,
In millions men to bondage would
    Professing Jesus' name.
The Spanish prince, exhorting thus,
    With glad and smiling cheer,
With sugared words, and gesture good,
    So pleased both eye and ear   500
That every man cried victory.
    This word abroad they blew,
A good presage that victory
    Thereafter should ensue.

---

[51] Ponder, think.
[52] Genoa.

The Turkish host in manner like
    Themselves they did array,
The which two Bashas did command
    And order every way.
For Portav Basha[53] had in charge
    To govern all by land,   510
And Ali Basha[54] had by sea,
    The only chief command,
These Bashas in the battle were,
    With mo[55] than I can tell
And Mahomet Bey[56] the right wing had,
    The left Ochiali fell.[57]
Then Ali Basha visied[58] all
    With bold and manly face,
Whose tongue did utter courage more
    Than had alluring grace.   520
He did recount amongst the rest
    What victory Turks obtained
On caitif[59] Christians, and how long
    The Ottoman's race had reigned.
He told them als, "how long themselves
    Had victors ever been,
Even of these same three Princes small,
    That now durst so convene,
And would ye then give such a lie
    Unto your glories past   530
As let your selves be overthrown
    By losers at the last?

---

[53] Pertew Mehemet Pasha, commander of the center of the Turkish fleet, and not the land forces.

[54] Kapudan Ali Pasha, admiral of the Turkish fleet.

[55] More.

[56] Viceroy of Alexandria.

[57] "Fell," meaning evil. Ochialli, or "Aluch Ali," Pasha, commander of the left-wing squadron of the Turkish fleet, earned this sobriquet because he was a renegade Christian originally from Calabria who rose to be viceroy of Algiers.

[58] Viewed.

[59] Base, despicable.

This victory shall Europe make
        To be your conquest prey,
And all the rare things thereintill,
        Ye shall carry away.
But if ye leese,[60] remember well
        How ye have made them thrall,
This samin way, or worse shall they
        Demaine[61] you one and all,   540
And then shall all your honors past
        In smoke evanish quite,
And all your pleasures turn in pain
        In dolor your delight.
Take courage then, and boldly to it,
        Our Mahomet will aid,
Conducting all your shots, and strokes,
        Of arrow, dart, and blade.
For nothing care but only one
        Which only doth me fray,[62]   550
That ere with them we ever meet
        For fear they flee away."
This speech did so the army please,
        And so their minds did move,
That clicks of swords, and rattle of pikes,
        His speeches did approve.
The glistering clear of shining sun
        Made both the hosts so glance,
As fishes' eyes did reel to see
        Such hues on seas to dance.   560
But Titan shined on eyes of Turks
        And on the Christian backs,
Although the wavering wind the which
        But seldom settling takes,
The Turks did second ever still
        While but a little space

---

[60] Lose.
[61] Demean.
[62] Make me afraid.

Before the choke, ô miracle,
  It turned into their face,
Which Christians joyful as a seal
  And token did receive,   570
That God of hosts had promised them
  They victory should have.
How soon a cannon's smoky throat
  The seas did dindle[63] all,
And on Bellona bold and wise,
  And bloody Mars did call,
And that the sounding clear of brass
  Did als approve the same,
And kindled courage into men
  To win immortal fame.   580
But what? Me think I do intend
  This battle to recite,
And what by martial force was done
  My pen presumes to write,
As if I had yon bloody God
  And all his power seen,
Yea, to describe the God of Hosts
  My pen had able been.
No, no, no man that witness was
  Can set it out aright,   590
Then how could I by hearsay do,
  Which none can do by sight.
But since I rashly took in hand,
  I must assay it now,
With hope that this my good intent
  Ye readers will allow.
I also trust that even as he
  Who in the sun doth walk
Is colored by the samin sun,
  So shall my following talk   600
Some favor keep of martial acts,
  Since I would paint them out,

---

[63] Sound.

And God shall to his honor als
    My pen guide out of doubt.
This warning given to Christians they
    With Turks' yoke here and there,
And first the six aforesaid ships
    That were so large and fair,
And placed were in the former ranks
    Did first of all pursue   610
With bullets, raisers, chains, and nails,
    That from their pieces flew.
Their cannons rummished[64] all at once,
    Whose mortal thudding drave
The fatal Turks to be content
    With Thetis for their grave.
The fishes were astonished all,
    To hear such hideous sound,
The azure sky was dimmed with smoke,
    The din that did abound,   620
Like thunder rearding rumling rave
    With roars the highest heaven,
And pierced with pith the glistering vaults
    Of all the planets seven.
The piteous plaints, the hideous howls,
    The grevious cries and moans,
Of millions wounded sundry ways,
    But dying all at once,
Conjoined with former horrible sound,
    Distempered all the air,   630
And made the seas for terror shake
    With braying everywhere.
Yet all these unacquainted roars,
    The fearful threatening sound,
Joined with the groaning, murmuring howls
    The courage could not wound
So far of Turkish chieftains brave,
    As them to let[65] or fray

---

[64] Rumbled.
[65] Prevent.

With boldest speed their grevious harms
     With like for to repay,   640
Who made their cannons bray so fast
     And hagbuts crack so thick,
As Christians dead in number almost
     Did countervail the quick,
And sent full many carcages[66]
     Of seas to lowest ground,
The cannons' thuds and cries of men
     Did in the sky resound.
But Turks remained not long unpaid
     Even with their proper coin,   650
By bitter shots which Christians did
     To former thundering join.
Dead drop they down on every side,
     Their sighing sprights eschews,
And crosses Styx into disdain,
     To hear infernal news.
Yea, scarcely could the ancient boat
     Such number of souls contain,
But sobbed underneath the weight
     Of passengers profane.   660
While here the Father stood with Son,
     A whirling round doth bear
The lead that dings the Father in dross
     And fills the Son with fear,
While there a chieftain shrilly cries,
     And soldats doth command,
A speedy pellet stops his speech,
     And stays his pointing hand,
While time a clustered troop doth stand
     Amassed together all,   670
A fatal bullet them among
     Makes some selected fall.
The hideous noise so deaf'd them all,
     Increasing every still,

---

[66] Carcasses.

That ready soldats could not hear
    Their wise commanders will,
But every man as Mars him moved,
    And as occasion served,
His duty did the best he might,
    And for no peril swerved,   680
Their old commanders' precepts past
    They put in practice then,
And only memory did command
    That multitude of men.
Thus after they with cannons had
    Their duty done afar,
And time in end had wearied them
    Of such embassed war,[67]
A rude recounter[68] then they made,
    Together galleys clipped,   690
And each on other rashed[69] her nose,
    That in the sea was dipped.
No manner of man was idle then,
    Each man his arms did use,
No 'scaping place is in the seas
    Though men would Mars refuse.
The valiant knight with cutlass sharp
    Of fighting foe doth part
The bloody head from body pale.
    While one with deadly dart   700
Doth pierce his enemy's heart in twain,
    And other fierce doth strike
Quite through his fellow's arm or leg,
    With pointed brangling[70] pike.
The cannons leaves [sic] not thundering of,
    Nor hagbuts shooting still,
And seldom powder wastes in vain
    But either wound or kill.

---

[67] Debased, i.e., fighting at a distance.
[68] Encounter.
[69] Crashed.
[70] Shaking.

Yea, even the simple foreseats fought
      With beggar's bolts[71] anew,   710
Wherewith full many principal men
      They wounded sore and slew.
While time a Christian with a sword,
      Lets out a faithless breath,
A Turk on him doth with a dart,
      Revenge his fellow's death,
While time a Turk with arrow doth,
      Shoot through a Christian's arm,
A Christian with a pike doth pierce,
      That hand that did the harm.   720
While time a Christian cannon kills
      A Turk with threat'ning sound,
A hagbut hits the cannoner,
      Who, dead, falls to the ground.
The beggars' bolts by foreseats casten,
      On all hands made to fly,
Jaw-bones and brains of killed and hurt,
      Who wished (for pain) to die.
The clinks of swords, the rattle of pikes,
      The whir of arrows light,   730
The howls of hurt, the captains cries [sic]
      In vain do what they might,
The cracks of galleys broken and bruised,
      Of guns the rumbling bear[72]
Resounded so, that though the Lord
      Had thundered none could hear.
The sea was varnished red with blood,
      And fishes poisoned all,
As Jehovah, by Moses' rod,
      In Egypt made befall.   740
This cruel fight continued thus
      Uncertain all the while,
For fortune oft on either side,
      Did frown and after smile,

---

[71] Presumably, a kind of weapon or missile appropriate for slaves.
[72] Roar.

It seemed that Mars and Pallas both
    Did think the day too short
With bloody practice thus to use
    Their old acquainted sport.
For as the slaughter aye increased,
    So did the courage still,   750
Of martial men whom loss of friends
    Enarmed with eager will,
The more their number did decrease,
    The more that they were harmed,
The more with Mars then were they filled
    With boldning[73] spite enarmed.
Now up, now down on either side,
    Now Christians seemed to win,
Now overthrown, and now again,
    They seemed but to begin.   760
My pen for pity cannot write,
    My hair for horror stands,
To think how many Christians there
    Were killed by pagan hands.
O Lord, throughout this labyrinth
    Make me the way to view
And let thy holy threefold spright
    Be my conducting clue.
O now I spy a blessed heaven,
    Our landing is not far.   770
Lo, good victorious tidings comes
    To end this cruel war.
In all the time that thus they fought,
    The Spanish prince was clipped
With Ali Basha, whom to meet
    The rest he had o'erslipped.
And even as throughout both the hosts,
    Dame Fortune varied still,
So kythde[74] she 'twixt those champions two,
    Her fond inconstant will.   780

---

[73] Emboldening.
[74] appeared, revealed herself.

For after that the castles four
     Of galleys both, with sound,
And slaughter huge, their bullets had
     In other made rebound,
And all the small artillery
     Consumed their shots below
In killing men, or else to cut
     Some cable strong or tow.
Yet victory still uncertain was,
     And soldats never ceased   790
(With interchange of pikes and darts)
     To kill, or wound at least.
In end, when they with blood abroad
     Had bought their meeting dear,
The victory first on Spanish side
     Began for to appear.
For even the Spanish prince himself
     Did hazard at the last,
Accompanied with boldest men,
     Who followed on him fast,   800
By force to win the Turkish deck,
     The which he did obtain,
And entered in their galley syne[75]
     But did not long remain.
For Ali Basha proved so well,
     With his assisters brave
That backward faster than they came
     Their valiant foes they drave,
That glad they were to 'scape themselves,
     And leave behind anew   810
Of valiant fellows carcasses,
     Whom thus their enemies slew.
The General, boldened then with spite,
     And varnished red with shame,
Did rather choose to lose his life
     Then tine[76] his spreading fame.

---

[75] Soon.
[76] Lose.

And so of new encouraged
     His soldiers true and bold,
As now for eagerness they burn
     Who erst were waxed cold.   820
And thus they entered in again
     More fiercely than before,
Whose rude assault could Ali then
     Resist not anymore,
But fled unto the fort at Stevin
     For last refuge of all,
Abiding in a doubtsome fear
     The chance he did befall.
A Macedonian soldier then
     Great honor for to win,   830
Before the rest in earnest hope
     To Basha bold did rin[77]
And with a cutlass sharp and fine
     Did whip me off his head,
Who lacked not his reward of him
     That did the navy led.
The General syne caused fix the head
     Upon his galley mast.
At sight whereof the faithless host
     Were all so sore aghast,   840
That all amazed gave back at once,
     But yet were stayed again,
And never one at all did 'scape,
     But taken were or slain,
Ochiali except, with three times ten
     Great galleys of his own,
And many of the knights of Malt[78]
     Whom he had overthrown.
But if that he with his convoy
     Had missed a safe retreat,   850

[77] Run.
[78] Malta.

No news had Selim but by bruit[79]
    Heard ever of this defeat.
When thus the victory was obtained,
    And thanks were given to God,
Twelve thousand Christians counted were
    Relieved from Turkish rod.
O Spanish prince,[80] whom of a glance
    And suddenly away
The cruel fates gave to the world
    Not suffering thee to stay.   860
With this the still night sad and black
    The earth overshadowed then,
Who Morpheus brought with her and rest
    To steal on beasts and men.
But all this time was Venice town
    Revolving what event
Might come of this prepared fight,
    With doubtsome minds and bent.
They longed, and yet they durst not long
    To hear the news of all,   870
They hoped good, they feared the evil,
    And kest[81] what might befall
At last the joyful tidings came,
    Which such a gladness bred,
That matrons grave, and maids modest,
    The marketplace bespread.
Anon with cheerful countenance
    They dress them in a ring,
And thus the foremost did begin
    Syne all the rest to sing.   880

CHORUS VENETUS

Sing praise to God both young and old
    That in this town remain,

---

[79] Rumor.
[80] Don John, who died suddenly.
[81] Guessed.

With voice and every instrument,
      Found out by mortal brain.
Sing praises to our mighty God,
      Praise our deliverer's name,
Our loving lord, who now in need,
      Hath kythd[82] to be the same.
The faithless snares did compass us,
      Their nets were set about,   890
But yet our dearest Father in Heaven,
      He hath redeemed us out.
Not only that, but by his power,
      Our enemy's feet they slayed,
Whom he hath trapped, and made to fall
      Into the pit they made.
Sing praises then, both young and old,
      That in this town remain,
To him that hath relieved our necks
      From Turkish yoke profane.   900
Let us wash off our sins impure,
      Cast off our garments vile,
And hant[83] his temple every day,
      To praise his name awhile.
O praise him for the victory,
      That he hath made us have,
For he it was revenged our cause,
      And not our army brave.
Praise him with trumpet, piphre[84] and drum,
      With lutes, and organs fine,   910
With viols, gitterns, cistiers[85] als,
      And sweetest voices syne.
Sing praise, sing praise both young and old,
      Sing praises one and all,
To him who hath redeemed us now,
      From cruel pagan's thrall.

---

[82] Revealed.
[83] Haunt.
[84] Pipe.
[85] Zithers.

In hearing of this song methinks
      My members waxes [sic] faint,
Nor yet from dullness can I keep,
      My mind by no restraint.   920
But lo, my yrni[86] head doth nod,
      Upon my adamant breast,
My eyelids will stand up no more,
      But falls [sic] to take them rest.
And through my weak and weary hand,
      Doth slide my pen of lead,
And sleep doth else possess me all,
      The similitude of dead.
The god with golden wings through ports
      Of horn doth to me creep,   930
Who changes ofter[87] shapes transformed
      Than Proteus in the deep.
How soon he came, quite from my mind,
      He worldly cares removed,
And all my members in my bed,
      Lay still in rest beloved.
And syne I heard a joyful song
      Of all the feathered bands
Of holy angels in the heaven,
      Thus singing on all hands.   940

CHORUS ANGELORUM

Sing, let us sing with one accord
      Hallelujah on high,
With every elder that doth bow
      Before the Lamb his knee.
Sing four and twenty all with us
      While Heaven and earth resound
Replenished with Jehovah's praise
      Whole like cannot be found.

---

[86] Iron.

[87] Morpheus, who changes shapes more often than Proteus.

For he it is, that is, and was,
     And evermore shall be,   950
One, only one, unseparate,
     And yet in persons three.
Praise him for that he create hath
     The heaven, the earth and all,
And ever hath preserved them since
     From their ruin and fall.
But praise him more, if more can be,
     That so he loves his name,
As he doth mercy show to all
     That do profess the same.   960
And not alanerlie[88] to them
     Professing it aright,
But even to them that mix therewith
     Their own inventions slight.
As 'specially this samin[89] time
     Most plainly may appear,
In giving them such victory
     That not aright him fear.
For since he shows such grace to them
     That thinks [sic] themselves are just,   970
What will he more to them that in
     His mercies only trust?
And sith that so he uses them
     That doubt for to be saved,
How much more them that in their hearts
     His promise have engraved?
And since he doth such favor show
     To them that fondly[90] pray
To other mediators than
     Can help them any way.   980
O how then will he favor them,
     Who prayers do direct

---

[88] Only.
[89] Same.
[90] Foolishly.

Unto the Lamb, whom only he
    Ordained for that effect?
And since he doth revenge their cause
    That worship God of bread
(An error vain the which is bred,
    But in a mortal head),
Then how will he revenge their cause
    That only fear and serve   990
His dearest Son, and for his sake
    Will for no perils swerve.
And since that so he pities them
    That bear upon their brow,
That mark of Antichrist, the whore,
    That great abuser now,
Who does the truest Christians
    With fire and sword invade
And make them holy martyrs that
    Their trust in God have laid?   1000
How will he them that thus are used,
    And bears upon their face
His special mark, a certain sign
    Of everlasting grace?
Put end unto the travails (Lord)
    And miseries of thy Saints,
Removing quite this blindness gross
    That now the world so dants.[91]
Sing praises of his mercy then
    His superexcellence great,   1010
Which doth exceed even all his works
    That lie before his seat.
And let us sing both now and aye
    To him with one accord,
O holy, holy God of Hosts,
    Thou everliving Lord.

Thus ended was the angels' song,
    And also here I end.

---

[91] Daunts.

Exhorting all you Christians true
     Your courage up to bend, 1020
And since by this defeat ye see
     That God doth love his name
So well, that so he did them aid
     That serv'd not right the same.
Then though the anti-Christian sect
     Against you do conjure,
He doth the body better love
     Than shadow be ye sure.
Do ye resist with confidence,
     That God shall be your stay 1030
And turn it to your comfort, and
     His glory for now and aye.

FINIS

INDEX

ROBERT APPELBAUM

NOTES ON CONTRIBUTORS

ROBERT APPELBAUM teaches at the University of San Diego, and he received his Ph.D. from the University of California, Berkeley in 1996. A fiction writer as well as a literary critic, his work has appeared in such journals as *Shakespeare Quarterly*, the *George Herbert Journal*, *Utopian Studies*, *Early Modern Literary Studies*, *Free Associations*, and *Fiction International*. He is currently completing a book entitled *The Look of Power: Ideal Politics and Utopian Mastery in Seventeenth Century England*.

SANDRA J. BELL is an assistant professor at the University of New Brunswick at Saint John. She received her Ph.D. from Queen's University in 1995. Professor Bell has co-edited *Sixteenth Century Prose and Poetry* with Marie H. Loughlin (Broadview Press, forthcoming), and she has an essay on James's *Lepanto* in *Other Voices, Other Views: Expanding the Canon in English Renaissance Studies*, ed. Mary Silcox, Helen Ostrovich, and Graham Roebuck (Newark: University of Delaware Press, 1999).

PETER C. HERMAN has written *Squitter-wits and Muse-haters: Sidney, Spenser, Milton and Renaissance Antipoetic Sentiment* and has edited three anthologies: *Rethinking the Henrician Era: New Essays on Early Tudor Texts and Contexts* (Urbana: University of Illinois Press, 1994), *Opening the Borders: Early Modern Studies and the New Inclusivism, Essays in Honor of James V. Mirollo* (Newark: University of Delaware Press, 1999), and *Day Late, Dollar Short: The Next Generation and the New Academy* (Albany: SUNY Press, 2000). He has published essays or has work forthcoming in such journals as *SEL*, *Criticism*, and *Texas Studies in Literature and Language*. He is an associate professor at San Diego State University.

LISA HOPKINS teaches at Sheffield University, and is the author of two books, *Queen Elizabeth I and her Court* (London: St. Martin's, 1990) and *Women Who Would Be Kings: Female Rulers of the Sixteenth Century* (London: St. Martin's, 1991). In addition, she has published many articles in such journals as *Shakespeare Quarterly*, *Connotations*, *Shakespeare Studies*, and *Comparative Drama*.